Golden Hands

ENCYCLOPEDIA OF

DRESSMAKING

Collins   Glasgow   &   London

William Collins Sons & Co Ltd
London · Glasgow · Sydney · Auckland
Toronto · Johannesburg

First published in this edition 1972
Completely revised, new metric edition
First published 1977
Second reprint 1979
ISBN 0 00 435040 5

Printed in Great Britain by William Collins Sons & Co. Ltd.

CONTENTS

Generally speaking

Skirtmaking

Toile-making

Blousemaking

Dressmaking

Know-how

CONTENTS *(Continued)*

Sewing for children

ACKNOWLEDGEMENTS

Photographers:

Malcolm Aird   John Carter   Chris Lewis   Tony Moussoulides
Peter Watkins   Clive Boursnell   Richard Dormer
Sandra Lousada   Peter Rand   Jim Williams   Camera Press
Trevor Lawrence   Philip Modica, Fotopartners
Michael Stuart

Text:

Elizabeth Baker   Alison Louw   Valerie Punchard

Our thanks are due to Vogue Pattern Service and The Butterick
Publishing Company for permission to reproduce photographs of
completed garments from their range of patterns.

Introduction

Here is a dressmaking book which can be used by readers on every level and adapted to the individual's specific needs. At last there is a book which assumes nothing of the reader: she may be an experienced dressmaker looking for a reference book on techniques and finishes, or one new to dressmaking whose greatest need is straightforward know-how. Certainly every woman who takes pride in making clothes with fit and flair – or who hopes to – will find many aspects of dressmaking clarified and potential problems eliminated.

Unlike so many books of its kind, this one lays the groundwork by presenting equipment and basic tools, and shows how to make your sewing machine work for you. A range of natural and synthetic fabrics, and their particular qualities and capabilities, is reviewed to give the dressmaker greater scope in using these to best advantage.

One invaluable lesson to be learned by everyone who uses the Golden Hands Encyclopedia of Dressmaking is the importance of completing each step carefully and accurately. And the book's logical progression of techniques and garments makes it so much simpler. Before proceeding with the mechanics of sewing, you learn to chart your own measurements, and take into account any figure problems which will need special attention. These are really the fine points which result in an attractive, well-fitting garment and defy the world of mass-produced fashion to match them.

An indispensable feature within the book is the Golden Hands Graph Pages, a set of basic graphs including a dress, skirt and blouse. We give instructions for making basic and well-fitting garments from these graphs; one can then adapt the pattern to make several other designs. However, the reader will gain as much satisfaction in applying methods and techniques learned from the book to her own use of commercial paper patterns; she need not feel limited to the selection of patterns offered within the Graph Pages.

The final chapters of the book deal with making clothes for children; these are easy to make, practical and, not the least important, attractive. They are a sure temptation for any reader who realizes the money-saving potential in sewing for children.

But the only way to satisfy your curiosity fully about the many aspects of this book is to glance through it. And then we dare you to go no further . . .

Chapter 1

The basic tools for successful sewing

Generally Speaking

Any sewing aid which is specially designed to make your work easier is a good idea. But now that the home dressmaking industry offers you practically every gadget imaginable, it's often difficult to decide which is really necessary and it is easy to waste money. Here is a list of the basic aids which you will need for the simplest dressmaking, and which will help you to achieve more advanced results.

Basic equipment

Sewing machine. The most important piece of equipment in the sewing room is, of course, the sewing machine. Whether it is a treasured family heirloom or a gleaming new model, it is very important that the machine stands on a firm base at a comfortable working height, and that a light shines directly on the needle when stitching.

Needles. Size 8 for dressmaking. Size 9 for bead embroidery and sewing fine fabrics such as silks or chiffons. Size 7 for heavier sewing such as stitching on buttons. Use either the medium length sharps or long straw needles, whichever suits you best.

Pins. Steel dressmaking pins, at least 2·5cm or 3cm long, are the best. Nickel-plated pins may bend during use and could damage fine cloth. Glasshead pins are very sharp (they're made from needle rejects) but have limited use since the heads break easily.

Scissors. You'll need a good pair of sharp cutting shears, with handles that comfortably fit the hand (left-handed shears are available for those who need them) also a pair of small dressmaking scissors to use while making up.

Tailor's chalk. At least two pieces are essential for marking, one white, one blue.

Tape measure. A good tape measure shouldn't stretch so use one made from glass fibre.

Tracing wheel. This is used for marking pattern outlines on to fabric. Choose one made from steel with sharp points.

Thimble. A steel-lined thimble is best since it gives longer wear. It should fit the middle finger of your sewing hand.

Triangle. This is also known as a tailor's square and is used to obtain fabric grain lines in pattern making.

Ruler. This is used for measuring hems and connecting points for straight seams. It should be firm and straight.

Iron. A good medium-weight iron with thermostatic controls is essential. Use cleaning spirits to keep the base of the iron clean.

Ironing board. This should stand firmly and have a smooth-fitting cover, such as a folded blanket covered by a layer of smooth sheeting, securely attached under the board. Covers made of heavily dressed cloth are not suitable since when wet, the dressing can be transferred to the iron.

Press cloth. A 60cm square piece of finely woven cotton or lawn is essential for steam pressing. Thicker cloths hold too much moisture and may harm the fabric. A good press cloth should be free of imperfections such as holes, frayed edges and prominent grains, all of which can easily be transferred to the fabric being pressed. Also, it shouldn't contain any dressing because this will stick to the iron and mark the fabric.

Press board. This is necessary for pressing pleats and flat surfaces. You can make one quite simply from a square of cork about 75cm by 50cm (a bath mat is excellent!). Pad it with a folded blanket and sheeting.

Buying a new sewing machine?

A sewing machine is a big investment so if you're thinking of making a purchase, it is important to know the types which are available and what they will do.

There are many makes of sewing machines on the market, all differently priced, but today's machines fit into three main categories: straight stitch, swing needle (or zig-zag) and swing needle automatic. Here are some tips on what to expect from each type of machine.

Straight-stitch. This machine sews only with a straight stitch and most will sew in reverse as well as forward. Some attachments come with the machine and others can be obtained at extra cost. Ask about this when buying. Straight-stitch machines are in the lowest price bracket and prices vary according to quality.

Swing needle. This machine does zig-zag stitching in addition to straight stitching. The zig-zag stitch is useful for finishing seams, hems, making lace insertions and buttonholes. Some swing needle machines have an automatic buttonhole reverse and most come with a good range of attachments. These machines are in the medium price range.

Swing needle automatic. This machine has all the facilities of the straight-stitch and swing needle but it can also do embroidery. Various effects can be achieved by inserting special discs into the machine or by engaging settings which are built into the mechanism. These are the most expensive machines to buy.

How to choose a machine

If you need a machine for light dressmaking only, any of the previously mentioned types, straight-stitch, swing needle, or swing needle automatic, will be suitable.

If you want a general-purpose machine to cope with all the household sewing and mending, be sure that the machine you choose will take heavy work.

If you need a machine for tailoring, it is advisable to choose from the straight-stitch and swing needle ranges only. A fully automatic swing needle machine has only a limited use for tailoring.

Testing

In most cases, it is possible to test a machine at home for a few days and this will give you a chance to see if it is really suitable for your needs. If you do have a machine on approval, first of all read the instruction manual carefully to see if there are any restrictions on how you can use the machine.

Here is your opportunity to try the machine on different types of cloth, especially those you are most likely to be working with later on. If you are testing the machine for heavier work, remember to stitch over double seams in a medium-thick cloth. See that the machine passes the work through evenly; that it does not hesitate in front of the seams or jump off when it has stitched through the thickest part.

It is important to test the speed of the machine. For instance, if you think you will be doing a lot of household sewing, particularly items like sheets, bedspreads, and curtains which have long, monotonous seams, then you will want a machine that can cope with this work quickly as well as correctly.

Do not be misled by a claim that a machine will 'wear in'. Many machines are set at one speed only, but some of the newest and most expensive have a built-in gear to increase the stitching rate. You can adjust the speed slightly by regulating machine controls, but transmissions vary and some machines will operate faster than others. By learning to operate the controls, you will always be able to use a very fast machine at slow speeds but if a machine stitches slowly it is because the transmission is low geared. When you're testing, make sure that the pressure foot and tension are at the correct setting. Settings vary with different manufacturers, and these details will be pointed out in the manual. For more information on sewing machines, and how to use them to their best advantage, see Chapters 2 and 3.

How to find the correct thread number and needle size
Many machines are tested, and set, to work best at a certain thread number. Therefore, find out from the manual which are the recommended numbers for that machine.

To help you, here is a chart setting out the comparisons between the British and Continental sizes.

British thread number	Metric count	British needle sizes	Continental needle sizes	Type of material
36 } 40 }	63 } 67 }	16	100	Heavy fabrics
50	84	14	80-90	Medium fabrics
60	100	11	60-70	Light-weight fabrics

Stitch size and tension
To obtain the correct stitch size and tension (the tightness balance between both threads) adjust the controls on the machine as shown below.

For the top thread feed control, adjust the dial on the front of the tension spring, which reads from 0-9. The higher the number, the tighter the thread feed.

To adjust the tension on the bobbin, loosen or tighten the tiny screw on top of the bobbin case which holds down a spring in the shape of a little steel clip.

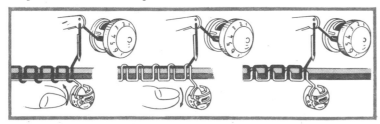

Different gauges of sewing thread, such as silk, cotton and mercerised cotton, can affect stitch size and the tension. So, before making a garment, always test the stitches on layers of the material you are preparing to sew.

Finally, having tested the performance of the machine, before buying, satisfy yourself that it carries a good guarantee.

Chapter 2
What your sewing machine can do

Generally Speaking

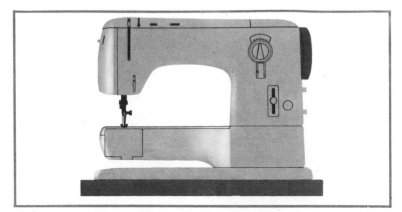

A free arm machine, useful for stitching narrow parts of a garment ▲

Machines today can produce exciting effects, in a few minutes, which would take hours of working by hand. Their potential has been briefly introduced in the previous chapter, but there are many more things today's machines can do and this chapter sets out to help you find which type you want. Buying a machine is an important once-in-a-lifetime purchase—it's important to assess your needs before making a choice.

Think before you buy

Before buying a machine ask yourself the following questions:
a. How much do you expect from your machine?
b. How much sewing do you do?
c. How much are you prepared to spend?
The more a machine can do the more expensive it becomes, and it is quite pointless spending money on facilities which you will never use. So read on further, look at the pictures and note the things you know you would use: then set about finding the machine which answers your needs in the price bracket you can afford.

Practical sewing
All that most people will need for everyday dressmaking is a machine with a good straight stitch and a reverse for ending off seams, a good zigzag with adjustable width, and one which makes clear neat buttonholes. A machine which tacks is also an advantage. In the way of attachments, the zipper foot, the roller foot and the buttonhole foot are the most used.
The zipper foot. This is constructed to enable you to sew right up to a zip edge without the zipper teeth being under the presser foot. The zipper foot is usually provided with a new machine as part of the purchase. When buying a zipper foot you will, of course, make sure that it is for your particular make of machine.
Roller foot. This has two roller-type wheels with a rough surface— very useful when sewing on materials like PVC and leather which can be difficult with an ordinary straight-stitch foot where the machine sticks, jumps forward, sticks again. But with a roller foot you can control the feed with ease. The roller foot is also very good for sewing pile fabrics such as velvet, corduroy and mohair.
The buttonhole foot and button plate. Some buttonhole feet are specially grooved so that the buttonhole can pass underneath. It is an advantage if the foot is made of plastic so that you can see the work through it.
The button plate is for sewing on buttons, which may be helpful if you have a lot to sew on, but hand-sewing is usually efficient enough.

Further practical sewing
Hems. The rolled hem foot is ideal for edgings of scarves and for very fine rolled hems on chiffon. The foot does all the work for you

▲ *A special foot for narrow braiding* ▲ *Special zipper foot in action*
▼ *Lace trim stitched with a zigzag* ▼ *Programmed scalloping cuff trim*

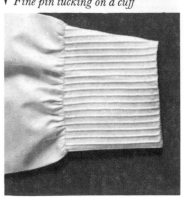

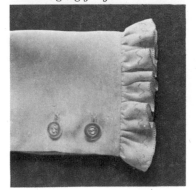

▼ *Fine pin tucking on a cuff* ▼ *Fine zigzag for frills*

8

▲ *Programmed machine embroidery*

▲ *Machined tailor's tacks*

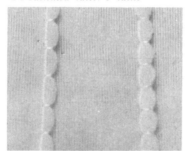
▲ *Shell edging on fine fabric*

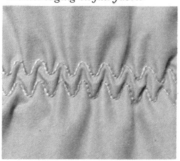

▲ *Pin tucks, eyelets and scalloping*

▲ *Serpentine stitched elastic*

by rolling and sewing in one operation.

There is also a blind hemming or blind stitch foot for making hems on medium-weight fabrics. But, on the whole, hems are better done by hand.

Darning. A darning foot and plate for darning household linen and clothes.

Gathering and shirring. Most machines have a special foot which will gather and shir all fabrics.

Tailor's tacks. As you can see from the picture there are machines which do tailor's tacks like the hand-worked version.

Bias binding. The binder foot sews on the bias binding and binds the raw edge in one operation.

Industrial overlocking. Some of the fully automatic machines do overlocking which is similar to industrial overlocking. This is not quite the same as a zigzag finish. There are no gaps between the stitches at the edge, thus eliminating all possibilities of fraying.

Running stitch or 3-point zigzag. A number of automatic and semi-automatic machines can perform this stitch. It is ideal for sewing fabrics which fray easily, like linen or any loosely-woven fabric, and is also used on stretch towelling. It has the function of a neatening stitch. The serpentine stitch is similar to the 3-point zigzag and is used for putting on elastic as shown here.

Sewing for decoration

Many machines today do some embroidery and a quick look at the machine manual will tell you all you need to know about this.

Some have discs or cams which are inserted into the machine and contain the blueprint of the pattern, while others have a dialling system programmed into the machine.

As you can see from the examples there are ways of decorating with a machine other than embroidery. For instance, on the cuffs shown here a narrow zigzag is used to edge a fine fabric—it is also used to sew on lace. Here are a few of the more useful decorating effects:

Pin tucking. A special grooved tucker foot used with twin needles was used for the example shown on this page. The spacing of the tucks can be easily varied.

Eyelet foot and plate. This is for making eyelets, as shown in the illustration.

Shell edging. A special programmed stitch was used for the shell edging in the example.

Free arm or flat bed

Having decided what you want your machine to do and the type of machine you are going to buy, you may then be confronted with yet one more choice, namely whether to buy a free arm or a flat bed machine. The difference between these two machines is slight. The free arm is usually a little more expensive and only comes in portable models whereas cabinet models are all flat bed. A free arm machine can be useful when you are stitching narrow parts of a garment, such as sleeves and cuffs, and particularly if you are going to flat fell the seams as these sections will fit round the arm of the machine. All free arm machines have a special plate which you can put round the arm to make a flat bed for supporting the work.

Sewing classes

Having bought a new machine you will want to make full use of it. Many companies give free lessons on how to use their machines and these lessons are worthwhile attending.

Summing up

The chart (left) covers all the special features discussed in this chapter and will help you see at a glance the type of machine which will be the most useful for you.

Type of machine ▶	Straight stitch	Swing needle	Automatic semi	Automatic fully
Straight stitch and reverse	✓	✓	✓	✓
Zigzag with adjustable width		✓	✓	✓
Tacking	✓	✓	✓	✓
Adjustable stitch length	✓	✓	✓	✓
Zipper foot	✓	✓	✓	✓
Roller foot		✓	✓	✓
Buttonholes and button plate		✓	✓	✓
Rolled hem foot	✓	✓	✓	✓
Blind hemming			✓	✓
Darning		✓	✓	✓
Gathering	✓	✓	✓	✓
Shirring	✓	✓	✓	✓
Tailor's tacks			some	some
Bias binding		✓	✓	✓
Industrial overlocking				some
Running stitch or 3-point zigzag		some	some	some
Serpentine stitch			some	some
Pin tucking		some	✓	✓
Eyelet foot and plate			some	some
Shell edging			✓	✓

Chapter 3

Needles, threads and stitches

Generally Speaking

With the wide and ever increasing range of fabrics on the market, both in natural and man-made fibres, it is important to realize that there is now the right sewing thread for every type of fabric. Successful dressmaking depends on using the right thread because if both thread and fabric share the same characteristics, they can be laundered together, ironed at the same temperatures and will also shrink and stretch together.

Types of thread

The natural threads are silk and cotton. Cotton thread is mercerised or unmercerised. Mercerised cotton, such as Sylko, is specially treated to give it lustre and greater strength. Silk thread is an all-purpose thread and combines strength with elasticity.
Of synthetic threads, the most commonly used are those made from polyester fibre, such as the Terylene thread Trylko.

Thicknesses

Threads, whether natural or synthetic, are produced in various thicknesses: the higher the number the finer the thread. The most commonly used thickness is 40, but for finer fabrics 50 or even 60 can be used. When machining, it is important to remember that whatever you use on the spool you should also use on the bobbin.

Sewing synthetics

When sewing man-made fibre fabrics, and mixtures of natural and man-made fibres, a synthetic thread should be used.
Synthetic thread is usually stronger than natural thread and an interesting feature is its stretchability, which is particularly important when sewing fabrics with stretch, such as synthetic jersey. With these fabrics a great deal of stress is put upon the seams during movement and activity, so if the thread can stretch with the fabric it minimises the chance of broken stitching.
Synthetic thread is also suitable for sewing fine leather which has a good deal of stretch in it.

Sewing cotton and linen

For these fabrics a mercerised cotton thread is used for most purposes. If you sew cotton or linen fabric with a synthetic thread, it would not be able to withstand the heat required for pressing and would melt.
Unmercerised cotton is used for tacking; not having the polished surface of mercerised cotton it does not slip out as easily.

Sewing wool and silk

Wool can be sewn with silk thread or a mercerised cotton. Always sew pure silk with a fine, lustrous pure silk thread.

Fabric	Fibre	Thread	Needle sizes Hand-sewing	Machine	Stitches per 2·5cm
Fine such as lawn, georgette, voile, chiffon, organdie, net, lace	synthetic and mixtures	synthetic 60	9	9 to 11	12 to 15
	cotton and linen	mercerised 50	9	9 to 11	12 to 16
	wool	mercerised 50 or silk	9	9 to 11	12 to 16
	silk	silk	9	9 to 11	12 to 14
Light-weight such as poplin, gingham silk, cotton	synthetic and mixtures	synthetic 60	8–9	11 to 14	12 to 15
	cotton and linen	mercerised 50	8–9	11 to 14	12 to 15
	wool	mercerised 50 or silk	8–9	11 to 14	12 to 15
	silk	silk	8–9	11 to 14	12 to 15
Medium-weight such as gabardine, brocade, tweed, water proofed	synthetic and mixtures	synthetic 60	8–9	11 to 14	10 to 12
	cotton	mercerised 50	7–8	11 to 14	12 to 15
	linen	mercerised 40	7–8	11 to 14	12 to 14
	wool	mercerised 50 or silk	7–8	11 to 14	12 to 14
	silk	silk	7–8	11 to 14	12 to 14
Heavy-weight such as coatings, canvas, heavy furnishing fabrics	synthetic and mixtures	synthetic 40	6	16 to 18	10 to 12
	cotton	mercerised 40	7–8	14 to 16	10 to 12
	linen	mercerised 40	6–7	14 to 18	10 to 12
	wool	mercerised 40 or silk	7–8	14 to 16	10 to 12
	silk	silk	7–8	14 to 16	10 to 12
Some special fabrics					
velvet	synthetic and mixtures	synthetic 60	8–9	11 to 14	10 to 12
	cotton	mercerised 50	7–8	11 to 14	10 to 12
	silk	silk	7–8	11 to 14	10 to 12
fine leather and PVC		synthetic 40		14 to 18	8 to 10

Threads for decorative stitching

For decorative stitching, such as saddle stitching, topstitching, channel seaming and some hand-worked buttonholes, buttonhole twist is used. This is a special, thick silk used to emphasize stitching and is not to be confused with button thread, which is an extra strong waxed thread used to sew buttons on men's clothing, overalls or shoes.

Having stated the importance of using the same thread on both the bobbin and the spool, buttonhole twist is an exception. It is used either on the bobbin or on the spool. Just remember four things about buttonhole twist.

1. If used on the spool, slacken the spool tension.
2. If used on the bobbin, slacken the bobbin tension.
3. If used on the spool, stitch from the wrong side of the garment to achieve the desired effect on the right side of the work.
4. A thicker needle and larger stitch length is required.

In most cases, a 40 mercerised cotton is a suitable companion thread to buttonhole twist but the best advice is to experiment first with your own machine to find the right combination.

Threads for sewing furnishing and upholstery fabrics

Here a very strong durable thread is needed because it has to stand up to a great deal of stress and hard wear. A 70% Terylene and 30% cotton fibre mixture, such as Dewhurst's Strong Thread, is ideal for this work. In this thread the cotton is wrapped around the polyester fibre, otherwise the very strong polyester strands used would cut the fibres of the fabric. In appearance it is similar to button thread.

This thread is also used on canvas, thick leather and suede.

Other threads

There are other threads on the market, such as embroidery threads, invisible thread, and so on, but this chapter concentrates on those which are most used in dressmaking.

A word on colour

Always choose a thread one or two shades darker than the fabric as this will work in lighter, becoming the same colour as the fabric.

Needles

It is important to use the correct size needle for the particular thread and fabric. As a general rule, the lighter the fabric, the finer the needle should be. The chart here shows you at a glance the needle and thread sizes for various weights and types of fabric. There are also different types of needle. A ball point needle is specially made for knitted fabrics so that the needle will not cut the fibres of the fabric and cause it to run. There are spear point needles specially made for leather and suede.

Keep a range of hand-sewing and machine needles handy in various sizes and always remember to keep them sharp and straight —don't wait for your needle to break before changing it.

Tension and stitch length

Many sewing faults are traced back to old machine needles and the use of the wrong thread and tension. Therefore, once you have chosen the fabric, thread and needles, and before you start sewing on the garment, test on a double scrap of the same fabric to find the correct tension. Also test the stitch length to see if it has the right appearance, counting the stitches per 2·5cm as given in the chart. If you see the fabric puckering it may mean there are too many stitches to 2·5cm in which case you will need to make the stitches larger. Test until you are satisfied—it is well worth while.

A Vogue Couturier Pattern reflects the result of perfect seaming ▶

Chapter 4

Generally Speaking

How do you measure up?

The main point to aim for in dressmaking is a really perfect fit. So first, you must know exactly what your personal measurements are. All paper patterns are made to standard sizes but even if you are among those with perfect proportions you may have to make slight pattern adjustments. You'll find a chart set out on the facing page containing all the measurements you will need to use, with instructions on where to take them. Before filling it in enlist the help of a friend or a willing husband and you'll soon have your personal measurement chart to keep by you as you will constantly need to refer back to it while you are dressmaking.

Taking your measurements

Study the first two columns carefully before you start so that you will be familiar with all the measuring points, then take the measurements over a smooth-fitting dress, or slip. You will need to pin a length of 13mm tape or straight seam binding round your waist before you start. This helps you to obtain exact bodice length measurements.

Make sure you do not measure tight but allow the tape to run closely over the body without dropping. Of course, you will be using your non-stretch metric tape! It's a good idea to take measurements more than once for complete accuracy and also to take them towards the end of the day, if you intend to make evening clothes, because body measurements can vary between morning and evening. You could even divide the 'Your Measurements' column into a.m. and p.m.!

Why your pattern is larger than you

When you measure through any paper pattern, you'll find that it is larger than your own measurements. This is because every pattern has tolerance, (or ease) built in, so that the garment cut from that pattern feels easy and comfortable during wear.

The standard allowance for tolerance is 5cm for bust, 2·5cm for waist and 5cm for hip measurements, but these amounts vary according to the fit of a garment and the fabric used for making up. Here are two simple examples.

If you use a bulky fabric, the standard allowance for tolerance must be increased by at least 2·5 cm to 5cm to allow the bulk of the fabric to settle around the figure. A loosely fitting style, on the other hand, will have extra tolerance built in to it and the extra amount required will already have been added to the standard tolerance in the pattern. If you measure through the Golden Hands blouse pattern, which is a semi-fitted style, you can check this for yourself.

You'll be coming across the term tolerance, or ease, frequently in the following chapters where you'll also discover its importance, particularly during the fitting stages of dressmaking.

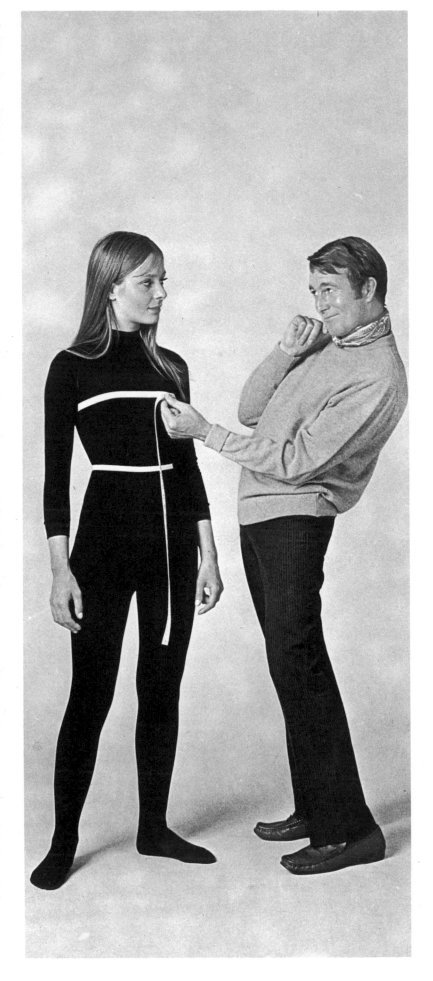

		Where to measure	Your measurements
1.	Bust	Over fullest part of bust and around back	
2.	Waist	Lay tape into natural waist curve	
3.	Hips	Over highest part of seat and thickest part of thighs	
4.	Shoulder	From neck to imaginary armhole seam	
5.	Shoulder across back	From armhole seam to armhole seam	
6.	Centre back length	From nape of neck to waist	
7.	Centre front length	From base of neck to waist	
8.	Front length (i)	From centre shoulder to waist	
9.	Front length (ii)	From centre shoulder to highest point of bust	
10.	Width across front	From armhole seam to armhole seam, half way between shoulder and bust line	
11.	Width across back (i)	From armhole seam to armhole seam over shoulder blades	
12.	Width across back (ii)	As 11, with arms extended forward	
13.	Armhole	Over shoulder point, around underarm, back to shoulder, with arm against body	
14.	Side-seam	From armhole to waist line	
15.	Underarm sleeve-seam	From lowest point of armhole to wrist with arm extended outwards 45°	
16.	Outside sleeve length	From point half way between shoulder and underarm seam, over bent elbow, to wrist	
17.	Sleeve length to elbow	From shoulder point to elbow	
18.	Neck (i)	Around base	
19.	Neck (ii)	Around neck	
20.	Forearm	Around fullest part of arm muscle	
21.	Wrist	Over wrist bone	
22.	Top arm	Around fullest part	
23.	Centre back full length	From nape of neck into waist, to hem	
24.	High hip	About 8cm below waist line over hip bone	
25.	Skirt length	From waist line over side hip to hem	
26.	Trouser depth of crutch	From centre front waist line through crutch to centre back waist line	
27.	Trouser inside leg	Stand with legs spread Measure from inside crutch to below ankle bone (Finished length depends on heel height worn.)	

Checking up on dressmaking terms

Ease. To hold in fullness without showing gathers or pleats.

Face. To finish raw edges with matching shapes.

Grain. Lengthwise, or warp threads running parallel to the selvedge. Crosswise, or weft threads running across fabric from selvedge to selvedge.

Interfacing. Fabric between facing and garment to support an edge and hold a shape.

Interlining. Inner lining between lining and outer fabric for warmth or bulk.

Marking. Indicating pattern detail on fabric. Showing seam allowance for cutting. Showing fitting corrections.

Nap or **pile.** Fibrous surface given to cloth in finishing.

Notch. Small 'V' cut in the seam allowance to eliminate bulk in outward-curving seams.

One-way fabrics. Fabrics where the surface interest runs in the same direction. This includes prints, nap or pile as well as warp-knitted fabrics.

Pile. Raised woven-in surface on velvets and fur fabrics.

Slash. To cut along a given line to open a dart or a fold.

Slip-tack. To tack a seam through a folded edge from the outside to match perfectly plaids or stripes for stitching.

Snip. A small cut made either at right angles or at a slant to the raw edge of a seam allowance to enable it to spread and follow a stitched curve.

Stay stitches. A line of stitches made by hand or machine to prevent stretching.

Tacking. A continuous row of long, hand or machine stitches to hold two or more layers of fabric together.

Tailor's tacks. Tacking stitches made with double thread where every second stitch forms a loop. Can be made in one continuous row or over a few grains of the weave, to form a single tack. Used only to mark pattern detail through two layers of fabric.

Top-stitching. A line of machine stitches made on the outside of a garment parallel to an edge or seam.

Chapter 5

Coming to grips with your figure

Many people make their own clothes so that they can achieve the perfect fit which is so important for a really good-looking garment. So, before you start making your own clothes, it is essential to know your personal figure type, and to be aware of any problems you may have. You can then select styles to flatter your figure, which make the most of your good points, and draw attention away from your faults.

Most of us have figure problems. Some are merely a matter of bad posture which can be corrected with a little practice, but others are fitting problems which require some adaptation of pattern and designs. If you work on the basis that almost any design can be adapted to any figure (except in extreme forms of fashion), then all you have to do is recognise your own particular size and problem and take this into consideration when cutting and fitting. But, of course, certain styles will be more flattering to one figure than to another. In this chapter we have given suggestions with each of the three main figure types to help you to make the most suitable choice of style and fabric.

With this knowledge, you can create a perfect picture whatever your figure problem, and feel really confident that your whole appearance is pleasing.

Which type are you?

There are three main figure types, which the chart on this page illustrates: the figure with standard body measurements, the figure with a large bust and the figure with large hips. You'll be able to identify yourself with one of these whether you're tall or short, small or large or anywhere in between.

What is your problem?

Having decided your figure type, you may have particular figure problems like narrow, very straight or sloping shoulders, a rounded back, high tummy or a neck that's set forward. Some figure problems need special attention, and will affect your choice of style as well as requiring careful fitting, while others are only a matter of making minor alterations to your pattern, and do not greatly affect the style of dress you should choose.

The two most common problem figures, which involve adaptation of style, are illustrated on the facing page, with suggestions for choosing suitable styles. All fitting problems will be dealt with in more detail in later chapters.

To find out which figure type you are, stand in front of a mirror, perfectly relaxed, just wearing your normal underwear and compare yourself to the figures illustrated.

Standard body measurements

The figure of standard proportions has a bust 5cm smaller than the hip measurement. So, whatever your size, if you have this proportion, standard sizes will fit you without much alteration.

The choice of your clothes will depend on your height and whether you are broad or slim. If you are slim, perfectly proportioned and of average height, you are lucky and can wear almost anything you like. If you are large, wear garments that fit to the body, with well-fitting shoulders, as unnecessary bulk increases the impression of size. Avoid horizontal stripes and gathered, full skirts. If you are short and plump, always aim to achieve an elongating effect in the way you dress. This does not depend on the length of a garment, but on the vertical design detail. If you wear a belt or separates they should match.

If you are tall and thin, soft styles, blouses, pleated, gathered or flared skirts, wide belts, tweeds and fluffy fabrics are all good for you.

Large bust

If your bust measurement is more than your hip measurement you are top heavy and yours is merely a fitting problem. Buy patterns to fit your bust, and take them in by the necessary amount at the hips. The best designs for you are those which minimise the width across the top. You should avoid any bulk such as gathers and folds, shoulders should fit well and fabrics over the bust should be smooth. Scoop necklines, which break up the area, are most effective on your figure type. If your hips are really slim then you will look good in skirts made from tweeds and other heavily textured materials.

Figure ◀Types

Figure Problems ▶

Large hips

The most feminine figure type is often referred to as pear-shaped. You are the girl with a good bust line and trim waist, but with larger than standard proportioned hips. To make your own clothes, buy patterns to fit your bust measurement and when you cut your garment, add to the width of the skirt pattern round the hips.

A-lines in skirts and dresses and fitted bodices with full skirts are good for you. Remember that you will create an illusion of all-over smallness if you accentuate the smaller proportions of your top half and camouflage the fuller part of your body, especially if the outline of your garment flows into a little more width towards the hem. Straight skirts and dresses need very well fitting blouses or bodices, perfectly plain and without too much ease. The soft blouse look is not the right style for you unless you are really thin.

Rounded back, very sloping shoulders, a neck that is set forward, and a high tummy

If this is your problem, your figure needs the very best support you can afford. Then it's a question of adapting the designs you choose.

As you appear narrow across the top and wide across the hips, triangular-shaped designs are ideal for you because they fit across your smallest points and skim over larger areas.

Never wear tuck-in blouses, but adapt them to short over-blouses, making sure that they are carefully proportioned to the length of your skirt.

Your neck is a very important point to watch, because it will always appear short. Avoid high or large collars and aim for a neat, clear line. Adapt designs to a flat, fitting collar, a soft, narrow roll or even a plain, finished line around the base of your neck. If your neck is very thin you can wear a close-fitting roll or mandarin collar if you like.

Bust larger than hips, flat tummy and very straight shoulders

If this is your problem, adapt the designs you choose. You will look best in fitted garments, without the bulk of gathers and folds. If you are broad or short, avoid waist-seams and belts.

Always aim to minimise the width across the bust line, choosing soft, wide neck lines on a straight, fitted dress. Keep trimming high above, or well below, the bust line. Draping should be used sparingly and be asymmetrical, leaving the bust line well defined. A-line dresses (semi-fitted at waist and hips) will do nothing for you, since the line will be lost, but you can adapt this line to a fitted dress flared gently at the hem. Make a point of choosing toning colours for your blouses and skirts and beware of shirt blouses, which can look very masculine on you.

Always choose a well-fitting shoulder line, with the armhole-seam high on the shoulder to lessen the appearance of width. Avoid wide or short sleeves which will add to the width.

Chapter 6

Understand your dress stand

Generally Speaking

Dress stands are an invaluable aid to the home dressmaker. At those times when you need to check an inaccessible area and there is no friend at hand, a dress stand can come to the rescue. Dress stands can be bought in many sizes and shapes and most women with standard measurements can find a stand which will suit their shape and which needs no alteration.

But if you do have a figure problem your clothes will need even more adjusting and a stand is of even greater value. Since you cannot buy a stand incorporating the problem it will require certain adjustments. These you can make yourself very easily and quickly by padding, as this chapter will show.

Of course, when choosing a stand you will make quite sure that no part of it is larger than any of your measurements—it is one thing to pad out the stand but quite another to make it smaller.

What you will need

Have at hand some tailor's wadding (a roll of cotton wool will do, provided it is not too soft), some old nylon stockings, a small upholstery needle, plenty of pins and one or two old nylon jersey slips which you won't mind cutting up. The slips are for covering the stand, so if you want to give it a more decorative look buy a length of pretty printed nylon jersey instead.

If you have the problem of sloping shoulders you will also need a pair of ready made cotton wool shoulder pads.

With these items you can pad out the stand to suit your figure—whatever your requirements.

Padding the top half of the stand

Using a bodice toile. Make yourself a bodice toile with all the ease pinned off as shown in Toile-making Chapter 22.

To find out which areas of the top half of the stand need padding pull the toile over the stand, then mark each area where the toile does not fit properly with tailor's chalk. Remove the toile.

Cutting the padding. Lay the wadding down flat then cut out layers of wadding large enough to cover the whole of each marked-out area. The only area not covered this way is for sloping shoulders which are dealt with separately below.

If one layer of wadding is not sufficient to correct the shape it will require building up with more layers.

Cut all the layers for one particular area to the same shape as the first but reduce them in size so that you graduate the shape to follow the contours of the body (figure 1).

Pin all wadding layers firmly in position (figure 2).

The edges of the layers of wadding will at this stage form sharp ridges since they are the same thickness all the way through.

So pluck out the edges until each layer tapers into the shape required.

Stitching the padding in place. Cut up the nylon stockings into single layers large enough to cover each padded area.

Stretch and pin the nylon over the padding then slip the toile over the stand again to check that it is padded correctly.

Remove the toile and sew the nylon in place using a small upholstery needle (figure 3). Sew to the stand and avoid catching the wadding in the stitches as the thread will gather it up and distort it. You may well find you are unable to remove all the pins used for holding the wadding in place. This does not matter—the ones that remain can be left there for good, or they may eventually work out.

Sloping shoulders. For this figure fault you will need to raise the shoulder line on each side of the neck, so for this use the cotton wool shoulder pads.

Slip the toile over the stand to check that the bust line of the stand is in line with the bust line of the toile.

You will find that the outer shoulder rests on the stand while the inner shoulder rises above it. Pin off the excess fabric on the inner shoulder so that the shoulder line fits correctly on the stand. Now the bust line of the toile and the bust line of the stand should coincide.

If the bust lines do not coincide padding may make a difference of about 2·5cm either up or down. But if the bust level varies by more than 2·5cm you must disregard the bust line fitting on the stand, fitting the bust line of your garments on yourself instead, and confine your fitting on the stand to the shoulder, which you adjust as follows.

Cut out a small shape from the thick end of the shoulder pad so that it will fit into the neck over the shoulder-seam of the stand (figure 4).

Pin the pad in position and check with the toile that you have achieved enough lift. If not, cut out pieces of wadding to the shape of the pad but smaller, and pluck out the edges of each cut shape to flatten it. Lay these pieces under the pads to build up the inner shoulder line until the toile fits correctly.

Cut sections from the nylon stockings to cover the pads and pin and sew in place as before.

Neatening the padded surface

If more than one area of your stand is padded it will now look rather lumpy. To give the stand the smooth appearance of a well rounded figure, and also to give you a good and easy surface to work on, here is how to quickly make a new cover for it.

The cover for the stand needs to be very close fitting, so use the toile pattern to cut out the stand cover.

Cut a bodice Back and Front from the nylon jersey, cutting both on the fold and leaving seam allowances on all seam lines. The amount of seam allowance needed depends on the amount of stretch in the jersey, but this can be trimmed as necessary afterwards.

Pin the Back and Front on the stand. When you are satisfied that the fabric sits firmly around the stand, and will not create folds when you run your hand over it, trim the seam allowance to about 6mm.

Overlap and pin the seam edges and hand-sew them together (figure 5a). Also hand-sew the armhole, neck and waist edges firmly in place.

Padding the hip line

To complete the adjustments to the stand you must, of course, also check that the hip line measurements are the same as your own. If you find that they need adjusting work as follows.

▲ **1.** *Wadding cut in graduating sizes* **2.** *Wadding pinned in place* **3.** *Covering the wadding* **4.** *Shoulder pads fitted for sloping shoulders* **5.** *Stages in covering the stand; a. covering the bodice; b. covering the lower area; c. the padded stand complete* **6.** *Skirt pattern adapted for stand cover*

Using the basic pattern from Skirtmaking Chapter 10, make a skirt toile, pinning off all the ease.

Slip the skirt over the stand and with tailor's chalk mark any areas that need padding.

Cut out layers of wadding and pad the hip area as you did for the top.

Since most adjustments to the hip line will take up fairly large areas you may find that a nylon stocking is not wide enough to cover each padded area. So pin the wadding sections very securely in place and use the nylon jersey fabric to make a solid cover.

To cut a well-fitting cover use the basic skirt pattern for your guide. But make the following adjustments to the pattern. Straighten the side-seams (figure 6), then fold away the ease by pinning a lengthwise fold down the middle of each pattern piece as shown.

Measure the length of the stand from waist to lower edge, allow a little extra length for adjustment, and cut the pattern to this measurement.

Using the adjusted pattern cut out the nylon jersey fabric, with Centre Front and Centre Back on the fold of the fabric, allowing seam allowances all round.

Pin the cover to the stand. Overlap the side-seams and hand-sew them together. The hip line cover must finish at the waist line. Hand-sew the waist line of the bodice and hip line covers together, having overlapped them with raw edges open (figure 5 b).

At the waist edge trim the raw edge close to the stitches then pin and tack a 13mm tape around the waist line (figure 5 c).

Firmly hand-sew the lower edge of the cover to the stand so that it cannot ride up.

Generally Speaking

Chapter 7
Fabrics made easy

Did you know that there are now pure wool tweeds and suedes that you can pop safely into a washing machine? Or that men's jackets can be baked like hot potatoes in the oven to set their shape for ever? Or that tweeds can now be knitted and that socks are being made with a permanently anti-smelly finish? It would be difficult to imagine what dress departments, fabric shops, not to mention laundry bills, would be like without the enormous advances made over the last twenty years in the textile industry by the fibre manufacturers, spinners, weavers and knitters, who are spending millions of pounds on developing even more fibres and fabrics.

It's worth making the effort to find out what a fabric is made of and how it is put together. You may also be missing out on some of the truly marvellous discoveries which are daily making fabrics more exciting, easier to look after—and sometimes cheaper.

To begin with, there are two basic points to get straight. First, it's important to know whether a fibre is man-made or natural, or a blend of both. In a world which is more and more labour-saving minded and price-conscious, man-mades do have some definite advantages. They are easy to care for and their production quality and cost can be closely controlled. But there are no man-made fibres which combine the best of the innate qualities of natural fibres. For example, many man-mades are non-absorbent which makes them inclined to be sticky and sweaty to wear, and they lack the thermal qualities which make the naturals warm in winter and cool in summer. Man-made fabrics also tend to create static electricity which attracts dirt.

In many cases the answer lies with blends which combine the best qualities of both natural and man-made fibres. (The increasingly popular cotton/polyester blends for shirts give the tough crease-resistance contributed by polyester combined with the cool comfort of cotton.)

The second point to get clear is what we all mean by names. If you think of satin, you probably imagine a fabric with a smooth, shiny surface. In fact the word satin not only describes the appearance, but is also the name of the basic weave which produces this finish. It could be all silk, all nylon, all acetate, or a blend. So the names in the Fabric Guide that appears on page 19 indicate the appearance of the weave or knit, but the fabrics can usually be made up in any fibre, or combination of fibres—though there are a few exceptions to this such as calico which is always cotton.

This question of weave and knit is becoming increasingly complicated. Most fabrics traditionally were woven, with a warp and weft thread. Now knitted fabrics, that is, jersey, are booming and this is a faster and sometimes less expensive method of production than weaving. Knitting machinery is getting so sophisticated that several different types of fabrics which used to be thought of exclusively as weaves—like twills, crepes and tweed-textures—can now also be found made in jersey fabrics.

However, most people still think of appearance in terms of cotton, linen, wool and silk. In the Guide, weaves and knits have been grouped together in categories most commonly associated with these natural fibres. One always thinks of tweeds as wool, but you would be surprised how many are made from acrylics or acrylic/wool blends these days.

So when you go shopping, first know what kind of woven or knit appearance you want, and what qualities you expect of it—then ask your shop assistant to give you full details of the fibre mixture, and the finishes.

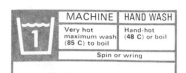

White cotton and linen articles without special finishes.

Cotton, linen or rayon articles without special finishes where colours are fast at 60°C.

White nylon.

Coloured nylon; polyester; cotton and rayon articles with special finishes; acrylic/cotton mixtures.

Cotton, linen or rayon articles where colours are fast at 40°C. but not at 60°C.

Acrylics; acetate and triacetate, including mixtures with wool; polyester/wool blends

Wool, including blankets and wool mixtures with cotton or rayon. Silk.

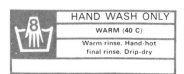

Washable pleated garments containing acrylics, nylon, polyester or triacetate, glass fibre fabrics.

Processes and finishes

Crease resistance. Almost all fabrics have a tendency to crease and some, like pure linen, crease far more than others. To counteract this, the yarn or fabric is chemically treated to give it added springiness and resilience. Most crease resist finishes radically alter the structure of the fibre throughout its life. Drip-dry and minimum-iron usually applies to garments like shirts and underwear and indicates that they should shed their creases if they are hung out to dry after washing. The question of whether to iron or not to iron applies equally to non-iron, wash n' wear, as well as drip-dry and minimum-iron. Although you won't have to give your clothes the thorough going over a madras cotton shirt requires, they will look crisper and smarter if you do iron them lightly.
Trade marks *Dumure* Minicare* Calpreta* Tebilized**

Machine washability. What is so wonderful about machine washability, you may ask yourself as you empty your Monday load into a tub of warm, soapy water. Practically everything—when you consider that the fabric in question is pure wool tweed and pure wool jersey and knitwear. But machine washability doesn't mean that there is a special breed of non-shrink sheep. The men behind the Woolmark guarantee have devised a process of treating wool yarn which prevents shrinkage. What to look for is Machine Washable or Washable, Shrink-Resistant on the label, followed by detailed washing instructions. More miraculous perhaps than machine washable wool is the machine washable suede. This is a beautifully soft specially treated leather with a fine suede finish which can be tossed into a washing machine without losing its shape or special suede feel. It can be bought in small, medium or large skins (0·56m sq, 0·65m sq, 0·74m sq).

Pre-shrunk. Fabrics can stretch quite badly in manufacture. To correct this, and to prevent them shrinking when washed at home, they are pre-shrunk as part of the finishing process. The pre-shrunk process often combines the same qualities as drip-dry and crease resist finishes.
Trade mark *Sanforized* Rigure* Tebilized**

London shrunk. A famous finishing process applied to wool suitings which are moistened and then allowed to dry out naturally. This leaves them in the ideal condition for tailoring.

Permanent press. To permanently pleat wool, the fabric is chemically 'processed' and then fixed by steam pressing. More rigorous treatment can be given to man-made fibres and special blends. They are soaked with chemicals and then 'cured' by literally baking them at high temperatures in ovens! This process permanently sets pleats and creases and is particularly suitable for skirts and men's trousers.
The heat treatment is now being applied as well to entire garments which claim never to crease, wrinkle, stretch or lose their shape and are also fully machine washable. At the moment this heat treatment mostly applies to men's wear, especially trousers.
Trade marks *Koratron* Evvaprest**

Fashioned. Fully fashioned denotes that knitwear or stockings have been 'fashioned' into shape on the knitting machine. Semi-fashioned applies to knitted garments that are only partially fashioned.

Moth-proofing. As far as the British Trade Descriptions Act (which came into force at the end of 1968) is concerned, there are distinct differences between moth-proof and moth-proofed. The first denotes fabrics which are inherently moth-proof: for example no moth has the right kind of digestion to cope with acrylics or polyesters. The second applies to wool fabrics, something moths are especially fond of, and indicates that a garment is treated against moth for life. If you suspect repeated washing or dry cleaning has removed the proofing, you can buy a tin of anti-moth or fit moth balls in your cupboard. Some people actually like the smell!

Flame-proofing. By law, young children's and old people's night clothes have to be treated for flame resistance. However, this can wash out if you use soap or a detergent containing soap. One of the best answers is to make night clothes in Courtauld's new flame-resistant fibre, Teklan. Teklan can be woven or knitted into warm, hard-wearing fabrics in a whole range of pretty colours. Always wash flame-proofed fabrics according to the directions.
Trade marks *Teklan* Proban**

Rain-proofing. When does a shower become a downpour? When you discover your raincoat is only water repellent, and not, as you might have hoped when you bought it, waterproof, and you get very wet. Water repellent, or the words rain resist or showerproof sewed on to a tab inside your raincoat can mean it has been treated with silicones to resist a certain amount of water. Waterproof means one hundred per cent resistance to rain and that the article is made from a rubberized or plastic-covered fabric or treated with wax. **NB.** This term can be only applied to garments which have reinforced seams!
Trade marks *Scotchgard* Aqua 5**

Lustre finishes. A few years ago, when crisp cotton with a shiny finish was in fashion, resins and starches were applied to them to give a lustre. This gloss finish is now primarily applied to furnishing fabrics in the form of glazed chintz.
Trade mark *Everglaze**

Useful definitions

Bulking or high bulk. A process which fluffs out the fibres of the yarn to give extra softness, stretch and absorbency. It also gives a pleasant, deeper texture particularly in knitted fabrics made from acrylics or polyesters.

Count. The yarn count indicates the thickness or fineness of cotton, wool or linen yarns. Traditionally, the higher the count the finer the yarn; with Tex, however, which is replacing counts, the lower the finer applies.

Denier. The same as count, but is used for silk and man-made filament yarns. As in stockings, the lower the denier figure the finer the yarn.

Mercerized. Cotton yarns, specially treated under tension, to make them extra strong, colourful and lustrous.

Spun yarns. Made from fibres spun to various thicknesses—from the softly spun yarns used for nice Shetland sweaters (woollen spun) to the fine, tight, smooth yarn (worsted spun) used for fine worsted suitings.

Warp. The lengthways threads in woven fabrics.

Weft. The widthways threads (left to right) in woven fabrics.

Natural fibres

	qualities	ways to wash
Cotton	*Cotton comes from the ripe, fluffy seed-pod of the cotton plant.* Cotton is a cool, strong fibre, easy to wash, absorbent and therefore extremely pleasant to wear. Great advances have recently been made with easy-care finishes.	All cottons will be washable under Codes 1, 2 or 4, depending on their finish and colour fastness.
Linen	*Linen is spun from the fibrous stalks of the flax plant.* Linen fabric is very tough, absorbent and cool to wear. Its strength actually increases in washing—thus its age-old use for sheets and household linen. Pure linen does crease, but new blends with man-made fibres and the development of crease-resistant finishes are making linen much more of an all-purpose fibre.	If washing is advised Codes 1, 2 or 5 will apply. It is important to pay special attention to the instructions because the treatment or finish given to linen fabrics may vary considerably.
Wool and animal fibres	*Wool fibre comes from fleece of the sheep. Other animal fibres include the luxurious, and expensive, alpaca (alpaca goat or S. American llama),: cashmere (very soft goat), vicuna (vicuna llama from S. America), mohair (crisp shiny fibre from the angora goat, used for men's light-weight suitings), and angora (angora rabbit).* Wool has inherent warmth and resilience. The most versatile of fibres, it can be spun and woven into both the lightest crepes or heaviest coatings and is cool in summer, warm in winter.	Dry cleaning is recommended unless the article is stated as washable.
Silk	*Silk comes from the filament spun by the silk-worm for its cocoon.* The most luxurious of fibres, silk has a lustrous, live quality and takes colour to a deeper intensity than any other fibre.	Silk should be dry-cleaned unless stated as washable, when Code 7 is advised (warm water, do not rub, spin-dry, do not wring).

What are man-made fibres?

Fibre family name	qualities	ways to wash
And Trade Names		
Acetate Dicel, Lansil, Lancola, Lo-Flam Dicel	*Acetate is derived from cellulose, the raw materials of which are cotton linters or wood pulp.* Regarded as the most silk-like of the man-made fibres in wide use. Acetate drapes well, and is woven into satins, taffetas, brocades and surahs. It is extensively used for silk-like jersey, and linings.	100% acetate fabrics can be washed easily, in *warm* (not hot) water at Code 6. They should be washed frequently to avoid over-soiling, then ironed with a warm iron while still damp.
Acrylic Acrilan, Courtelle, Orlon, Dralon, Novacryl	*Acrylic fibres are produced from acrylonitrile, a liquid derived from oil refining and coal carbonisation processes.* Easy-care and crease-resistant, acrylic fibres most closely resemble wool and are very popular for knitwear and light, washable tweeds.	Acrylic fibres wash easily, under Codes 6 or 8, and dry quickly. A cold rinse should always be given before drying, to avoid creasing. Always iron *dry*—do not dampen for ironing.
Modacrylic Teklan, Dynel	*Based on derivatives of oil refining and coal carbonisation processes.* Modacrylic fibres are used for both garment and industrial fabrics. Teklan, strong, hard-wearing and flame-proof is very practical for children's clothing.	Washing at Code 6 is a simple matter, but only a cool iron should be used when the article is quite dry.
Elastomeric Lycra, Spanzelle	*These are stretch yarns with a high degree of elasticity, based on segmented polyurethane.* Elastomeric fibres are used in foundation garments, swimwear and stockings.	These fibres are always combined with others which dictate the washing instructions. Hand wash or minimum machine wash is recommended. Do not iron.
Nylon Bri-Nylon, Blue C Nylon, Tendrelle, Celon, Enkalon, Perlon	*Nylon's raw materials are benzene from coal, oxygen and nitrogen from the air and hydrogen from water.* Nylon is extremely strong and has inherent elasticity. It can be spun into fine silk-like fibres which make it ideal for stockings and lingerie. Its crease-resistance and quick drying qualities have given nylon a large share of the men's shirt market.	Knitted as well as woven nylon fabrics shed creases and are easy to wash and quick to dry. White nylon should be laundered according to Code 3. Coloured nylon at Code 4. It is often drip-dry and minimum or non-iron.
Polyester Terylene, Crimplene, Dacron, Trevira, Terlenka, Tergal, Diolen	*Polyesters are made from ethylene glycol and terephthalic acid, derived from petroleum.* A very strong fibre, polyester is frequently found as a blend with wool or cotton. Used alone, polyester is often 'bulked' or 'crimped' as with Crimplene, and knitted to give a durable and practical fabric.	Woven or knitted into jersey fabrics, polyesters should be washed at Code 4, usually drip-dried and ironed only with a warm iron when necessary.
Triacetate Tricel, Tricelon, Arnel	*Primary raw materials in the manufacture of triacetates are wood pulp and cotton linters.* Triacetates have a dry, crisp silky handle and slightly shiny finish. They have easy-care qualities and are crease-resistant.	Always washable, at Code 6 or Code 8 for permanently-pleated fabrics, triacetates are quick drying and require little or no ironing. Must not be dry-cleaned with trichlorethylene.
Viscose Rayon Sarille, Fibro, Zantrel, Evlan, Triple A	*With a wood pulp base, viscose rayon is a cellulosic fibre and is probably the most widely used of all man-made fibres.* Rayon is the old 'art silk' rayon and is still used to-day for linings or 'brushed' as a cheap wool substitute. It is also used as a blend where its absorbency is balanced with a stronger but non-porous fibre.	100% viscose rayon fabrics may be treated at Codes 2, 4, 5 or 7, depending on the particular fibre content of the fabric, and individual instructions must be followed carefully. A medium-hot iron is usually suggested.

Chapter 8

Linings, interlinings and interfacings

Generally Speaking

In dressmaking the correct choice of under fabrics—linings, interlinings and interfacings—is most important and makes all the difference to the finished result. The wrong choice can be disastrous, so to help you avoid such disasters this chapter sets out to explain the difference between these under fabrics, the function of each type, and what to use. Remember that you need an under fabric which can be washed or dry cleaned successfully with the garment, so always check this important point when buying.

Linings

A garment and its lining are made up separately and when the lining is not stitched into the seams it is replaceable.

Choosing the correct lining fabric can sometimes be confusing, but if you bear in mind what you expect the lining to do for the garment in question this should help you to make the right decision.

Functions of a lining
There are several functions which a lining can perform, the general function being to tidy up the inside of a garment. A lining also prevents a garment from coming into direct contact with the body and so helps it to wear longer.

Linings help garments to hang well by ensuring that they slide over those areas where there is a tendency to cling. They add bulk to a garment and so help garments to keep their shape. Linings also help to prevent creasing and seating, but for greater protection against these a garment has to be mounted or interlined.

The difference between lining and interlining
Interlinings are mounted onto the fabric and made up as one, whereas linings are constructed separately. And although the practice is widespread, the outside fabric should not be mounted onto the lining fabric.

Different fabrics are used for lining and mounting. Whereas there needs to be a perfect marriage between a top fabric and its interlining, this is not the case with a separately constructed lining, and it is rare for lining fabrics to be suitable for mounting.

In addition, mounting with an unsuitable fabric will often prevent you from working the outside fabric properly, such as in pressing when the outside fabric may require greater heat than the lining can stand. So if you want a mounted dress lined you should line it in addition to mounting it.

Methods of attaching linings
Most linings are made up separately from the garment and then attached to the neck line and armholes by hand (figure 1), or caught in with the facings by machine.

Couture touch. Couture dressmakers assemble a lining by hand

and sew in each section over the corresponding section of the garment (figure 2). This avoids creating any folds and creases which a separate and loose lining often makes. In addition, the lining has more anchorage to the garment, friction is reduced to a minimum and the lining will therefore last longer.

Strictly speaking this time consuming task is a labour of love, but it is well worth the effort. While you may not want to go in for this sort of finish it does help to explain one reason why couture garments are so expensive and last so long.

Types of linings
Here is a chart giving suitable lining and fabric combinations.

Linings		
Outside fabric	**correct lining**	**substitute lining**
Cotton: dress-weight cotton suit-weight cotton	pre-shrunk treated lawn tricel taffeta	jap silk (washable)
Linen	jap silk	imitation jap silk
Pure silk	pure silk according to weight	rayon or tricel taffeta
Wool	pure silk or rayon taffeta	
Man-made fibre fabrics	tricel taffeta	

Interlinings or underlinings

The term interlining is often applied to that layer of fabric, between the outside fabric and the lining, which adds warmth to a garment. But interlinings in dressmaking are fabrics used for mounting. Used in this sense the terms interlining and underlining are synonymous and you will often find the term underlining used instead of interlining.

Functions of interlinings
Interlinings are used to help prevent creasing, stretching out of shape and seating, to give body to fabrics and are particularly important for a sculptured look. With interlinings direct hand-sewing to the outside fabric is avoided, thus giving that exclusive couture finish.

In addition, there are some fabrics which would not wear successfully if they were not mounted, such as a number of soft and loosely-woven suitings and coatings, and the soft tweeds mentioned in Skirtmaking Chapter 19 for the bias skirt. Such fabrics are not just mounted, but are properly backed with the interlining sewn to the wrong side of the outside fabric permanently before the garment is made up.

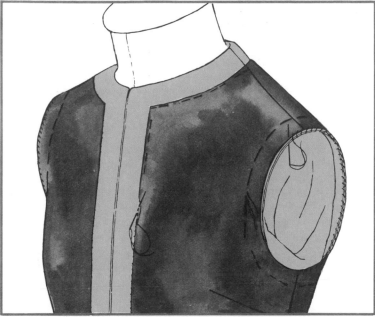

▲ 1. *Attaching a lining to the neck line and armholes by hand*

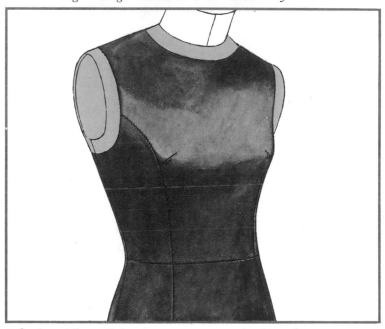

▲ 2. *Assembling a lining the couture way, section by section*
▼ 3. *Tacking an interlining to the wrong side of the top fabric*

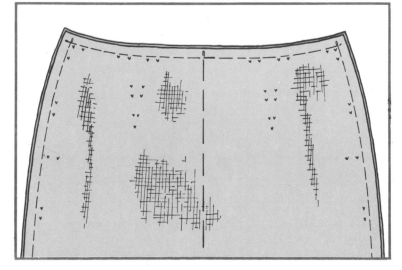

Applying interlinings

Interlinings are tacked to the wrong side of the top fabric before stitching (figure 3) and then top fabric and interlining are made up as one.

To neaten interlined seam allowances oversew them by hand. Always avoid machine finishes as they tend to curl the two layers of fabric, so creating a thick and hard seam edge which makes an impression through the fabric and often shows up quite definitely on the outside.

To stop interlinings folding up inside hems it is necessary to prick stitch fabric and interlining together just below the hem line before the hem is turned up (figure 4). Also, when sewing the inner edge of hems and bias facings to a mounted garment do not sew through to the outside fabric, but catch the interlining fabric only to give the outside a smooth finish.

Facings should be caught lightly to seam allowances only and not be firmly sewn in place, so work under the facing edge and hand-sew loosely.

For the method of backing see Skirtmaking Chapter 19.

Types of interlinings

The correct combination of outside fabric and interlining fabric is most important and compromises can be disastrous.

Unfortunately, many of the interlining fabrics used by the couture are not readily available, and in any case they can be very expensive indeed. They are mostly made of pure silk and often cost more than the outside fabric, which is why interlined dresses are so very expensive.

However, here are a few interlining fabrics which are easily obtainable and reasonably priced.

Interlinings	
Outside fabric	**suitable interlining**
Silk, rayon, fine wool, cotton and linen	pure silk organza or a soft jap silk
Heavier dress and suit-weight wool	soft lawn or mull

▼ 4. *Left: oversewing interlined seams by hand. Right: prick stitching interlining and top fabric together just below the hem line*

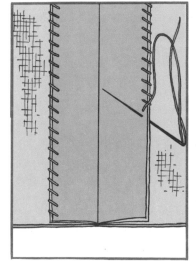 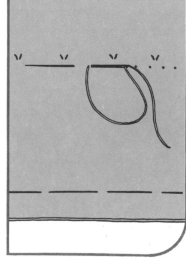

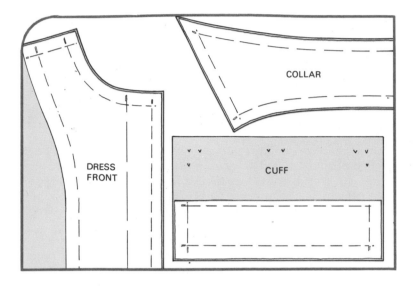

Interfacings

Areas such as collars, lapels, cuffs, belts and opening edges are interfaced to maintain their shape (see above). Interfacing strengthens, prevents stretching, and adds body and crispness without bulk.

The choice of interfacing is large and selecting the right one needs practice. The wrong choice of interfacing can mar the finished appearance of a garment however beautifully made it otherwise might be (figures 5, 6 and 7).

Dressmaker's and tailor's interfacings
To help you in your choice you need to understand that there is a difference between dressmaker's interfacings and tailor's interfacings—this will greatly reduce the list of possibilities and so make the choice easier.

Dressmaker's interfacings can be used for most fabric weights, but tailor's interfacings need the expertise of a tailor to combine and work them successfully.

Dressmaker's interfacings are those which you can stitch in with the seams, and tailor's interfacings are worked onto the wrong side of the outside fabric and stop at the seam lines.

Canvas is of little use to the home dressmaker—this is best left to the tailor as he knows how to work it.

Functions of interfacings
The following chart gives you a guide to the type of interfacing which goes with a particular fabric. But do realize that interfacings also come in different weights and degrees of stiffness and some, like soft pre-shrunk lawn, are not stiff at all. The difference between a very stiff collar and a soft one is in the interfacing, so the correct weight and stiffness to choose will be determined by the function it has to perform. You might even need more than one type of interfacing in a particular garment.

Some interfacings are designed for special jobs. A very stiff interfacing such as permanently stiffened cotton, for example, is used for belt making or to form a firm inside support for a full skirt.

In Blousemaking Chapter 28 it is suggested that interfacing and top fabric should be bought together, and a simple method of testing for the correct choice is given which is worth while stressing. If you are striving for a soft effect place an edge of the interfacing into the folded edge of the top fabric, and if the fabric rolls over the interfacing in a gentle, soft roll it is the right interfacing to use. If sharp points and a hard edge are formed you have chosen the wrong interfacing.

Interfacing fine and see-through fabrics
A problem with fine fabrics can sometimes be the shadow caused by an interfacing. If a lawn interfacing is appropriate for the fabric you are using it is available in different colours so you can choose a shade to match the fabric.

For see-through fabrics use pure silk organza which is so colourless that it can be used for most fabrics.

Types of interfacings
Apart from the many woven interfacings such as lawn and calico there are also the iron-on, woven interfacings and non-woven interfacings about which it is useful to know something.

Iron-on interfacings. These must be used with the greatest of care since not all fabrics will react favourably to them. Unfortunately, once they are ironed on these interfacings do not always stay permanently in place, and sometimes work loose unless they are stitched to the fabric around the edges. Also, as they become detached they will decrease in stiffness and eventually you will have no more support than an ordinary mull or lawn would have given you. They do, however, save working long rows of tacking when making up.

Do not use iron-on interfacings on large areas as they are not designed for this, and be particularly careful to find out if the one you buy can be washed and dry cleaned.

Non-woven interfacings. These usually carry the manufacturer's recommendation for use and combination with fabrics. There is little to add, since they are tested and designed for use with special fabrics. So ask for the right type and weight for the particular fabric you are using and for the function the interfacing has to perform.

Non-woven interfacings, too, should not be used on large areas.

Interfacings	
Outside fabric	**correct interfacing**
Dress weight: cotton linen wool	pre-shrunk treated lawn iron-on or non-woven interfacing as recommended by the manufacturer
Suit-weight: cotton linen wool	treated cotton interfacing, such as bleached calico iron-on or non-woven interfacing as recommended by the manufacturer
Man-made fibre fabrics	non-woven interfacing as recommended by the manufacturer for very light fabrics (lawn, voile, etc) pure silk organza
Pure silk	fine lawn or pure silk organza
See-through fabrics	soft organdie or pure silk organza

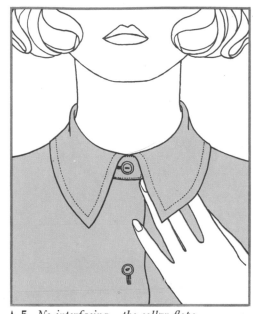

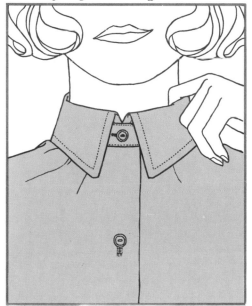

▲ **5.** *No interfacing—the collar flops*
▼ **6.** *Interfacing much too stiff—collar chokes*

A Vogue pattern, interlined to perfection ▶
▼ **7.** *The right interfacing—the right look*

Chapter 9

Meet the basic stitches

Most sewing in the realm of dressmaking today can be done on your sewing machine—the more sophisticated the machine the greater the variety of stitches to choose from. However there are times when hand-sewing comes into its own, especially when it concerns finishing seams, hems and other fine detail. It is here, too, that you can give your clothes the couture, custom-made look sadly lacking in so many off-the-peg garments.

On these two pages you will find all the stitches you will need to do just that. Some of them will be shown again when they relate to a specific technique.

Back stitch

This is a very firm stitch and is worked by taking the needle and thread back one stitch on the side facing you, inserting the needle just in front of the preceding stitch. The resulting stitch at the back is twice the length of the top stitches.

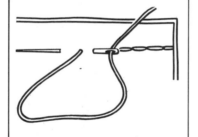

Blanket stitch

This is a commonly used stitch for neatening seams on all sorts of woollen materials. It is worked from left to right over the raw edges. It is an alternative to the zig-zag stitch of the sewing machine.

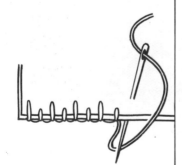

Blind stitch.

This is a more closely worked version of invisible hemming stitch.

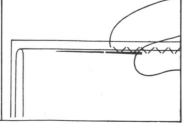

Even tacking

This stitch is used for seams which will take quite a lot of strain during fitting. Use suitable length of stitch and thickness of thread to suit the material. An occasional back-stitch will help where firm tacking is essential.

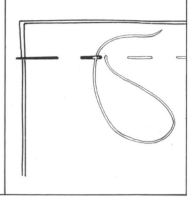

Felling stitch

Felling is a form of hemming one piece of fabric to another piece. The edge can be folded or left raw. While it is a very strong stitch, it has the added advantage of a neat look.

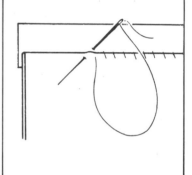

Herringbone stitch

This is the ideal stitch for turning up single hems when you are using non-frayable material and also for tacking facings. Work from left to right of work, taking a small stitch in the hem and then a one-thread stitch in the fabric.

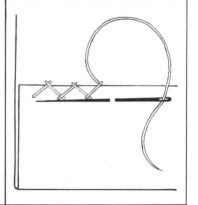

Invisible hemming

The rule to remember when turning a hem is to keep the stitches loose. If the thread is pulled tight, it will leave indented marks on the right side. Take up very little thread from the garments and a good deep thread from the hem. Leave a small loop every four or five stitches which will ease out during wear. Start and fasten off on the hem, never the garment.

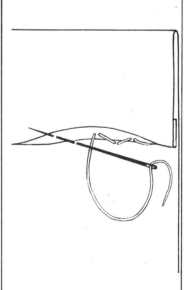

Overcast stitch

This is the usual way of neatening cut edges and, of course, stops them fraying. As you can see from the diagram, it is worked diagonally, with small evenly spaced stitches.

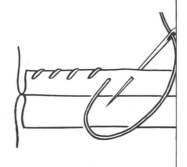

Prick stitch

This is a version of back stitch, worked over a single grain of fabric, forming a tiny surface stitch.

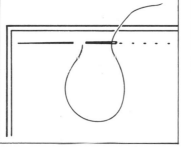

Running stitch

The most elementary of all sewing stitches, this is used when seaming and gathering. Weave needle in and out (as shown in the diagram) before pulling the needle through.

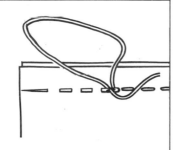

Slip stitch

This stitch gives an invisible finish and is worked in an almost straight line as opposed to the zigzag motion of a felling or hemming stitch.

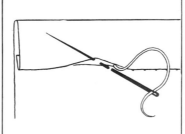

Whip stitch

This is a very fine oversewing stitch worked from right to left. It can be used to finish off the edge of very fine fabrics by turning under the edge 3mm and whipping to look like very fine cording.

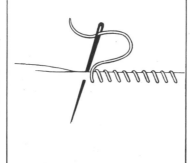

Ball section of press-stud

Socket section of press-stud

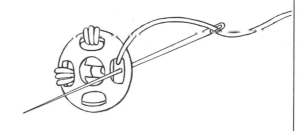

Sewing on press-studs. Sew on ball section of the press-stud first to the upper section of the opening. Press against the lower section of the opening leaving a tiny mark to show the position for the socket section. Oversew into one hole two or three times passing the needle under the stud to the next hole until each hole has been firmly stitched.

Ball section of press-stud goes on front part of opening and socket section goes on back

Chapter 10

Theme and variations on a simple skirt

Every one of the elegant skirts shown here can be made from one single pattern, and you can even make that yourself. So instead of having to buy seven different patterns, you simply adapt this one to make the style of skirt you want. The basic skirt pattern is a simple flared style, but in later chapters you will discover how this pattern can be used to make all the variations sketched here. With the length of skirts and the moods of fashion constantly changing, you can be certain that this is one pattern which will go to any length to suit your needs.

What you wear with your skirt is important and demands careful thought, because an unsuitable combination can spoil the effect of any garment. Of course, there is an enormous variety of clothes to choose from for wearing with a skirt, but a collection of blouses provides the ideal answer and gives you the scope to choose the perfect partner for the length and style of skirt you wear. The blouses sketched here are some variations on the basic blouse from the Golden Hands Graph Pages, and you will find instructions for making all of them are given in later chapters. If you make blouses and skirts, you can have fun choosing colour schemes and you'll be surprised how many different outfits you can make up if the colours are carefully chosen to match or complement each other and fit in with the rest of your wardrobe.

An introduction to drafting

Making your own pattern may sound like a formidable task, but if you work from a graph you'll discover it is fun and very easy—in fact drafting from a graph is the simplest form of pattern making. This chapter starts off with the simple flared skirt, and if you follow the step-by-step instructions carefully, you can't go wrong. Read on and you will see some of the advantages of making your own pattern. The graph is for a 92cm hip, 66cm waist and 58cm length, but you will find the instructions give all the information you need for altering the size of the graph pattern to your own measurements, including full instructions which give the secrets of lengthening and shortening a flared skirt.

Although you will make the pattern to your size, your individual proportions may not be standard and you will need to make certain alterations to the pattern. So when you have cut out and tacked the skirt, the following chapter describes fitting in detail and shows how to transfer any alterations to the skirt pattern. You will then have an individual pattern which takes all your personal skirt fitting problems into account.

You can use this corrected pattern to make the skirt variations illustrated here. And, because the pattern fits you perfectly, there should be very little fitting to do when you use it again for making up other variations of the basic style.

Theme: the flared skirt...

Straight

4-gore

6-gore

Knife pleated

Dirndl

Bias cut

...Variations

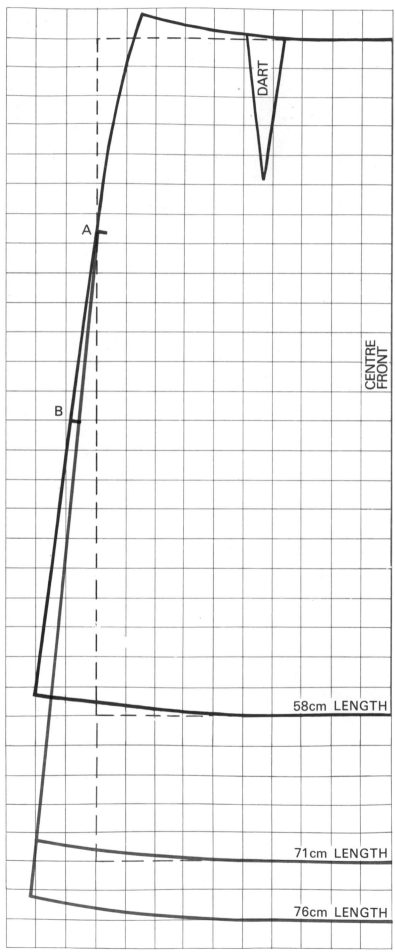

DART

A

B

CENTRE FRONT

58cm LENGTH

71cm LENGTH

76cm LENGTH

Pattern making from a graph

To make the pattern, you will need the following equipment:
- ☐ Ruler
- ☐ Tape measure
- ☐ Tailor's square, or a 45° set square from most stationers will do just as well
- ☐ Soft pencil
- ☐ Large sheet of brown packing paper, with lengthwise grain lines, from stationers

To make a pattern from a graph, just count the squares and translate them into centimetres. Here, we use a rectangle of dotted lines to make it easy to obtain the pattern shape, the position of the darts, and the curves. The size of the rectangle is based on the length of the skirt and the hip measurement. The pattern shown on the graph is for size 92cm hips and a 66cm waist. Instructions on changing the size and length of the pattern are given at the end of this chapter, so read first and then take action. Each square represents 2·5cm square. It is worth noting that if you prefer, you can work in inches, in which case each square represents one square inch. The easy way to do this is to use an inch/centimetre tape.

How to copy the rectangle and obtain your pattern shape
First, fold the edges of the paper under 2·5cm, along the lengthwise grain lines, to give a strong working edge. Starting with the black rectangle for the front, count the squares on the Centre Front line of the graph. Measure this distance on the folded edge of the paper and mark in pencil starting 10cm from the top. Then, count the squares along the horizontal dotted lines and measure the distance on the paper, making two more pencil marks opposite those on the folded front edge. Connect these points using a ruler making this the dotted vertical line, marking it as it appears on the graph.
At this stage, it is very important to double check that the distances between the folded edge and the dotted vertical line are equal, top and bottom, or the pattern will become uneven.
To make the horizontal lines, lay the tailor's square on the folded edge and your first pencil marks, and draw dotted lines across to complete the rectangle.
Make the rectangle for the back skirt section in exactly the same way. These rectangles now give the guide lines to count from, to obtain the pattern outlines and the position of the darts.
Points A and B are balance marks. These marks are important and have to meet when you stitch the skirt seams together.
For the waistband, mark out a strip 3cm wide and 33cm long, as shown on the graph. This is half your waist measurement. For the waist-band to fit snugly, no tolerance is allowed.

How to alter the graph size
If the size on the graph is too small for you, it is quite easy to increase it. This is how to do it.
Make the patterns as before, but instead of making the fold on the grain line of your paper 2·5cm, increase the fold to 5cm. Next, refer back to your measurement chart in Chapter 4 for your waist and hip measurements, remembering to add the tolerances given to your own measurements.
Then divide the difference between your measurements and those

Graph pattern of skirt front for size 92cm hip showing 58cm length in black, and 71cm and 76cm lengths in red. Each square = 2·5cm square.

on the graph by eight (this is because you are working on half sections of the pattern only). For example, to increase the pattern to a 102cm hip and a 76cm waist, you will have to add 10cm to the graph pattern size—10cm divided by eight means that you will have to add 12mm to each centre line and side-seam. To add 12mm to the centre lines, unfold the edge of the paper by this amount. To add 12mm to the side-seam, measure outwards from the given line and draw a new line. Make sure that the point where side-seam and waist-seam meet stays the same distance from the upper horizontal line of the rectangle.

How to alter the graph length
The graph pattern shows a 58cm length skirt in black and 71cm and 76cm lengths in red.
To increase the length to 71cm or less the rectangle is increased to the desired length and the pattern made as before. This gives the same flare at the hem as in the shorter version.
For lengths over 71cm the flare needs to be increased. To do this, first draw up a skirt 71cm long as above. Then extend the line of flare by the required length as shown for the 76cm length skirt.

Cutting out the pattern
You are now ready to cut out the pattern. Before cutting out, be sure that you have marked the folded edges, Centre Front and Centre Back, and balance marks. Cut round all the shapes—cut into the darts, too. It is best to transfer this pattern on to stiff white paper (from stationers) since the original will be used later to obtain all the outlines for the other skirt styles you will make.

Fabric requirements
In the next chapter you will be cutting out your skirt. Here is how to calculate the amount of fabric you will need, depending on the width you have chosen.
140cm width—for sizes 87cm, 91cm and 96cm hips, your skirt length, measured over side hip, plus 20cm for seam and hem allowances and waist-band.
For 102cm, 107cm and 115 cm hip, one and a half times your skirt length, measured as above, plus 20cm.
70cm or 90cm width—twice your skirt length, measured over side hip, plus 28cm for seam and hem allowances and waist-band.
N.B. 70cm fabric is not suitable for hip sizes over 96cm.

Choosing your fabric
Having made the pattern and worked out the amount required, it is time to choose your fabric and get everything ready for cutting out.
When choosing fabric, make sure it's easy to work and practical to wear. When you buy, make sure you ask for skirt or suit weight cloth. Our choice was a worsted woollen gabardine, but you could choose from any of the following:
☐ Firmly woven worsted woollens, cottons and linens
☐ Fine grain tweeds, such as hand-woven Irish or Scottish
☐ Firm man-made fabrics, like acrylics (Courtelle, Acrilan)
☐ Mixture fabrics, such as wool or linen, which have been blended with nylon, acrylics, or polyesters (Terylene, Dacron)
   You will also need:
☐ Sewing thread
☐ Hooks and eyes, size 3
☐ 18cm zip fastener
☐ 1 metre stiff grosgrain ribbon, or petersham 2·5cm wide.

Graph pattern of skirt back for size 91cm hip showing 58cm length in black, and 71cm and 76cm lengths in red. Each square = 2·5cm square.

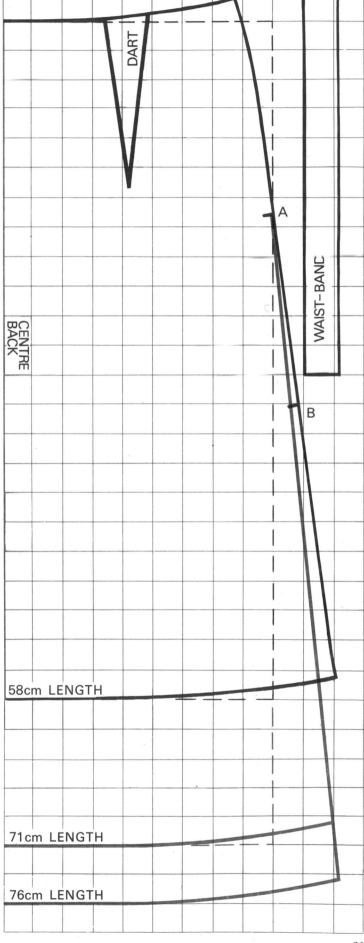

Chapter 11

Preparing to sew the skirt

Having bought your fabric and made the basic skirt pattern from the graph in the previous chapter, you are now ready for the important stages of cutting out the skirt.

Here is the equipment you will need:

☐ 1 reel of tacking cotton, No.50
☐ Cutting shears
☐ Tailor's chalk
☐ Pins and needles
☐ Firm table surface

Preparing the fabric

It is essential that the fabric is perfectly smooth before you begin to cut. If it has become creased through packing and folding, press the whole length carefully, using a table surface or press board rather than an ironing board. Leave the fabric folded lengthways with right sides together, and steam the creases out on the wrong side of the fabric using a damp but not wet cloth. Press both sides of the folded length.

Set up your cutting area on a table large enough to take the full folded width and length of the fabric, and fold the fabric as shown in the following layouts and instructions. If you don't want to use a table top, a sheet of hardboard, 120cm wide by 120cm long, will provide you with an excellent cutting surface.

If the fabric is 140cm wide, unfold it so that it lies flat on the table. Then, for a hip size of under 102cm, refold the fabric with wrong side out, so that the selvedges (finished edges) meet at the centre fold line. Smooth out the layers of material towards the new folds to make sure the fabric lies perfectly flat, then secure the selvedges to the centre crease with pins. For size 102cm hip or more, simply fold over the selvedges until the pattern width is accommodated (see layout far right).

For narrower fabrics, fold lengthwise, selvedges together, smooth out and pin.

Laying on the pattern

Before laying on the pattern pieces, make sure you have marked all pattern details such as Centre Front, Centre Back, and the balance marks on the side seams.

Place the Centre Front and Centre Back lines of the skirt on the fold as shown in the appropriate layout.

Pin both pieces around the edges, making sure they lie flat and are firmly anchored through both layers of fabric.

Since the pattern is cut without seam or hem allowances, leave enough room round each piece for 19mm seams and 6·3cm hem.

Marking the pattern detail on the fabric

Before cutting, transfer the shape of the paper pattern to the fabric by marking round the edges with continuous tailor's tacks. Once you become more familiar with paper patterns and working on fabrics, you can mark pattern details after cutting.

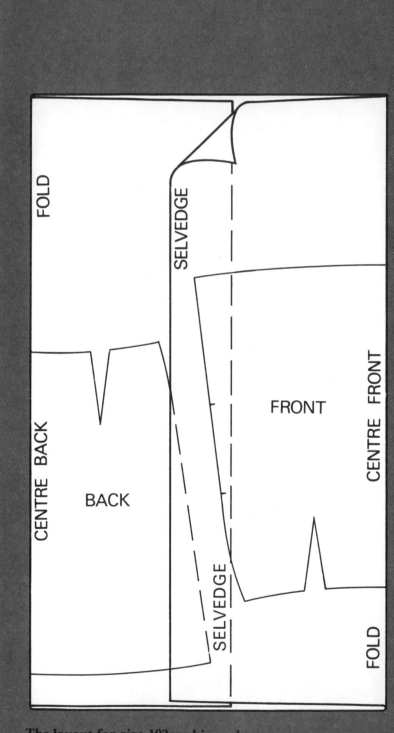

The layout for size 102cm hip and over, on a 140cm wide fabric

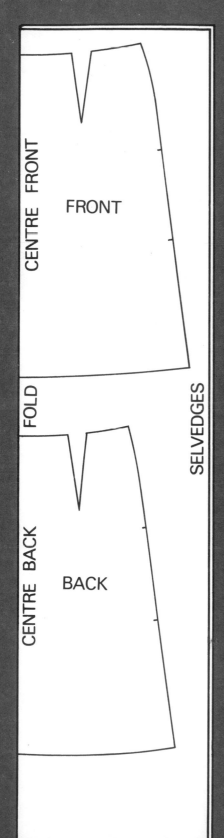

CENTRE FRONT

FRONT

FOLD

SELVEDGES

CENTRE BACK

BACK

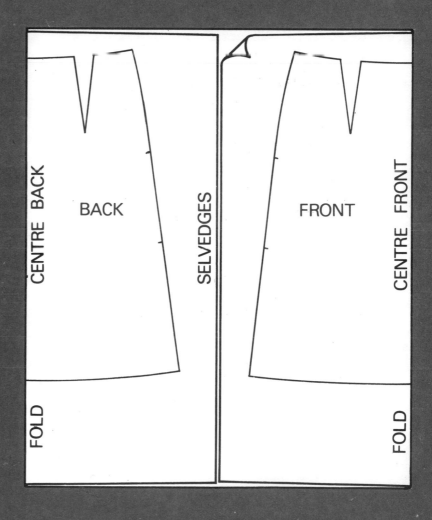

CENTRE BACK

BACK

SELVEDGES

FRONT

CENTRE FRONT

FOLD

FOLD

The layout for sizes 87cm, 91cm and 97cm hip on a 140cm wide fabric

The layout for 68cm and 90cm wide fabric.
On a 68cm width this layout is for sizes 87cm, 91cm and 97cm hip only

Making continuous tailor's tacks

Thread the needle with tacking cotton, pulling it through so the ends meet and the cotton is doubled. Make the stitches 13mm long, leaving a loop about the size of your finger tip on every other stitch as shown.

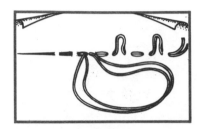

Make tailor's tacks carefully round the pattern and into the darts. Make a single tailor's tack to mark the balance marks A and B, using a double thread, and make a back stitch leaving a loop.
Before cutting, you must add on the hem and seam allowances. Add 6·3cm for the hem and 19mm for the seams. You can mark these with pins or tailor's chalk. A chalk line is the best method, provided the edge of the chalk is kept sharp by scraping it with a knife, as a thick line can alter the width of your allowances.

Cutting

This is a magic word for even the most experienced dressmakers. It is the point of no return—check once again that all markings and allowances are correct and the fabric is perfectly flat.
Insert the shears from the top edge of the fabric and cut along your pin or chalk lines with firm, short movements through both layers of fabric. As you cut, keep the fabric flat and firmly in position with your hand alongside the shears. This prevents the fabric lifting, which would cause your seam allowance to shift and alter the correct measurement on each edge.
After cutting, set aside the remaining fabric which you will be using later for making the waistband.
Remove the patterns.

Separating the layers

Separate the layers of fabric held together by the tailor's tacks by pulling them apart gently along the tacking lines. This will flatten the loops on the top fabric to give enough room to insert the scissors between the layers and cut through the tacks. Be careful when doing this not to cut the skirt fabric.
When you unfold the skirt pieces, the seams and hem line will have a row of tailor's tacks to guide you.

Tacking for fitting

To tack your skirt together, start with the darts, creasing them down the centre, so that both rows of tailor's tacks meet evenly to form a sewing line. Pin. Working from the top edge of the skirt towards the points of the darts, tack them together with small tacking stitches. Use single cotton and make flat stitches. Secure ends well with a double back stitch.
Working on a flat surface, place the Back and Front pieces together with right sides facing and seams coinciding. Make sure the balance marks on the hipline on the Back and Front correspond and that both layers of fabric lie flat. Pin seams together.
Hold the pinned seams up and if one side puckers and makes the seam swing out instead of hanging straight, unpin the seam and gently stroke out the fullness. Pin again.
Still working on a flat surface, tack the right side-seam. On the left side-seam measure 18cm down from the waist-seam line and leave open for the zip fastener. Tack the rest of the seam.

The expert touch

After tacking the darts and seams, press the seams open with very light strokes, so they will lie reasonably flat for fitting. The importance of pressing as you go can't be stressed enough because it really does make all the difference.
A complete guide to fitting comes in the next chapter.

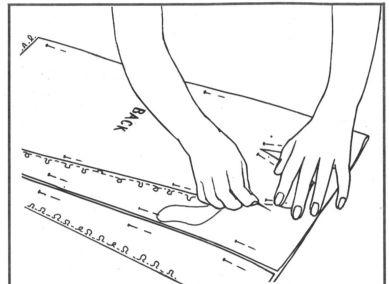

Marking the pattern outline

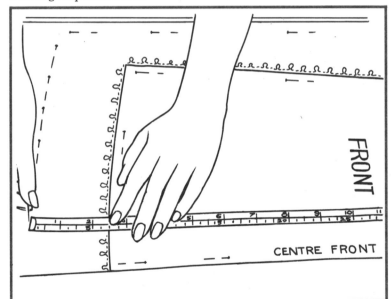

Pinning the hem allowance

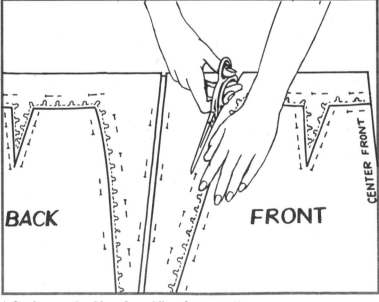

▲ *Cutting out the skirt after adding the seam allowance*

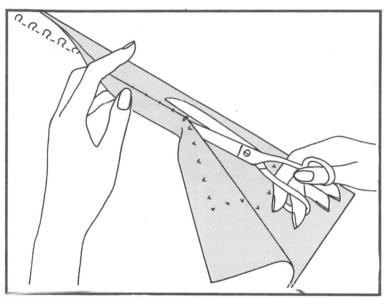

Separating the layers of fabric

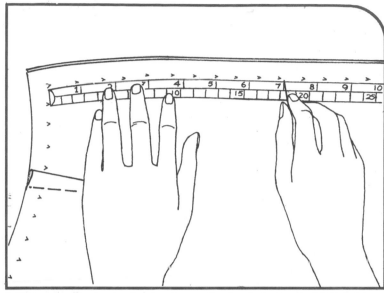

▲ *Measuring the opening for the zip*   ▼ *Two looks for the finished skirt*

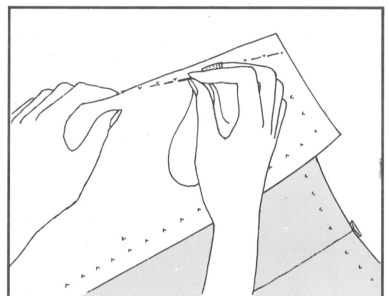

Tacking the darts

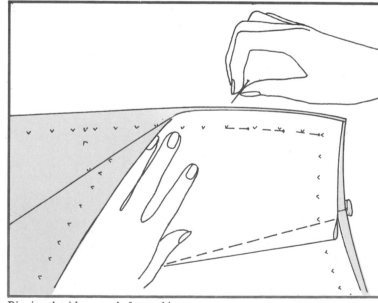

Pinning the side-seams before tacking

Chapter 12

When it comes to fitting- persevere!

Your skirt is now ready for fitting. It is a good idea to find someone to help you with this because although it is possible to fit yourself, it is not always very easy to do if you have a difficult fitting problem, or, for instance, if you need to pin and make adjustments to the back section.

Slip your skirt on and pin together the opening for the zip, in the seam-line. Then adjust the skirt around your waist and lay the ribbon or petersham on to the waist-seam marking, and pin it.

Your skirt should fit closely to the figure around the waist and hips and fall to a gentle flare at the hem—it should not fit tightly at any point. Now comes the moment to get things absolutely right. The guide here shows some of the common faults, and on the next two pages you find out in detail how best to correct them.

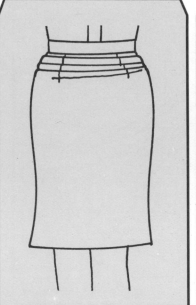

1. 'Pulling' lines across waist and hips
The skirt is too tight around the body.

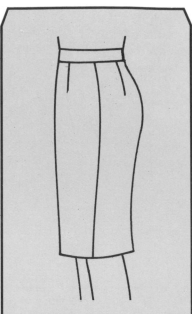

2. The skirt pulls in below the seat
The skirt is just too tight over the seat.

Fitting guide

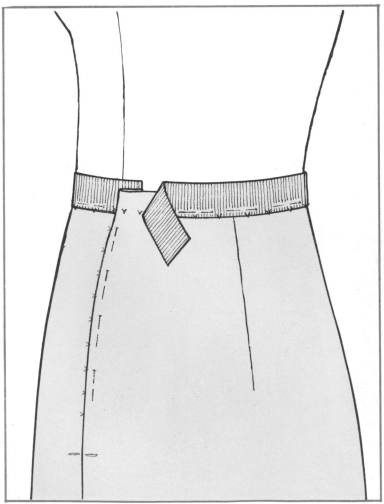

Undo the skirt and pin new side-seams all the way down.

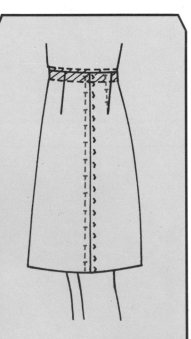

Pin new side-seams on the back section.
Take any extra width at the waist into the back darts.

3. The skirt hangs loosely around the body
It is simply too big.

4. Creases below waist line at the front or back
At the back it's usually the combination of a long waist, and a high seat.
At the front it's because your natural waist line tends to dip.

5. The skirt juts out at front or back hem
This means you have either a high tummy or a high seat.

6. Skirt juts out at front and back hem, and side-seams hang inwards
This usually means that your waist is larger in proportion to your hips.

Faults and their causes ▲ ..... *and how to correct them* ▼

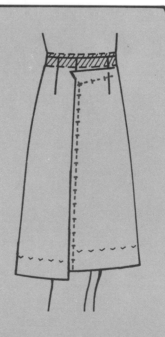

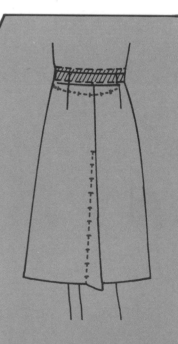

Pin away the fullness into the side-seams. You may also have to let out the darts to allow the skirt to hang properly. If you do, take the extra material into the side-seams.

The waist line requires re-shaping. Pin a crease across on the fabric below the waist-band. Do not pull the excess up under the waist-band as this will result in an incorrect waist fitting.

Pin a small crease towards the side-seam on the section which juts out, enough to give you the correct hang.

Pin a crease, below the waist-band and across the side-seams so that the skirt hangs straight. Do, however, watch your hip-line as this may need to be taken in. If so, pin away the amount into the side-seam.

Tracing your alterations

Take your skirt off very carefully to avoid displacing the pins. Mark the alterations by tracing over the pins with long stitches in tacking cotton, taking care to catch in only one layer of material at a time. Trace the alterations on both sides, so that you do not loose all the markings when you take out the pins.

Remove the petersham, marking any alteration you may have made to its length.

Marking and correcting after fitting

Now you are ready to correct and mark the skirt for stitching. The diagrams on the right show how to do this, taking each fitting in the same order as before.

Code:
- □ small ticks = the original line of tailor's tacks
- □ red dashes = alteration lines
- □ scissors = where to trim off surplus material

Is one hip higher than the other?

If you have one hip-bone higher than the other, first cover all the main faults mentioned in this chapter and then prepare the skirt for a final fitting.

You will then see how your high hip-bone affects the general hang of the skirt. If it is not affected you need only let out the seam slightly over the high hip in order to accommodate the higher curve.

If you find, however, that the hang of the skirt is affected, then you will need to adjust it on the opposite seam as well, by lifting into the waistband.

Transferring alterations to paper pattern

Once you have marked and corrected the skirt, it's a good idea to transfer the fitting corrections to the paper pattern straight away, so that when this pattern is used again you can be sure of a really good fit.

To do this, measure all the alterations and draw them on the pattern in pencil. You can cut out the alterations to the waist line curve after first having made sure you have marked the pattern accurately.

If the skirt was taken in, mark the alterations to the side-seams in pencil against the side-seam on the pattern. Do not cut this off, since the same skirt made in another fabric may well fit you. Just make a note of it so that when you re-cut, you can tack the skirt inside the side-seam line.

If you had to let out the side-seams, extend the paper pattern by attaching a strip of paper down the full length and draw the alteration on to it.

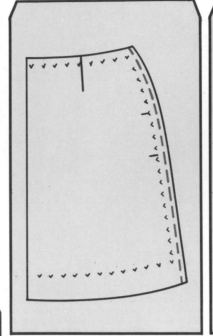
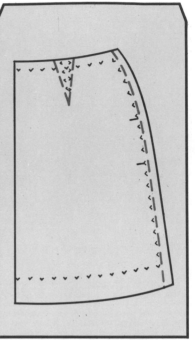

Fitting guide

1. Letting out side-seams on both sections

Undo these seams all the way down and fold the pieces on centre lines, as they were after cutting.

Measure the difference between the original side-seams and the alteration marks on both the left and right sides of each piece of the skirt. On each piece, add the difference together, halve it, and measure this figure out from the original side-seams, using pins or chalk. This is very important. When pinning the skirt, you might have taken up unequal amounts. The skirt would then be unbalanced if made up to the pin marks. Make a new line of tailor's tacks. Remove original markings.

N.B. When pinning seamlines, remember it's a good idea to lay the work flat on a table and bend down to look into the pin line at table level. You will be able to see if even one pin is out of line.

2. Letting out side-seams on back section

Work as for (1), but on the back section only.

Next, the darts.

You have already trace-tacked the extra amount to be taken into the darts. Now lay the back skirt section flat, right side up, and measure the distance between the trace-tacks at the top of each dart. Add these figures and divide into four. Turning the skirt section wrong side up, pin this amount off from the darts, starting at the waist line. Allow the fullness to run into the original stitching line.

Tailor's tack over the pins to make a new stitching line.

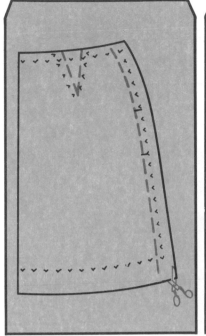
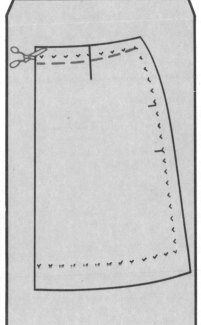
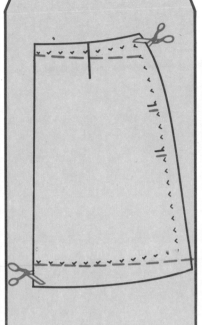
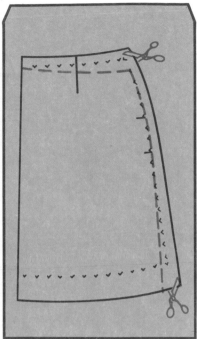

Take note ..... Take action

3. Taking in the side-seams

Work as for (1) but instead of measuring out from original side-seams, measure in.

Let the darts out on the front and back sections in equal amounts. Pin off the surplus into the new side-seam, starting at the waist line and tapering into the seam at hip level. Tailor's tack over this new line of pins. Mark the corrections with new lines of tailor's tacks and trim away surplus to correct seam allowance.

4. Re-shaping the skirt at the waist line

Turn the skirt inside out. Fold front and back sections on centre lines. Pin the side-seams together and pin along the waist line.

Measure along the depth of the crease between the trace-tacks and, starting with the full depth at Centre Back or Centre Front, pin a new waist line through the double layer, gradually curving up into original seam line so that the curve ends at the side-seam.

Make a new line of tailor's tacks along the pin line and remove the original markings. Cut through tailor's tacks to separate layers and trim off any surplus material, leaving correct seam allowance.

5. Lifting a skirt that juts at the hem

Undo the side-seams and to correct the jutting section displace the balance marks 13mm upwards. The depth of the crease you pinned when fitting may not be quite correct since the skirt was tacked together at the side-seams and you may need a greater displacement than 13mm. Try the skirt on again, and check. Take care when you've reached the right amount of lift, you may find it necessary to take in the side-seam on the lifted section. Finally, level the waist and hem line. To do this, always level to the section which remains unaltered. In this way, if you lifted the front section, level this down to the back section and vice-versa.

Make the new lines of tailor's tacks. Trim off surplus leaving correct seam allowance.

6. Lifting skirt at top of side-seams

If it is necessary to take in the side-seams, do this first. Unpick skirt sections and lay them together, right sides facing. Measure the amount to be taken in. There will be more at the hem and less at the hip with the line disappearing into the waist.

Use a ruler to chalk out a straight line from hem to hips and then pin a gentle curve from waist to hips. Make a new line of tailor's tacks along pins for the side-seams and cut away surplus, leaving correct seam allowance. To re-shape waist line, pin and tack side-seams together in new line, then fold skirt on centre lines and pin side-seam to side-seam, and darts to darts. Pin along waist-seam.

Measure out depth of crease between trace tacks and pin new line from side-seam tapering into original waist line.

Make new lines of tailor's tacks. Cut off surplus material. Cut through tailor's tacks to separate layers.

Chapter 13

Give your skirt a neat finish

Having re-tacked the seams and darts after alteration, and tried your skirt on again for a final check you are now ready to stitch the darts and seams.

In this chapter you will find out how to put in the zip properly, step-by-step, and how to stitch your darts for a really professional finish. And just to get you started, the illustration on the left shows you how your skirt should look when it is finished.

Seams and darts

Thread your machine with the same colour as your skirt, and test stitch length and tension on a double scrap of skirt material. It helps when stitching darts and seams to remember the shape of the human body. At no point where clothes cover us is there a sharp corner. Even the thinnest figures have gentle contours, so, when stitching the seams, always aim to run the straight lines into the curves slowly. To switch direction suddenly will cause an unsightly pucker.

Stitch the darts and side-seams, and allow the dart ends to run out smoothly.

Start at the top of the side-seams and stitch just outside the tacking lines. If you stitch over the tacking, it will be very difficult to remove and also, as there is some give in tacking, your skirt might be too tight.

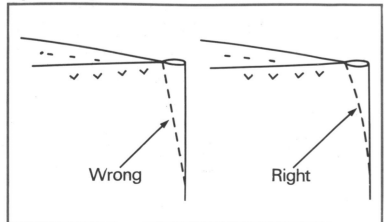

The right and wrong way to stitch skirt dart

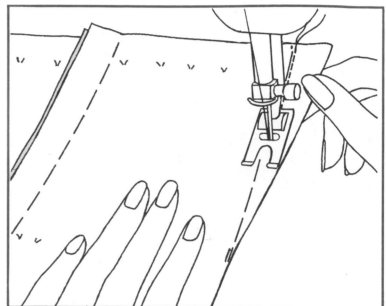

Stitching the darts

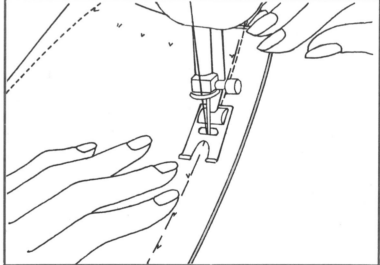

Stitching the side-seams

Pressing hints

Pressing in dressmaking is quite different from ironing when it is just a question of smoothing out a surface. Pressing means fixing a certain shape which you have taken the trouble to fit and stitch. To retain this shape, use a lifting and pressing movement and adjust the pressure according to the weight and texture of the fabric. Some fabrics, such as woollens and linens, require a heavy pressure to stay in position—others, such as rayons, silks, and man-made fibres, need only light pressure.

If you use a damp cloth for steam pressing, do not keep the iron in the same place until the cloth is dry, but lift and press again repeatedly, until all the steam has gone. Even if you are working on fabric which does not need steam, it is a good precaution to use a dry cloth under the iron.

With some of the new man-made fibre fabrics, it is a good idea to ask for washing and pressing instructions when buying the fabric. As a general rule all fabrics made of man-made fibres should be pressed with a cool iron.

With mixtures of natural and man-made fibres, the seams may be difficult to press properly. In this case, use heat applicable to the base fabric, making sure at the same time that the fabric is protected by a cloth throughout the pressing.

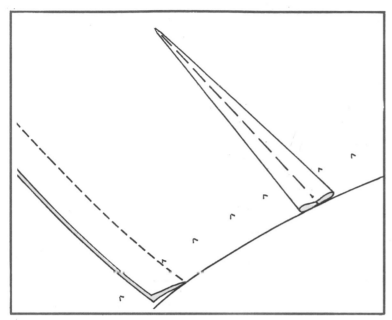

Dart tacked flat ready for pressing

Pressing the darts and side-seams

Some darts are turned to face the centre of the garment and are pressed in that position—others are cut open to within 5cm of the point and pressed open. But the darts on the flared skirt are pressed flat, with the centre of the dart over the dart seam, which shows a neat flat finish from the outside.

Fold the dart centres to dart seams, pin and tack. Lay the pressing cloth (damp or dry, according to the fabric you are using) over the darts and press gently. Take out the tacking and press again, to fix the shape.

Next, the side-seams. Remove all tacking other than the balance marks, lay the skirt over the ironing board and press the seams open, starting at the bottom. Do not press the side-seams downwards. The flare in the skirt means that the fabric is cut slightly on the cross towards the hem—and if you press into the seam starting from the top, you could stretch it.

When you have pressed the seam open and flat, you may find when you lift the edges that they have left impressions. Remove these by laying the damp cloth under the seam edges and, without touching the seam crease, press out the impressions.

Seam finishing

After the seams have been stitched and pressed, they must be neatened off, to prevent fraying during wear.

There are various ways of doing this. If you are using a firmly woven fabric, use the zig-zag stitch on your sewing machine to

overcast the seams. Again run up the seam edges, not down, because as with pressing, these edges could stretch if they are not stitched in the right direction. If you do not have a swing needle machine, oversew the raw edges by hand.

Putting in the zip

First, tack the zip opening closed on the seam lines and press open carefully, as for a seam. Take out all the tacking and press again to remove any impressions made by the tacking cotton. As the seam is now open, take great care not to stretch the edges. Undo the zip and with right side of the skirt facing you, lay the back seam edge of the skirt to the outer edge of the right-hand zip teeth, and pin. When fitting a zip, never stretch the seam over the zip, as this will cause it to wave. Also, the zip and the seam should never be at equal tension; the zip must always be held taut. If the opening turns out to be too short, undo the seam a little more to accommodate the zip fully.

Pin across the seam to catch the zip tape. After pinning, you should see the fabric rise a little over the tape between the pins. Tack the right-hand zip teeth into the back seam edge of the skirt securely, with firm small stitches. Using the zipper foot on your machine, stitch the zip in, about 3mm from the edge.

Close the zip after stitching and lay the front seam edge to cover the zip teeth completely, far enough to meet the stitching line on the back seam edge. This will allow for recession when it is stitched in, and yet still ensure that the material covers the zip completely. Start pinning the front seam edge to the zip from the bottom of the zip up, putting two or three pins across seam edge and zip tape. Then pin the top of the zip to the seam, before pinning the rest. By doing this, you will easily be able to see how to distribute any fullness you might have had in the seam. If there is too much, ease this out towards the top. (It should never be more then 6mm) Trim off after stitching, so that both top edges are level. Tack zip in firmly and machine stitch about 9mm from seam edge.

Then, take out all the tacking and with a cloth gently press, wrong side up. This applies to metal zips only. Nylon zips need only the lightest touch when being pressed.

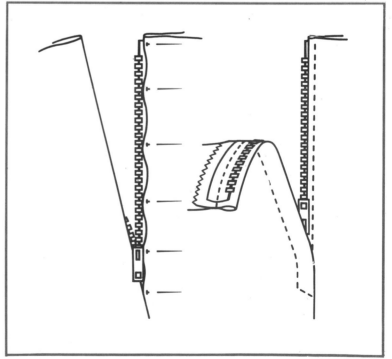

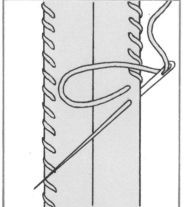

Overcasting by hand

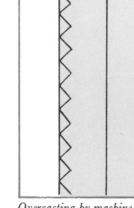

Overcasting by machine

The skirt back seam edge pinned to the zip   *The zip stitched into position*

Making skirt hangers

For looped hangers cut two 15cm lengths of straight seam binding to match the skirt. Fold double to form loops. With loops pointing downwards, pin the ends 13mm over waist seam line, on the inside of the skirt, just behind the zipper on the back and 3·8cm from the right side-seam on the front. Tack into position.

For flat stitched hangers cut two strips of silk or lining 10cm long and 2·5cm wide. Fold lengthwise and machine stitch 9mm from the fold. Pull them through with a small safety pin and press flat. These are attached after the waist-band is finished (see paragraph on waist-band fastening on opposite page).

Putting on the waist-band

Cutting out the waist-band

Use the fabric from the bottom of the skirt length and fold it in half, selvedges together.

Lay the waist-band pattern to the fold and pin, first making sure that the fabric is lying perfectly flat. If, as a result of the fitting, you need to add to the length, now is the time to do it. Cut out the waist-band, adding the same seam allowance as on the skirt, 19mm. Cut the tailor's tacks to separate the layers.

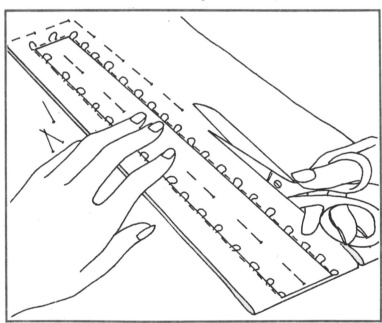

Cutting the waist-band

Stitching on the waist-band

First, measure the waist-seam on the skirt and make a mark exactly half way. This mark will be just in front of the right side-seam, as all side-seams in dressmaking are laid towards the back by 2·5cm on either side. The skirt waist line should be 2·5cm wider than the waist-band. Mark the centre of the waist-band and pin into place on the skirt waist-seam, matching centre marks. Then, lay the end of the waist-band to the zip opening in the seam line, back and front, making sure that the waist-band is level with the seam edges at the opening.

The skirt waist-seam is fuller than the closely fitting waist-band because the skirt needs more ease immediately below the waist-band to fit smoothly.

Distribute the fullness evenly between the centre mark and both ends of the waist-band, taking care not to make creases. Tack into position on the seam line. Remove all tailor's tacks. Stitch the waist-band into place as close as possible to the tacking line.

Mark the centre of the petersham or ribbon, and lay it along the upper seam marks on the right side of the waist-band. Tack firmly and stitch. The petersham or ribbon may be a little tighter than the fabric waist-band. This happens through the natural spread of the fabric and will disappear when the stiffening has been turned under. Do not tighten the fabric waist-band, as this could make the finished waist-band buckle.

Remove all the tacking, trim the waist-seam on the skirt to 9mm, as the double layer would be too thick, and press the seam into the waist-band on the wrong side.

Turn under the seam edges on the front and back of the waist-band level with the zip opening.

Fold over the petersham or ribbon, and pin.

Pin and tack the petersham to the waist-seam and stitch by hand.

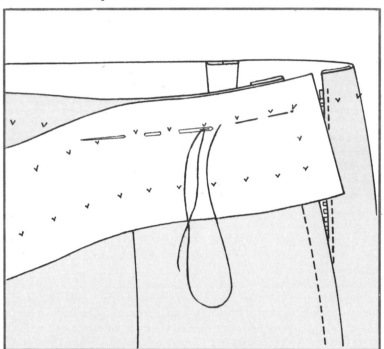

Tacking the waist-band into position

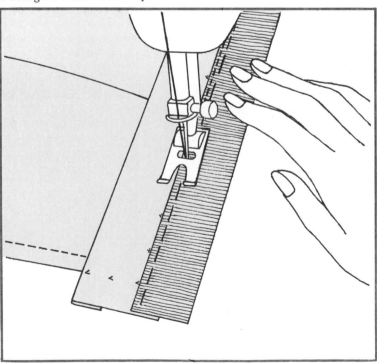

Stitching the petersham to the waist-band

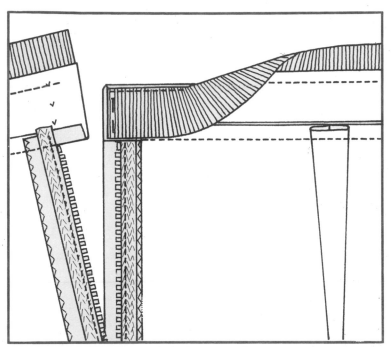

Folding over the petersham and pinning

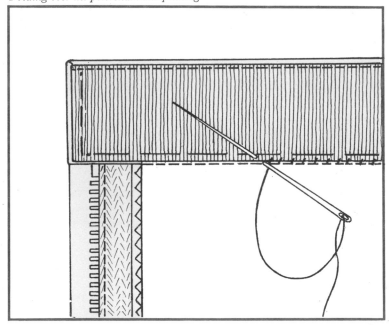

Stitching the petersham by hand

Waist-band fastening

Stitch two No.3 hooks and eyes on the inside of the waist-band, one at the top and the other just above the waist seam. Sew the eyes on the back edge, and hooks on the front. For the eye, the loop should come over the edge 2mm. Hand sew over the sides of the loop and through each ring separately. Set the hooks back 5mm. Stitch under the hook, over the double wire, and then through each ring separately. The hooks and eyes are sewn on in this way to prevent the skirt gaping when the give in the hand sewing makes them move towards each other slightly.

If you are using flat skirt hangers, now is the time to fit them lengthwise to the inside of the waist-band. Do not loop them. Turn hangers under 13mm at each end, pin one on the back, just beyond the opening, and one on the front, beyond the halfway mark. To test their position, put the skirt on a clothes hanger. If the waist-band droops, adjust the front skirt hanger until the waist-band is level. Stitch on securely by hand.

Turning up the hem

First, pin the hem up on the line of tailor's tacks to check that the length is correct and that the hem is straight. If you have to level the hem or alter the length, ask a friend to help.

Before taking out the pins, trace along the crease of the corrected length with long tacking stitches. Take out the old tailor's tacks to avoid confusion.

Before stitching the hem, make sure that the depth is even all round—measure this carefully and cut off any surplus.

Machine finish the edge with zig-zag stitch, or overcast by hand, making sure you do not stretch the full sides.

Pin up the hem to the new line from the inside and tack about 13mm from fold edge. When pinning up a hem, always lay it on a table and insert pins towards hem at right angles to it. This allows you to distribute any fullness evenly and prevents a twist on the finished hem.

Press the hem lightly with a cloth before stitching, remembering to press out the impressions left by the edge. Tack again about 13mm from the top edge, to hold the hem in place for hand sewing. Taking the full depth of the hem into your hand and, without creasing it, turn over 6mm of the upper edge with your thumb. Stitch invisibly behind the hem, taking up very little thread from the skirt and a good, deep thread from the hem.

Don't pull the stitches tight, as this will show through to the outside. And, to give an important couture tip, leave a little loop about every four or five stitches, which will ease itself into the other stitches. Always secure the ends of your stitches on the hem, never on the outside fabric.

Remove all the tacking, and press the hem for the last time. Leave the hem lying flat, and not over an ironing board, as this would make little puckers on the outside.

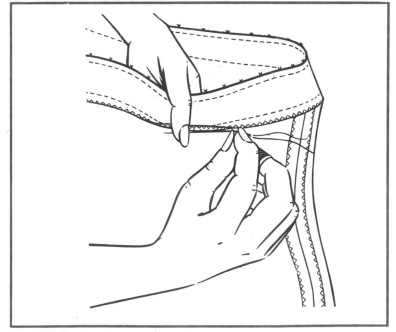

Hand-sewing the skirt hem

Pressing for finishing

This gives the final touch to the skirt. Turn it inside out and make sure you have removed all the tacks. Always use a cloth (damp or dry, depending on your fabric) and press the waist-band firmly into place, still keeping the skirt flat. Then pull the skirt over the ironing board and press, leaving out the hem.

Chapter 14

Fine finishes

So far only one method has been given for finishing the waist-seam of a skirt but there are many other ways of doing this. Not all the methods serve the same purpose: each is designed to do a specific job, so that once you know how to do the various finishing methods you will be able to adapt them to your personal needs. Because of their particular qualities, some fabrics dictate the way in which they must be finished, but the waist-bands described here can be used successfully on all the fabrics suggested for skirts in Skirt-making Chapter 10, p31 and are the most commonly used.

The waist-band with enclosed stiffening

First, make a paper pattern for the waist-band.
Length: to find the length, measure your waist and add 5cm for wrap.
Width: the stiffening, or petersham, should be 2·5cm wide, and the waist-band must be twice as wide as the stiffening, plus 6mm. The 6mm is taken up when the waist-band is turned over the top of the stiffening.
So, for a size 66cm waist, the pattern will be 71cm by 5·6cm.
Don't add tolerance to the waist-band unless you like it loose.
Lay the pattern on single fabric. If you use a strip of fabric from the side of the skirt layout, check the grain lines. In many fabrics the fact that the grain on the waist-band runs in a different direction from the skirt does not matter, but if the fabric you are using has a marked grain it is a point to watch.
Pin the pattern on to the fabric and mark around it with long, flat tacking stitches.
Add 19mm seam allowance all round and cut out.

WRAP	BACK	FRONT

How to mark out the fabric waist-band

Tacking and stitching

The wrap of a waist-band always goes to the back of a skirt. With the right side of the fabric facing you, mark off 5cm from the left seam line and then mark the centre between this point and the right seam line. With right sides facing, raw edges level, place the waist-band to the skirt and pin, letting the wrap extend over the opening. Tack and sew in place.
Cut the petersham, or other stiffening, exactly to the length of waist-band pattern, that is, with wrap but without seam allowance. Again, mark off 5cm from the left and find the centre of remainder. Pin and tack the petersham over the seam allowance of waist-band and skirt with the bottom edge of the stiffening just meeting stitching line. Stitch in position along edge of stiffening.

Fold the seam allowance at each end over the stiffening, so making the front edge level with the zip opening, and tack. Fold the waist-band over the stiffening and fold under the seam allowance along the lower edge of the waist-band. Pin and tack to skirt along the stitching line. Hand sew into position with firm stitches and slipstitch turned in ends to close. Remove tacking.

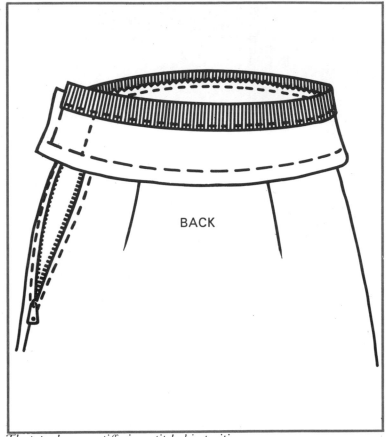

The petersham, or stiffening, stitched in position

Attaching hooks and eyes

The hook and eye fastening for this waist-band is slightly different from the one used for the flared skirt.
Using two No.3 hooks and one eye, first stitch one of the hooks to the front edge of the waist-band, about 6mm in, and make a bar by hand on the back of the waist-band, level with the zip opening, as shown. When the zip is closed the waist-band will fasten in line with the side-seam.

How to make a bar

The bar goes across the centre of the waist-band in line with the hook and is stitched from the top towards the bottom.
Thread the needle with a strong machine twist, pull it double and make a knot at the end. Insert the needle from the back and return it into the fabric about 13mm further down, placing the tip of your thumb-nail under the thread as you pull it through to prevent it becoming too tight. This tack makes the foundation of the bar. Now return the needle to the top of the tack and repeat the stitch four times, taking care not to pull the thread tight at the back. Then before you make the buttonhole stitch, work over the back threads and stitch them firmly down to the fabric to prevent the bar stretching.
Buttonhole stitch over the tacks as shown, keeping your thumb-nail tip under the threads to avoid catching the fabric in the stitches. Make the stitches close together and fasten them off at the back when you have completed the bar. If the knot is unsightly, cut it off now.

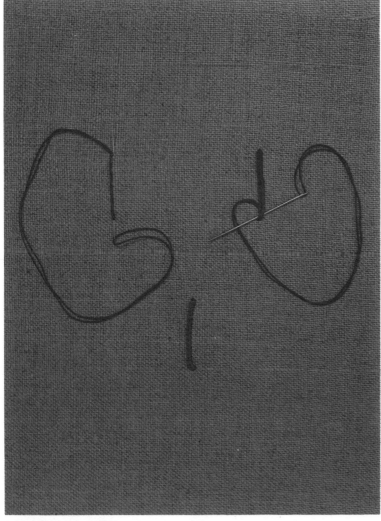

Making the bar tack

Finishing the fastening

Stitch the eye to the edge of the wrap, on top of the waist-band and not underneath it, leaving the eye extending as shown.

To find the correct position for the second hook, close the zip and

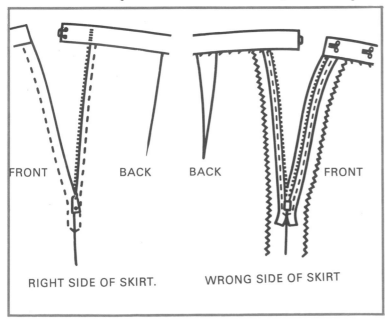

RIGHT SIDE OF SKIRT.   WRONG SIDE OF SKIRT

The finished waist-band with the correct setting for the hooks and eyes

the hook and bar, and place the second hook on the inside of the front waist-band 3mm further in from the eye.

When you stitch the hooks, eye and bar into position, make sure that the stitch catches through to the stiffening for extra hold, but do not stitch through to the outside. It is important not to place the second hook 5cm from the front edge of the waist-band (the length of the wrap) because, depending on the thickness of the fabric, this measurement sometimes alters slightly and the fastening might stretch. The strain would then break the hand-made bar, which only holds the top of the waist-band down.

Hangers for this waist-band can be either one of the types in Skirtmaking Chapter 13 p42.

The soft waist-band

So far the two most popular methods of making a stiff waist-band have been covered, but you may prefer one without stiffening which is soft and less constricting.

This type of waist-band should not be deeper than 2·5cm because it would turn over at the top. And, for extra support, the waist-seam allowance on the skirt must be the same as the width of the waist-band, or else it will wrinkle. It will also wrinkle if it is too tight, so the soft waist-band must fit around you less snugly than the stiff waist-band.

Using the previously prepared pattern, add 2·5cm tolerance and work exactly as before, leaving out the stiffening.

The hidden waist-band

The waist-bands made so far are visible and are fixed to the top of the skirt. This waist-band is hidden.

Since this waist-band is not supported by fabric, it is advisable to use a wider petersham than you have used for the others.

The best width to work on is 3·8cm with or without whalebones. If you use the whalebone-stiffened one, make sure that the openings of the little whalebone slots are at the top edge of the waist-band, otherwise the bones will gradually work out.

This type of waist-band must be curved and fit to the body.

To obtain the curve

Don't pleat the petersham, since this only results in a nasty kink in the waist-seam, but use the following method:

Cut the length of petersham to the amount you require for your waist size plus 13cm. Lay it flat on an ironing board and press over the petersham with a hot iron and damp cloth. Before the steam dries remove the cloth and gently pull the lower edge of the petersham into a curve. Dry the damp on the petersham with a

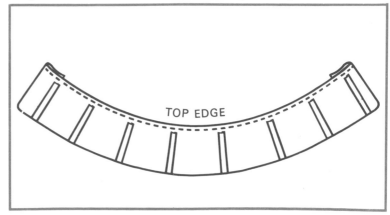

TOP EDGE

The whalebone petersham, correctly curved, and ready to use

hot iron, fixing the shape and pressing in the fullness around the top edge. To stop this edge from stretching when you attach it to the skirt, run a stay stitch through it on the machine, feeding it into the machine from the front and letting it run out behind the needle, without pulling it.

Now measure the inner curve to the length that you need for your waist size. Add 2·5cm at each end, and cut off the remainder. Turn each end under 13mm then fit the band to your waist. It should lie around your body closely but not tightly.

Tacking and stitching to the skirt
Take out the marking for the original seam allowance of 19mm on the skirt waist-seam, and mark a new line 9mm from the top edge. This is necessary because, as you turn the waist-band under, it will take up some of the length. This would make your fitting incorrect. Following the sketch, lay the short, inner curve of the petersham to the inside of the new waist-seam line and stitch into position close to the edge of the petersham. Cut a length of straight seam binding in a matching colour, 13mm shorter than the top edge of the petersham, and lay it over the raw waist edge on the right side of the skirt and the petersham, leaving 6mm at each end uncovered. The lower edge of the binding must cover the row of stitches.

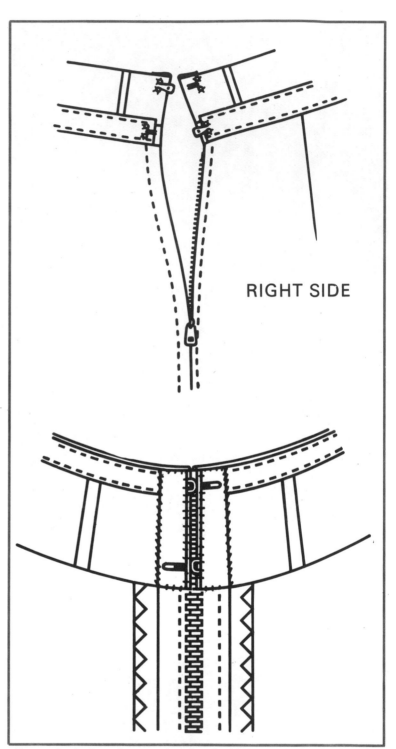

Above: the hook and eye setting for the hidden waist-band with seam binding covering the raw edges
Below: hidden waist-band fastening with neatened edges, seen from inside

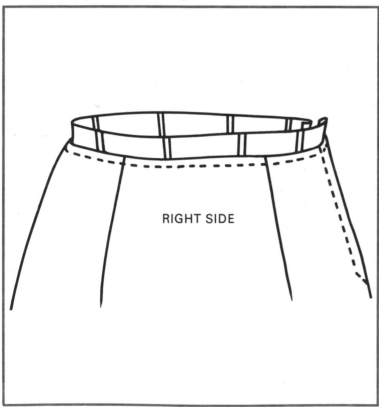

The curved petersham stitched to the inside of the waist-seam

Tack and stitch into position on both edges, avoiding the whalebone insertions, by lifting the presser foot and passing the work under the needle to the other side of the bone.
Turn the waist-band to the inside of the skirt and tack along the upper edge.

Hooks and eyes
To fasten this waist-band, use No.3 hooks and eyes on the edges of the waist-band opening and place a hook to an eye and an eye to a hook. Since the waist-band must not fit tightly into the waist, this method will ensure that they cannot come undone. They must be stitched to the outside of the waist-band, otherwise the top hook could not be done up.

Turn the petersham and seam binding to the inside. To neaten off the edges cut two strips of seam binding 6·3cm long. Turn under 13mm at each end and stitch them over the edges of the waist-band, covering the raw edges at the top, and passing them under the hook-bars as you see below. Slipstitch in place all round. If the skirt fabric is heavy, you may find it an advantage to machine stitch along the folded edge at the top of the skirt, to prevent the waist-band from working up over the top. On normal skirt weight fabric, though, it should be quite enough to attach the bottom edge of the petersham in a few places, such as the seams and darts, with a light holding stitch.

Hangers

If you want skirt hangers use the flat type, as described in Skirt-making Chapter 13, for this waist-band, but ideally this waist finish should hang on a spring-loaded skirt hanger.

Zip in a straight seam

Although the overlap type of zip opening (the one used on the simple flared skirt) is the most commonly used in side-seams on skirts, you may wish to put a zip into the centre back or centre front seam of a skirt. In this case, the zip will have to be stitched in so that the stitching lines are equal on both sides.

Prepare the opening by tacking the seams together and pressing them carefully, as for the side-seams.

Remove the tacking. Open the zip to the bottom, and lay it in the skirt opening so that the seam edges just cover the zip teeth on both sides. Tack the zip into position.

To make sure that the seams lie perfectly flat and don't push each other up, close the zip before you machine it in. If the seams do push up, take the seam edges back a fraction until they lie flat still keeping the zip completely hidden. Start machining about 9mm from the seam edge on one side, and stitch down until you are level with the zip end. To make the mitre at the end, turn the work and stitch towards the seam. Pivot the work on the needle and return on the other side in the same way.

This method of inserting a zip is most successful when it's used on a straight seam. But for a curved seam, the overlap on one side is safer, since the equal distance of the stitching line on both sides —down into and then up into the grain, over the rigid tape of the zipper—would tend to drag the seam and make it twist.

Since skirt zips are always of the heavier variety, it is not advisable to insert them by hand, other than in very fine fabrics where you would use a dress weight zip.

A word about the invisible zip

To insert this type, you must first of all have the right zip presser foot for your sewing machine to enable you to put in the zip properly. Carefully follow instructions to get the correct finish. Without the correct presser foot the result will not be satisfactory.

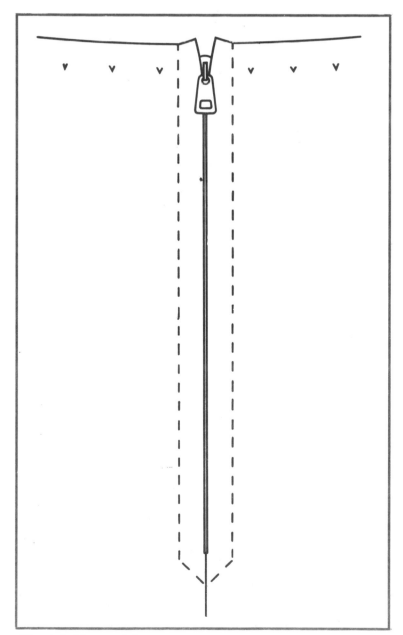

Zip stitched in a straight seam

Zip in a curved seam

Chapter 15

Focus on hems

Making a hem is not just a method of tidying up to complete the garment. The length of a skirt is often such a fashion point that the eye is immediately drawn to the hem. Stitches which show, or an uneven length, are instant giveaways so that an immaculate hemline is essential if your garment is to have a professional look. Each type of hem has a definite function and gives the final hold to the outline. Some garments need extra weight at the hem to make the skirt hang properly, so the depth of the hem has to be considered. Garments made from extra-fine fabric, such as chiffon or voile, need a finely rolled hem for a soft, light, wispy look. Special hems like these come in Know-How chapters.

The basic dress and skirt are finished with a conventional hem which is correct for the firm fabric used. However it is the fabric, together with the cut of the garment, which dictate the method to be used for finishing the hem and there are many different techniques for doing this.

Rules which will always apply to hem-making

Here are some basic rules which must be followed whenever you are making a hem.

The most important one is the pinning up of the hem in the right way—this is where you can make or mar it.

Always pin at right angles to the hem however wide or narrow it is. Never slant the pins or place them parallel to the hem turning because this could cause a shift in the layers of fabric you are pinning together and result in a nasty twist in the finished hem which will spoil the hang of the garment as well as look ugly.

Always work with the hem lying flat on a table so that the weight of the garment is supported. By working in this way you will be able to see that the hem is straight along the turning. Or, if you are working with a curved hem, you will be able to see that the fullness is evenly distributed with the fluting directed straight towards the raw edge. If the fluting is twisted or forced to one side it will make a kink in the turning and the hem will finish up with a series of points.

Always tack the hem about 13mm from the lower edge. Make stitches between 13mm and 2·5cm long, depending on the fabric and which size holds it in position best. Never pull the stitches tight.

Always give the hem a light pressing (steam press only if the fabric requires it) and shrink in any fullness around the raw edge. Be careful not to press too hard over the tacking stitches as they might leave impressions in the cloth which are difficult to remove.

Always press with the hem lying flat on the ironing board making sure that the garment is supported over the back of a chair so that it cannot drag away from the iron. Never pull the skirt over the ironing board.

Always press the hem from the wrong side—it should never be necessary to press it from the right side.

▼ *The wrong way and the right way of pinning a hem. Always place pins at right angles to the hem, never horizontally as in the top picture*

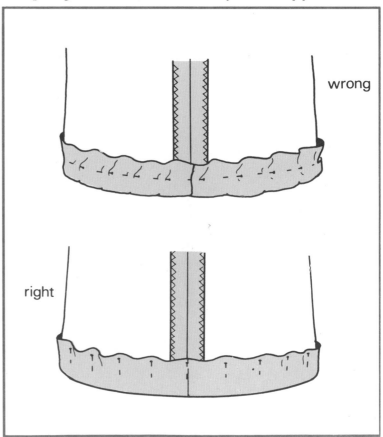

The flared hem

When you are faced with a hem which is curved and you have too much fullness to shrink, or you are using a fabric which will not shrink at all, make the hem as narrow as possible, sometimes as narrow as half the width of the normal hem allowance.

Then, using a small running stitch, gather in the fullness along the raw edge and draw it up to fit the skirt. Fasten the stitches off well so that the hem will not stretch again.

To finish the raw edge of this type of hem, don't use the machine zigzag but oversew by hand. After a final press over the sewn edge, stitch the hem in place using the invisible hemming method shown in Skirtmaking Chapter 13, p43.

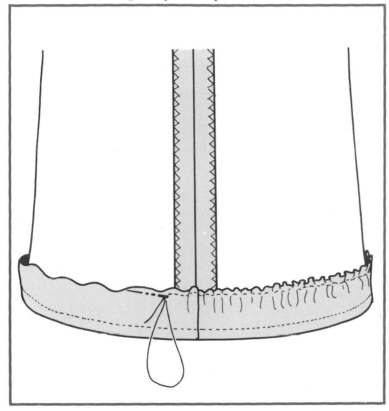

▲ *On a flared hem fullness must be gathered with small running stitches*

The hem with a straight folded edge

When the hem is straight and you are using a light-weight fabric, simply turn the raw edge under 13mm and use a slip stitch to sew it to the skirt. This method applies mainly to fine cotton fabric or to special hems where extra weight is needed to help the shape of the skirt. A good precaution is to press the folded edge first but be very careful not to stretch it as it is possible to stretch a straight edge under heat and pressure.

The pleated skirt hem

When a hem has to endure a lot of hard pressing, such as with pleated skirts, it is important to make the hem finish as flat as possible. You can never completely avoid leaving an impression on the hem with hard pressing but by making the hem flat, the marking will be less obvious. So use a herringbone stitch. This means you need not oversew the raw edge, except when the fabric frays a lot, and the hem will be as flat as you can make it.

The hem in thick fabrics

If you are working with a heavy tweed or other thick fabric, oversewing is not quite enough to finish off the raw edge of the hem — it should be bound. You can buy bias binding already cut and turned under which is ideal for this purpose, but make

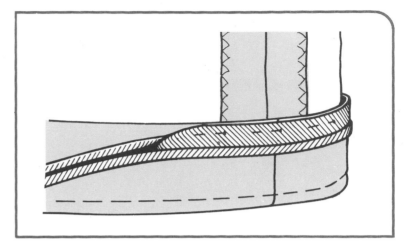

▲ *How to pin bias binding to the raw hem edge when using a thick fabric*

sure you ask for rayon bias binding as cotton bias binding is usually too stiff.

Prepare the hem in the usual way. Then take the bias binding, unfold one edge and pin and tack it to the outer hem of the skirt, with the raw edges level. Stitch the binding to the hem using a slightly longer machine stitch than you normally use for the seams. Fold the other edge of the bias binding over the hem edge and sew into position along the back of the hem with a running stitch. Press the bound edge before you begin sewing the hem to the skirt.

Although the stitches already covered are those most commonly used for hems, you often need a stronger stitch for heavy fabrics because the friction between the two layers of fabric is greater. Therefore, to make the hem secure and also to allow for the movement, use an invisible herringbone stitch and sew with a slightly stronger thread.

To do this, turn the hem edge back as for the hem on the flared skirt and work the herringbone stitch, catching the material from the garment and the hem each time.

In some fabrics you may find that the bound edge is too thick to turn back easily. Therefore, turn the whole of the hem under and herringbone stitch along the crease between the garment and the bound edge, as shown.

When you have finished and taken out all the tacking threads, you will see how you can move the hem without it being loose or dropping out of line.

▼ *How to work herringbone stitch under a bound hem edge*

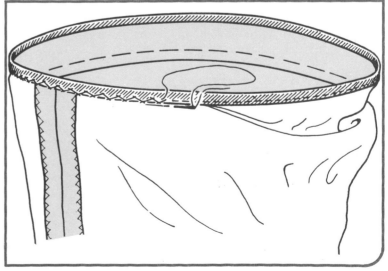

Chapter 16

One pattern-many skirts

Knee-length, midi or long, gored or dirndl–which is right for you? Here you see how easy it is to experiment by manipulating the basic skirt pattern of Skirtmaking Chapter 10. It is transformed into a four-gore skirt, itself adaptable to a choice of lengths, and a dirndl. There is a pleated variation in the next chapter. Once you have mastered these styles you can try adapting the pattern even more yourself.

The four-gore skirt

The making up stages for this skirt are the same as for the simple flared skirt in Skirtmaking Chapters 10 to 13, except that you allow for, and stitch, a Centre Front and Centre Back seam.

Fabric requirements

For 140cm width — your skirt length plus 20cm for sizes 87cm to 106cm hip.
For size 115cm hip, allow 23cm extra.
For 90cm width — twice your skirt length plus 28cm for all sizes (87cm to 115cm hip).
For 70cm width — twice your skirt length plus 38cm for sizes 87cm to 106cm hip.
For size 115cm hip, twice your skirt length, plus 61cm.
You will also need an 18cm skirt zip and matching thread. Remember to buy hooks and eyes, seam binding and petersham or stiffening, if necessary, for the waist-band.

Layout and cutting notes

Using the flared skirt pattern from Skirtmaking Chapter 10, select the correct layout for your size and fabric width. Remember that the Centre Front and Centre Back seams should always be cut on the straight grain of the fabric.
Before you cut out the skirt cut the fold to the length of the pattern. This will help you to remember to leave an allowance for the Centre Front seam.

Making up

Mark around the pattern with tailor's tacks. Add 19mm seam and 6·3cm hem allowances all round. Then follow the tacking, fitting, sewing and finishing instructions for the simple flared skirt with the addition of a Centre Front and Centre Back seam.

Top stitching

If you want to give the centre seams added importance top stitch them before you put on the waist-band and sew the hem up. Using a slightly thicker machine twist to make the stitches stand out from the fabric, run a parallel row of stitching 9mm from the seam, to each side of it. You can also do this by hand, using a 6mm running stitch.

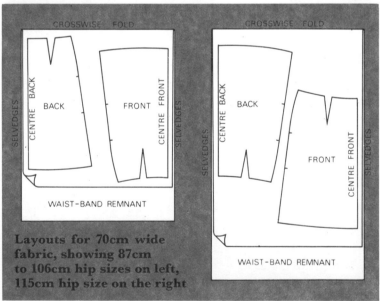

Layouts for 70cm wide fabric, showing 87cm to 106cm hip sizes on left, 115cm hip size on the right

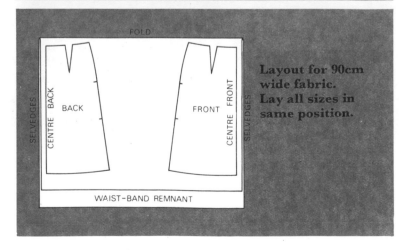

Layout for 90cm wide fabric. Lay all sizes in same position.

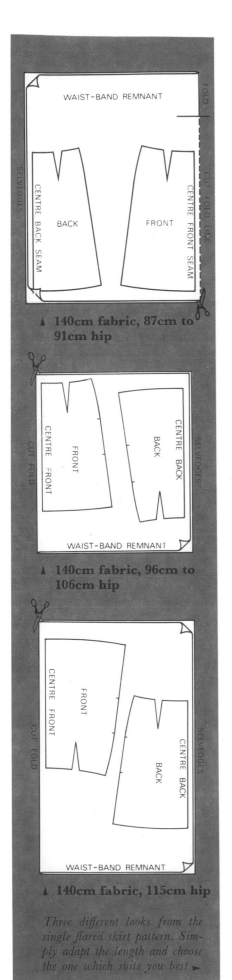

▲ **140cm fabric, 87cm to 91cm hip**

▲ **140cm fabric, 96cm to 106cm hip**

▲ **140cm fabric, 115cm hip**

Three different looks from the single flared skirt pattern. Simply adapt the length and choose the one which suits you best ▶

The dirndl skirt

There isn't an easier skirt to make than the gathered dirndl. You can make it from a strip of fabric about 1¼ times your hip measurement or, if the fabric is fine enough, you can use more for greater fullness. But to take the guesswork out of making this skirt use the pattern for the basic flared skirt pattern in Skirtmaking Chapter 10 as a guide.

Fabric requirements

For 140cm width — your skirt length plus 18cm for all sizes (87cm to 115cm hip).
For 90cm width — twice your skirt length plus 28cm for all sizes (87cm to 115cm hip).
For 70cm width — twice your skirt length plus 28cm for size 87cm hip.
For sizes 90cm and 95cm hip, twice your skirt length plus 35cm. NB This style is only flattering to sizes over 95cm hip if the waist is small and neat. These sizes cannot be cut from 70cm width without seams at the Centre Front and Centre Back.
You will also need an 18cm zip, 13mm wide straight seam binding and matching thread. Remember to buy hooks and eyes and petersham or stiffening, if necessary, for the waist-band.

How to prepare the pattern

Preparing the pattern is simple. To obtain the fullness for the gathers, just lay the basic pattern on a sheet of paper and square it off, as the diagram shows. Remove the basic pattern and mark the skirt sections, Back and Front.

Layout and cutting notes

After selecting the correct layout for your size and fabric width, place the squared off pattern pieces on the fold of the fabric as indicated, mark around them and mark the centre lines on the skirt. Cut out the fabric remembering to make 19mm seam allowances and 6·3cm hem allowances.

Making up

Stitch the side-seams and insert the zip.
Make a row of stitches for gathering the waist either side of the waist-seam, 6mm apart, on the right side of your skirt. It is important to stitch on the right side of the fabric because you must always pull up gathers from the wrong side. When machining the gathering stitches engage the longest stitch setting on the machine and slacken off the upper tension; this makes it easier to draw the threads of the lower stitches into gathers.

The waist-stay

Before you gather the skirt waist, first prepare a stay tape, or a waist guide.
Cut a length of 13mm seam binding the length of your waist plus 2·5cm for tolerance.
Mark this strip by measuring against the original basic pattern as follows. Starting with the left end of the tape, measure off the Back section of the basic pattern from side-seam to centre (excluding the width of the darts). Mark this measurement on the tape with tacking cotton. This mark will be the Centre Back. From this mark, measure off the same amount again to find the position of the opposite side-seam.
Then, using the Front section of the basic pattern and starting from the opposite end of the tape, measure and mark from side-seam to the Centre Front and from the Centre Front to side-seam as before.
When you have finished marking the tape, pin it to the side-seam and centre marks on the skirt.

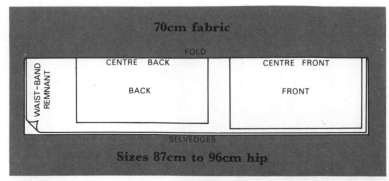

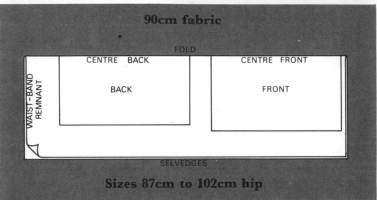

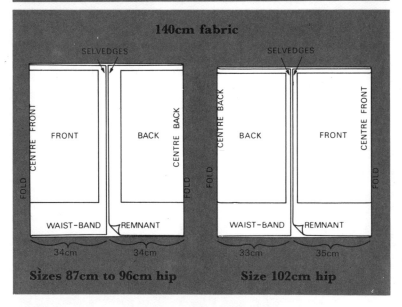

Preparing the waist-seam for the waist-band

Pull up the gathers by picking up the thread ends of the two rows of machine stitches and gently ease the fullness into even gathers along the waist line between the pins. Pin, tack and stitch the tape to the skirt.

Notes on stitching gathers

When you are stitching gathers to a straight piece of fabric, always make sure the gathers are uppermost. If you leave them out of sight, under the straight fabric, you'll find there is a tendency for them to get caught up into the seam — they'll tilt and bunch, because you will not be able to hold them out of the way of the machine needle.
If, sometimes, you cannot avoid leaving gathers out of sight or under the work, make a row of tacking stitches either side of the seam line, to stop them from moving.
Now that you've prepared the waist-seam, you are ready to stitch on the waist-band.

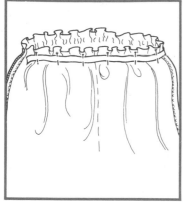
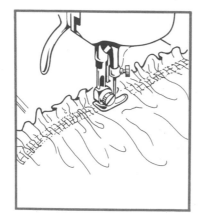

▲ *Waist-stay pinned into position*   ▲ *Stitching waist-stay over gathers*
▼ *How to prepare the pattern for the dirndl by adapting the basic skirt*

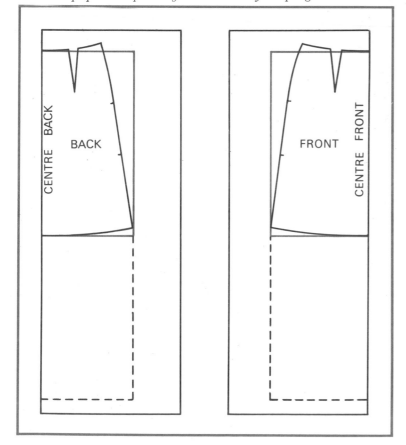

CENTRE BACK
BACK

FRONT
CENTRE FRONT

Versatile waist-bands

You can use any of the waist finishes (except for the invisible waist-band) as in Skirtmaking Chapters 13 and 14 for the dirndl skirt because the waist-bands are attached by using centre markings. This means that, regardless of the position of the seams in relation to the waist-band, provided you always make the centre marking on the skirt opposite the opening and match this to the centre marking on the waist-band, you can put the zip where you like, in the side-seam, the Centre Back, or Centre Front seam.

Evening dirndl

The dirndl is an ideal style to make up as a long evening skirt and preparing the pattern is, again, very simple. Measure the side length from waist to floor. When doing so, be sure to put on the shoes you will be wearing with the finished skirt, because a high heel can take up as much as 8cm or 10cm. Then, all you need to do is to add the extra length to the pattern by extending it from the hem, indicated by the dotted lines in the diagram.

Chapter 17

Knife-pleated skirt

A knife-pleated skirt—another variation of the basic pattern —flatters any figure.

Suitable fabrics
The fabric you use for a pleated skirt should be crease resistant but it should also be capable of taking a sharp crease under pressure and steam. Worsted woollens are particularly suitable; so are some acrylic fibres such as Courtelle; polyester fibres such as Terylene, Dacron and Trevira; linens, firmly woven tweeds and a number of mixture cloths, mostly obtainable in the narrower widths.
Before buying any fabric, it's a good idea to ask if it will pleat well.

Fabric requirements
For 140cm width—twice the skirt length plus 28cm for all sizes (87cm to 115 cm hip).
For 90cm and 70cm widths—four times the skirt length plus 53cm for all sizes (87cm to 115cm hip).
You will also need an 18cm zip and matching thread. Remember to buy hooks and eyes, seam binding and petersham or other stiffening if you need them for the waist-band.

Adapting the basic pattern
To begin, make a copy of the flared skirt pattern in Skirtmaking Chapter 10 to use as the basic pattern but do not cut out the darts—just mark them in pencil.
Using the ruler, extend the balance marks on the Front and Back right across the pattern pieces, as illustrated.
The extended balance marks become meet marks for the

pleats to ensure that they will lie flat and hang well when stitched and pressed.
To obtain the cutting line on the pattern, measure the distance from the Centre Front and Centre Back lines to the lowest point of the dart. Measure and mark off this distance all the way down to the hem, making a series of pencil marks parallel to the Centre Back and Centre Front.
Connect these marks with a ruler, taking the line through the centre of the darts right up to the waist line, and down to the hem.
Now mark the pattern sections on either side of the new cutting lines, as Front, Side Front, Back, Side Back. This will help you to avoid putting the wrong pieces together when you lay out the pattern.
Cut the pattern pieces on the cutting lines.

Knife-pleated skirt in Trevira ▶

▼ *Front pattern, with cutting line*

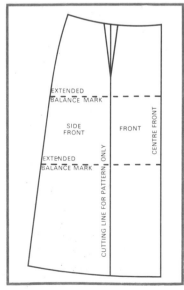

Layout on 140cm width

Leave the fabric folded and lay it flat on the cutting table, allowing enough area to work on one complete section of the skirt at a time. Starting with the Front section of the pattern, measure 6·3cm from the fold and pin a line parallel to the length of the pattern pieces.

Lay the Centre Front line of the pattern to the pin line and pin the pattern down on to the fabric.

Then, measure 13cm from the cutting line of the Front section and similarly mark the distance to the length of the pattern piece with a pin line.

Lay the cutting line of the Side Front section of the pattern to this pin line, securing the section with one or two pins so it cannot move. Using the ruler, lay it to the line of extended balance marks and make sure they go straight across both Front and Side Front pattern pieces.

Now lay out the back skirt sections in the same way.

Make whatever adjustments are necessary to ensure that the pattern sections line up correctly, and then pin them down securely on to the fabric.

Layout on 70cm or 90cm widths

Open up the fabric to the full width and length on the cutting table. Fold in half so that the raw edges meet as shown in the layout diagram.

A point to watch—if you have bought a fabric with a nap, or a one way design (this means the surface interest on the fabric goes in one direction, up or down), you must cut the length in half across the width, turn one layer and lay it in such a way that the surface interest runs in the same direction.

Before cutting make sure the right sides of the cloth are facing each other because many a fine length has been spoilt by laying it up carelessly. Otherwise you will find after cutting that you have two right sides or two left sides and cannot match them up to make a whole garment.

When you lay on the Front and Back pattern sections you must allow an extra 19mm for a seam on the fabric before you measure out the centre line pleats. This is because the Centre Front and Centre Back are now on a selvedge and not a fold as in the 140cm width. Having done this, you can proceed in exactly the same way as described for the 140cm layout.

To prepare for cutting

Now it is time to cut out the darts on the pencil lines. Make sure that you curve them into the cutting line at the ends—don't let them finish on a sharp corner as this will make the pleat seam poke out at the end of the dart.

Tailor's tack around all the pattern pieces, not forgetting the balance marks on the pleat lines as well as the side-seams.

Mark out 19mm seam allowance along the side-seams and mark out a 6·3cm hem.

When marking and cutting the seam allowance at the waist edge, more than the usual 19mm is needed. So do not follow the curve of the waist line, but allow the normal seam allowance at the side-seam and waist line point and then cut straight across to the centre on both back and front. This gives you an extra 19mm seam allowance at the deepest point of the curve.

You will see when you have pleated the skirt that because of the curves of the side darts and waist line extra seam allowance is needed to catch the right pleat at the front and left pleat at the back into the waist-band.

Mark the normal waist line of the pattern on the fabric and leave the trimming of any excess seam allowance till after the skirt sections have been pleated.

After you have removed the pattern pieces, connect the balance marks with long lines of tacking stitches.

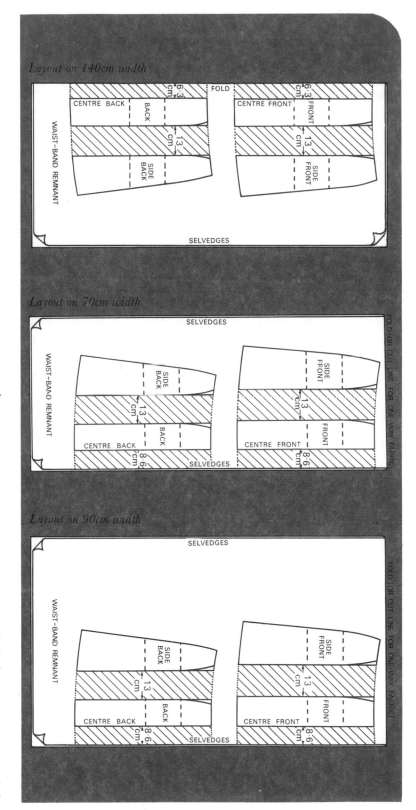

Pleating the skirt with soft pleats

Before you separate the layers of the skirt sections, you must first decide which way you are going to pleat the skirt.

One way is to lay the pleat lines together, tack them all the way down and then stitch them like a seam as far as the hip line, about 18cm from the waist, and press the pleat to one side from the inside of the skirt. This sort of pleating will give the skirt a soft look. If you are going to do it this way, you'll have to mark a fold line between the pleat lines of the Centre Front and Side Front sections as shown in the illustration.

Pleating the skirt with tailored pleats

If you prefer a crisp, tailored look, lay the pleats from right to left on the outside of the skirt, matching the balance marks and tacking them down securely along the edge.

Press them very lightly into position and top stitch about 2mm in from the edge, as far as the hip line.

Don't press the pleats in very sharply at this stage, but make up the skirt first.

When making the waist-band any of the methods in Skirtmaking Chapters 13 and 14 are suitable.

Special finishing notes for the pleated skirt

1. When you fit the skirt, do so with the pleats tacked together. Turn back to the skirt fitting guide in Skirtmaking Chapter 12. When you have corrected the faults, fit the skirt again with the tacking removed and the pleats loose. They should hang straight and closed—not jutting forward or pulling open. If you see the pleats spreading, fan-like, towards the side-seams, you will need to lift the skirt and pleats into the waist, until the pleats hang straight. If you see one pleat hanging badly, then this will need to be pulled up from the inside.

2. Before you stitch on the waist-band, make sure the pleats are caught flat and firmly into the seam, then trim seam allowance.

3. If you've cut the skirt with a Centre Front seam, refer to the side-seam in the child's pleated skirt in Skirtmaking Chapter 20 for the hem finish. But the easiest way to finish off the hem is to leave about two widths of the hem unstitched at the bottom of the seam in the pleat, make up the hem, and then stitch through all layers to the bottom edge of the hem as shown.

4. When turning up the hem, work hem at inner crease of the pleat about 6mm shorter, as illustrated, to stop pleats showing.

5. Before you press in the pleats finally, make sure that you have removed all tacking threads and tailor's tacks.

6. Sometimes pressing the thickness of pleats might make impressions on the fabric, which show on the right side. To remove these, carefully press under the pleats, on the wrong side.

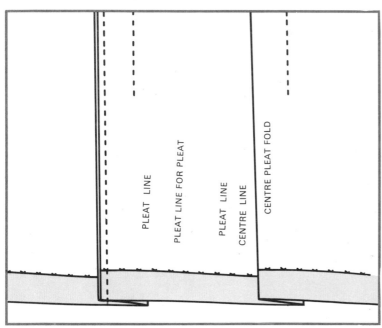

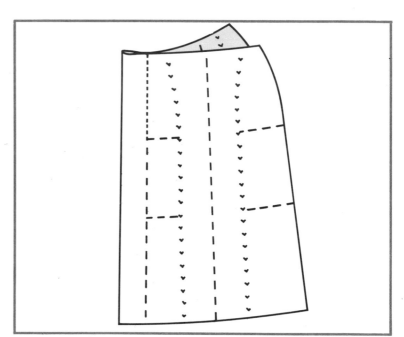

Pleating so the pleat lines meet on inside of skirt, making soft pleats ▲
Pleating from right to left on outside of skirt, making tailored pleats ▼

Hem finish for the seamed centre pleat ▲
Finished hem for pleated skirt, showing raised inner points of pleats ▼

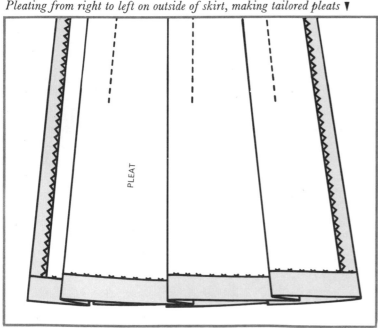

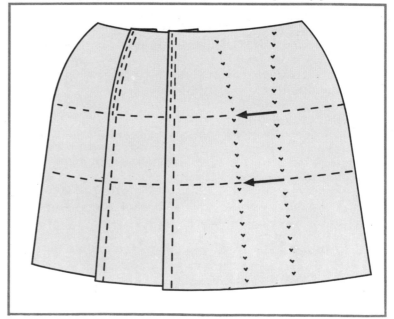

Chapter 18

The six-gore skirt

Here the basic·skirt pattern is converted to a six-gore, or panelled version which can be made up in three different styles. Add a little flare· to the panel seams and it becomes a skirt with a young and lively swing, very flattering for the larger figure. Or leave all the panels straight and just make a beautifully tailored six-gore skirt. The third version has straight panels and a knife pleat on each side of the back panel. For all three versions, use the pattern for the knife-pleated skirt in Skirtmaking Chapter 17.

Version 1 — six-gore with flared panels

Extending the pattern
Pin strips of paper 5cm wide along the panel-seam edges on all pattern pieces, as shown in diagram 1.
To make the flare, measure 2·5cm out from the point where the hem and side-seam meet. Using a ruler connect the hip line to this point to make the new panel-seam line. Extend the hem to the new seam line.

Suitable fabrics
All the fabrics suggested for the basic skirt in Skirtmaking Chapter 10 are suitable for the flared six-gore skirt.

Fabric requirements and notions
These fabric amounts are for a 58cm skirt length.
140cm width, without one way—1·30 metres for sizes 87cm, 90cm and 95cm hip; 1·40 metres for sizes 102cm to 115cm hip.
90cm width, without one way—1·60 metres for sizes 87cm to 115cm hip.
70cm width, without one way—2·20 metres for sizes 87cm and 90cm hip; 2·30 metres for sizes 96cm to 107cm hip; 2·40 metres for size 115cm hip.
For one way fabrics—add about one extra skirt length to all the above fabric amounts.
Extra length: if you want the skirt to be longer (or shorter), add (or subtract) the amount to (from) the above amount as follows: on 140cm and 90cm widths—twice the difference in length; on 70cm widths—three times the difference in length.
Notions: you will need an 18cm skirt zip, belt stiffening and matching thread.

Cutting out
Choose the correct layout for your size and fabric width from the next page. Place the pattern pieces on the fabric as indicated. The shaded sections on the 70cm layouts indicate that you have to lay the cloth full width on the cutting table and use a complete Back and a complete Front pattern. To do this, make a copy of the half patterns, join them along the Centre Back and Centre Front and lay them on single fabric. This is called an open layout. Add 19mm seam and 6·3cm hem allowances and cut out.

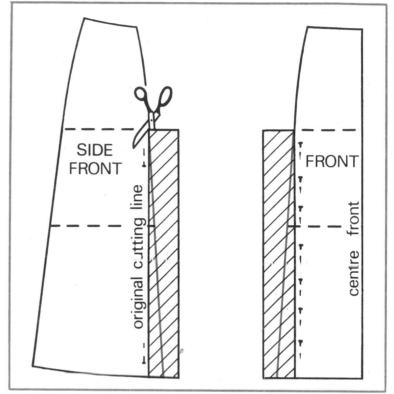

▲ **1.** *Extending the panel-seams to increase the flare*

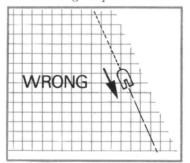

▲ **2.** *Left: stitching into the bias* ▲ *Right: stitching with the bias*

Stitching the seams on the bias
Because the flare on the skirt has been increased, the seams now slant towards the bias. This is not a true bias such as for the bias cut skirt, since the seams do not run at a 45° angle to the straight of the grain (see diagram 2).
It is a good precaution to stitch such seams with the bias, ie, from the hem upwards. Stitching into the bias can make the top layer of fabric stretch, thereby gathering or dragging the underlayer, and making the seams hang badly.
Generally, seams should be stitched from the top of a garment downwards, because there is often a little fullness in the fabric, caused by the finish or the weave, which cannot be detected until the two layers have been firmly joined by machine stitching. If the seams were sewn upwards from the bottom, such fullness would be passed into the waist line, neck or armholes, seriously upsetting the fit.
Pressing out the fullness before sewing may seem the obvious answer but not all fabrics benefit from being pressed first. If the weave is slightly uneven, the fabric can be distorted. Pressing before cutting should do no more than remove creases.

Fitting
Tack the side- and panel-seams. Try the skirt on and follow the fitting instructions for the basic skirt in Skirtmaking Chapter 12.

Taking in at the waist. If you need to take in the waist do not deepen the darts along the panels (ie, the curved parts of the seams). Leave the panel-seams as they are and make one small dart in each side front and side back piece, half-way between panel- and side-seams. If you take this fullness into the curve of the panel-seams at the top it can create the impression of a big stomach and high seat and the curve becomes too steep to form a good line.

Topstitching the panels

Topstitching the panels gives the seams a little extra support and emphasises the flare at the hem. You will see from diagram 4 just how effective the topstitched panels look.

If you are topstitching the panel-seams they must be prepared. Trim the seam allowances on the Front and Back panels to 6mm as shown, but do not trim the seam allowance on the side back and side front sections. Fold the untrimmed allowance over the trimmed one, and tack flat into position.

With the right side of the skirt uppermost, run a row of machine stitches on the panels only, about 13mm to 19mm from the seam. This will look best if you use a slightly heavier machine twist and a larger stitch setting.

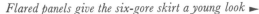

Flared panels give the six-gore skirt a young look ►

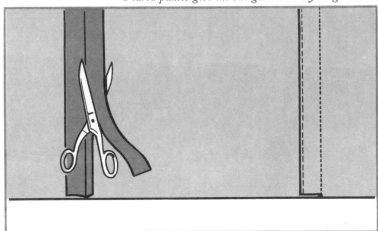

▲ **3.** *Trimming the panel-seams*   ▼ **4.** *The top-stitched panel-seams*

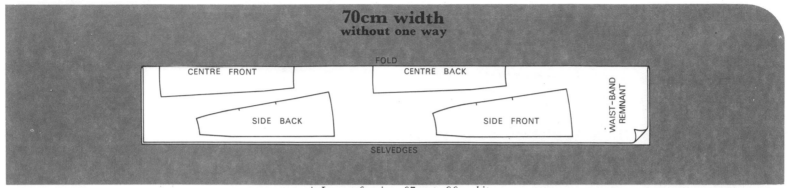

70cm width
without one way

FOLD

CENTRE FRONT · CENTRE BACK

SIDE BACK · SIDE FRONT

WAIST-BAND REMNANT

SELVEDGES

▲ *Layout for sizes 87cm to 90cm hip*

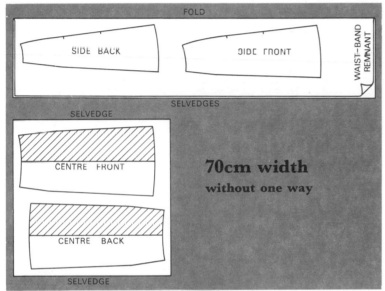

70cm width
without one way

FOLD

SIDE BACK · SIDE FRONT

WAIST-BAND REMNANT

SELVEDGES

SELVEDGE

CENTRE FRONT

CENTRE BACK

SELVEDGE

▲ *Layout for sizes 96cm to 107cm hip with open lay*

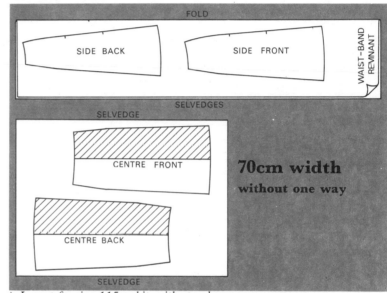

70cm width
without one way

FOLD

SIDE BACK · SIDE FRONT

WAIST-BAND REMNANT

SELVEDGES

SELVEDGE

CENTRE FRONT

CENTRE BACK

SELVEDGE

▲ *Layout for size 115cm hip with open lay*

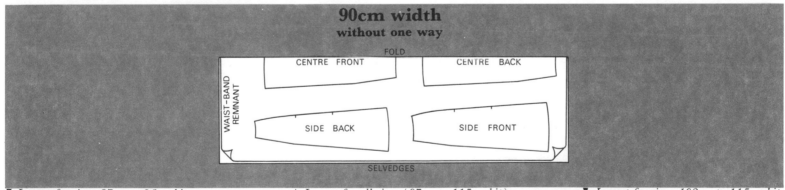

90cm width
without one way

FOLD

WAIST-BAND REMNANT

CENTRE FRONT · CENTRE BACK

SIDE BACK · SIDE FRONT

SELVEDGES

▼ *Layout for sizes 87cm to 96cm hip*   ▲ *Layout for all sizes (87cm to 115cm hip)*   ▼ *Layout for sizes 102cm to 115cm hip*

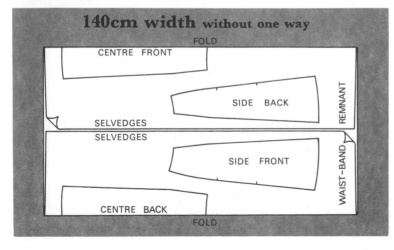

140cm width without one way

FOLD

CENTRE FRONT

SIDE BACK

REMNANT

SELVEDGES

SELVEDGES

SIDE FRONT

WAIST-BAND

CENTRE BACK

FOLD

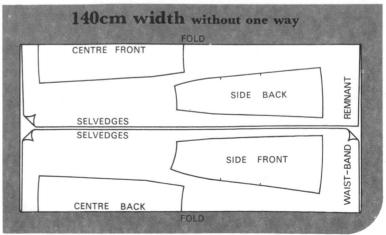

140cm width without one way

FOLD

CENTRE FRONT

SIDE BACK

REMNANT

SELVEDGES

SELVEDGES

SIDE FRONT

WAIST-BAND

CENTRE BACK

FOLD

Chapter 19

The bias cut skirt

You will have noticed that the use of the basic skirt pattern from Skirtmaking Chapter 10 is wide and unlimited. In this chapter you will see what happens when you turn the pattern grain lines by 45 degrees and cut the skirt on the cross or bias of the fabric, and if you prefer a little extra flare on the hem, this chapter will tell you how to add it. Fabrics for bias cut skirts have to be chosen carefully—and you will find that plaids and checks will give you interesting effects.

Making the pattern for the bias cut skirt

It is easier to use complete Back and Front pattern pieces when laying out the bias cut skirt. So fold two pieces of paper in half, large enough to accommodate each basic pattern piece. Lay the Back and Front on the paper with the Centre lines on the folded edges. Pin down the pattern pieces securely. Draw round the outlines and remove the pattern.

If you are going to add extra length to the pattern, do so now. Unless you want to increase the flare, cut out the new pattern. When it is unfolded you will have a complete Front and Back section for the skirt.

Adding 10cm to the basic flare

Extend the point where the hem and side-seam meet outwards by 2·5cm. Using a ruler connect the hip line to this point and draw a line for the new side-seam. Then extend the hem line to meet it. Cut out the pattern along the new lines and unfold it.

Marking the grain lines for the bias cut skirt

To make sure that you place the pattern correctly on the fabric when cutting, mark the grain lines as follows.

With the pattern pieces still folded, place a set square along the fold as you see in the diagram. The diagonal opposite the right angle is the grain line. Draw it on the pattern, then unfold the pattern and extend the line.

The new grain line becomes the straight of grain and the old grain line, which is also the Centre line, goes through the bias of the fabric. This ensures that the skirt is cut on the true bias.

Suitable fabrics for bias cutting

When choosing fabrics for garments cut on the bias you need to be a little more selective.

First decide on the effect you want to achieve.

If you want the bias cut to play its true role with a soft, clinging and figure hugging effect, choose a soft crepe.

If you are cutting on the bias for the effect it has on a pattern such as a check or plaid you will have to be very careful when choosing the design. Stripes can also be cut on the cross, but are difficult to match in the seams on a narrow flare such as this.

When choosing plaids or checks it is essential that you find a regular check, that is, the check must be a perfect square. If it is

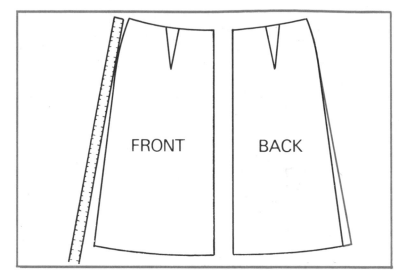

Increasing the basic flare

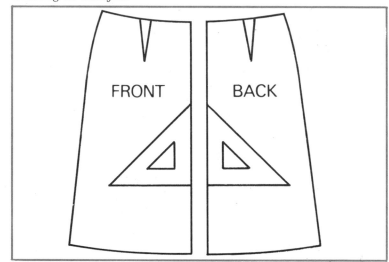

Finding the straight of grain on the pattern with a set square
Folding the fabric to see if the check is perfectly square

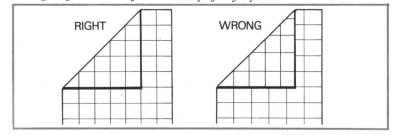

not, the skirt will look as though the diagonal is not true and will result in differing slants on each side of the seams.

It is often difficult to detect an irregular check, when the difference in length of the sides is minute. If the weave is prominent enough, make a quick count of the amount of threads in the warp and the weft that make up a square. If they are equal and the design still looks a little irregular, fold the fabric diagonally as shown in the diagram so that one selvedge meets the straight of the grain. All checks along the folded edge should have equal amounts of the squares showing.

The weight of the fabric is also important. There is always some drop in bias cut fabrics, and a heavy fabric can result in a drop which distorts the pattern and looks very ugly indeed.

So, when choosing slightly heavier fabrics, look closely at the weave. If it is a firm weave the strength of the weave will assist the cloth in keeping its shape.

Fabric Requirements

You will need more fabric when cutting a garment on the cross than on the straight of grain.

Here are the amounts for sizes 61cm and 66cm waists:

For a 90cm wide fabric you will need approximately three times the skirt length.

For a 140cm wide fabric you will need approximately 2¼ times the skirt length.

Allow an extra 0·15 metres for each size larger, that is, for a 71cm waist allow 0·15 metres, for a 76cm waist allow 0·25 metres. In addition, if you have had to make the pattern wider to fit you, allow another 0·15 metres.

The above amounts do not allow for pattern matching for which you must add one extra fabric pattern depth for each pattern piece. If the fabric has a pattern where one colour runs down or across the pattern and does not form part of the definite check or plaid, allow an extra half skirt length.

Preparing the fabric for cutting

On a regular check or plaid the diagonal is obvious. But where the diagonal is not obvious, it is best to mark the direction of the bias on the fabric first.

Straighten and trim the raw edges on both ends of the fabric along the grain as shown in Skirtmaking Chapter 20. Then unfold the fabric and lay it full width, face down, on a cutting table.

Take the top right hand corner and fold it towards the lower left until the raw upper edge meets left selvedge. Pin edges together. The fold line is the true bias for the fabric. Use long tacking stitches to mark it.

Next, unfold the fabric and, using the whole Front skirt pattern, position it over the tacking line (see diagrams a,b). The Centre Front line should coincide with or run parallel to the tacked line. To allow for a drop in the fabric which could make the skirt slightly narrower, mark out 3cm for seams in case you have to let them out. Chalk or pin the seam allowances and the usual hem allowance. Mark round the pattern using a flat tacking stitch without loops as the fabric is single.

Mark the bias at the other end of the fabric in the direction shown in diagrams a,b and lay out and mark up the Back pattern. If you cut the skirt from fabric which has a prominent colour running down or across it, reverse the folding of the fabric from right to left when finding the bias for the Back section, and use the alternative layout c as a guide.

Making up the bias skirt

The instructions are the same as for the basic skirt in Skirtmaking Chapters 11 to 13 except that you will need a little more time as the skirt has to hang. After you've tacked the skirt together, and before fitting, it is important to leave it to hang for at least 24 hours. The drop in the fabric should be dealt with now so that the fitting and the hem level will not be affected.

Hang it from three loops of tape, one pinned to each side and one in the centre of the waist. Better still, if you have a dressmaker's stand, slip the skirt over it and pin it to the stand around the waist.

Fitting the bias skirt

You will see that a skirt cut on the bias does not present the same fitting problems as one cut on the straight of the grain. The bias is more pliable and inclined to mould itself to the figure, so a lot of faults disappear in the soft hang of the fabric.

The skirt may appear tighter than the pattern size. If so, use the extra seam allowance to let it out.

The waist darts should be reduced to a minimum. Let them out as far as you can so they will be as short as your figure shape allows.

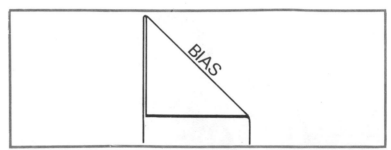

Finding the bias on the fabric

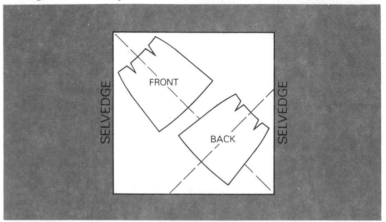

Layouts for a. 140cm wide fabric without one way b. 90cm wide fabric without one way c. 90cm wide fabric with one way

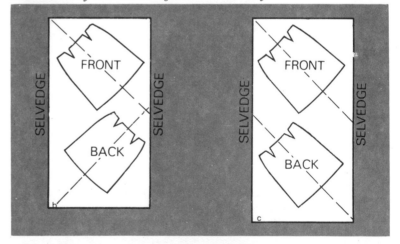

Take the surplus into the side-seams or, if this causes strain, ease the fullness into the waist-band.

This is a delicate fitting point and needs a little perseverance to get the right result. But when you have achieved it, you will see that the effort was worth while. Trim seam allowances to 19mm Do not fit for length at this stage.

Stitching the seams in the bias skirt

There are precautions applied to stitching seams which run into a bias and were covered in the previous chapter. These precautions, however, do not apply when stitching the seams in the bias cut skirt.

Just observe the following points and all should be well:

1. Do not pull the bias cut seams through the machine as you are stitching, but just guide the fabric gently through the machine.

2. Slacken the tension on the presser foot so there is less likelihood of the fabric layers being pushed or dragged in opposite directions.

3. Before tacking the seams, insert pins at right angles to the seam line to prevent the fabric layers from slipping. Then tack, using small but not tight stitches.

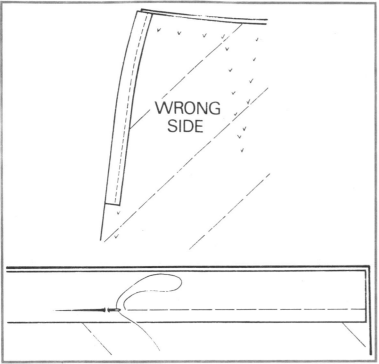

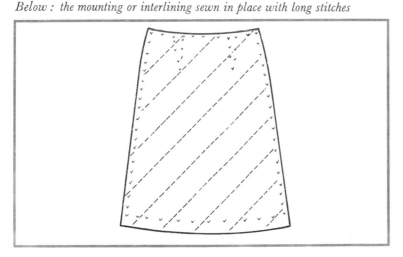

Above : inside of the zip opening with lining strip
Centre : detail of the lining strip along the zip opening
Below : the mounting or interlining sewn in place with long stitches

Pressing the stitched bias cut seams

When pressing the seams, never use a pushing movement: always press, lift and press, or else the seams may stretch and bulge.

Putting in the zip

There are two ways to prepare the opening for the zip. One is to run a tacking stitch in double cotton along the seam line of the opening, back and front, before tacking the side-seams together. This method may not give sufficient firmness to heavier fabrics. If this is the case use the following method: cut two 2·5cm wide strips of lining material on the straight of the grain, to the length of the opening. Use one strip on each side of the opening, laying it to the edge of the 19mm seam allowance on the wrong side of the fabric, with 6mm projecting over the seam line. Make sure the work is lying flat while you prepare the opening so that the fabric does not pucker.

Sew on the strips with long running stitches just inside the seam line catching only a thread or two from the top fabric. Stitch the side-seam, catching down the bottom edge of the strips and press. Tack the seam allowance under carefully and insert the zip before

removing any of the tacking threads.

Stitching on the waist-band

To make the waist-band use one of the methods shown in Skirt-making Chapters 13 and 14. Before you finally stitch it to the skirt try the skirt on again with the waist-band tacked in place.
Never make a tight-fitting waist-band for this type of skirt because the bias cut will cause the skirt to roll up over the waist-band.

Lining the skirt

To help the skirt retain its shape during wear, make a smooth fitting lining.
Cut it to the same pattern with the Centre Back and Centre Front on the straight grain of the fabric.
The lining should be an easy but perfect fit. Sew the lining so that the seams and darts face towards the body when it is sewn into the skirt. If they face the skirt they will make impressions which show on the outside. Skirts cut on the bias tend to show everything!

Mounting the fabric

In mounting, two pieces of fabric are stitched to one another and handled as one.
Mounting or interlining bias cut fabrics is a very difficult task and requires a lot of dressmaking know-how.
If done incorrectly it can have disastrous results, such as the bias cut fabric dropping in huge folds over the mounting. So mounting should be avoided except for one instance.
Mounting or interlining becomes essential if you use one of the light-weight, high bulk tweeds which contain a high percentage of mohair or simulated mohair and where the weave is rather open. They are very cosy and warm and when cut on the cross they can be worn by many figure types without looking bear-like and clumsy. Using the skirt pattern, cut an interlining from lawn or soft pre-shrunk cotton, cutting it on the bias as you did for the top fabric. Pin and tack the mounting to the inside of each skirt section, using very long tacking stitches along the straight of the grain.
To support the fabric permanently it is necessary to anchor the interlining or mounting to the fabric. Use matching thread and make rows of stitches along the straight grain of the fabric about 10cm to 13cm apart, as shown in the diagram. The stitches should be about 2·5cm long on the mounting surface of the fabric, should only just catch the skirt fabric, and should not show on the outside of the garment at all. Do not pull them tight.
After mounting, make up and fit the skirt as before.
This type of skirt also needs a lining. Here are two ways to do this.
1. Make a loose lining cut on the straight of the grain as before.
2. Make a lining from heavier taffeta which is cut on the cross and the same as the skirt. Stitch the darts so that they face the inside of the skirt and slip stitch the lining to the skirt over the hem. This leaves the inside of the skirt very neatly finished. But when you have the skirt dry cleaned, remember to unpick the lining from the hem otherwise the seams, which often fold to one side during cleaning, cannot be pressed properly.

Pressing bias cut garments

Always press along the straight of the grain. Pressing into the bias can distort the fabric and result in very ugly bulges which no amount of shrinking and pressing will get rid of.
Place the garment over an ironing board and turn the work as you proceed, so that the straight of the grain is always before you.
Let the work cool down a little before moving it on. This is particularly important when there are raw edges, such as the hem edge, still unfinished. If the weight of the fabric is allowed to drag the work, you will find that the warmth from the iron will carry on doing its work and make the hem edge look rather fluted.

Chapter 20

Basic pleating for skirts

Skirt – making

Inside every small girl is a fashion expert in the making and every mother ought to encourage her daughter to develop good dress sense. She may be tied to a school uniform during the week which is all the more reason to allow her to indulge her fancy a little in her spare time. The best way to learn is by sheer trial and error which can be fun but expensive if you have to buy every item, especially considering the rate children grow. As no one wants a wardrobe full of expensive mistakes, dressmaking is the obvious answer. Here is a swinging pleated skirt any little girl will love. Whether you add the optional shoulder straps or not will depend on the shape of her tum. Later chapters include more clothes to make for children, boys as well as girls.

A word about little girls' fitting problems

Before you start it's as well to go over the basic shape of little girls and the skirt fitting problems that arise as a result of their shape at this age.

The skirts will not stay up or they ride up and jut out so that the front looks shorter than the back and pleated skirts look particularly clumsy because all the pleats tend to jumble up in front.

Let's look at the reasons for the bad fitting.

If you stand a little girl sideways on, you will notice that the curve of the spine through the waist towards the seat is concave and that the tummy is quite high and curves from the abdomen to the chest. This happens with most little figures. There is no waist line and although there is a difference in the measurements around the body, the extra centimetres are taken up by the height of the seat and by the upper thighs.

The hip bones are not sufficiently developed to stop the waist-band of a skirt from falling down and the roundness of the tummy encourages the skirt to ride up if the waist-band is tight. The only way to counteract this is to attach narrow straps to the waist-band which are worn over the shoulders and crossed at the back so that they don't slip down. For a child with narrow or sloping shoulders, it may be necessary to stitch a brace across the front of the straps to hold them in position.

Although the straps are strictly functional they can look an attractive part of the skirt if made in the same fabric. They are versatile too, as jumpers and shirts can go under or over the straps.

With the straps doing most of the work, the waist-band can be made quite loose so that the skirt will hang better.

Although you might think an elasticised waist-band is a good alternative to the straps, it pulls the waist-band tightly into the figure and only makes the problem worse. The reason for using an elasticated waist-band is to give easy expansion and not simply to hold up the skirt.

The pleated skirt made up in a woven Courtelle ▶

How to work out basic pleating

In basic pleating, the length of the pleat fold is the same as the pleat distance (or half the pleat depth). Therefore you require three times as much fabric as the measurement you are fitting. This could be a waist or hip measurement but in the case of a small child it is the waist measurement. Here's how to work it out.

How to work out pleating for the given width

In pleating a skirt from one width of fabric, the length of the fold is *not* equal to the pleat distance. Apply what you have learned about basic pleating but remember, you are working on a given width of 140cm. As you work it out this time, compare the two charts.

Use this column to work out the pleating yourself for a child's skirt in 140cm width. Just fill in the spaces.

Basic pleating	Example	Given width	Example	Fill in
1. Take the waist/hip measurement loosely and add the correct ease.	For example: making a skirt for a 58cm waist measurement with the pleats 2·5 cm apart 58cm + 5cm = 63cm	**1.** Take the child's waist measurement loosely and add 5cm for ease.	For example: making a skirt for a 58cm waist measurement with the pleats 2·5cm apart. 58 + 5 = 63cm	…cm + 5cm = …cm
2. Multiply by three. This gives you *the amount of fabric needed for pleating.*	63cm × 3 = 189cm	**2.** You are working on a given width of 140cm fabric. Deduct 13mm seam allowance from each end.	140cm — 2·5cm = 138cm	140cm — 2·5cm = 138cm
3. Decide on the distance you want between the pleats and divide the waist/hip measurement plus ease by this figure. This gives you *the total number of pleats.*	63cm ÷ 2·5cm = 25 pleats	**3.** Decide on the distance you want between the pleats (for small children 2·5cm pleats are best) and divide the waist measurement plus ease by this figure.	63cm ÷ 2·5cm = 25 pleats	(Pleat distance = …cm) …cm ÷ …cm = …pleats
4. Deduct the waist/hip measurement plus ease from the amount of fabric needed. This gives you *the amount of fabric to be divided into pleat depths.*	189cm — 63cm = 126cm	**4.** Deduct the waist measurement plus ease from the amount of pleating fabric.	138cm — 63cm = 75cm	138cm — …cm = …cm
5. Divide by the number of pleats. This gives you *the depth for each pleat.*	126cm ÷ 25 = 5cm	**5.** Divide by the number of pleats.	75cm ÷ 25 = 3cm	…cm ÷ … = …cm pleat depth

The all-round pleated skirt for 2- to 7- year-olds

This is a pleated skirt made from just one width of 140cm fabric and therefore quite inexpensive to make. This little skirt has a full round of pleats calculated in such a way that you can get it out of the shortest possible length of fabric. But before you can work out the pleating for it, it is necessary to know how to work out pleating in general.

Suitable fabrics

The fabric used for a pleated skirt should be crease resistant but should take a sharp crease under pressure and steam.

Worsted wool, Terylene, Dacron and a number of mixture cloths, linens and firmly woven tweeds are good for pleating.

If you want a really hard-wearing, hard-washing and pleat-retaining fabric, you can't make a better choice than from the range of woven Courtelles or some other acrylic fibres. They can be machine washed and still retain the sharp crease of the pleats needing only the slightest touch with a warm iron to make the garment as good as new. What is more, you can pleat woven Courtelle permanently yourself.

When you buy the fabric always remember to ask if it pleats well and whether it needs washing or dry cleaning.

Fabric requirements

For 2- to 7-year-olds—140cm width only, the skirt length plus 23cm. Measure the strap length and if this measurement is more than 68cm you will need an extra 8cm of fabric.

If you wish to use a narrower fabric, to obtain the correct length for pleating you must allow the skirt length plus 8cm for each extra width you cut.

You will also need two No.2 hooks and eyes, one press fastener size 0 and matching thread.

Preparing the fabric before cutting

Before you start cutting the pleated skirt, it is essential that the fabric is perfectly square in the grain. To square the fabric to the grain, use the thread-drawing method illustrated and cut the fabric along the line of the drawn thread.

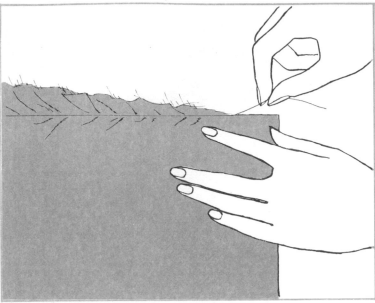

▲ *Finding the straight of the grain by drawing a thread out of the fabric*
▼ *Cutting along the straight of fabric using drawn thread line as a guide*

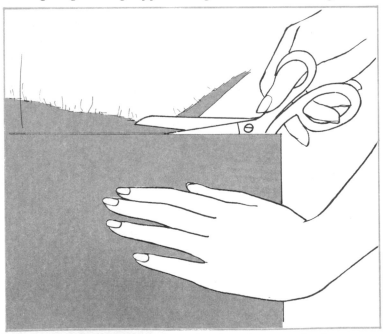

If you are using a weave where the thread cannot be drawn, or it is hard to see the direction of the grain, the easiest way to square the fabric is with a tailor's square or set square and ruler.

Carefully place the selvedge along the straight edge of your cutting table and smooth out the rest of the fabric over the table. Take great care not to force it in any way. Lay the tailor's square to the selvedge near the raw edge, then lay the ruler along the top line of the square and draw a chalk line right across the fabric.

To check that the fabric is perfectly straight, repeat the operation about 25cm further down and measure the distance between the two chalk lines. The measurement should be the same on the selvedge and right across the fabric. Cut the fabric on the line nearest the raw edge and brush off the other chalk line. The fabric should now be perfectly square for cutting.

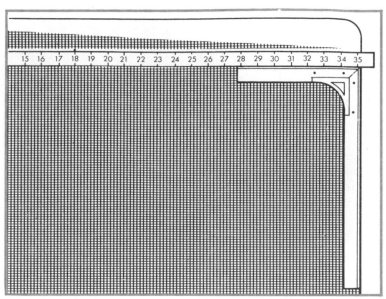

▲ *How to straighten the grain using a tailor's square and ruler*

How to cut the skirt

Making a pleated skirt from one length of 140cm width is so simple that you don't need a paper pattern.

Open out the fabric to the full width across the cutting table. Measure the length of the skirt along the selvedge, allowing 5cm for the hem and 19mm for the waist-seam, then take this measurement right across the fabric marking a straight line with pins or chalk. Cut along this line. Put the remaining fabric aside for the straps and waist-band.

Make the hem first before you start pleating. Turn up 5cm along the cut edge of the fabric and tack. A 5cm hem is quite deep enough since it is almost impossible to lengthen a pleated skirt after a lot of hard wear and washing and in any case, you will be able to adjust the length sufficiently from the straps.

When stitching the hem, leave 8cm at each end just tacked—don't stitch yet.

Press the hem and remove all tacking stitches except for those at the ends. Turn the fabric right side up and lay it flat on the cutting table with the hem nearest you.

Starting the pleating

Have the pleating chart open in front of you with the measurements you need to use. Pleat from left to right marking each pleat line with a line of pins.

Measure a 13mm seam allowance on the left selvedge and make a pin line.

As the skirt opening will be on the inside of a pleat it is necessary to start with a half pleat which means halving the pleat depth. Do this and pin the amount off from the seam allowance pin line. Now make the whole pleats starting with the pleat distance followed by the pleat depth.

Repeat until you have marked off the required number of pleats, less one (this is 24 in the example), all the way across the fabric. The last pleat (25th in the example) is the top of the opening so for this you need only measure out the pleat distance. Turn under the remaining fabric and selvedge.

Having measured out the pleats, check to make quite sure that you have made the right calculations for fabric width and body measurements.

Fold along each pleat distance line, bring fold over to the right to fall on the pleat depth line and tack down securely.

Make sure the hem line and waist line remain straight.

Tack the end pleat fold under.

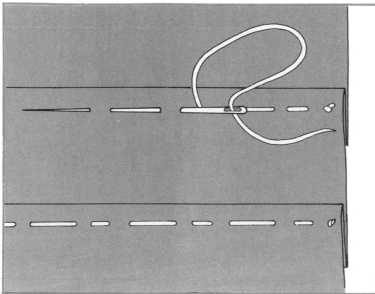

▲ *Tacking the pleats down using a long and a short stitch*

NB When you're tacking down lots of small pleats or any folded edge on springy fabric, use the tacking stitches illustrated. Make a short stitch between each long stitch to give extra hold.

Pressing

Lay the pleated fabric, still flat and open, over a press board, making sure that the ends which cannot be accommodated are supported. Press, using a damp cloth and warm iron.

To secure the upper edge of the pleating, make a row of machine stitches just above the waist-seam. Remove all tacking stitches except those holding the end pleat and press the pleats in again, more firmly, taking care to press each pleat in its original crease.

Stitching the side-seam

To stitch the side-seam of the skirt, lap the end pleat over the halved pleat depth you measured out from the left selvedge and tack it in position.

Turn the skirt to the wrong side. Use the seam allowance pinned on the left selvedge for the seam line guide since you may have a little less or more fabric in the pleat depth on the right selvedge. Leave an opening 8cm long at the top, unfold the hem and stitch the selvedges all the way down.

Press the seam open for 10cm, from the bottom edge, so that you can finish the hem.

Now snip the selvedges towards the seam, just above the hem, and press both selvedges together all the way up.

Oversew the snip with fine hand stitches to prevent fraying.

Finishing the opening

To finish the 8cm opening, turn back the selvedge seam allowance on the back of the skirt (the left end when you were pleating) to the length of the opening. Sew it down by hand using a herring-bone stitch.

Snip the selvedge on this side towards the seam so that it will lie flat. The front turning, or right end, remains just folded and need not be stitched back.

To prepare the waist-seam

Make a mark opposite the left opening. Then make running stitches along the back waist-seam, pull up the stitches and gather in 2·5cm. This will give the skirt a little fullness around the seat to stop the pleats from spreading.

Because of gathering the fabric at the back of the skirt, the mark opposite the opening has shifted towards the back so, before attaching the waist-band, you must make a new mark. Otherwise, the waist-band will not go on evenly.

Measure out the distance half-way between each side of the opening and the mark opposite, and make two more marks.

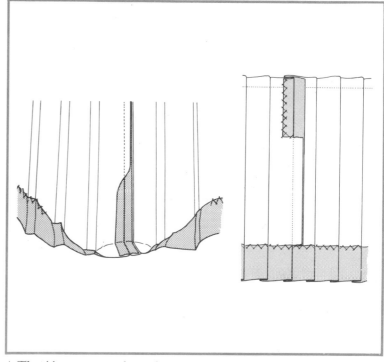

▲ *The side-seam pressed open in the hem*   ▲ *Finished·side-seam and opening*

These are to indicate the Centre Front and Centre Back.

To obtain the correct length for the waist-band, measure along the top edge of the skirt and cut a strip of fabric 8cm wide and the same length plus 13mm seam allowance at each end. You will not need any extra wrap because it wraps in the depth of the pleat.

Fitting the skirt

Tack on the waist-band and try the skirt on the child. Pin on two lengths of tape for the shoulder straps, crossing them at the back. Mark the lengths needed on the tape.

The skirt should hang almost free around the figure.

If you see that there is a pronounced drop at the back, try easing the skirt up into the waist-band at the back. Be very careful though, not to drag the fullness of the pleats from the sides of the skirt. If this happens, do not take the skirt up any further.

Stitch on the waist-band and finish with hooks and eyes for the fastening. Stitch a press fastener inside the fold of the opening so that it won't gape.

Attaching the straps

Measure the length of the straps from the tape used for the fitting and add 15cm to the length. This makes room for adjustment for 2 to 3 years of growing.

Cut two strips of fabric 8cm wide to this length. Fold them in half lengthways, pin the edge into position and hand-sew with very small hemming stitches leaving one end open.

Turn in the raw end to neaten and hand sew firmly to the inside of the waist-band about 5cm to either side of the Centre Front and Centre Back marks on the skirt.

Now give the skirt a final pressing to seal in the pleats. Pay special attention to the pleat which goes through the hem in the side-seam. The thickness of the seam inside the hem will need extra pressure to crease in the pleat.

Chapter 21

Fling yourself into kilt-making

The most famous of all pleated skirts is, of course, the Scottish kilt. An authentic kilt is very full and heavy and made from metres of fabric but there are many ways this can be pared down and still resemble the original.

This chapter gives you a simple method for working out the pleating and calculating fabric requirement for any size, and for skirt lengths up to 58cm. But if you hanker after the glamour of the full length version shown here, you can make it from a commercial pattern and use Golden Hands pleating know-how to help you achieve perfect results.

Choosing your fabric

Although kilts are associated with Scottish tartans, they can be made in other fabrics, including plain cloths, provided that the fabric pleats well (see the suggestions for the knife-pleated skirt and child's pleated skirt in Skirtmaking Chapters 17 and 20).

The authentic fabric for kilts is a fine wool and because of the amount of fabric used it is best not to choose anything too heavy or bulky.

If you are choosing a man-made or mixture cloth for the·adult kilt, do make sure that it will respond to being pressed and moulded as a natural fibre does. This is important if you want to make the best of the fitted lines on this pleated garment.

Points on pleating

The kilt is fully pleated, which means the length of the pleat fold is the same as the pleat distance (see Skirtmaking Chapter 20).

As it is quite a bulky garment to make and handle it is a good idea to practise first on a child's kilt, then you can make one for yourself from the same working sequence.

Working out the pleating

This requires a little mathematics, but it is simple if you follow the step-by-step chart shown here. First, take note of the following points:

1. The kilt is fitted so calculate the amount of fabric needed by the hip measurement, which is the largest part of the body it has to cover.

2. The width of the plain front panel is in proportion to the hip measurement and takes up about one quarter of the circumference. This can be varied, however, to suit your own taste. When dividing measurements for the panel, calculate to the nearest centimetre—it is so much easier.

3. Allow plenty of ease when you take the hip measurement as the thickness of the layers of fabric will take it up. The chart shows you how much ease to add.

4. The calculations for the adult and the child's kilt are the same and are based on a 140cm wide fabric.

Full length for glamour. A Vogue Pattern made in Menzies tartan ▶

What to do	For example:	For your own use
	making a kilt for a 76cm hip and 63cm waist, with 20cm panels and 2·5cm pleats	
1. Take the hip measurement and add 8cm ease.	76cm + 8cm = 84cm	. . .cm + 8cm = . . . cm
2. Deduct the width of the panel. This gives you the area to be pleated and also the number of pleats.	84cm — 20cm = 64cm (25 pleats)	. . .cm — . . .cm = . . . cm (. . . pleats)
3. Multiply by three. This gives you the fabric needed for pleating.	64cm × 3 = 192cm	. . . cm × 3 = . . . cm
4. Add twice the panel width (the kilt has a double wrap over).	(20cm × 2 = 40cm) 188cm + 41cm = 229cm	(. . . cm × 2 = . . . cm) . . .cm + . . .cm = . . . cm
5. Add the seam allowance (13mm) for each pleated section to be joined together.	229cm + 2·5cm = 231·5cm	. . .cm + . . . cm = . . . cm
6. To neaten and finish the upper front panel add 13cm	231·5cm + 13cm = 244cm	. . . cm + 13cm = . . . cm
7. To neaten the under front panel add 2·5cm	244cm + 2·5cm = 246cm = the total width of the skirt.	. . . cm + 2·5cm = . . . cm

How much fabric to buy

The example in the chart gives a skirt width of 246cm which easily fits across two widths of 140cm fabric, or twice the skirt length. But if the total width of the skirt exceeds 265cm, an extra skirt length is needed for the additional pleats. There will, of course, be an extra seam which must be allowed for.

For the total amount add 9cm on each skirt length for the waist-seam and hem allowance, and 6cm–8cm for the waist-band.

If you are buying a check or tartan make sure that the pattern can be matched across all sections and that you buy sufficient to enable you to do this.

As explained, all the instructions for working out the fabric in this chapter are based on a 140cm width. It is possible, however, to use narrower fabric, but there will be more seams in the pleating.

Royal Stewart tartan gives this girl's kilt an authentic Scottish air ►

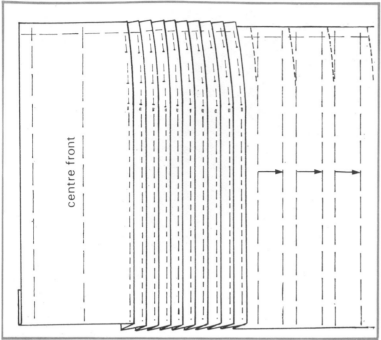

▲ *Above diagram shows tacked pleats. Hem is turned before pleating*

Preparing to pleat

Study figure 1, which is the pleating diagram. You will notice that there is an inverted pleat at the inner edge of the upper front panel. This is an extra pleat not accounted for in the pleat number, but allowance was made for it in the 13cm added for neatening and finishing the upper front panel, when calculating amount. The inverted pleat enables the panel to lie flat and hang well. The pleat sequence for the kilt remains the same for all sizes apart from the measurement for the panels and the number of pleats. The pleating diagram indicates a left hand fastening: for right hand fastening, simply reverse the reading of the diagram.

Making the kilt

Cutting. Prepare the fabric for cutting as for the child's pleated skirt in Skirtmaking Chapter 20. Measure and mark the skirt lengths across the fabric, add hem and waist-seam allowances and cut.

Making the hem. Make the hem first, before pleating, leaving 8cm to each side of the seam(s) just tacked. Press.

Pleating. With the fabric right side up and following figure 1, mark all the pleat lines, seam lines and edges with tacking. Also mark the Centre Front on both panels. Where the fabric is to be joined finish with a half pleat depth and seam allowance and start the next section with a seam allowance followed by half a pleat depth.

Starting with the left panel pleat from left to right pinning as for tailored pleats (see Skirtmaking Chapter 17). Make the inverted pleat by folding the upper front panel edge to meet the fold of the last pleat.

You are now ready to tack the pleats. Since the skirt is fitted from the hip line into the waist, tack each pleat from hip line to hem only and leave the top pinned for tapering.

Stitching the seams. Join the skirt sections making sure as you tack and stitch each seam that it forms the inside crease of the pleat. Finish the hem at the base of each seam. (See the side-seam for the child's pleated skirt, Skirtmaking Chapter 20).

Tapering the pleats
The chart here shows you a simple way of calculating how much to taper each pleat.

What to do	For example 64cm waist, 76cm hip	For your own use
1. Add 5cm ease to the waist measurement.	**64**cm + **5**cm = **69**cm	... cm + 5cm = ... cm
2. Find the difference between this figure and the hip measurement plus ease (8cm)	**84**cm — **69**cm = **15**cm	... cm — ... cm = ... cm
3. Divide the amount equally by the number of pleats (don't forget the inverted pleat!)	**15**cm ÷ **26** pleats = about 6mm for tapering each pleat	... cm ÷ ... pleats = ... mm

The dash lines indicated on figure 1, show you how to taper the pleats. Roll under the edge of each pleat and bring it to meet the distance line of the next pleat. Be sure that each pleat runs back into the original line at the hips.

The fitting
Tack the top of the pleats firmly into position and press the pleats all the way down.

Cut a waist-band the full length of the waist edge and tack it to the kilt.

Try on the kilt, and wrap the panels so that the Centre Front lines meet. There must be enough ease for the panels to stay fully wrapped and not pull away from each other.

Use the fitting hints for the knife-pleated skirt in Skirtmaking Chapter 17 when you look at the pleats. You will find the skirt fitting guide in Skirtmaking Chapter 12 useful too.

Mark any faults and correct them, unless you find you need to cut a curve for the waist—this should be done after you have stitched the pleats.

Finishing the kilt
Stitching the pleats. Remove the waist-band and topstitch each pleat close to the edge, from the waist to the hip line. Press.

Curving the waist. If you need to cut a waist curve, do so now. With the panels wrapped in position, fold the kilt in the Centre Front lines and pin it together along the waist line. Curve the waist following the instructions in Skirtmaking Chapter 12. Tack the top of the pleats along the new seam line.

Fringing. To finish the upper front panel you can make your own fringe from the kilt material.

Cut a strip about 5cm wide, a little longer than the length of the panel. Carefully lift out the threads from one edge until the fringe is about 19mm wide. Lay the fringed strip on the facing fold line of the upper panel as shown in figure 2 and stitch along this line. Neaten, then hand-sew the inside raw edge to the facing.

Finishing the panels. Fold under the 8cm facing on the upper front panel and the 2·5cm turning on the edge of the under panel over the hem. Tack and hand-sew as shown in figure 3.

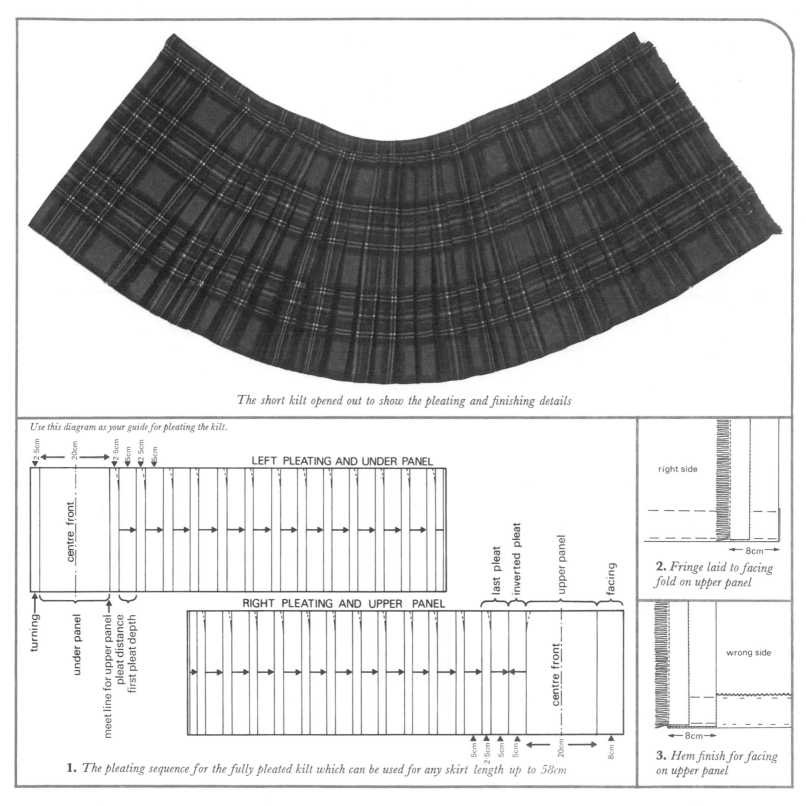

The short kilt opened out to show the pleating and finishing details

Use this diagram as your guide for pleating the kilt.

LEFT PLEATING AND UNDER PANEL

RIGHT PLEATING AND UPPER PANEL

1. *The pleating sequence for the fully pleated kilt which can be used for any skirt length up to 58cm*

2. *Fringe laid to facing fold on upper panel*

3. *Hem finish for facing on upper panel*

Fastening the waist-band. Before you attach the waist-band, consider the way you want the kilt to fasten. You can fasten it with a hook and eye but if you want to be traditional, make a tab and buckle fastening. Choose the size of buckle you require and then make the tab to enable it to fit neatly.

The tab should project about 13cm from the end of the waist-band and there are two methods of attaching it, depending on the type of waist-band you are making.

Method 1. If you are making a waist-band with an elasticised back, the tab must be attached before you finish the end of the waist-band. Make the tab a fraction narrower than the waist-band, insert the raw edge into the end of the waist-band on the upper front panel, then stitch twice across the end to secure it.

Method 2. If you are making a plain waist-band, cut the tab slightly longer than 13cm and make both ends pointed. Lay one pointed end on to the end of the waist-band and topstitch neatly following the shape of the point.

For both methods, the buckle can be stitched straight on to the waist-band in line with the tab, or you can make a belt end for it and then sew it securely to the waist-band. Use strong hooks and eyes or a trouser hook and bar on the under panel to hold the wrap in position.

Chapter 22

Fitting with a toile

This chapter introduces a new method for fitting—the toile (pronounced twahl), a mock up version of the final garment. This method is used by couturiers and professional dressmakers to ensure perfect fit.

Once you have made your own personal blue-print you can put your scissors into expensive material without the nagging doubt at the back of your mind, "Will it fit?"

Make your basic pattern from the Blouse Graph Pattern on pages 84 and 85. There will undoubtedly be variations between it and your actual measurements so check back carefully with your figure chart on page 13.

The completed bodice toile

A toile saves endless fitting problems later on and you can use this same toile when making up commercial paper patterns, to check where they need altering.

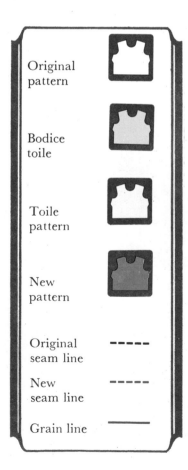

▼ The basic blouse pattern
This is used to make . . .

▼ . . . the bodice toile
This is a mock garment, a fitted bodice in this case.
The alterations on the toile are used to make . . .

▼ . . . The toile pattern
This is a waist-length version of the basic pattern from which you cut . . .

▼ . . . the new pattern
This is your personalised adjusted and corrected pattern from which the blouse is cut.

Original pattern

Bodice toile

Toile pattern

New pattern

Original seam line   - - - - -

New seam line   - - - - -

Grain line

Making a bodice toile

You may have a suitable plain remnant from which you can make your toile. Or a used sheet with enough sound material left to make your mock-up blouse would do, bearing in mind that the material you use must be firm enough to stand sewing and fitting. Alternatively you will need 1·15 metres 90cm wide calico or sheeting which you can buy from dress fabric shops or large department stores. You will also need paper for patterns, a tailor's square or 45° set square, two pencils (one coloured).

 Making the toile pattern

Measure your length from the neck to the waist line, back and front (see Dressmaking Chapter 2), and mark off these measurements on the Back and Front patterns.

Lay the Back and Front patterns together at the side-seam with the lower stitching line of the side bust dart meeting the balance mark on the Back. Draw a pencil line across both pattern pieces to connect the waist line marks. This will give you the pattern length required to make the toile.

Lay these pattern pieces on a large sheet of paper. Draw round the edges and into the darts. Mark the waist line and balance marks. Then copy the pencilled waist onto the toile pattern.

Cut out and trim the toile pattern at the waist.

 Cutting the bodice toile

Fold the calico or sheeting lengthwise. Place the Back section of the toile pattern to the fold line and the Front section to the selvedges.

Allow at least 2·5cm seam allowance at all seam edges, except at the Centre Front where it wraps over, and at least 5cm at the waist.

Transfer all the pattern markings on to the fabric, then cut out and remove the pattern.

Open up the cut fabric pieces and draw in the grain lines of the fabric with coloured pencil.

 Marking the grain lines on the toile

To find the lengthwise grain, measure about 9·3cm in from the Centre Back and the Centre Front lines and draw a line parallel to each of these.

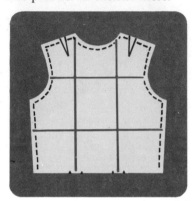

To find the crosswise grain on each piece, lay a tailor's square or 45° set square to the Centre Back and Centre Front and draw lines across the fabric half-way between the waist line and the side bust dart and half-way between shoulder and underarm-seam.

 Fitting the toile

Pin and tack the shoulder and side-seams and darts. Do not tack the pleats in the waist line, they will be pinned into darts when you fit the toile.

Try on the bodice over a slip. Pin the fronts together down the Centre Front line.

Always start fitting from the shoulders downwards, working towards the waist.

NECK AND ARMHOLES

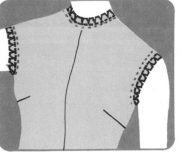

1. Problem The toile is tight and pulls or is raised round the neck or armholes.
Correction If it's the neck line that is tight, snip into the seam allowance. Pencil a new neckline on the toile around the base of the neck and snip to this line until the garment sits without straining.
The correction is exactly the same for the armholes.

2. Problem Thin arms. The armhole is too large.
Correction Raise the underarm curve into seam allowance.

3. Problem Thin neck. The neckline is too large.
Correction Use the seam allowance on the toile to mark the correct position for the neckline. If the neckline is still not the right size, you will have to tack strips of fabric round the neck on which to mark the new line

SHOULDERS

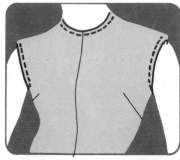

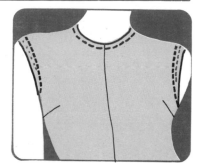

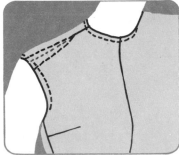

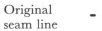
4. Problem Straight shoulders.
The fabric strains at the outer end of the shoulder-seam.
Correction Undo the shoulder-seam and let it out.

5. Problem Sloping shoulders.
The seam rises above the shoulder at the outer edge and there are often drag lines from the inner shoulders towards the underarm.
Correction Take the surplus material into the shoulder-seam. Snip the seam allowance around the underarm curve, lifting the material on the Front until you have a smooth fit. Do the same for the Back and watch the crosswise grain.

6. Problem Shoulders too wide or too narrow.
Correction To find the position for the armhole-seam, follow the crease of your underarm round the front on to the top of outer shoulder points. Continue working this line towards the back. When halfway down the back move your arm forwards very slightly and continue to work towards the crease of the underarm. This is to allow ease for movement.

BACK

7. Problem Rounded back. This often accompanies round shoulders.

The horizontal grain lines tilt down towards the side-seams.

Correction Undo the side-seams. Lift the Back side-seams until the grain is straight, and pin. Use the balance marks as a guide to see that you get the same lift on each side. Un-pick the shoulder-seam, then lift the fullness around the armhole into the shoulder-seam by deepening the dart. If the problem is very pro-nounced, undo the shoulder darts and take the depth of the darts and the surplus fabric into the neck line by making two darts to each side of the Centre Back.

Repin the shoulder-seams and mark a new armhole line to match up with the line on the Front, because the original line will have moved in on the shoulder. Re-mark the under-arm line, which has also been displaced, but allow plenty of width across the back.

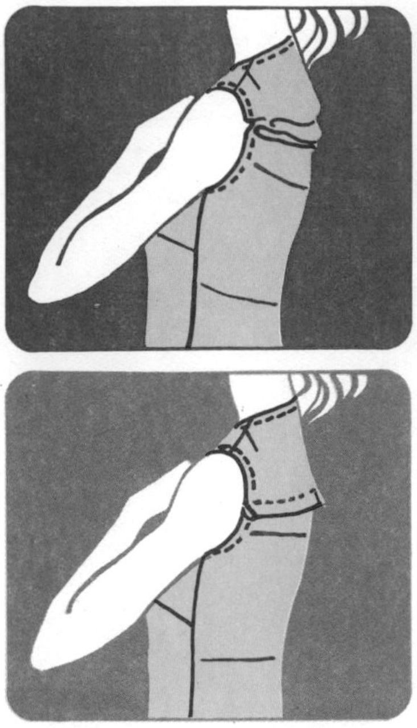

8. Problem Straight, very erect back.

The horizontal grain lines drop at the back towards the centre.

Correction If the drop is between the neck and under-arm, pin a fold right across the Back, starting at the Centre, until the grain runs straight. Any fullness below that point can be let down into the waist-seam, but only as far as the straight of the grain will allow. If this isn't enough you will have to pin another fold line, tapering off towards the side-seams, below the armhole.

IMPORTANT!

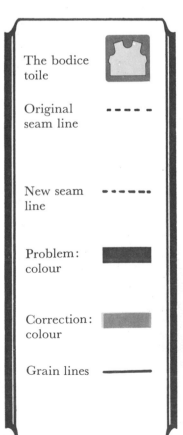

The bodice front should hang straight from the shoulders now and is ready to be fitted into the waist.

Pin off the ease and fullness into the side-seams, beginning at the underarm edge. It must be a comfortable but not a loose fit over the bust.

The fullness below the bust should fall straight towards the waist line.

Pin the side-seam off into the waist without causing the full-ness under the bust to be pulled sideways.

Then, starting at the waist, using the pleat marks as your guide, pin this fullness into darts which should finish on the point of the bust.

Lengthen the pleat marks in the Back also into darts.

The bodice toile

Original seam line — - - - -

New seam line - - - - - -

Problem: colour ▬▬▬

Correction: colour ▬▬▬

Grain lines ▬▬▬

BUST AND WAIST LINE

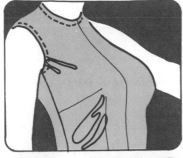

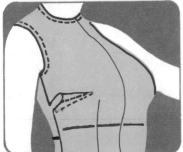
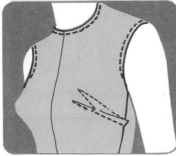

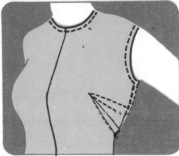

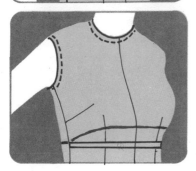

9. Problem Full bust.
Usually shown by drag lines from the bust towards the side-seams at the waist line.

Correction Pin a tape in a straight line across the front of the toile, starting and ending at the seam line on the lower grain line. Allow the grain line, but not the tape, to rise when the bust has taken it up. Mark the toile along the edge of the tape, using a different coloured pencil so that you cannot confuse this line with the grain line.
Remove the tape.

Undo the side-seams and lift the fabric into the side bust dart on the lower stitching line only.
Check the crosswise grain line on the lower half of the toile and don't pin any more into the side dart than will allow the grain line to run straight.
The side-seams will now be shorter, so pin a new line for the waist.

10. Problem Side bust darts in wrong position. The dart should run towards the point of the bust.

Correction If it is higher or lower, drop it or raise it.

11. Problem Shallow bust. The point of the side bust dart creates fullness over the bust and does not run out smoothly. You will notice that the lower grain line curves downwards towards the Centre Front.

Correction Undo the side-seams and let out the side bust dart on the lower stitching line, allowing the fabric to drop into the waist until the grain line runs straight.
Repin the side-seams, taking in the surplus width from the front.
Your armhole may need re-shaping around the front.

12. Problem Underarm bulge.
Pulling under the armhole.

Correction Slant the side bust darts by making them a little lower at the side-seams. Let out the side-seams between the underarm dart and the armhole line.

Finishing the toile
The grain lines should now be perfectly vertical and horizontal and the bodice should fit well.
Finally lay a narrow seam tape round your waist and pin it to the toile. Mark in your correct waist line if it has altered.

Balancing the toile corrections

Mark all pin and pencil lines with tacking cotton.

Remove the pins and unpick the toile.

Fold the Back on the Centre Back line, matching all edges, and place the Fronts together. Compare the alterations on the left and right side of each

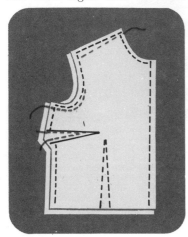

bodice piece. Even out any differences, as for the skirts in Dressmaking 6, except where you have made alterations for uneven sides.

Trace the new lines on both sides of the toile.

Pin and tack together again for a final check.

Preparing the toile

Unpick the tacking on the toile. Cut off all seam allowances and cut out the area between the stitching lines of all darts.

Cut the Back of the toile along the Centre Back line, unless you have made adjustments for uneven sides. (See notes for 'Uneven sides' in the chart.)

As the left and right bodice pieces are now the same, you need only work with that half which corresponds to the pattern.

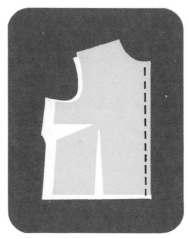

With the right sides of the toile pattern and the corresponding toile pieces uppermost, lay the toile Front section on the pattern Front and the toile Back on the pattern Back.

Having pinned off the ease on the side-seams in the last chapter, you will see at once that the pattern is much wider than the toile. Shirt blouses must have an 8cm to 10cm ease over the bust, and to make them blouse at the waist they are cut with very little shaping. Ignore the under bust dart on the toile until later, when you will be shown how to alter the pattern to fit larger bust proportions.

Making the new pattern

Preparing the new pattern

Place the original basic Back and Front patterns on a large sheet of paper and draw round

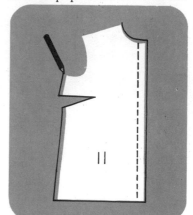

them. Draw into the darts and transfer all markings on to the new pattern. Allow enough room round each piece for corrections.

Original pattern	
Bodice toile	
Toile pattern	
New pattern	
Original seam line	-----
New seam line	-----
Grain line	———

NECK AND ARMHOLES

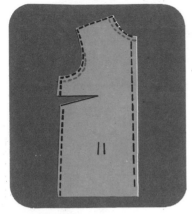

1. Problem The toile is tight round the neck or armholes.
Altering pattern Mark the new neck line or armhole on to the new pattern.

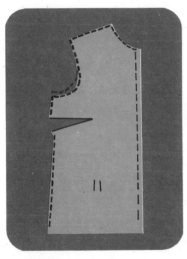

2. Problem Thin arms.
Altering pattern Mark the new underarm-seam on the new pattern.

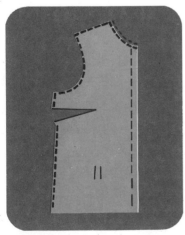

3. Problem Thin neck.
Altering pattern Mark the new neck line on the new pattern.

SHOULDERS

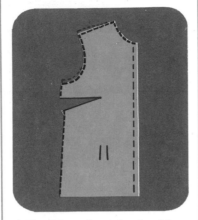

4. Problem Straight shoulders.
Altering pattern Mark the new shoulder line on the new pattern. If the armhole is now too large it must be raised at the underarm.

5. Problem Sloping shoulders.
Altering pattern Mark the new shoulder line on to the new pattern. If the armhole is now too small it must be lowered at the underarm.

6. Problem Shoulders too wide or too narrow.
Altering pattern Mark the new armhole line over the shoulder on to the new pattern.

BACK

7. Problem Rounded back.
Altering pattern The Back pattern needs extra length between the base of the neck and the waist. If you have only deepened the shoulder dart, make the new dart length on the toile pattern and adjust the shoulder-seam and armhole line.

If the problem is pronounced and you have pinned neck line darts, pin the Centre Back of the toile pattern to the Centre Back of the new pattern.

Measure the distance from the neck to the highest point of the curve on your back and make a straight pencil line across pinned toile pattern at this point.

Unpin the top part of the toile pattern and cut along the pencil line to within 6mm of the armhole.

Measure the extra depth of the darts you pinned on the toile at the neck (that is, the depth of the new darts less the depth of the discarded shoulder dart), and open up the slash across the pattern by this amount.

The toile pattern has now swung outwards and away from the Centre Back line, so use the Centre Back line of the new pattern as your guide. Lay the toile to this line and copy all the fitting alterations. Complete the neck line in a shallow curve as shown, connecting the shoulder line to the new Centre Back. Adjust the shoulder-seam as pinned.

Mark the two neck darts on to the new pattern, otherwise the neck line of the new pattern will be too large.

8. Problem Straight, erect back.
Altering pattern If there is too much length between the shoulder and armhole, pin a fold across the toile pattern to the same depth as on toile.

If there is too much length between the armhole and waist line, mainly concentrated in the centre of the back, pin a dart across the toile pattern, about 10cm above the waist line, beginning on the Centre Back line and tapering towards the side-seam, to the depth of the one pinned on the toile.

On the blouse, you need only correct extra length between shoulder and armhole and adjust armhole on the new pattern to preserve original shape. For corrections below the armhole, lay toile pattern on new pattern. Shorten the Centre Back line by the depth of the pleat and let out the side-seam by the amount the Centre Back line is tipped forward.

BUST AND WAIST LINE

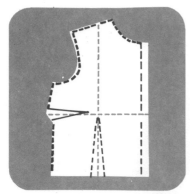

9. Problem Full bust.

Altering pattern All the corrections for a full bust are transferred from the toile on to the toile pattern. Using the toile pattern as a guide, a corrected toile pattern is drawn up, then this corrected toile pattern is used to make the new pattern, using the Basic pattern as a guide to allow for the ease required.

Transfer the markings for the darts and side-seams from the fitted toile on to the toile pattern.

On the Front toile pattern, draw a straight line from the waist upwards through the point under the bust dart and a line across the pattern through the point of the side bust dart.

Cut the pattern on the pencilled horizontal line only.

Lay the Front toile pattern to the straight edge of a sheet of paper.

Move the bottom half of the toile pattern away from the top half the distance between the crosswise grain markings and the coloured line from the tape. Pin both pattern pieces to the straight edge of the paper along the Centre Front line. Cut the pencilled vertical line to within 6mm of the shoulder line.

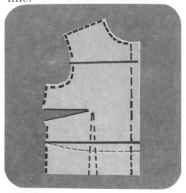

To find the distance by which the pattern should be spread, make the following small calculation:

Measure the depth of the under bust dart in the waist line and deduct 5·6cm (the normal depth for an underbust dart). Beginning with the lower side section, spread the pattern outwards by this amount. Pin into position.

To obtain the extra depth required for the side bust dart, pivot the upper side sections of the pattern until the distance between the cutting lines on the side-seam is the

amount by which you have lengthened the pattern, plus the extra depth of the side bust dart.

Find the pointed ends of the darts in the centre of the pattern spread. Use the toile to mark in the depth of the darts.

Lay the toile over the pattern and check the dart position. If you had to raise or lower the darts, transfer the new position to the pattern.

Straighten the shoulder line before cutting out the new toile pattern.

Remember that the upper and lower stitching line of the side bust dart must be of equal length and that you will have to make adjustment to the lower side-seam.

Cut out the correct toile pattern.

To adjust the new pattern, lay the corrected toile pattern along the Centre Front line of the new pattern. The corrected toile pattern will be smaller, because there is no ease on it. Use the corrected toile pattern to adjust the new blouse pattern and add the ease on to the side-seam, which must be

19mm on both Back and Front. This must be measured from the top of the side-seam on the pattern and taken all along the side-seam. Mark in the alteration to the darts.

Check the size of the armhole. The ease in the blouse should continue over the bust. So when you lay the toile pattern on to the new pattern, the lower armhole curve should be 13mm outside the armhole line of the toile pattern and should taper into the armhole on the toile pattern at the underarm, half-way along the armhole towards the shoulder. Always remember to measure the length of the side-seams after adjustments, and level them up to the length, which has remained static. The extra length is added to the hem line of the new pattern.

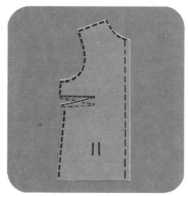

10. Problem Side bust darts in wrong position.

Altering pattern Using the toile, draw in corrected dart positions on the new pattern.

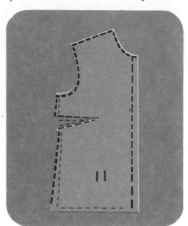

11. Problem Shallow bust.
Altering pattern Copy the new dart and side-seam, allowing 19mm for ease, and adjust the length on the new pattern,

trimming off the extra length on the Front hem line.

Reshape the underarm if necessary.

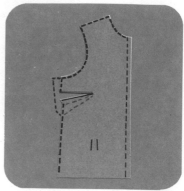

12. Problem Underarm bulge.
Altering pattern Correct the slant of the underarm dart on the toile pattern.

To let out the top of the side-seam on the pattern, fold the lowered dart in the stitching position.

You will see that the lower stitching line of the dart projects over the side-seam. The amount by which it projects gives the extra width needed at the top of the side-seam.

If you had to take more fabric into the dart, don't forget to adjust the lower edge of the pattern accordingly.

Transfer corrections on to the new pattern.

UNEVEN SIDES

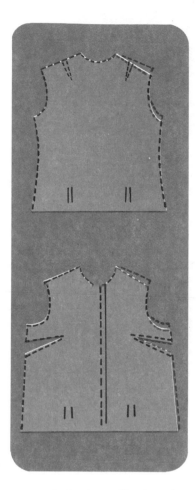

If you find after adjusting the toile that you have pronounced differences, such as one sloping shoulder or one high shoulder, or one side of the bust larger than the other, make corrections as follows:

First compare and balance all the fitting alterations on the toile, with the exception of the differences.

Draw up the other half of the new Back and Front patterns identical to the first half. Cut out the pattern pieces, leaving 2·5cm seam allowances all round and 5cm at the hem. Join the Back pattern sections along the Centre Back line and pin the Fronts together along the Centre Front line. Correct the new pattern, making the adjustments each side of the pattern as required.

Trim the pattern along the new seam lines.

When cutting, you must unfold the fabric and use the complete Back and the complete Front of the pattern.

ALTERING THE SLEEVE PATTERNS

If you have made the armhole larger or smaller you will of course have to alter the sleeve pattern by the same amount. Most sleeves need only minor adjustments and these can usually be done when fitting the cut-out sleeve. But here are four pattern adjustments which must be done before cutting, because they affect the shape of the sleeve cap as well as the fit of the sleeve.

Thin upper arm

Pin a small vertical pleat about 13mm deep (depending on the size of the armhole alteration) through the centre of the sleeve pattern. Pin the pleated pattern on to a sheet of paper and pencil round it for the new pattern.

Large upper arm

Cut the pattern through the centre from the hem to the top of the cap. Pin the pattern to a sheet of paper, spreading the pattern pieces apart by the required amount. Pencil around the spread-out pattern for a new sleeve pattern.

Heavy shoulder

Slash the pattern vertically from the shoulder to the hem edge. Pin the pattern to a sheet of paper and spread it by the required amount, tapering it towards the hem into the original pattern line. Pencil round the spread pattern pieces for a new sleeve pattern.

Straight shoulder and large upper arm

Work as for large upper arm, but also raise the cap of the sleeve by the same amount you let out of the shoulder-seam if the underarm-seam has not been raised.

Here are four pretty styles which can be made from the Golden Hands Blouse Graph. Instructions on the previous pages will ensure a perfect fit.

Chapter 23 About commercial paper patterns

Toile — making

Commercial paper patterns are the greatest invention since the sewing machine as an aid to successful home dressmaking, and no sewing course which didn't teach you how to use them would be complete. In using the specially designed patterns from the Golden Hands Graph Pages you have become familiar with pattern shapes, how to adjust them for fitting, and how to adapt them to other styles. Now is an appropriate moment to introduce commercial paper patterns into Golden Hands dressmaking and in using them show you how you can apply all the knowledge you have gained so far. This chapter may help to dispel some of the mystique which surrounds commercial paper patterns.

Facts about commercial paper patterns

Today commercial paper patterns are as near perfect as you can ever expect them to be and the home dressmaker now has the best of all worlds—a perfect combination of design and fabric as well as a better, more lasting finish, and clothes which are so much cheaper.

The drafting and grading of commercial paper patterns has reached such a high level that if you are a standard size you can make a dress without trying it on at all and yet achieve a reasonable fit.

As far as sizing is concerned, you may well find that one particular name of pattern fits you better than another but, apart from small differences in detail, they are all very similar, as the big pattern companies adhere strictly to an international sizing code.

There was a time when the name on a pattern catalogue was an indication of its fashion content, but this is no longer so. The pattern industry is a very competitive one and each company caters for a variety of tastes and requirements. Also, changes in fashion can now be translated speedily and effectively into paper pattern form, making each catalogue as exciting as a shop window.

The cost of patterns varies according to the design or the contents of the pack. Some cost slightly more because there are several variations in one pack while with others it is the individual design which is expensive (as with Vogue Couturier patterns), and the cost of the pattern should be compared with the end result. You cannot expect to have an exclusive design for the price of a mass produced one—the cost is relative and you get what you pay for.

When choosing a design decide the purpose of the dress and choose accordingly. For casual outings choose a simple but good design and leave the special, more complicated, designs for those occasions when you want to look beautifully dressed. This way you really will enjoy making and wearing your clothes.

Reading a commercial paper pattern

In the pattern envelope you will find sheets of tissue paper with shapes printed on them: these are the pattern pieces. Sometimes they are all printed on one sheet, if so cut them out but leave a margin round the outlines.

If you are not sure what all the lines and symbols mean, take a pattern from the Golden Hands Graph Pages and place it beside the commercial paper pattern. Compare and identify the markings. Here the Basic Blouse Pattern and Vogue Pattern 1000 are used (figures 1 and 3).

The lines. Commercial pattern pieces are outlined by a heavy line inside of which is another, lighter line. This inner line may be broken or continuous. These double lines are the seam and cutting lines, the space between them, usually 16mm, being the seam allowance with the inner, lighter line as the seam line. When there is only one line it indicates that the line has to be placed and cut on a fabric fold or no seam allowance is needed.

Hem lines are rarely given, but the hem allowance is written against the solid line at the bottom of the pattern.

Inside each pattern piece you will find a variety of lines—stitching lines, lengthening and shortening lines, darts and grain lines. The lines usually carry wording to say what they are, but if in doubt find the key to them on the instruction sheet.

Although the major pattern companies are now producing printed patterns only, you may still come across some patterns which have perforated markings instead of printed lines. If so, lay the pattern on a hard dark surface and read the key to the perforations. Then connect the relevant perforations with pencil lines so that you can see at a glance where the seams, darts and other lines are. Apart from the fact that these patterns are perforated instead of printed they are cut to size exactly as the others, with seam allowances included.

Read the key to the perforations carefully and if you still find them confusing and want to make quite sure that you will not make any mistakes when cutting, mark the seam and dart lines with a red pencil—that is red for danger, do not cut!

Symbols. Looking at the printed pattern you will see a number of symbols—large dots and tiny dots, diamonds, triangles and squares. These all have a meaning, some have to be matched to another symbol of the same shape either on another pattern piece or on another stitching line on the same piece, such as with darts. The diamonds along the seam lines or seam allowances are the balance marks, and by having them printed in groups they are also a code to the seam in question.

On perforated patterns you will find cut out 'V' notches and perforated symbols in varying shapes and sizes. These have the same meaning as on the printed patterns.

The symbols are very important indeed and using them as they are meant to be used will help you to avoid making time-wasting mistakes.

Personalizing commercial paper patterns

You will now find out just how valuable the bodice toile is (see previous chapter).

If you have not already made one, you should do so now and then transfer all the fitting corrections to the Golden Hands Basic Blouse Pattern. This will save you endless time and trouble later.

To correct the commercial paper pattern for fit, lay it over the corrected pattern made from the graph to see what adjustments are necessary.

If you have to make drastic alterations, such as those for a rounded back, pin the toile under the pattern and make the adjustments using tissue paper or soft wrapping paper and sticky tape. Remember that the toile has no seam allowance so take this into account before cutting out the new shape.

Adjustments to length should also be made at this stage. Lengthen or shorten the pattern as shown in previous chapters. If the seams are shaped always connect them carefully to avoid 'stepping 'when you cut out the fabric.

Fitting alterations to sleeves are covered later in this chapter.

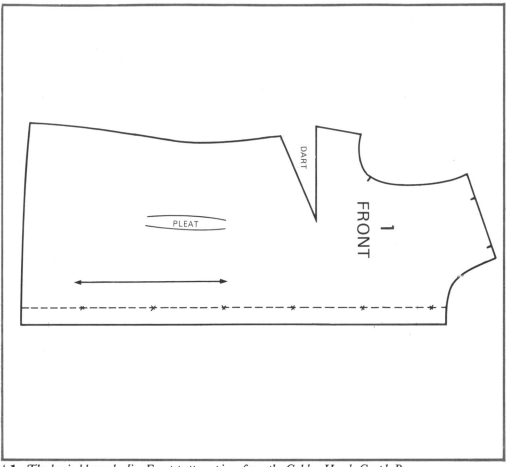

PLEAT

DART

1
FRONT

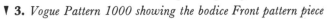

▲ **1.** *The basic blouse bodice Front pattern piece from the Golden Hands Graph Pages*

▼ **3.** *Vogue Pattern 1000 showing the bodice Front pattern piece*

▲ **2.** *The second skin bodice toile without ease*

▼ **4.** *The Vogue Pattern dress toile with ease*

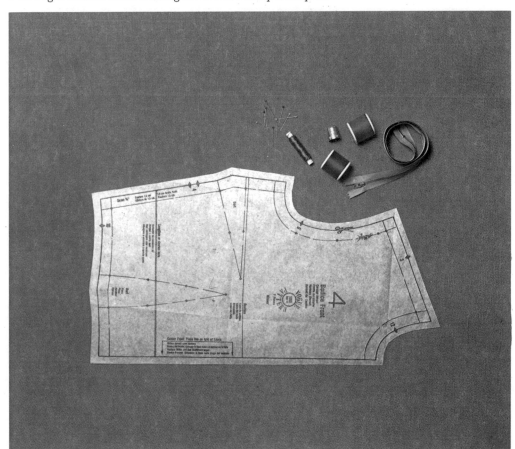

Use your personalised Vogue 1000 dress toile for fitted styles from any commercial paper pattern

The toile pattern can be used with front and back fastening bodices.

The instruction sheet

Each commercial paper pattern comes with an instruction sheet. Use this to identify the pattern pieces needed for making up the particular version you have chosen. The sheet also contains layouts for all sizes and fabric widths.

The actual making up instructions on the sheet are merely a guide to the assembling of the various sections and the finish of the garment.

Throughout this book the Golden Hands step-by-step making up instructions include preparing the garment for fitting. So, using the instruction sheet, first read 'tack' where it says 'stitch' as you prepare the garment to be fitted. Then read through the instructions again, step-by-step as you make up the garment, and you will find that they really help the dressmaking to go easily and smoothly.

Making up a dress from a commercial paper pattern

Vogue Pattern 1000 has been chosen to give you a full working example of how to use a commercial paper pattern. This pattern is of a simple waisted dress which is 'Vogue's guide to perfect fit of fitted garments'.

It is being made up as a dress toile which can later be used to adjust other patterns (figure 4).

This dress toile differs from the Golden Hands bodice toile (figure 2) which is made without ease to help you make the correct adjustments for figure faults. The dress toile, however, not only incorporates the fitting corrections which you should already have copied but also includes ease (or tolerance) so that you can make sure there is enough room for movement.

Do not dispense with your bodice toile when you have made the dress toile because you will find later that both have their uses.

Cutting out

Make the dress toile from unbleached calico or soft sheeting, buying the amount stated on the pattern envelope. Do not use old, heavily used · fabric because the results will not be the same.

The pattern has seven pattern pieces. Lay them out on the fabric as shown on the pattern layouts.

Start pinning the pattern on the fabric. Here you will encounter your first snag. Patterns made from tissue paper do not have the same resistance to creasing as the firm home-made patterns. Therefore, to avoid losing on your pattern size, hold down the centre of each pattern with two or three pins or, if it is laid to the fabric fold, pin it at right angles to the fold at

intervals of about 25cm. Smooth the pattern out towards the seams.

To check how much the pattern decreases in size, make a chalk line along the pattern edge, before pinning further, then pin it down all round and see how much the pattern has moved in. If it has moved by 3mm or more you will need to cut outside the cutting line otherwise at least 13mm from the size of the pattern will be lost.

When you lay out the pattern pieces leave a small margin between them even though the seam allowances are already marked on the pattern. Should the fabric fray a lot it is wise to cut a little more than the given seam allowance.

Cut out the pattern.

Marking the pattern detail

The seams cannot be marked with continuous tailor's tacks, as for the Golden Hands patterns, because of the inclusion of the seam allowance, so make small slits through the pattern along the stitching lines, at about 13cm intervals, and make single tailor's tacks through them. For the balance marks make a tailor's tack at right angles to the seam line.

The symbols are best marked with different coloured threads. But do make a note of what each colour represents on the symbol key to prevent confusion later.

One very important point to remember: where darts are marked with solid lines only always make a tailor's tack where the dart goes across the seam line. Sadly, it is all too easy to take up a little more, or less, in the darts than specified and you will then find the seams do not match.

Assembling the dress from the instruction sheet

With the fabric details clearly marked you are ready to start assembling the dress. Lay the instruction sheet before you as you work and following the text and diagrams, pin and tack the seams.

When you get to the facing stage, stop. Join the skirt to the bodice along the waist-seam ready for fitting.

Since the waist-seam is always a very delicate fitting point, even on the slimmest of figures, it is essential that you fit it with a waist petersham. This need not be put into the finished garment, where it may be too stiff for your requirements, but it is the only safe way to check at the fitting stage that the finished waist-seam will be in the right place.

Cut a strip of 2·5cm wide petersham ribbon to the length of your waist plus 2·5cm for fastening over and adjustment. Pin and tack it to the waist-seam of the dress, easing in the tolerance of the waist line evenly. The seam should run along the centre of the petersham.

Leave a small piecc unstitched at the back to each side of the opening so that you can fold the seam allowance along the opening and fasten the ends of the petersham.

Fitting the waisted dress

Having copied all the fitting adjustments made from the Golden Hands pattern on to the commercial paper pattern, only the new fitting problems associated with fitted dresses are left to be checked.

The ease or tolerance requirement is very important and varies according to the figure. Even standard sizes may not find enough ease in a fitted garment, so it is important that all figure types fit the dress. Fasten the back opening all the way up, then move around. Sit, stoop, then stretch your arms forwards to make sure that the stress on the seams does not distort or split them.

If you want really fitted sleeves your arm movement is restricted at all times as is your waist by a fitted waist. To compensate a little for these restrictions allow plenty of ease (no bulk though) over the bust and across the back, set in the sleeves really high and make sure that the sleeve head is not tight across the upper arm.

Another important point to watch when making a fitted dress: always fit the dress after meals because body measurements change during the day. Many an evening dress fitted in the morning has been too tight and uncomfortable to wear at night. Victorian ladies used to stay in bed until after midday if they wanted to look really slim at night!

Altering the sleeve pattern to fit

Thin arms (figure 5). Make a pleat along the centre of the sleeve pattern as shown in the correcting of the short sleeve pattern in Toile-making Chapter 22, p79.

Large arms (figure 6). Cut through the pattern as shown in the correcting of the short sleeve pattern in Toile-making

▼ *5. Altering the sleeve pattern for thin arms*

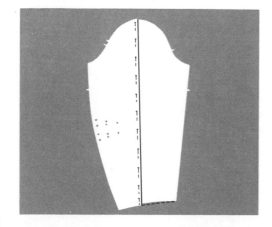

Chapter 22, p79. Make a new pattern.

Muscular forearm and top arm (figure 7). Slash the pattern from hem to seam line at the crown of the sleeve head. Spread the pattern sideways by the required amount as shown. This will form fullness between the crown and underarm which should be lapped and pinned to enable the pattern to lie flat. Make a new pattern adding the amount of the fullness pinned off to the crown of the sleeve head.

Large upper arms (figure 8). Cut the pattern as shown and spread it outwards by the required amount. Draw a new pattern.

Very straight arms (figure 9). If, at the fitting stage, you find there is a lot of fullness at the back of the sleeve head and that the curve of the sleeve does not follow the arm, move the crown of the sleeve forward by moving the balance mark, which meets the shoulder-seam line, back by 13mm or more. If this only shifts the problem of fullness from one place to another then correct the sleeve head by pinning off the required amount and then correct the pattern. Slash into the sleeve-seam on the pattern as shown, then pleat off the required amount across the sleeve head and redraw the pattern.

Finishing the toile

Finish toile following instruction sheet.

Mark in coloured pencil on the toile anything worth noting for further usc then keep the toile in a safe place because it will help you time and again to check the fitting of other patterns.

Adjusting the pattern after fitting

Transfer the markings from the dress toile to the pattern pieces where you have made adjustments to the fitting.

Using the pattern again

Although you can use a commercial paper pattern several times, once you have to start ironing it to get the creases out it is best to buy a new one. The creases can be ironed out but it seems that the paper shrinks and retains the width taken up by the creases.

It is not a good idea, though, to copy the pattern pieces on to firmer paper because there is no stiff edge to work around and the result could be very inaccurate, especially on large areas.

If you have to copy a pattern piece after a severe alteration, use soft wrapping paper which can be bought in rolls. Remember to continue both the cutting and seam lines on to the new pattern, otherwise you will lose the seam allowances where you made the alterations.

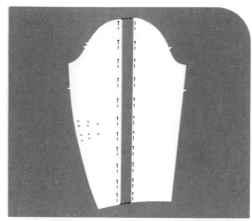

▲ *6. Altering the sleeve pattern for large arms*
▼ *7. Altering sleeve pattern for muscular arms*

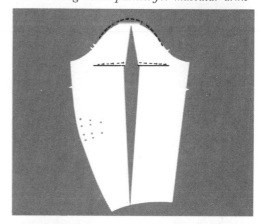

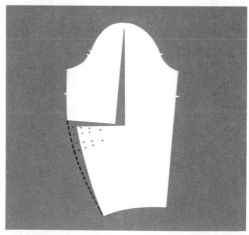

▲ *8. Altering sleeve pattern for large upper arms*
▼ *9. Altering sleeve pattern for straight arms*

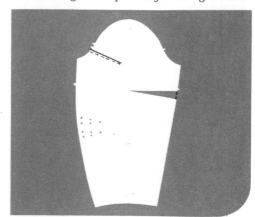

Basic blouse graph pattern

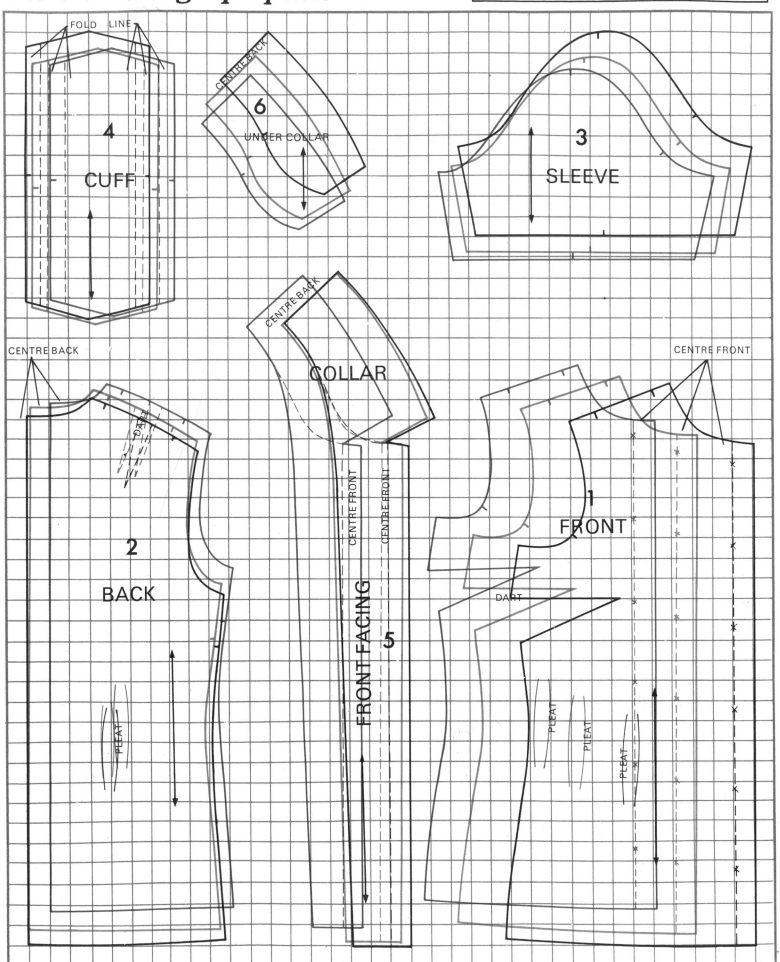

KEY

——— Size 82cm
——— Size 87cm
——— Size 90cm

⟷ Straight of grain
One square = 2·5cm

FOLD LINE

4

CUFF

6

UNDER COLLAR

CENTRE BACK

3

SLEEVE

CENTRE BACK

COLLAR

CENTRE BACK

CENTRE FRONT

2

BACK

CENTRE FRONT

CENTRE FRONT

FRONT FACING

5

1

FRONT

DART

PLEAT

PLEAT

PLEAT

PLEAT

The outlines given are the stitching lines.
Refer to page 117 for seam allowances
and check with the following chapters for
any variations.

KEY

Size 96cm
Size 102cm
Size 107cm

← → Straight of grain
One square = 2·5cm

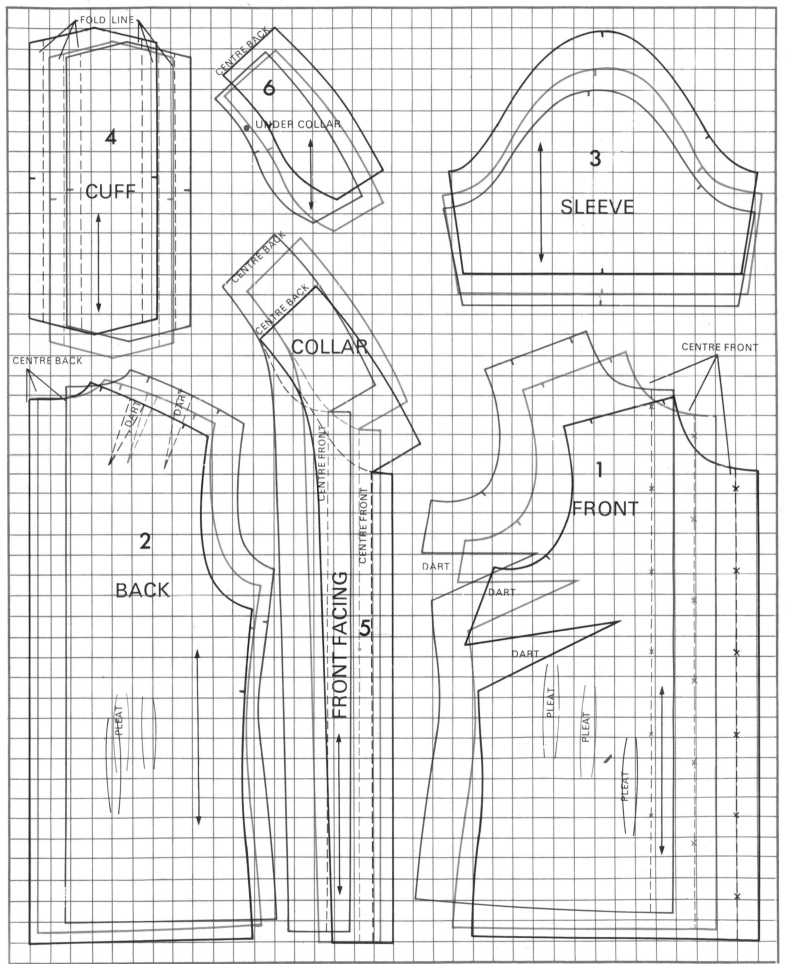

FOLD LINE

4
CUFF

CENTRE BACK
6
UNDER COLLAR

3
SLEEVE

CENTRE BACK
COLLAR
CENTRE BACK

CENTRE FRONT

CENTRE BACK

CENTRE FRONT
CENTRE FRONT
FRONT FACING
5

DART
DART

2
BACK

PLEAT

1
FRONT

DART
DART
DART

PLEAT
PLEAT
PLEAT

Chapter 24

The basic blouse

Here we give you instructions for making one of the most useful garments in every woman's wardrobe — the basic shirtneck, short-sleeved blouse. If you have already made the toile, remember to transfer all your corrections before cutting out the blouse —you will be assured of success at a fraction of the cost of an off the peg model. Instructions for making a variety of other exciting blouses are given on the following pages.

Choosing the fabric

The choice of fabrics for making blouses is exciting, because there is such a variety of light-weight materials available— plain, patterned or textured.
Here is a list of the most suitable fabrics for the basic short-sleeved blouse and variation shown here. The fabric needs to be crisp enough to hold the tailored shape of this blouse, but many other fabrics, which are not suitable for the basic style, will be included later for the other versions you see here. The first list has been especially selected for the beginner:
Firmly woven cottons: poplin, men's shirting, Swiss cotton, lawn, strawcloth, pique.
Linens: embroidered or other fine blouse-weight linen.
You can add the following to your list if you have a little practical experience in handling finer fabrics:
Silks, pure and artificial: shantung, Honan and fine Thai silk.
Man-made fibres: woven Crimplene and Courtelle or similar acrylic and polyester fibres; triacetate and rayon fabrics.

The amount

The amount needed for the basic green blouse with pointed cuffs is on the chart which appears below. For the floral, roll-sleeved variation the amounts are the same except for the following sizes, which all need 25cm extra: sizes 82cm and 87cm, 140cm wide fabric, without one way; sizes 90cm and 96cm, 90cm wide fabric without one way, 140cm wide fabric with and without one way; sizes 102cm and 107cm, 90cm wide fabric without one way, 140cm wide fabric with and without one way.

When you are buying your fabric, remember that you will also need four buttons and matching thread.

Blouse requirements

Sizes	cm 82	cm 87	cm 90	cm 96	cm 102	cm 107
	m	m	m	m	m	m
90cm Without one way	2·30	2·30	2·40	2·40	2·55	2·55
With one way	2·30	2·30	2·40	2·40	2·65	2·65
140cm Without one way	1·40	1·50	1·75	1·75	1·75	1·75
With one way	1·60	1·60	1·85	1·85	1·85	1·85

90cm Width With one way Sizes 90cm—96cm

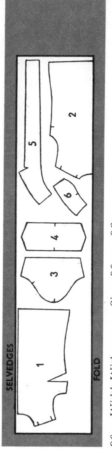

90cm Width Without one way Sizes 102cm—107cm

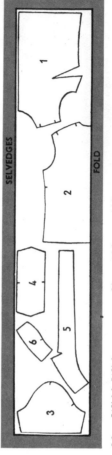

90cm Width With one way Sizes 102cm—107cm

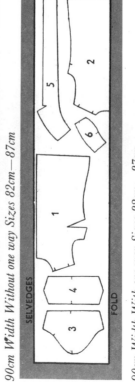

90cm Width Without one way Sizes 82cm—87cm

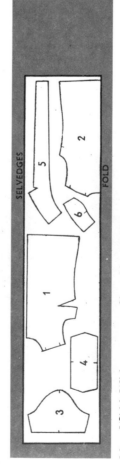

90cm Width With one way Sizes 82cm—87cm

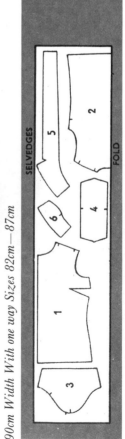

90cm Width Without one way Sizes 90cm—96cm

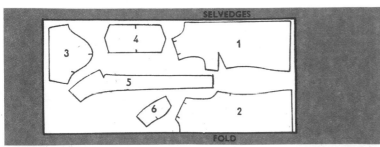

140cm Width With one way Sizes 82cm—87cm

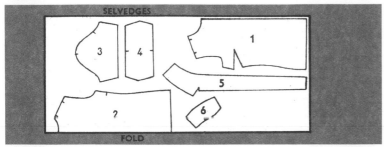

140cm Width Without one way Sizes 82cm—90cm

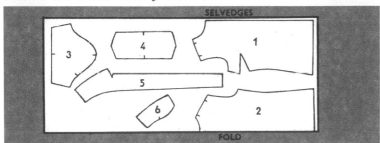

140cm Width Without one way Sizes 90cm—96cm

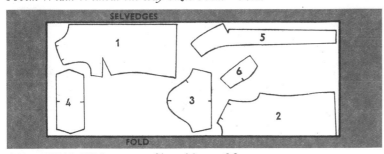

140cm Width With one way Sizes 90cm—96cm

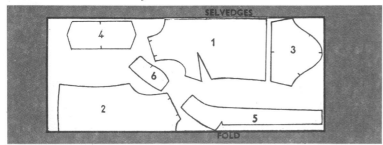

140cm Width Without one way Sizes 102cm—107cm

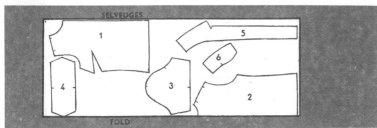

140cm Width With one way Sizes 102cm—107cm

Two moods of the basic blouse, instructions are given here for both.

Altering the collar

The collar fitting will not be affected by the alterations to the pattern except where your neck is larger or smaller than the pattern size.

Depending on whether the neck line has been altered at the Back or Front, or both, cut out the collar pattern along the broken lines indicated on the sketch.

Place the cut pattern on to a sheet of paper.

To make the collar larger, spread the pieces by the required amount and pin them in place.

To make the collar smaller, overlap the sections by the required amount and pin them in place.

To make a new pattern, draw round the pinned pattern and cut out.

Front facing, under collar, cuff

Any alteration to the collar must be transferred to the under collar.

If the Centre Front length of the pattern has been altered, alter the length of the front facing.

Any alterations made to the sleeve hems will affect the cuffs, so alter the cuffs accordingly.

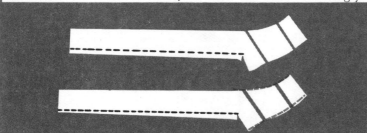

Before cutting — a word on seams

Shirt blouses are usually designed for hard wear and continual washing, and are therefore made in materials to withstand both. The seams must be strong to stand up to this treatment. So, for the blouses shown here, a flat-fell seam is used, where all the edges are stitched firmly in position.

Flat-fell seams are the traditional type of seaming for shirting.

Seam allowance

Previously, seam allowances have been 19mm. But to avoid double seam trimming and to give you the correct seam allowance for the flat-fell seam, allow only 16mm for seams.

Preparing the fabric for cutting

Green basic blouse with pointed cuffs. Straighten the fabric and fold it lengthwise, selvedge to selvedge. Use a large table for cutting out, to accommodate as much of the fabric as possible.

Select the correct layout from the Layout Sheet in the Pattern Pack and follow it carefully.

Pin all the pattern pieces securely on the fabric, with the Centre Back on the fold as indicated, and using any corrected new pattern pieces you have drawn up. If the fabric you are using marks easily, don't use too many pins.

Remember, the pattern has no seam or hem allowance, so mark these on the fabric round each piece. Allow 16mm for both seams and hems.

Cut out the blouse.

Floral, roll-sleeved variation. Before cutting out this blouse you will have to alter the basic blouse sleeve pattern as shown in the diagram. Place the pattern (or new sleeve pattern if you had to make one in the last chapter) on a sheet of paper about twice the length of the pattern, and draw round it. Remove pattern. Straighten the slope of the underarm-seam and extend it for 20cm. Mark the fold line 8cm down from the old sleeve edge.

Cut out the pattern along the new lines as indicated.

The cutting instructions and layouts are the same as for the basic blouse above except that you will not need the cuff pattern and will substitute the sleeve pattern you have just made for the one in the layout. The amounts given in Dressmaking chapter 16 will accommodate the extra length of the pattern.

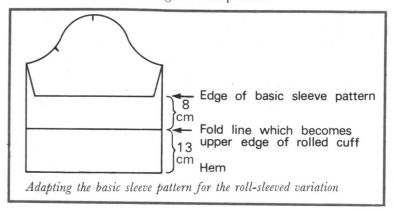

Adapting the basic sleeve pattern for the roll-sleeved variation

Edge of basic sleeve pattern

8 cm

Fold line which becomes upper edge of rolled cuff

13 cm

Hem

Marking the pattern details

Use continuous tailor's tacks to transfer all markings from the pattern to the fabric.

If you are working with fine fabrics, use a fine thread to avoid damaging the cloth. Make the tailor's tacks with a single thread and small stitches 6mm long. These will not fall out as easily as long stitches.

To make the dash lines on the cuff and the Centre Front on the facing and blouse, remove the patterns, measure the distance from the edge of the pattern pieces, and mark the fabric with pins. Tailor's tack along the pin lines.

Marking the curved dash line on the collar is optional: it is simply the dividing line between facing and collar. However, if you disregard it, be careful when machining that you stitch right into the point where the collar and Centre Front meet.

Marking the buttonholes at this stage is optional. These can be left until you are ready to make them. If you do mark them, use a contrasting coloured thread, so that you cannot confuse them with the Centre Front markings.

Remove all pattern pieces.

Pinning and tacking

Separate the pieces of fabric by cutting the tailor's tacks as previously shown. Use small scissors on fine fabrics, as they are less likely to snag the material.

Pin and tack the blouse bodice together for fitting.

First tack the underarm darts, remembering to taper the darts to the curve of the body.

Pin the shoulder-seams, disregarding the shoulder dart (unless you have fitted a shoulder dart to overcome the problem of a round back).

You will see, when pinning, that you have some ease along the back — this must be held in between the balance marks. Tack. If you find the material is too stiff to take the ease, pin and tack the shoulder dart indicated on the pattern, before tacking the shoulder-seam.

Pin and tack the side-seams.

Pin the pleats by meeting the stitching lines.

Fitting

Try on the tacked blouse and pin the Fronts together along the Centre Front line.

Check the fitting and make any alterations necessary. If you prefer less fullness round the waist, make the pleats deeper.

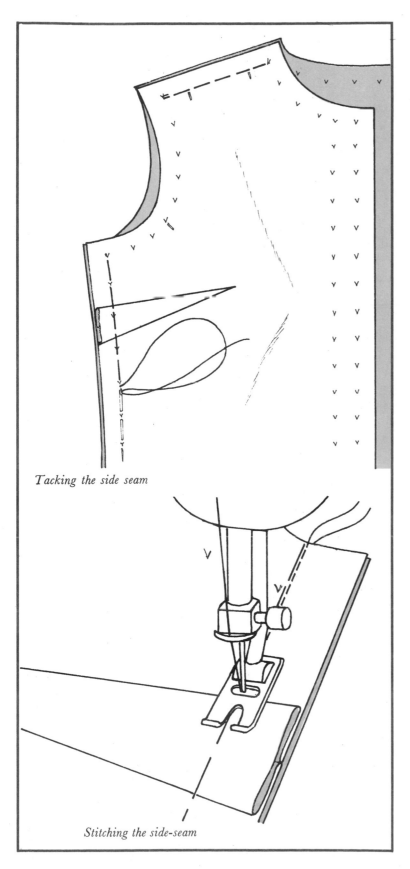

Tacking the side seam

Stitching the side-seam

Stitching

Unpick the side-seams and stitch the underarm darts. Fasten off securely at the ends. Flatten, by bringing the dart fold to meet the stitching line. Tack and press.

If you are using shoulder darts, stitch them, and press towards the centre.

Stitch the side and shoulder-seams.

Stitching the flat-fell seams

Press the side and shoulder-seams towards the back of the blouse, then trim the seam allowance, on the Back only, to 5mm, as these edges go inside the fell.

Turn under the edge of the seam on the Front by the same amount you trimmed off the Back.

Pin and tack over the trimmed seam edge.

Stitch the seams down, close to the edge.

Flat-fell seams can be worked on the inside of a garment or on the outside — both are correct.

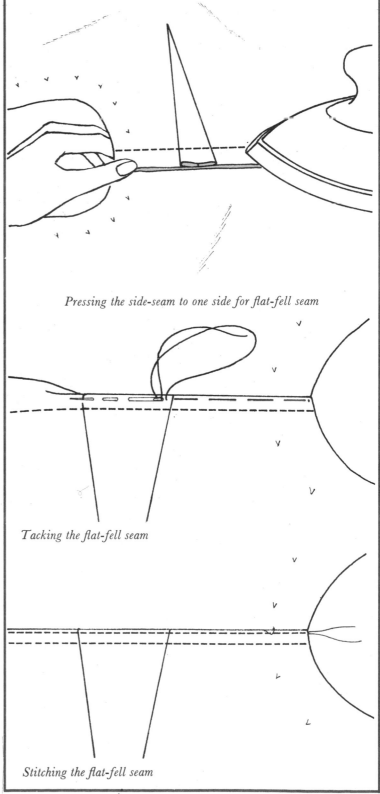

Pressing the side-seam to one side for flat-fell seam

Tacking the flat-fell seam

Stitching the flat-fell seam

Attaching the collar

Sew the under collar pieces together at the Centre Back. Press seam open.

Working with the under collar uppermost, pin it to the neck edge of the blouse, right sides facing. Match Centre Backs, and make sure the front edge of the under collar falls on the Centre Front of the blouse.

Tack in place. It is important to tack the collar down with small stitches because of the adverse pulling of the fabric along the neck line.

Stitch along the seam line and remove the tacking. Fasten off the threads securely at each end.

Snip the collar seam allowance where it meets the shoulder-seam of the blouse, to within a fraction of the stitching line.

Press the Back neck and collar-seams into the collar.

Snip into the seam allowance of the Front neck edge of the blouse, only. To enable you to stitch on the collar and facing in one movement, cut into the seam allowance of the neck edge at the Centre Front to within one or two grains of the stitches. Press seam open.

Be careful not to stretch the seam when pressing, and turn it carefully on a sleeve board to avoid making creases on the collar. By pressing the seam in this way you lessen the chance of ridges showing through the facing and collar.

Stitch the collar and facing pieces together at the Centre Back seam. Press seam open.

With right sides facing, pin and tack to the blouse, working with the under collar and blouse front uppermost. Make sure that the markings on both collar and under collar match perfectly. Stitch round the outer edge of the collar and down the fronts.

Having snipped the neck edge at the Centre Front, you can stitch into the corner of the notch on the top collar and facing by turning the seam allowance of the wrap on the neck edge out of the way of the needle before you stitch it to the facing.

You will notice that the top collar is slightly fuller than the under collar. This is to allow for the roll when it is turned out.

Carefully snip into the corner as shown, and cut across the points of the collar to take away the surplus fabric.

Turn the collar and facings to the inside and carefully tack round the stitched edges. Press the edges gently.

Turn in the seam allowance along the inside edge of the facings as far as the shoulder-seam. Pin and tack.

Neaten the edges by machine stitching close to the fold edge.

Turn under the seam allowance on the collar along the Back neck seam, pin and tack so that it lies just on the previous stitching line. Hand sew it down.

Press the collar from underneath.

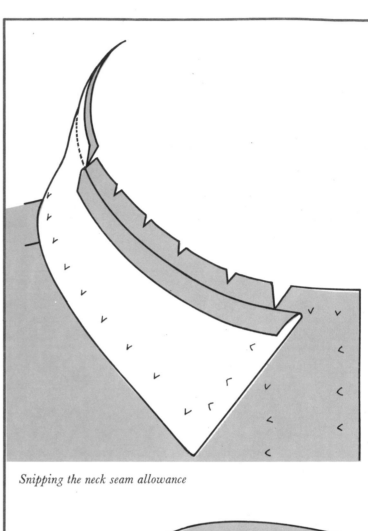

Snipping the neck seam allowance

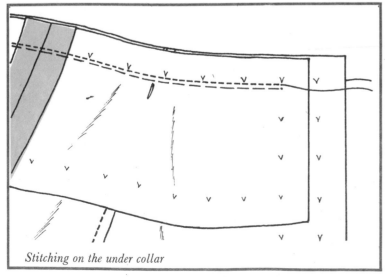

Stitching on the under collar

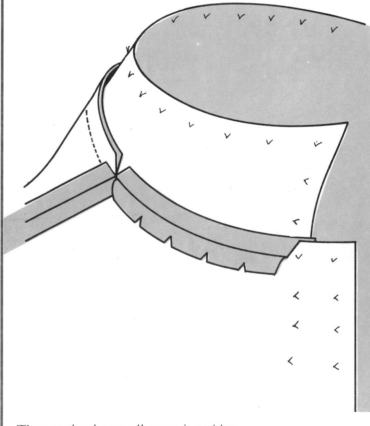

The pressed neck seam allowance in position

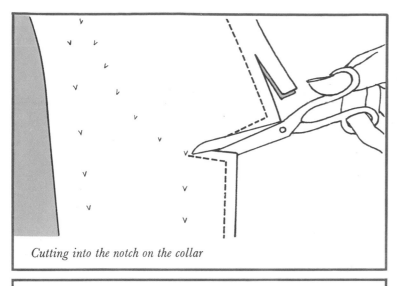

Cutting into the notch on the collar

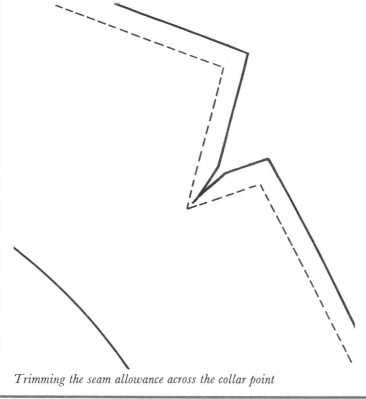

Trimming the seam allowance across the collar point

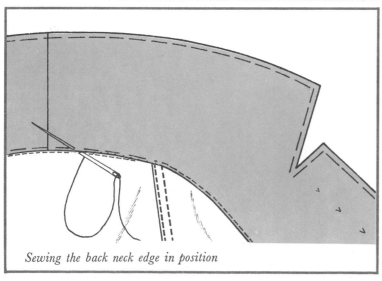

Sewing the back neck edge in position

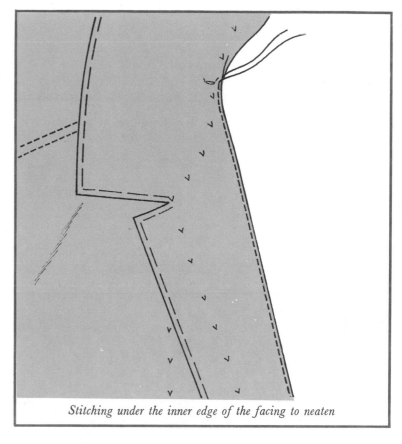

Stitching under the inner edge of the facing to neaten

The flat-fell seam

For a flat-fell seam, trim one seam allowance to 16mm and the other to 5mm.

Press seam allowance to one side with the wider seam allowance covering the trimmed allowance.

Turn under the edge of the upper seam allowance so it is level with the trimmed seam. Pin and tack over the trimmed seam edge.

Stitch close to the edge.

This seam can be worked on the inside or outside of a garment.

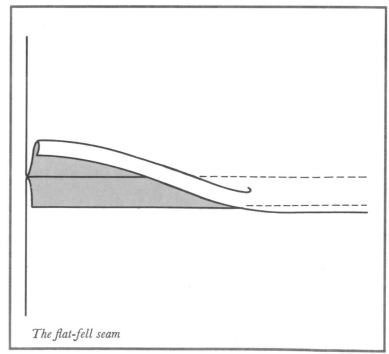

The flat-fell seam

Chapter 25

Finishing the blouses

The character of a blouse is determined by the fabric it is made in and the style of the collar and sleeves. The basic blouse and its variations are very casual-looking garments, but you will soon see how to change the effect by using a variety of sleeves and neck finishes described in later chapters. In this chapter we show you how to sew the sleeves and add the finishing touches. Again, the instructions for both blouses are the same, except where otherwise stated.

Making the sleeves
Pin, tack and stitch the sleeve-seams.
Prepare these seams for flat-fell seaming and sew, as you did on the bodice in Blousemaking Chapter 24, p89.
Make two rows of running stitches or machine gathering stitches around the cap of each sleeve, one to each side of the seam line.
Carefully draw up the ease, which is approximately 3·8cm to each side of the balance mark at the top of the sleeve and fasten off the gathering threads over a pin.
Try to shrink in the fullness by pressing. Place a press pad (available in store haberdashery departments) over the end of a sleeve board, lay the cap of the sleeve over it so that the sleeve hangs down and gently press the fullness into the fabric. You may need to use a little steam here, but make sure that the fabric will not mark.
Remove the press pad, pull the sleeve over the sleeve board and press the rest of it.

Setting in the sleeves
When pinning, tacking and stitching sleeves into armholes, always work from the sleeve and not from the bodice.
Pin in the sleeves, matching the side-seams to the sleeve-seams and the balance marks on the sleeve caps to the shoulder-seams. Any fullness on the sleeves should be evenly distributed without any folds or creases.
If the fabric is too stiff to take all the fullness, ease it out by deepening the seam allowance around the sleeve cap only and not on the underarm section.
Tack in the sleeves and stitch. Remove all tacking cotton, press the seams towards the blouse and trim the seams for flat-fell seaming. When you have completed the flat-fell seams. press carefully over the end of a sleeve board.

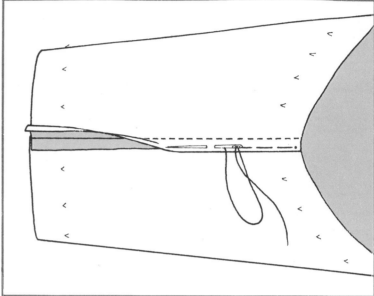

▲ **1.** *Tacking the flat-fell seam on underarm seam*
▼ **2.** *Making two rows of stitches on the sleeve cap*

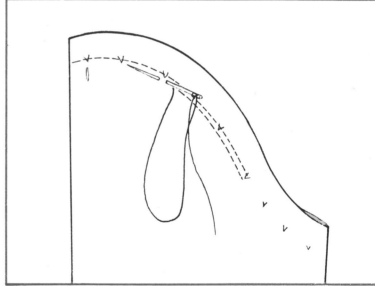

▼ **3.** *Drawing in the ease on the sleeve cap*

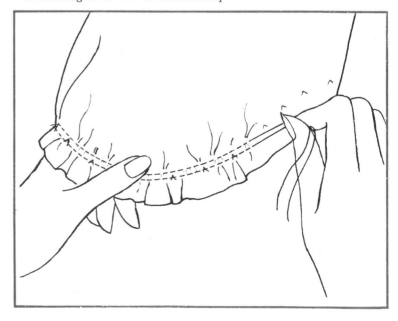

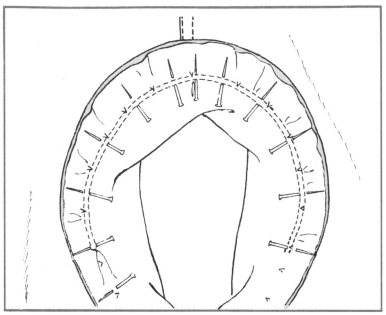

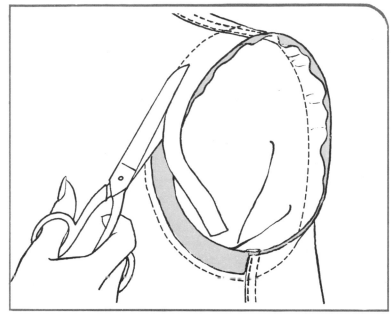

▲ **4.** *Pinning the sleeve in place*
▼ **5.** *Tacking the sleeve in place*

▲ **7.** *Trimming the armhole seam allowance*
▼ **8.** *Tacking the flat-fell seam round the armhole*

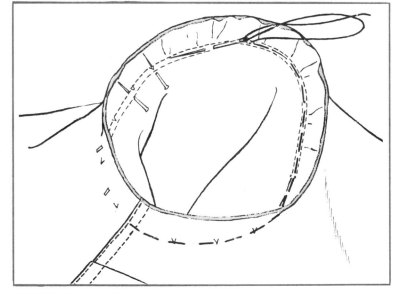

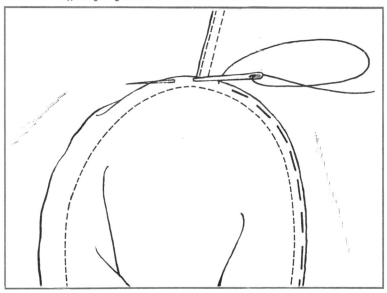

▼ **6.** *Stitching the sleeve in place*

▼ **9.** *Stitching the flat-fell seam round the armhole*

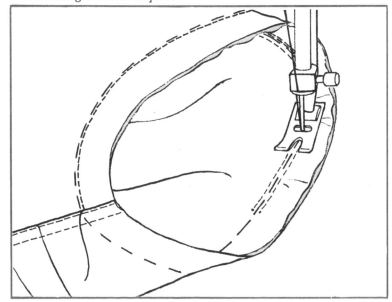

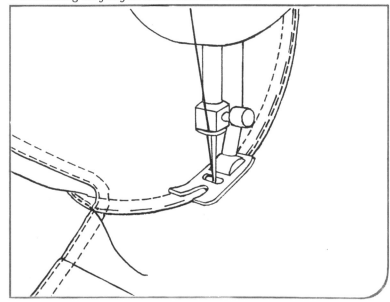

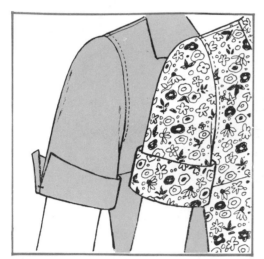

The pointed cuff and the roll sleeve

Making the cuffs
Green basic blouse with pointed cuffs

The outer solid lines on the cuff pattern are the stitching lines and the dash lines mark the fold, or roll, line. The balance mark meets the underarm seam.

Fold the cuffs lengthwise, right sides together, and stitch the ends, beginning at the dash roll lines and working towards the points. Fasten off the threads securely. Trim off the seam allowance across the points and turn the cuffs to the right side. Tack along the stitched edges and press flat.

Remove all tacking stitches. Turn under the seam allowance on one edge of each cuff and tack.

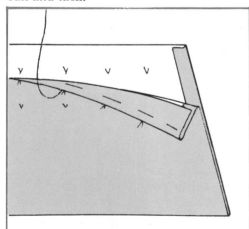

10. *Turning in one raw edge of the cuff*

To stitch the cuffs to the sleeves, place the raw edges together with the right side of the cuff to the wrong side of the sleeve so the cuff meets at the roll line but is a little apart at the seam line.

Pin and tack. Press the seam towards the cuff edge.

Lay the tacked cuff edge over the seam line and tack in place.

Machine stitch along the tacked folded edge.

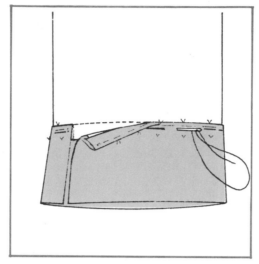

11. *Tacking the folded cuff edge over the seam line*

Remove all tacking stitches and turn the cuffs up on the roll line.

To hold the cuffs in position and stop the points from falling down, make a small bar 13mm above the roll line.

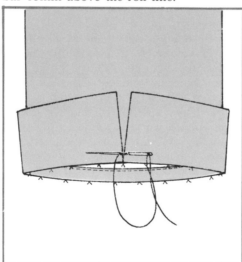

12. *Making a small bar 13mm above the roll line*

Floral, roll-sleeve variation

To make the deep hem, turn in the lower edge along the line marked 'upper edge of rolled cuff' (see pattern diagram in Blousemaking Chapter 24) and pin. Turn in the seam allowance on the raw edge to neaten. Tack and stitch in place. Press. To form the rolled cuffs, turn the hem up and over the sleeve so that the upper edge of the rolled cuff covers the stitching line.

Finishing touches

The blouse is finished except for the pleats, the hem, the buttonholes and buttons.

Pleats

Pin and tack the depth of the pleats on the inside of the blouse and stitch them. Press the pleats towards the centre on Back and Front.

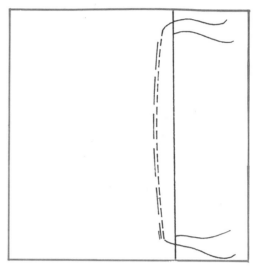

13. *Stitching a pleat*

Hem

Turn back the facings to the right side of the blouse and tack. Stitch the facings along the hem line, then turn them again to the inside.

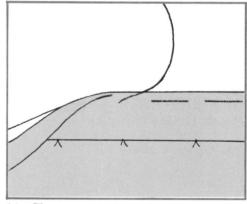

14. *Turning up the hem edge*

Turn up the rest of the hem. Turn in the raw edge so that the hem is 13mm wide and tack. Machine stitch close to turned in edge and through the facings (see picture).

15. *Stitching the hem edge*

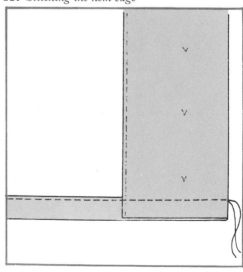

Top stitching

Top stitch the floral blouse down the fronts and round the collar.

Buttonholes

There are several types of hand-made buttonholes and each one is designed to do a certain job. For the blouse, use the buttonhole with a rounded end (this type is ideal for a button with a shank). At the rounded end the stitches are fanned out, leaving a close cluster on the edge which protects the fabric against the friction of the button movement.

Tack the facing to the blouse along the machine-finished inner edge so that it cannot move as you make the buttonholes. If you have made the blouse in a fine fabric, you will need to underlay the buttonhole with thin pieces of cotton fabric. But test first to make sure the pieces will not show through the blouse fabric.

After making the buttonholes as shown, trim the underlaid pieces as close as you dare to the buttonholes. This will avoid ridges when you press the front edge.

Position the buttonholes as indicated on the pattern, making sure that they extend 3mm over the Centre Front line.

Stitch the buttons to correspond on the opposite Centre Front line.

When you have removed all tacking cotton, give the blouse a final press.

The completed buttonhole

Hand-made buttonhole

The buttonhole described here has one bar and one rounded end.

Buttonhole length

For flat buttons, the buttonhole length should be the diameter of the button plus 3mm. For thick or domed buttons, add $1\frac{1}{2}$ times the thickness of the button to the button diameter.

Choosing the thread

For very close weaves make the buttonholes with ordinary sewing thread. Before you work on the garment, make a sample buttonhole to test the stitch on the fabric. If the fabric frays and the grain is coarse, use a heavier sewing thread or buttonhole twist.

Making the buttonhole

Mark the length of the buttonhole. Using sharp scissors, cut along the buttonhole length. The grain of the fabric will help you to cut a straight line. Oversew cut edges with shallow stitches. Starting with a length of thread long enough to complete the buttonhole, work buttonhole stitches from left to right along its length. Insert the needle into the back of the work and before pulling it through, bring the thread from the needle under the point to form a loop. Pull forward into a small knot, placing it on the cut edge. Do not pull the loops too tight or the edge will roll and the buttonhole will not meet properly.

The spacing of the stitches is important. If the stitches are worked too close together the edge will cockle. Judge the distance of the stitch by the thickness of the thread you are using and the grain of the fabric.

The depth of the stitch depends on how easily the fabric frays. A firm fabric can be worked with a very shallow stitch (2mm). If the fabric frays easily take a deeper stitch. Use your thumb-nail as a guide to help you regulate the depth.

Form a fan of stitches at the rounded end of the buttonhole (i.e. the end nearest the Front edge), keeping the centre stitch in line with the slit. Turn the work and carry on along the top edge.

At the end make a small bar across both rows of stitches.

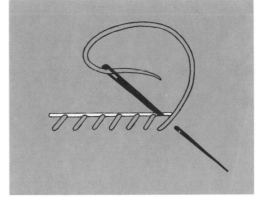

Oversewing the cut edges ▲
Working buttonhole stitch ▼

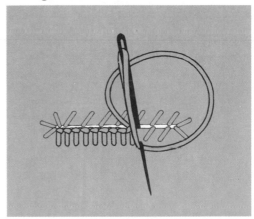

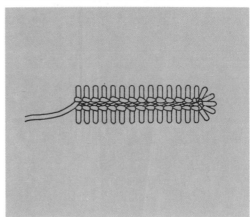

▲ *Buttonhole without bar end*
▼ *Detail of bar and fanned end*

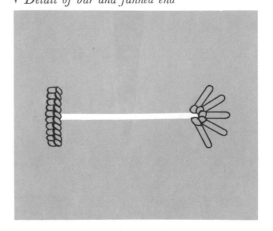

Accessories graph pattern

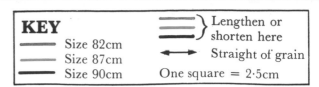

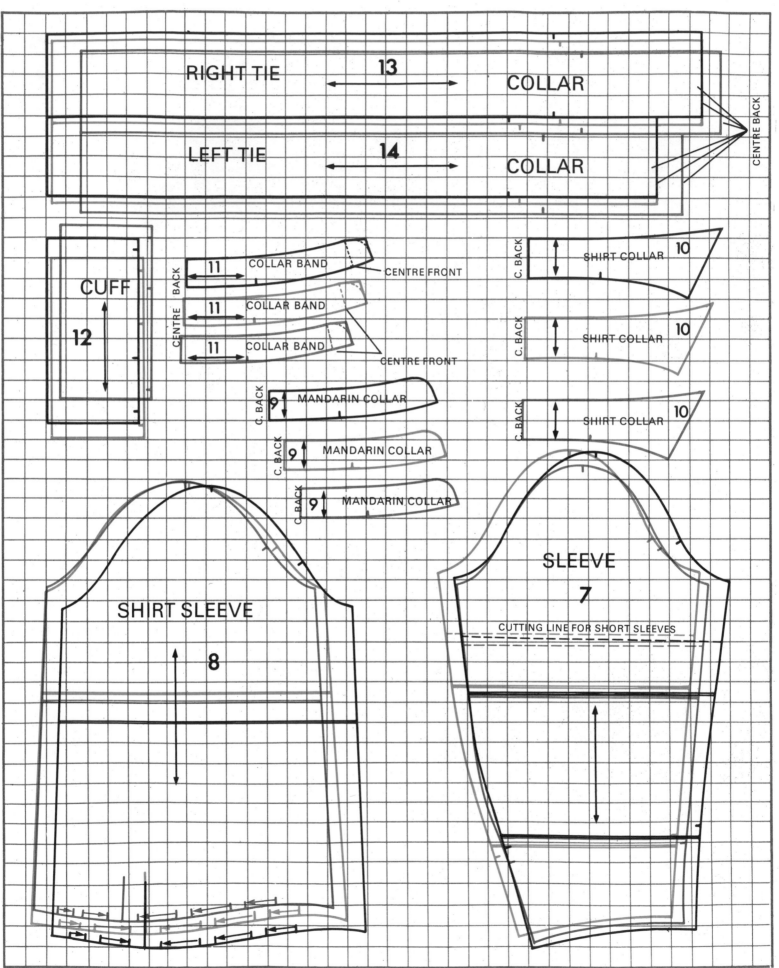

RIGHT TIE 13 COLLAR

LEFT TIE 14 COLLAR

CENTRE BACK

CUFF 12

CENTRE BACK

11 COLLAR BAND CENTRE FRONT
11 COLLAR BAND
11 COLLAR BAND CENTRE FRONT

C. BACK 9 MANDARIN COLLAR
C. BACK 9 MANDARIN COLLAR
C. BACK 9 MANDARIN COLLAR

C. BACK SHIRT COLLAR 10
C. BACK SHIRT COLLAR 10
C. BACK SHIRT COLLAR 10

SHIRT SLEEVE 8

SLEEVE 7
CUTTING LINE FOR SHORT SLEEVES

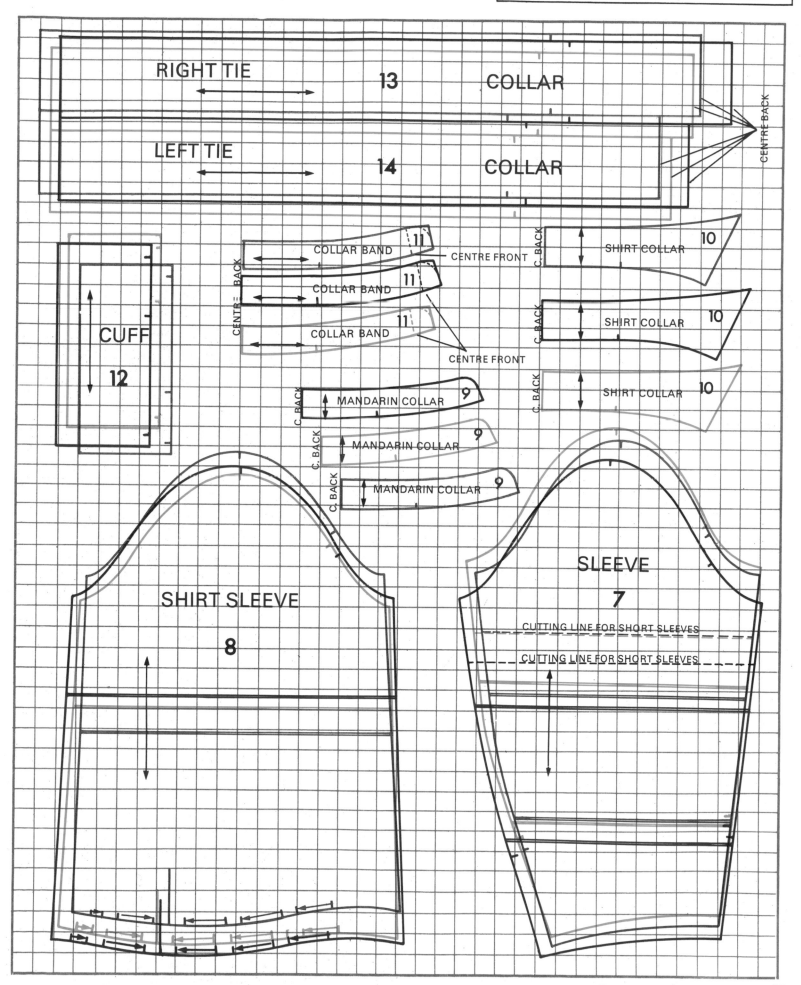

Chapter 26

Blouse making

Basic blouse into shirt

Here is another blouse conversion from the Golden Hands Blouse Graph which was given on pages 84 and 85. It is a traditional fitted shirt with tailored lines and classic good looks. This makes it a valuable addition to any wardrobe.

A feature of this shirt is the seaming. It is stitched with French seams which give a neat and durable finish—useful for garments like shirts which usually have to undergo frequent laundering.

Alternative cuffs are given too, so that you can choose between single or double cuffs when finishing the sleeves. Making instructions for the cuffs are in the next chapter.

The fitted shirt

Suitable fabrics

Plain and printed silk, cotton, linen or light woollen fabrics.

Fabric requirements and notions

- [ ] 90cm wide fabric—for sizes 82cm and 87cm, 2·65 metres; for size 90cm. 2·75 metres; for sizes 96cm to 107cm, 2·90 metres.
- [ ] For all sizes, 0·35 metres of interfacing. For silk fabric this should be preshrunk lawn—for other fabrics, a fine poplin.
- [ ] Buttons, 8 for single front buttoning, 12 for buttoning in groups of three. Allow 2 extra for linked button cuffs in both cases.
- [ ] Matching thread.

The shirt pattern

From the Basic Blouse Graph you will need pattern pieces 1 and 2, which are the Front and Back.

From the Accessories Graph you will need pattern pieces 8, 10, 11 and 12, which are the shirt sleeve, shirt collar, collar band and cuff patterns.

The shirt also needs a front facing which you make as follows. Lay the pattern Front on a piece of paper and draw round the shoulder, neck edge, front edge and lower edge. Remove the pattern and make the facing as shown in figure 3: it should be 3·8cm wide at the shoulders and 8cm wide at the lower edge. Unlike the basic blouse, this shirt is fitted and has back and front body darts. So if you have already made the toile in chapter 22, copy the darts on to the pattern pieces, otherwise the body darts will be fitted later using the pleat lines as a guide.

Cutting out the shirt

Select the correct layout overleaf, according to your size. Remember that the patterns have no seam allowance, so add 16mm seam and hem allowances all round. The seam allowance is not 19mm as for most of the other garments given so far, because less seam allowance is required for French seams.

For classic good looks the fitted shirt has few rivals

There are the following points to watch.

Decide what sort of cuffs you want. If you want them single (ie cuffs half the depth of the cuff pattern as figure 1) you will only need two cuff pieces. But if you want double cuffs (ie cuffs cut to the depth of the cuff pattern, folded over and closed with link buttons as figure 2) you will need four cuff pieces.

If you have chosen a striped fabric and wish to make a feature of the stripes, copy the other half of the collar pattern and join the two at the Centre Back. When laying out the collar pattern, place the lengthwise grain line on the pattern along the crosswise grain on the fabric.

Cut out the fabric and keep the remnants as you will use them later.

Mark the pattern details. Pay special attention to the collar and collar band details, the balance marks and the centre markings. The collar ends should meet on the Centre Front line, with the ends of the collar band meeting the edges of the shirt Front.

To hold in the fullness around the lower edge of the sleeves, you have a choice. If the fabric is soft, disregard the pleat markings

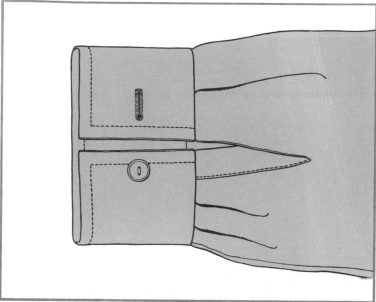

▲ **1.** *The single cuff with topstitching detail*

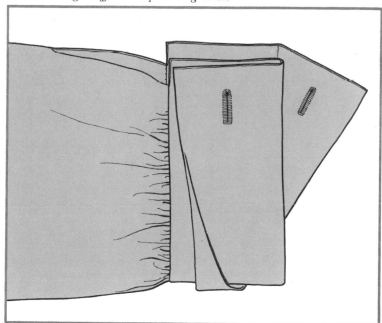

▲ **2.** *The double cuff for link buttoning*

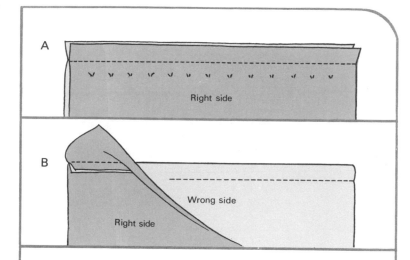

The French seam

The French seam is a double seam with the raw edges encased.

A. With wrong sides facing, first pin and stitch the seam 9mm from the seam line inside the seam allowance.
Trim and lightly press the stitched seam towards the Front. Turn the garment inside out.

B. Working on the wrong side, pin, tack and stitch along the original seam line, encasing the raw edges in the seam.

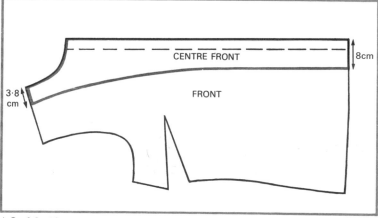

▲ **3.** *Marking out the front facing for the fitted shirt*

as you can simply gather the lower edge to fit the cuff, but for crisper and bulkier fabrics mark the pleat details.
Remove the pattern pieces.

Interfacing

To give the collar and cuffs that extra crispness which is required for a shirt they should be interfaced.
Cut one collar piece and one collar band from the interfacing with the Centre Back on the fold as indicated on the layout. If you are making double cuffs, cut two cuff pieces from the interfacing. If the cuffs are to be single, cut two pieces half the depth of the cuffs, as the interfacing needs to go only to the point where the cuffs are folded over.
Pin and tack each interfacing piece to the wrong side of a corresponding shirt piece. The interfacing should go on that piece which will be uppermost.

Fitting

Tack the darts, side and shoulder-seams and try on the shirt,

pinning it together along the Centre Front line. If you have not already marked the body darts on the pattern extend the pleat lines into darts, running them out smoothly at each end.
Make any alterations necessary following the fitting instructions for the toile in Chapter 22.
Try the sleeves for length with the cuffs tacked in position.

Making up

With right sides together pin, tack and stitch the facings to Front edges. Do not stitch them along the neck and hem edges. Turn the facings to the inside, edge-tack and press.
Stitch all the darts. Press the side bust darts flat and the under-bust and all the Back darts towards the Centre line.
Make French seams, as shown, on the side and shoulder-seams. Before machining the second row of stitches which encase the raw seam edges, press the edges lightly towards the Front and then stitch along the seam line.
Press the finished French seams towards the Front.
Turn up the hem as shown in Blousemaking Chapter 25, p94.

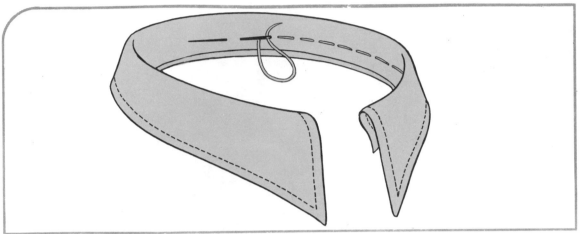

Making the collar

Working on a flat surface, place the top (interfaced) and under collar pieces together, right sides facing. Pin, tack and stitch along the front edges and the upper curved seam.

Trim the seam allowance to 6mm, trim across the corners and turn to the right side. Tack along the stitched edges and press.

If you want to topstitch the collar do so now, stitching 6mm from the edge.

Roll the collar in the position you would wear it, as shown in figure 4. You will see that the lower edge of the top collar rises above the edge of the under collar. Tack it firmly in this position along the seam line of the under collar.

▲ 4. *Rolling the collar and tacking along the lower edge* **▼ 5.** *Stitching the collar between the collar bands*

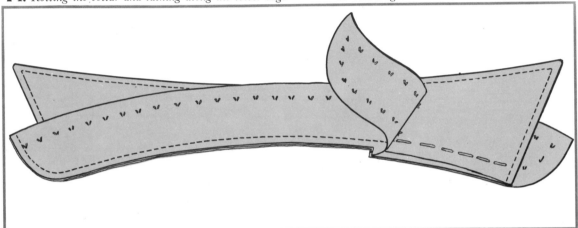

To complete the collar, stitch it to the collar band. Matching all markings, place the collar between the inner and outer collar band pieces as shown in figure 5 and stitch, leaving the lower edge open.

Trim the seam allowance on the stitched edges of the collar band to 6mm and turn to the right side. Tack along the stitched edges (figure 6) and press.

The ends of the collar band have now become the tabs for the button and buttonhole. Should you find that the tabs are too bulky, notch the seam allowance—this will help to flatten them.

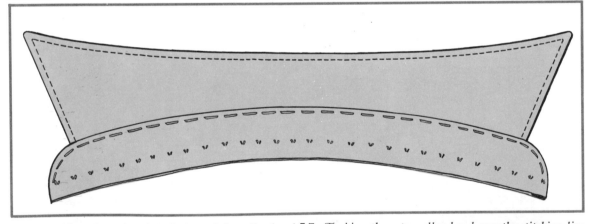

▲ 6. *Tacking along the stitched edges of the collar band* **▼ 7.** *Tacking the outer collar band over the stitching line*

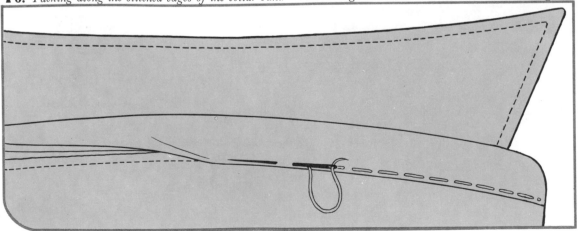

Stitching on the collar

Tack the front facing to the shirt along the neck line.

Pin the inner collar band along the inside of the neck line with the raw edges level, carefully matching the balance marks.

Tack, stitch and trim the seam allowance.

Turn under the seam allowance on the outer collar band, lay it over the stitching line to cover the machine stitches as shown in figure 7. Carefully slip stitch in place.

Be very careful when you hand-sew along the tab, because this part will show when the collar is buttoned.

Fitted shirt layouts

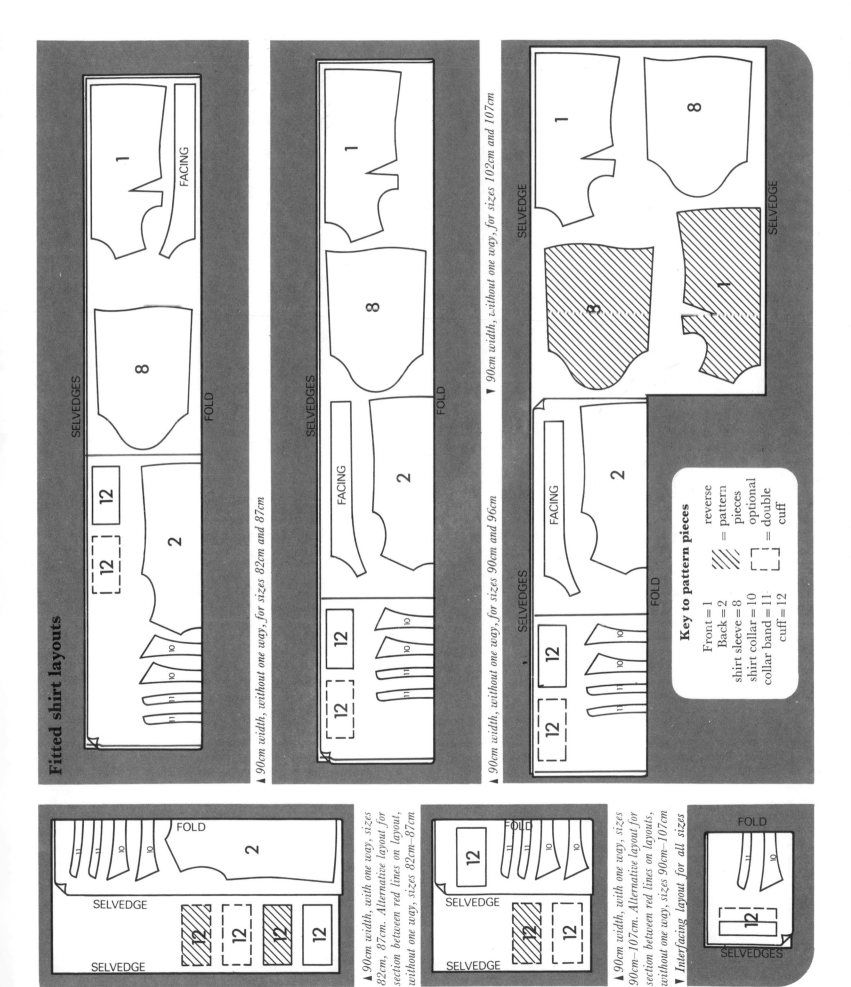

▲ 90cm width, without one way, for sizes 82cm and 87cm

▲ 90cm width, without one way, for sizes 90cm and 96cm

▼ 90cm width, without one way, for sizes 102cm and 107cm

Key to pattern pieces

Front = 1   reverse
Back = 2   ⟋⟋⟋ = pattern
shirt sleeve = 8   pieces
shirt collar = 10   optional
collar band = 11   ⌐⌐ = double
cuff = 12   cuff

▲ 90cm width, with one way, sizes 82cm, 87cm. Alternative layout for section between red lines on layout, without one way, sizes 82cm–87cm

▲ 90cm width, with one way, sizes 90cm–107cm. Alternative layout for section between red lines on layouts, without one way, sizes 90cm–107cm

▼ Interfacing layout for all sizes

101

Chapter 27

Tail of a shirt

This chapter continues with blouse conversions from the Golden Hands Blouse Graph. The fitted shirt is completed and is followed by instructions for making the shirt with tails, pictured overleaf. The shirt with tails is made up in a light-weight striped wool, it has flat-fell seams, single cuffs with link buttons and the body darts are omitted.

The shirt sleeve openings

Before you stitch the sleeve-seams, make the openings.

Here are two simple ways to do this.

A. The faced opening. This opening is suitable for both single and link buttoning.

To make a facing, cut a straight piece of fabric from the remnants, 5cm wide and 2·5cm longer than the opening indicated on the wrist edge of the sleeve pattern piece. Do not cut the opening yet. Lay the facing centrally over the opening line on the outside of the sleeve, right sides facing, and tack. Stitch the facing to the sleeve as shown in figure 1, carefully tapering into a point at the end of the opening.

Cut through the centre to within 1 grain of the stitches at the point. Turn the facing to the inside (figure 2), edge-tack or topstitch close to the edge and press.

Turn in the raw edge of the facing, tack and hem to the sleeve.

B. Opening with wrap extension. This opening is not suitable for link buttoning.

From remnants cut a straight strip of fabric 3·8cm wide and twice the length of the opening.

Cut the sleeve along the opening line (figure 3). Pin and tack the

▼ **1.** *Cutting through faced opening*

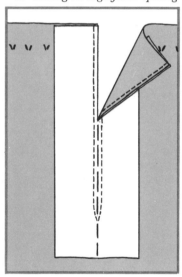

▼ **2.** *Tacking the faced opening*

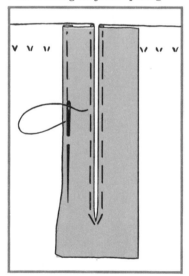

▼ **4.** *The facing for the wrap extension stitched to the sleeve opening*

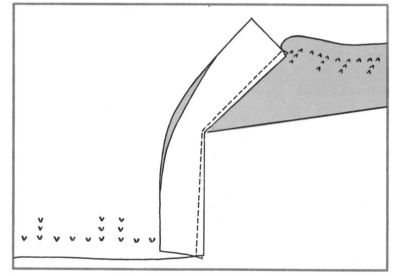

▼ *The fitted shirt*

▼ **3.** *Cutting the sleeve opening*

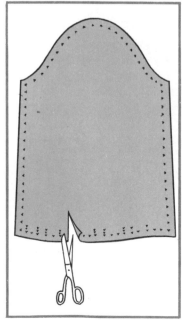

▼ **5.** *Pinning the wrap extension strip to the right side of the sleeve*

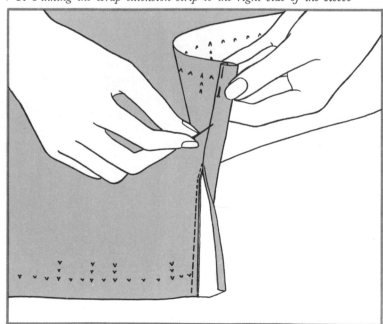

strip of fabric along the opening with the right side of the strip to the wrong side of the sleeve.

Stitch along the opening taking 6mm seam allowance on the facing but tapering towards the point (figure 4).

When you have reached the point, pivot the work on the needle, ease the fold to the back of the needle and stitch along the other side. Press the seam towards the strip.

Fold in the long raw edge of the strip, pin and tack it over the seam on the outside of the sleeve and topstitch (figures 5 and 6). Press the wrap to the inside of the sleeve as shown.

After finishing opening stitch sleeve-seams with a French seam.

Making the cuffs

A. Single cuffs. Fold the interfaced cuffs lengthwise, right sides facing, and stitch each side up to the seam allowance at the top edge. Trim the seam allowance and turn to the right side. Edge-tack and press.

If you want to make single cuffs with link buttoning, stitch the upper edge as far as the two outer balance marks before turning to the right side, as for the double cuff in figure 7. Snip the seam allowance at the balance marks and turn out.

B. Double cuffs. Pin the interfaced and plain sections together, right sides facing.

Stitch round the edges as shown in figure 7. Trim the seam allowance and across the corners. Snip into the seam allowance at the top edge as shown.

Turn the cuffs to the right side, edge-tack and press.

Attaching the cuffs

Gather or pleat the lower edge of the sleeves. The pleats should be folded in the direction of the arrows on the sleeve pattern.

Pin, tack and stitch the cuffs to the right side of the sleeves as shown in figure 8. (Make sure the interfaced section will be uppermost on the finished cuff.)

Turn under the remaining raw edge on each cuff, pin and hand-sew it over the seam on the inside (figure 9).

If you wish to topstitch the cuffs 6mm from the edge to match the collar stitching, do so now.

Stitching in the sleeves

Stitch the sleeves to the shirt with a French seam. Press the seam towards the sleeve.

▼ **6.** *The topstitched wrap extension with wrap pressed to the inside*

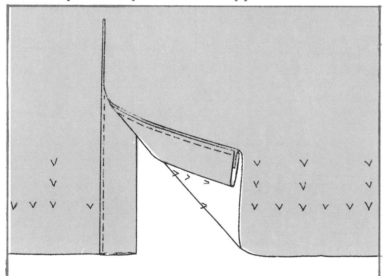

▼ **8.** *Pinning on the cuff to the right side of the sleeve*

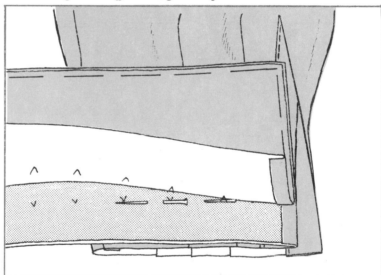

▼ **7.** *Stitched and trimmed double cuff before turning to the right side*

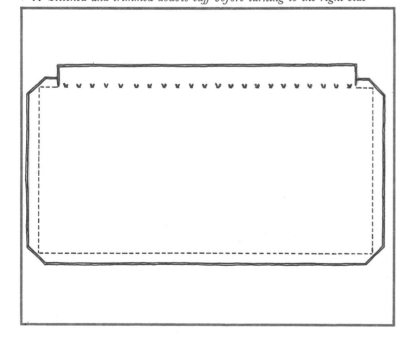

▼ **9.** *Hand-sewing the inside cuff edge over the seam line*

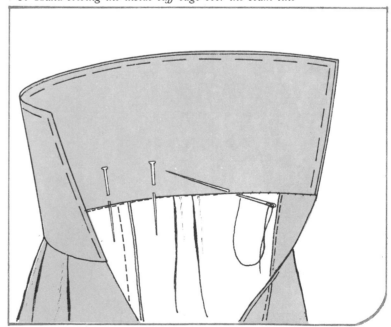

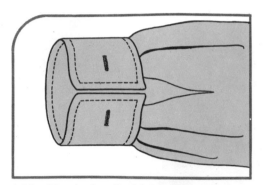

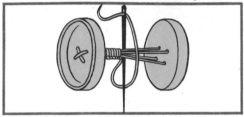

▲ **10.** *The single cuff with buttonholes for links*

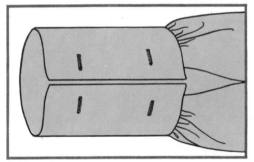

▲ **11.** *Making the button link*

▲ **12.** *The double cuff with buttonhole positions*

Buttons and buttonholes
Fitted shirt front. Follow the buttoning for the shirt with tails (see figure 13) or, for a more unusual effect, arrange the buttons in groups of three as shown in the sketch on the previous page. Because the shirt is worn tucked in it is best not to place buttons below the waist as these would bulge underneath a skirt.
Make the buttonholes as shown in Blouse-making Chapter 25 and sew on buttons to correspond.
Single, unlinked cuffs. Make a button-hole on each cuff on the edge furthest from the sleeve seam (see figure 1 in the previous chapter) and sew on a button to correspond.
Single, linked cuffs (figure 10). Make two buttonholes on each cuff. Make the button links as in figure 11, working the link as for the bar in Skirtmaking Chapter 14, pp44, 45.
Double, linked cuffs (figure 12). These need four buttonholes on each cuff. The thickness of the layers of fabric may cause the under cuff to pucker. So make the buttonholes which go to the top of the cuff 3mm closer to the edge than those on the underside of the cuff.
Make the button links as in figure 11.

104

Shirt with tails

Fabric requirements and notions
☐ 90cm wide fabric—for sizes 82 and 87, 2·90 metres; for size 90, 3 metres; for sizes 96 to 107, 3·10 metres.
☐ 35cm of interfacing in preshrunk lawn for silk fabric and fine poplin for other fabric
☐ 9 buttons, or 11 for link buttoned cuffs
☐ matching thread

The pattern
Use all the pattern pieces for the fitted shirt.
To make the tails, place the Front and Back bodice patterns on a sheet of paper at least 8cm longer than the pattern. Draw round the pattern then extend the side-seams for 8cm and draw in the new hem line on both pattern pieces as shown in figure 13.
Draw curves for the tails which taper into the side-seams as shown. To make sure the curve is the same on the Back and Front make a paper template, lay it on the extension of the Back and Front pattern pieces and draw in the new lines.
Then, at the top of the curve on the Back, add 13mm to the side-seam and taper into the curve as shown in figure 14.

▼ **13.** *The Front pattern extension and curve*

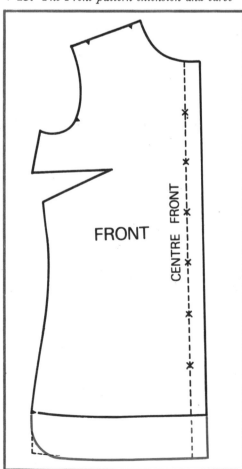

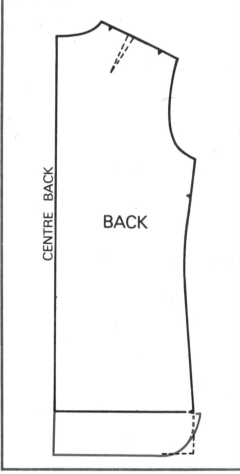

▲ **14.** *Back pattern with seam allowance extension*

Make a balance mark on the side-seams where the original pattern lengths end; this is the end of the side-seam stitching line.
Cut out the new patterns.

Cutting out
Use the cutting instructions and layouts for the fitted shirt in the previous chapter as a guide, making the necessary adjustments to take in the new pattern lengths. The shirt is sewn with flat-fell seams which like the French seam, require 16mm seam allowances.

Fitting
Follow the fitting instructions for the shirt in the previous chapter but omit the Back and Front body darts.

Making up
Follow the making up instructions for the fitted shirt but observe the following points.
1. Stitch flat-fell seams instead of French seams. The flat-fell seams are stitched as those in Blousemaking Chapter 24, but this time they are stitched with wrong sides facing and are folded on the outside of the garment, with the folded edge towards the Front.

2. Stitch the shoulder and side bust darts only.

3. Position the buttons and buttonholes as shown in figure 13.

4. The hem edge is finished at the side-seams as follows.

Hemming the tails. Stitch the side-seams to the balance marks, wrong sides facing. Then snip into the Front side-seam allowance at the bottom of the seams and trim the Front seam allowance for flat-fell seaming as shown in figure 15.

Fold the Back seam allowance over the trimmed Front seam. Pin and tack.

Pin and tack the hem on the Front to the wrong side. Machine stitch and continue the stitching into the folded flat-fell seam edge so that you stitch the hem and flat-fell side-seam in one operation (see figure 16).

Pin under the hem on the Back. When you reach the point where the side-seam and front hem merge, pin the folded edge of the Back hem in line with the side-seam as shown in figure 16. Like this, it will lie flat over the top of the front curve and give a neat strong finish. Tack and machine stitch in place.

Stitch across the top of the hem as shown to hold it firmly in place and to strengthen this point.

▼ **15.** *Snipping into the Front seam allowance*

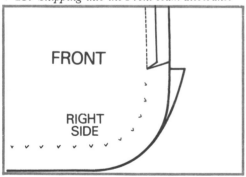

FRONT

RIGHT SIDE

▼ **16.** *The stitched tails at the side-seam*

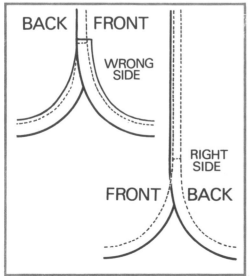

BACK | FRONT

WRONG SIDE

RIGHT SIDE

FRONT | BACK

Chapter 28

Blouse conversion

The tie-neck blouse, shown here in a luxurious printed silk, is a soft and feminine variation of the Golden Hands basic blouse. In making it you will be taken several steps further in your dress-making know-how. You will learn to apply couture finishes to a simple garment to turn it into something special, such as the finish on the sleeve openings which is specially for fine, soft fabrics. This chapter, which includes layouts, takes you to the fitting stage.

Suitable fabrics

You can use most of the fabrics mentioned for blouses in Blouse-making Chapters 24 and 26, but for the gentle style of this tie-neck blouse the texture should be a little finer and the fabric quite soft. For instance, if you want to use a poplin, as for the basic blouse, make sure it is the finer type.

Amounts and notions

☐ For amounts see layouts and note on tie collar overleaf
☐ Interfacing, 90cm width—the length of the blouse from the highest point on the shoulder to the hem plus 3·8cm for seams (see notes below)
☐ 8 buttons (you will need 2 more for link-buttoned cuffs)
☐ 1 small press fastener
☐ Matching thread

A note on interfacing

The texture of the interfacing is dictated by the top fabric: soft fabric, soft interfacing.

To see if the texture of the interfacing is correct make the following test. Place an edge of the interfacing into the folded edge of the top fabric, if the fabric rolls over the interfacing in a gentle, soft roll it is the right interfacing to use. If, however, sharp points and a hard edge are formed you have chosen the wrong texture of interfacing.

To help you in your choice select from the following:

☐ For soft, natural fibre fabrics choose a soft lawn or a finely textured pre-shrunk cotton, sold specifically for interfacing
☐ For soft fabrics in man-made fibres, pure silk organza is often the only choice, because an interfacing in a man-made fibre of the same type as the blouse fabric can result in edges which will not lie flat

The pattern pieces

For the tie-neck blouse you will need the following pattern pieces from the Golden Hands Graph Pages: from the Basic Blouse Graph Pattern the Front and Back pattern pieces, numbers 1 and 2; from the Accessories Graph the shirt sleeve, cuff and tie-collar pattern pieces, numbers 8, 12, 13 and 14.

The facing pattern

When making a garment in a soft fabric it is advisable to avoid unnecessary seams—the finished garment will look smoother. So, when making the tie-neck blouse, the Front and front facing are cut out as one.

First make a facing pattern as shown in Blousemaking Chapter 26, figure 3.

Then join the Front pattern piece to the facing pattern along the front edges by pinning them alongside each other over a strip of paper (figure 1). The line along the join becomes the fold line of the facing.

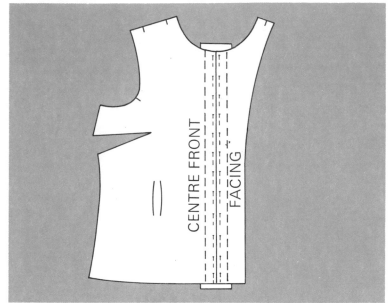

▲ **1.** *Joining the Front and front facing patterns along the front edges*

Cutting out

Blouse fabric. Select the correct layout for your size from those given overleaf. Decide whether you want single or double cuffs (Blousemaking Chapter 26) and a single or double width tie.

Pin the pattern pieces on to the fabric, mark out 19mm seam and hem allowances and cut out.

Mark all details on the fabric with tailor's tacks, using the methods shown so far.

After you have marked the blouse Front unpin and remove the facing pattern, then mark along the front edge of the Front pattern piece for the fold line. Remove all pattern pieces.

Interfacing. First cut or tear off the selvedges of the interfacing fabric.

Fold in half and pin the cuff and front facing patterns on to the double interfacing fabric. Cut a full cuff section or a half section only depending on your choice of cuff.

Mark out 19mm seam allowances along the Front, hem, neck and shoulder edges of the facing and along the cuff edges.

You will not need seam allowances along the inner edge of the facing or along the fold edge of the single cuff.

Cut out and mark the pattern details on the interfacing.

Remove the pattern pieces.

Choose pure silk for the soft, gentle lines of the tie-neck blouse ▶

Interfacing the Fronts for fitting

Pin and tack the interfacing to the wrong side of each blouse Front as shown (figure 2), allowing the seam allowance on the interfacing to go over the fold line on to the facing. Note that it is tacked both along the Centre Front and the fold line. Attach the interfacing to the blouse with prick stitches (Generally Speaking Chapter 9). Work the prick stitches in the seam allowance of the interfacing, just outside the fold line, so that they will not show on the top of the garment when the facing is turned under.

Turn the facing to the inside and tack along the fold line ready for fitting.

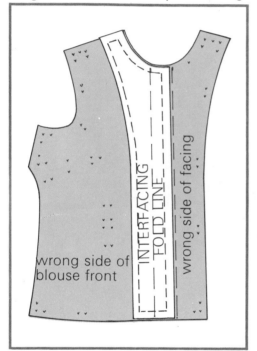

▲ 2. *The interfacing tacked to the blouse Front*

Fitting the blouse

Carefully pin and tack the blouse darts and seams and tack in the sleeves ready for fitting.

Make any corrections necessary (Toile-making Chapter 22).

Fitting the collar

It is also necessary to fit the tie-neck collar before making it up. The balance marks on the ties are only an approximate indication of where the ties begin when the collar is attached to the neck line, and they will fall about 2·5cm in from the Centre Front at each side.

It is always best to determine how far a tie collar should be attached to the neck line by fitting. A given length may be right for one fabric but may leave an unsightly gap in another.

Two ways to finish the ties are given here. They can be folded in half lengthways to achieve the effect in the picture, or made

double width and left unfolded with rolled hem edges. The latter is particularly attractive in transparent fabrics.

For both versions first stitch the collar sections together along the Centre Back line and press the seam open.

Folded collar version. To prepare this for fitting, fold the collar and ties in half lengthways, right sides facing. Pin and tack the seams of the ties as far as the balance marks.

With the collar still inside out, pin and tack it to the blouse neck line, matching Centre Backs, and with the balance marks falling on the Front neck edge 2·5cm in from the Centre Front at each side.

The wider collar. To prepare this for fitting fold the collar lengthways at the neck only. Pin and tack it to the blouse neck line, matching Centre Backs, and with the balance marks falling on the Front neck edge 2·5cm in from the Centre Front at each side (figure 3).

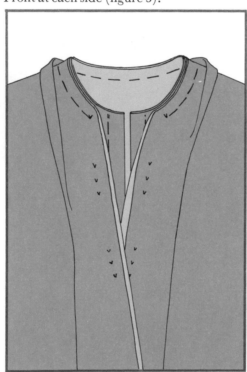

▲ 3. *Tacking on the wider collar for fitting*

Both versions. Try on the blouse again and tie a bow to see how far you need the collar stitched to the blouse at the neck edge.

The bow should lie comfortably in the opening and not be pushed forward through lack of space. If it is, the size of the space must be increased equally on each side.

If, however, the space is too large, just reduce the distance between the collar ends and the Centre Front of the blouse equally on each side.

Carefully mark the position of the collar ends on both the blouse and the collar.

Amounts

90cm width, without one way— sizes 82cm and 87cm, 2·55 metres; sizes 90 and 96, 3·45 metres; sizes 102 and 107, 3·55 metres.

90cm width, with one way—sizes 82 and 87, 2·75metres; size 90, 3·10 metres; size 96, 3·20 metres; sizes 102 and 107, 3·45 metres.

N.B. For transparent fabrics such as voile and chiffon buy extra fabric and double the width of the tie collar to make a really full bow.

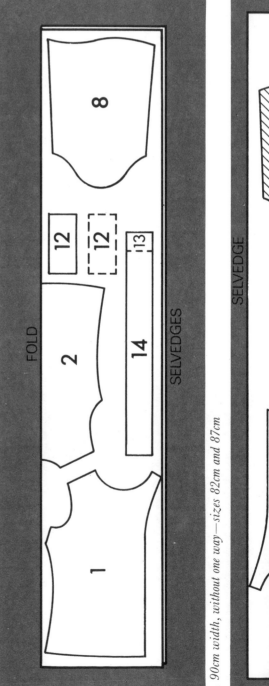

▲ *90cm width, without one way—sizes 82cm and 87cm*

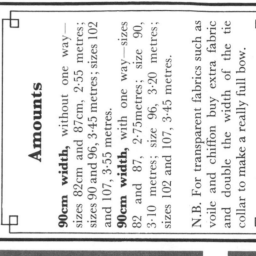

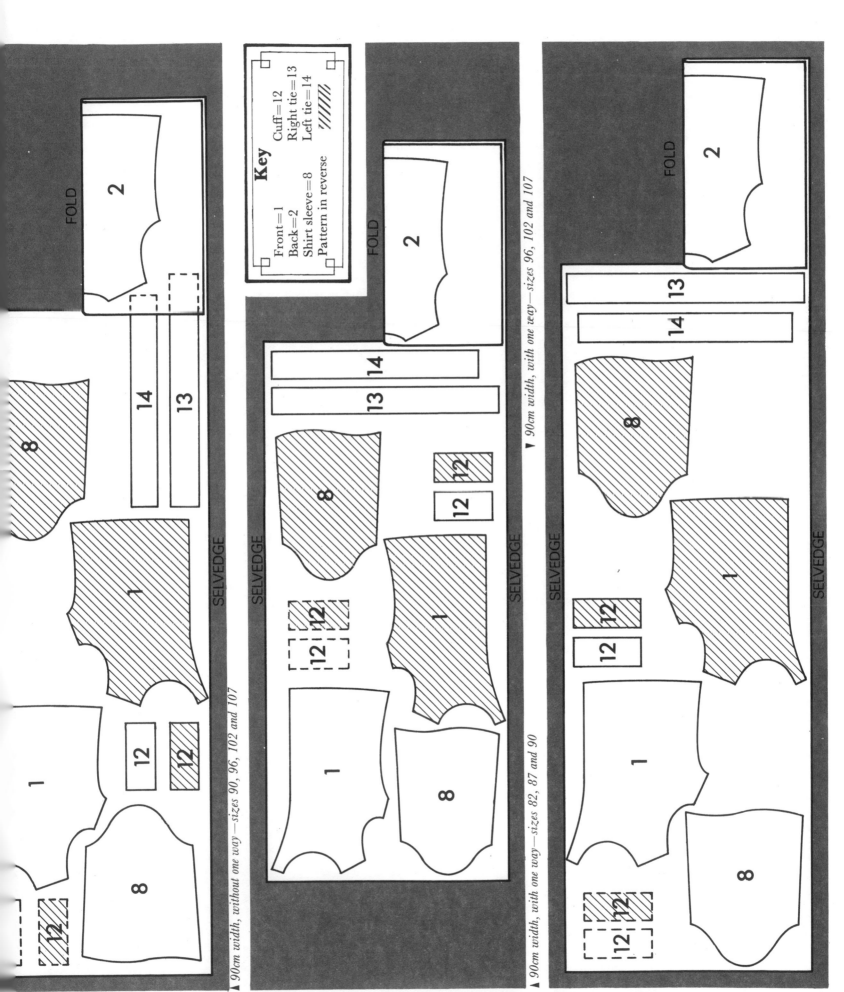

Key

Front=1   Cuff=12
Back=2   Right tie=13
Shirt sleeve=8 Left tie=14
Pattern in reverse ///////

▲ 90cm width, without one way—sizes 90, 96, 102 and 107

▲ 90cm width, with one way—sizes 96, 102 and 107

▼ 90cm width, with one way—sizes 82, 87 and 90

FOLD

SELVEDGE

109

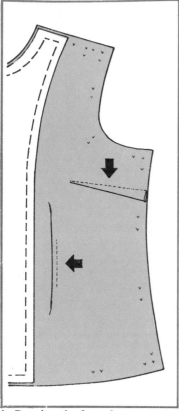

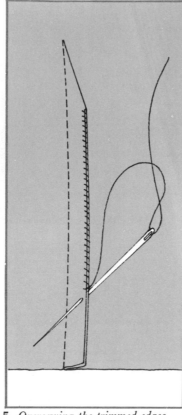

4. *Pressing the front darts*　　**5.** *Oversewing the trimmed edges*

Making up the tie-neck blouse

Stitch all the darts and press. The body and shoulder darts (if used) are pressed towards the centre, and the side bust darts are pressed downwards (figure 4). If you pressed the darts open in a soft fabric they would fold over or cockle because the fabric does not have sufficient body to hold them in place during wear.

If you are using a transparent fabric cut the depth of the darts to 8mm and oversew the raw edges very finely together (figure 5). Stitch the side and shoulder-seams and press them open.

Trim the seam allowances evenly. To neaten the raw edges fold them under 3mm and whip along the folded edge.

If the fabric is transparent press the seam allowance together towards the Front of the garment. Trim to 8mm and oversew as for the darts.

Finishing the front edges

Fold each facing along the fold line to the right side of the garment, unpicking the tacking along the fold line.

Pin, tack and stitch along the neck edge from the marking for the collar end to the fold line.

Snip the seam allowance to allow it to follow the neck line curve (figure 6) and at the end of the stitching line where it meets the collar mark.

Turn the facing to the wrong side, tack along the stitched neck edge and press.

Pin and tack the facing firmly to the inside of the blouse along the rest of the neck edge and along the inner edge and fold line. Fold under the seam allowance on the shoulder of the facing and trim to the width of the shoulder-seam on the blouse. Hand-sew to the seam line with small slip stitches.

Stitching the folded collar

Stitch the tie ends of the collar as far as the balance marks or the new marks made at the collar fitting (figure 7). If you want the

ends to be pointed, as in the photograph, taper the stitching as shown (figure 8).

Trim seams, snip off the seam allowance across the corners. Turn the tie ends to the right side, edge-tack and press.

Pin and tack the outside of the collar to the outside of the blouse, matching the Centre Backs and the collar end markings on the neck line. Stitch.

Trim the seam allowance to eliminate bulk and press the seam into the collar.

Fold in the raw edge of the inside of the collar along the seam line. Hand-sew it to the stitching line to cover the seam allowance.

Pay special attention to the ends of the collar-seam, making a small bar at each end for extra strength.

Stitching on the wider collar

For the wider single tie, trim the seam allowance to 6mm, except where the collar is attached to the neck, on both sides of the tie. Roll the trimmed edges.

To do this roll under the raw edges 3mm, then turn under again for 3mm and sew in place with fine slip stitches (figure 9).

Stitch on the collar as for the folded version.

The rolled sleeve opening

On finer fabrics it is not advisable to make the usual sleeve openings as shown for the fitted shirt (Blousemaking Chapter 27). They look heavy and the very narrow seam allowance inside the facings

▼ 6. *Snipped neck edge of facing*　　**▼ 7.** *Stitching the double tie*

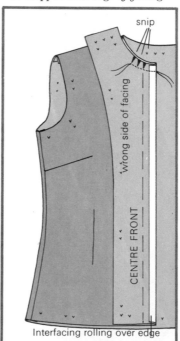

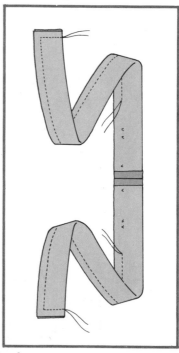

▼ 8. *Stitching the double tie for tapered ends*

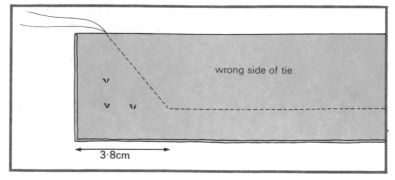

frays during wear because it cannot be double stitched. So for this soft blouse a special rolled opening is made.

First trim the seam allowance along the cuff edge of the sleeve to 13mm.

Then measure out the opening for the roll along the cuff-seam line 2·5cm to each side of the opening marking.

Starting at the centre of this 5cm opening, roll the seam allowance under for 6mm and turn it under again by the same amount. Let it taper out into the raw edges just beyond the mark on each side.

Hand-sew the small hem firmly in position (figure 10).

On very fine fabrics this roll should not be more than 3mm deep, but do not forget to trim the whole length of the seam allowance accordingly or the ends of the cuffs will slant downwards.

Finishing the sleeves

Stitch the sleeve-seams, press and neaten the seams.

Make the cuffs (single or double depending on your choice) as for the fitted shirt (Blousemaking Chapter 27) with the extensions for link buttoning, or without if you are buttoning over.

When attaching the cuffs work across the rolled edge as shown (figure 11).

Stitch the finished sleeves into the blouse and neaten the armhole-seam edges.

If the fabric is transparent trim the armhole-seam allowance and neaten as for the blouse.

The hem

A beautifully finished garment deserves a beautifully finished hem, so hand roll it.

Turn up the hem edge for 3mm and then another 3mm. Then, with small slip stitches, sew it to the blouse along the folded edge. Take the hem right over the front facings and do not fold them back as for the other blouses.

Stitch the ends of the hem securely and press.

Finishing

Hand-work buttonholes (Blousemaking Chapter 25) and stitch on the buttons. Sew on a small covered press fastener to the top corner of the wrap so that the point will not fall back during wear.

Covering a press fastener

To cover a press fastener cut two circles of fabric as shown (figure A) and work a gathering stitch round the outer edge of each.

Cover each half of the fastener by drawing up the fabric to the wrong side of it and, in the case of the ball section, piercing the ball through the centre of the fabric (figure B). Finish off the fabric at the back and stitch the press fastener on (figure C).

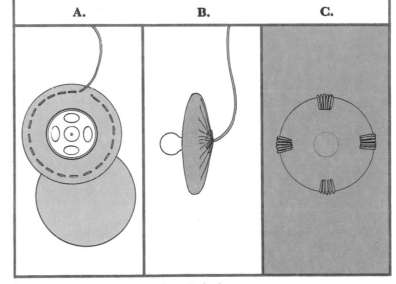

A.   **B.**   **C.**

▼ **9.** *Rolling the edges of the wider tie*

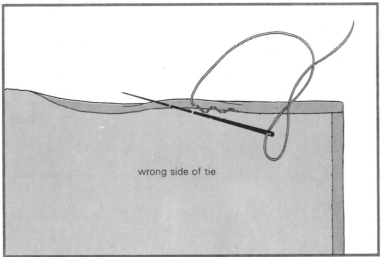

wrong side of tie

▼ **10.** *The hand-sewn rolled sleeve opening*

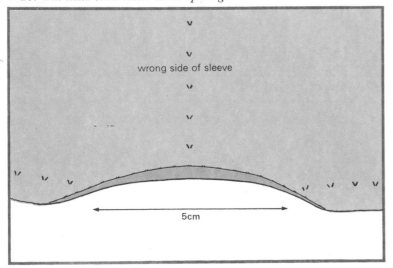

wrong side of sleeve

5cm

▼ **11.** *Attaching the cuffs at the rolled edge*

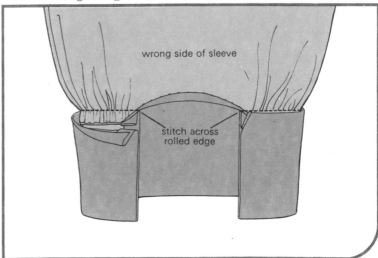

wrong side of sleeve

stitch across rolled edge

Basic dress graph pattern

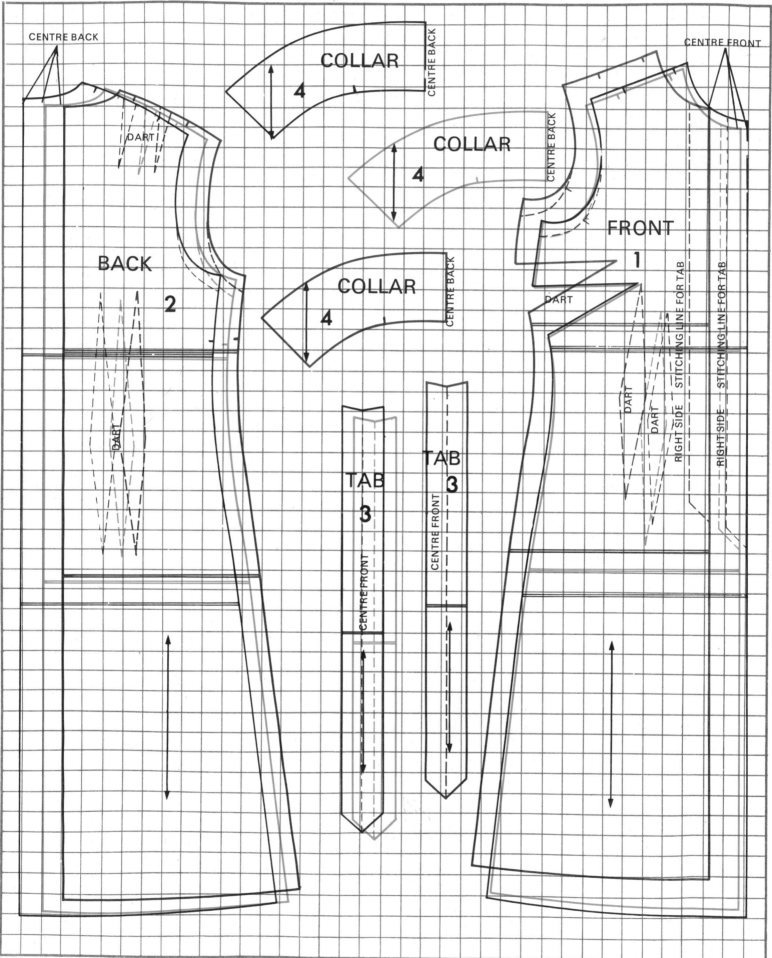

KEY
Size 82cm
Size 87cm
Size 90cm

Lengthen or shorten here
Straight of grain
One square = 2·5cm

CENTRE BACK

COLLAR
4

CENTRE BACK

COLLAR
4

CENTRE BACK

COLLAR
4

CENTRE BACK

CENTRE FRONT

FRONT
1

DART

RIGHT SIDE STITCHING LINE FOR TAB

RIGHT SIDE STITCHING LINE FOR TAB

BACK
2

DART

DART

TAB
3

TAB
3

CENTRE FRONT

CENTRE FRONT

DART

DART

The outlines given are the stitching lines. Refer to page 117 for seam allowances and check with the following chapters for any variations.

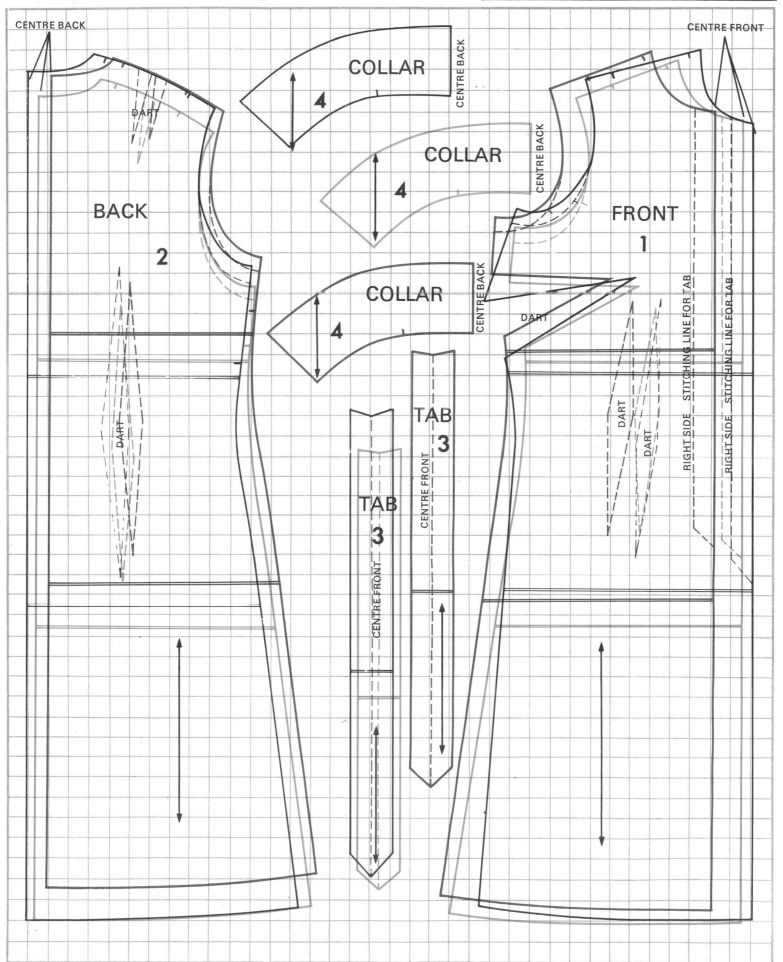

CENTRE BACK

CENTRE FRONT

COLLAR
4

CENTRE BACK

COLLAR
4

CENTRE BACK

BACK
2

FRONT
1

DART

DART

COLLAR
4

CENTRE BACK

DART

DART

DART

RIGHT SIDE STITCHING LINE FOR TAB

RIGHT SIDE STITCHING LINE FOR TAB

TAB
3

TAB
3

DART

CENTRE FRONT

CENTRE FRONT

Chapter 29

Dress-making

Begin with the basic dress

It is every would-be dressmaker's ambition to make a dress successfully but many give up in despair. They buy a pattern, cut out the fabric and plunge in and sew the seams without marking the pattern detail or tacking the garment for fitting. Halfway through they find that the garment does not fit and since they haven't transferred the pattern detail to the fabric there are no guide lines for altering the dress. Often the result is that the garment is thrown into the back of a drawer and forgotten. With more careful initial preparation there would be no need for discouragement and it would be a relatively simple matter to put things right.

The dress on the right, made from the Basic Dress Graph, has been designed with both the beginner and the accomplished dressmaker in mind. If you are a beginner you will find that all the stages of making a dress and detailed fitting instructions are given and also that the pattern pieces are kept to the minimum needed to assemble a dress. Everything is clearly marked and easy to identify. And, to prevent confusion at the cutting out stages, only the main pattern pieces are cut at first: the facings are cut as you need them.

Watch out for the tips for the experienced dressmaker too. The method used for finishing the inside of the basic dress, the neck lines, armholes and Centre Front fastening is that used by haute couture to limit bulk on these edges, especially when thick and weighty fabrics are being used. Other finishes are covered in later chapters.

Assembling the basic dress is clearly explained step by step. Therefore when you come to other dresses you will be able to refer to the techniques for putting on tab front fastenings, finishing and fitting contained in these chapters.

The basic dress

The basic dress with collar and tab front, shown here in blue wool, is cut from the Golden Hands Graph on pp112, 113.

The pattern is so versatile that you can make a whole wardrobe of dresses based on this one pattern. Being a semi-tailored dress the style lends itself to a wide variety of fabrics, the mood of the dress depending on the fabric and trimming used to make it.

Here are a few suggestions: for a sporty version, use a crisp fabric and top stitch collar and tab details; for parties use voile or silk; for more formal occasions extend the pattern to full length and make an evening dress in a glamorous printed silk.

Later chapters explain in detail how to use the basic dress to make various other attractive styles, which are only a few from the complete Golden Hands wardrobe of styles to make. However, for those of you who are advanced dressmakers, having the Graph Pages enables you to make any one of these dress conversions straight away.

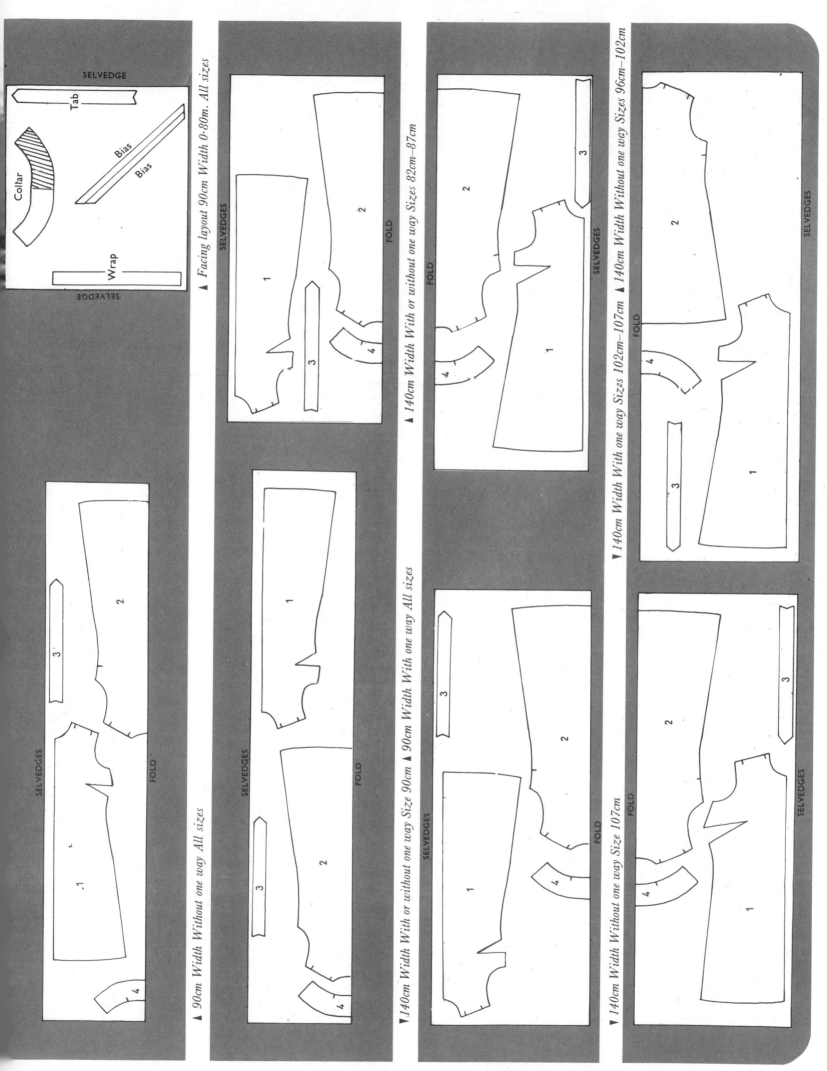

SELVEDGE

Tab

Collar

Bias

Bias

Wrap

SELVEDGE

▲ *Facing layout 90cm Width 0·80m. All sizes*

SELVEDGES

FOLD

1

2

3

4

▲ *140cm Width With or without one way Sizes 82cm—87cm*

SELVEDGES

FOLD

1

2

3

4

▲ *140cm Width With one way Sizes 102cm—107cm* ▲ *140cm Width Without one way Sizes 96cm—102cm*

SELVEDGES

FOLD

1

2

3

4

▼ *140cm Width With one way Sizes 102cm—107cm*

SELVEDGES

FOLD

3

2

1

SELVEDGES

FOLD

2

3

1

4

▲ *90cm Width Without one way All sizes*

SELVEDGES

FOLD

1

2

3

4

▼ *140cm Width With or without one way Size 90cm* ▲ *90cm Width With one way All sizes*

SELVEDGES

FOLD

1

2

3

4

▼ *140cm Width Without one way Size 107cm*

115

Choosing your fabric

If you're a beginner, use a firmly woven fabric which does not fray easily such as Shetland wool, fine tweed or a worsted woollen fabric. All these are easy to handle, retain their shape and will not slip about during making.

Here is a list of other fabrics which are also suitable for the dress.

☐ **Firmly woven cottons:** sailcloth, dress-weight poplin, strawcloth and piqué.
☐ **Linens:** dress weight, plain or embroidered.
☐ **Man-made fabrics:** cloth made from, or containing, acrylic or polyester fibre such as Crimplene or Dacron.
☐ **Woollen or wool mixtures:** Viyella, wool crepe and many traditional woollen dress-weight fabrics.

And here are some more expensive fabrics which require a little more dressmaking know-how.

☐ **Silks, pure and artificial:** shantung, Honan and Thai silk, foulard and brocade.
☐ **Cotton:** lawn, organdie and voile.
☐ **Woollen:** wool muslin (nun's veiling).

The basic dress can also be made from jersey fabric, with the exception of the silk or silk-type jerseys. Before buying jersey, test it by holding it up over your wrist. If there is a downward drag to the fabric—almost as though it is weighted—it is more suitable for softly draped styles and not for the semi-tailored style of the basic dress.

Fabric requirements and notions

Before buying the dress and facing fabric look at the amounts given at foot of the page. To face the woollen and silk fabrics use pure silk or rayon taffeta. Avoid triacetates or nylon because they will not stand as much pressing as is necessary on wool. For cotton and linen use poplin. Man-made fibre fabrics should be finished with fabric of equal weight, strength and texture. If your dress is washable, remember to buy washable facing fabric. You will also need the following notions: 8 buttons; 9 press fasteners size 0; matching thread.

Sewing psychology

Dressmaking needs careful planning. In order to be successful, each job must follow the preceding one in natural and logical succession. If you neglect the preliminaries, you may find yourself with an ill-fitting garment when it's too late to alter it. So, plan your dressmaking and remember to concentrate on doing the job in hand so that you can do the next one properly.

Dress requirements

Sizes	cm 82	cm 87	cm 90	cm 96	cm 102	cm 107
	m	m	m	m	m	m
90cm Without one way	2·40	2·55	2·65	2·65	2·75	2·75
With one way	2·55	2·65	2·65	2·75	2·90	2·90
140cm Without one way	1·50	1·60	1·85	1·85	1·85	1·95
With one way	1·50	1·60	1·85	2·10	2·20	2·30

In this way you will enjoy your work and the results will be good. It is also worth the extra time to read through the whole of each chapter before taking action because this will help your planning and avoid possible disaster later on.

Reading the Golden Hands pattern pieces

Make your paper pattern from the graph, transferring all the markings. Before cutting out the paper pattern spare a moment to look at it so that you can identify the pattern pieces and get to know what the markings mean. You may find it easier to study the pattern pieces on the facing page.

The four pattern pieces needed for the basic dress are the Back, Front, tab and collar patterns. Note the seam lines: the pattern is without seam allowance so the solid lines are also stitching lines. Look at the balance marks which will have to be matched. For instance, the balance mark on the side-seam of the dress Back meets the end of the side bust dart on the dress Front. The shoulder balance marks on Back and Front will have to meet when sewing the shoulder-seams.

Next, look at the dotted lines which indicate stitching lines and optional darts. The dart shown on the shoulder of the dress Back is optional as some fabrics will ease in between the balance marks but if you need more fullness across the back shoulder line, or if your fabric is too stiff to ease in, then you will need this dart for a smooth fitting shoulder line.

The long body darts are also optional and largely a matter of style and fashion, except for in the case of larger bust sizes when they become a must.

The long, pointed dotted line parallel to the Centre Front is the stitching line for the tab on the right Front and the meeting line for the tab on the left Front, when the tab is wrapped over for fastening.

The two double horizontal lines across the Back and Front are for lengthening or shortening the pattern. The dotted line on the tab pattern is the Centre Front and the dotted lines below the solid line of the lower armhole are stitching lines when making the dress with sleeves.

Cutting out the paper pattern

Cut out the Back, collar and tab pattern pieces along the solid outlines. Then cut out the Front, leaving a 13mm margin along the shoulder and side-seams, outside the solid pattern outline. Do not cut out the side bust dart.

Correcting the pattern length

As the pattern has been made without either seam or hem allowances it is easy to check the final length by slipping it over your right shoulder.

Dart the pattern at the side bust dart by pleating the lower seam line towards the upper seam line and secure with pins.

Lap the back shoulder-seam over the margin on the front shoulder-seam to meet the solid seam lines, and pin. Similarly join the side-seam.

Slip the pattern over your shoulder and stand sideways in front of a long mirror so that you can see the final length of your dress. If you need more or less length measure the amount you need, take off the dress and unpin it. Then make the length adjustments along the double horizontal lines.

The dress length is to the knee for a 162cm height. If you are taller or shorter and want to alter the dress to obtain this hem line level, use the double solid lines as described. If, however, you simply want the dress to be longer than knee length, you can add up to 13cm by using the double solid lines across the skirt of the dress. If this is not enough and you need more length still, just add that to the hem line.

To lengthen the pattern, cut the pattern along the horizontal lines and fix strips of paper between the pattern sections to make up the required length.

To shorten pattern, simply make a pleat along each horizontal line, to the depth of the required amount.

Re-pin the darts and the shoulder and side-seams and slip the pattern on once again for a final check to see that you have made the right adjustments.

Take out all the pins and cut off the margins on the dress Front. Also cut into the under arm bust darts.

Preparing the fabric for cutting

Prepare the fabric in the same way as for the basic skirt in Skirt-making Chapter 11. Smooth out any creases with a warm iron and a damp or dry cloth, according to the fabric type.

When working on longer lengths of fabric it becomes difficult to find a surface large enough to accommodate the full length, so use a chair back to support the rest of the fabric. This prevents any pull on the fabric on which you are working.

Check that the selvedges of the fabric are not tight and making the fabric cockle. If they are, make small snips through the selvedges only, about 5cm apart. If this doesn't make the fabric lie flat, cut off the selvedges altogether.

Select the appropriate layout from the special sheet and follow it carefully.

Leave enough room between pattern pieces for 19mm seam and 6·3cm hem allowances. Pin your pattern pieces down securely.

Beware—before you cut

Having studied figure types and problems in Generally Speaking Chapter 4 you may have discovered you need to make adjustments to your pattern before cutting out. Later chapters deal fully with pattern adjustments but because of the soft fit of the basic dress, figure problems are quite easily overcome, provided you take the following precautions.

Straight shoulders. For very straight shoulders add 13mm to the normal seam allowance towards the outer edge of the shoulder seam, as you may have to let it out.

Rounded back and sloping shoulders. For a slightly rounded back and sloping shoulders leave an extra deep seam allowance along the back armhole edge, about 3·8cm at shoulder level, tapering into normal seam allowance towards the underarm.

Thick-set neck. If you have a thick-set neck, measure your neck around the base, then measure the neck edge of the Centre Back to Centre Front of the pattern. This measurement should be 2·5cm larger than your own. If it is not, do not cut the collar until you have fitted the dress.

Large proportions. It is always a good idea to leave an extra seam allowance where you know your measurements are slightly larger than standard proportions. You can then make the necessary adjustments when you are fitting the garment.

Pinning the hem and seam allowances

Mark the hem and seam allowances with pins or tailor's chalk. Pin 19mm seams and 6·3cm hem allowances all round, and if you need to make any of the alterations just mentioned, add the additional allowances now.

Cut the extra seam allowance at the darts as shown in the top right-hand diagram.

You will notice the layouts given earlier in this chapter show extra width on the Centre Front seams. This is a double seam allowance of 3·8cm and you will see how to use this later. Leave on this double seam allowance when you cut out.

You are now ready to cut out the fabric. The pattern details will be marked after cutting.

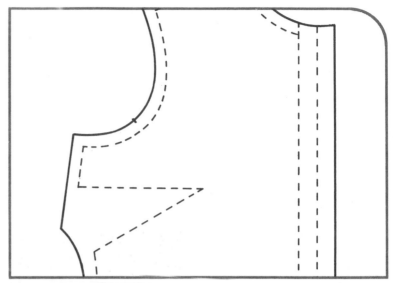

Add seam allowance at the darts ▲   *Basic dress pattern pieces* ▼

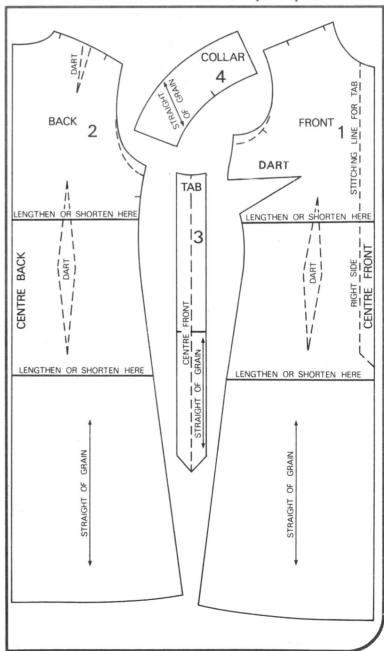

Chapter 30

The next step

The next stage of making the dress is to mark the pattern details on the fabric. For the skirt in Skirtmaking 11 these were marked before cutting to prevent the beginner being confused. In this case, however, it is easier to mark the details once the pieces have been cut out.

Marking the 'Golden Hands' pattern detail

First mark the details on the dress Back. Lay it on a flat surface and mark around the pattern edges with continuous tailor's tacks. Make single tailor's tacks at right angles to the seam edges to indicate the balance marks.

Next, the dash lines. Those on the Back indicate optional shoulder and waist darts and need only be marked if you are using them. To do so make short slits about 8cm apart through the pattern with a needle, along the dash lines. Make single tailor's tacks through each slit, being careful not to stitch into the pattern.

Mark the Centre Back fold line with a row of long tacking stitches as you will need this line to check the hang of the dress.

The dress Fronts are marked in two stages. First the general pattern details are marked and then the fastening details.

Mark the Centre Front line from hem to neck.

Make slits through the dash line of the tab stitching line and mark with single tailor's tacks. Mark the corner and point especially carefully because they have to match the shape of the tab. Similarly mark the waist darts if you are using them.

Tailor's tack round the rest of the pattern and into the darts. Mark the balance marks.

For the second stage the layers must be separated as described for the skirt in Skirtmaking Chapter 11, so cut through the tailor's tacks. Lay the right Front, right side up, on a flat surface in front of you. Mark the 19mm seam allowance along the Centre Front, from the hem upwards to where it meets the stitching line of the tab. Then mark a seam allowance along the tab stitching line and cut off the surplus as shown in the diagram.

With the left dress Front in front of you, right side up, look at the diagram carefully. You have already marked the Centre Front line and the meet line for the tab.

Halve the double seam allowance along the Centre Front and mark the line with long tacking stitches. Following the red line on the sketch, cut off the extra seam allowance from the lower edge on the Centre Front, where you don't need it. The extra seam allowance along the upper edge will provide you with enough wrap to fasten the dress.

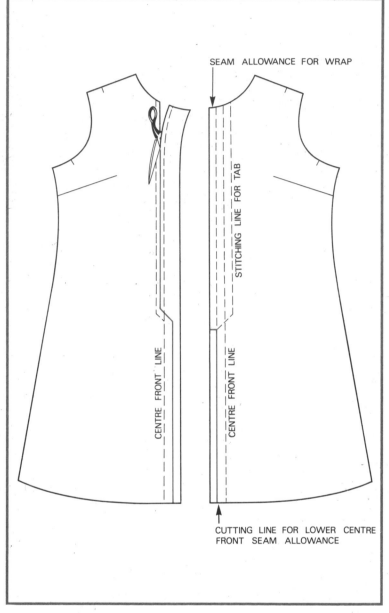

Preparing the right front (left)   Preparing the left front (right)

A wrap is usually half the width of the tab (that is 2·5cm here) and meets the tab stitching line when closed. But to simplify the cutting of your first dress a seam allowance width (19mm) only has been given and this is quite enough. Instructions for cutting a conventional wrap are given later.

On the tab make long tacking stitches round the outline and mark the Centre Front line.

Tailor's tack round the collar.

Remove the pattern pieces and separate the layers in the usual way.

Preparing for fitting

The dress is now ready to be pinned and tacked to prepare it for fitting.

Pin and tack the darts.

Pin and tack the Centre Front-seams from the pointed end of the tab stitching line to the hem.

Pin and tack shoulder and side-seams, carefully matching the balance marks.

Press the seams lightly and turn up the hem.

The fastening detail is not made up at this stage.

Fitting the dress

Before you start fitting, put on the underclothes you will wear with the dress when it is finished. Make sure your bra shoulder straps are adjusted correctly because if you alter them later your side bust dart will not fit properly.

Slip on the dress and pin the Centre Front opening closed by lapping the raw edge of the seam allowance on the right over the seam allowance for the wrap on the left Front.

Now look at the dress in a full length mirror. This is the time when most people wish they'd never started; your dress looks raw and bulky but don't despair—even experienced dressmakers have to remain very objective at this stage to avert the feeling.

When fitting, start from the top and work downwards. Here is a list of fitting stages in order.

1. The neck	5. The body darts
2. The shoulders	6. The side-seams
3. The armholes	7. The hang
4. The bust	8. The length

1. The neck

Make sure that the row of tailor's tacks around the neck, indicating the stitch line for the collar, lies flat around the base of the neck. If it is strained, or rises on the neck, carefully snip into the seam allowance until you have the required fitting. Do not snip too deeply, because the seam allowance will have to be trimmed and snipped again after you have stitched on the collar. Mark a new stitching line with pins.

2. The shoulders

If the dress lifts at the inner shoulder or feels tight over the top of the arm, it means that your shoulders are straighter than the standard slope of the pattern. Let out a little from the seam allowance on the outer edge of the shoulder line and taper into the original seam allowance towards the neck.

If sloping shoulders make the dress rise at the outer shoulder edge you will need to lift the seam. Start at the armhole edge and taper into the original seam towards the neck, until the shoulder line lies flat. This may tighten the armholes of the dress. If so snip the seam allowance carefully where it is tight, until the armholes feel comfortable, and pin a new armhole line.

3. The armholes

If the armholes feel tight and the dress shoulders are caught over the upper arms, your problem is large upper arms.

If the armhole is merely too tight, pin a new armhole line. But if the dress is held away from the neck through tightness around the armhole you must fit this in two stages.

First cut off the seam allowance from the armhole edge around the underarm and slip the dress on again. Then pin a new armhole-seam. If you have more than the normal seam allowance left outside the new pin line take the dress off and pin the armholes together. Mark the pinned armhole line through both layers of fabric and trim to the normal seam allowance. Try on the dress once more to make sure all is well.

Finally look at the armhole-seam line over the shoulders and make sure this is in the correct position.

4. The bust

The well made look of a dress does not depend on your figure, but on the way the dress is fitted to it. So always take the trouble to fit your dress really well, especially over the bust line. The dress should fit smoothly and not strain, even when you are moving. Look at the dart points; these should be in line with the highest point of the bust. If not, pin them higher or lower as required.

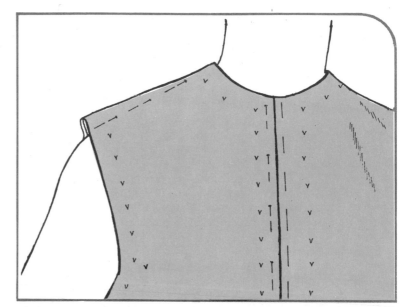

Lifting the shoulder seam

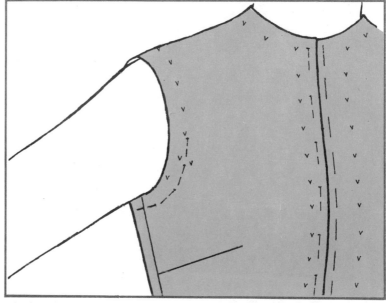

Pinning a new armhole seam
Altering the bust dart

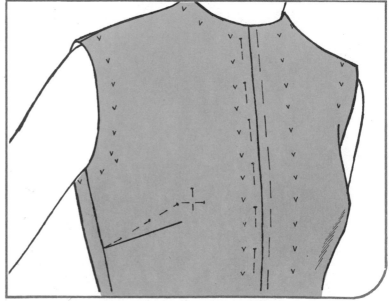

Small adjustments can be made by altering the angle of the darts, but if you have to alter them by more than 13mm it is best to move the whole dart by that amount.

When you have made the necessary adjustments move about, swing your arms to see how much room you require for movement. Also sit down as this can tighten the bust line of the dress if you have a large bust.

5. The body darts

If you have used the body darts to make your dress fit more closely, make sure the front darts run towards the bust line and finish just under the highest point of the bust.

The body darts in the back should finish about 5cm above the seat. The deepest curve must go through the waist line and not above or below it as this would leave strain lines.

6. The side-seams

Stand sideways in front of a mirror and look at the way the side-seams hang. They should run in a straight line all the way, fitting close to the body at bust level, bypassing the waist and gently flaring towards the hem.

A swing towards the front may be caused by a large bust which will be dealt with under point 7. If this is not the case and they swing towards the front or back of the dress, it may be that when tacking the side-seam you eased one side into the other. If so unpick

the side-seams and tack them again making sure that both sides are smooth and flat.

If the dress is too loose, adjust it by pinning off the fullness from the side-seams.

If your dress is too tight, let out the side-seams.

7. The hang

With the help of a hand mirror look at the back of the dress. The line of tacking stitches along the centre back line should hang straight. If it is dragged sideways through tightness let out the dress at the side-seams.

If the tacking line hangs towards the right or left and this is not caused by tightness you will have to lift the corresponding side-seam until the tacking line hangs straight. To do this, unpick the side-seam and lift the dress Back into the armhole till the hang is straight. This may leave your armhole too large. If so pin the surplus into the shoulder-seam.

The hang of the dress can effect the side-seams. A large bust for instance will pull the dress up in front making it jut forward at the hem and pull the side-seam towards the front. Unpick the side-seams and lift more fabric into the underside of the side bust darts. If this gives you too much width in the side-seams over the hips pin off into the seam.

A rounded back can cause the same trouble at the back of the dress. To counteract this, unpick the side-seams and lift the dress

Fitting the dress

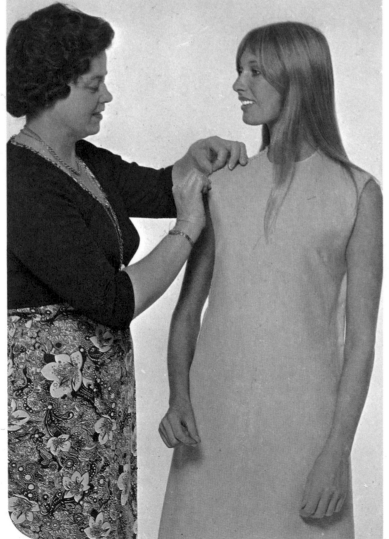

Stitching the dart

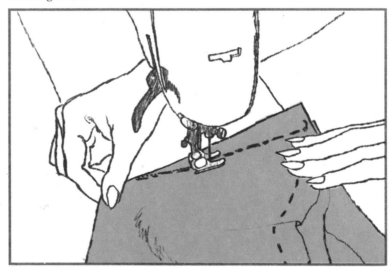

Pressing the dart

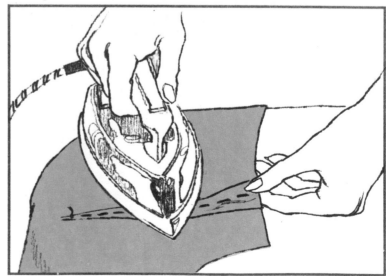

Back into the armholes, making sure that you lift it evenly on both sides. Use the balance marks as a guide.

It is difficult to guess the amount to lift, so start by lifting the Back by 2·5cm, re-pin the side-seams and slip the dress on again and you will then see if the drag towards the underarm has been corrected. If not, lift the dress Back a little more.

This adjustment gives you surplus width around the armhole at the back. Lift this surplus into the shoulder-seam by first deepening the dart and then making the Back shoulder seam slope down a little more, otherwise it will poke out at the armhole point of the shoulder-seam.

Line up the armhole-seam on the Back to the armhole-seam on the Front, which you will be able to do because you have added extra seam allowance when cutting out the fabric.

8. The length

Adjusting the hem is the final stage in the fitting.

If you have adjusted the hang of the dress on one side, level the hem line on that part of the dress with the hem line on the other side.

Marking the corrections

Trace the pin lines, which indicate the new fitting, with tacking cotton, tracing on each side of the new seam line where the fabric

Pinning the tab sections

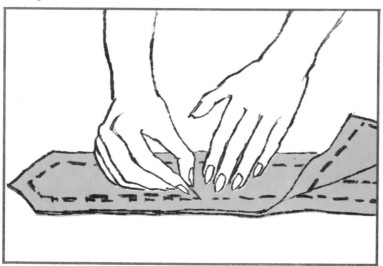

Tacking the tab along the stitched edge

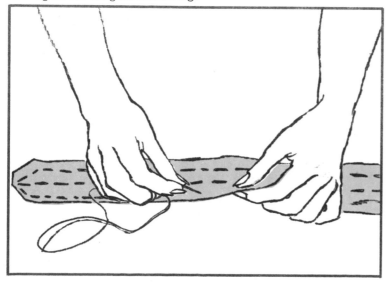

is double, taking care not to catch in both of the layers at once.

Then unpin and unpick the tacked seams. Make sure the fitting corrections are the same on both sides of the dress as shown for the skirt alterations in Skirtmaking Chapter 12, unless of course your figure is uneven, when you must fit each side to the shape of your body. Mark the pattern too for future reference.

When all the corrections are done, tack the dress together again and make a final fitting.

Stitching

You will be cutting out the under collar and the facings for the Centre Front, tab and armholes as you need them so have your facing fabric and layout ready.

Test the machine stitches on a scrap of dress material.

To help you plan your work and show you how the making up and finishing progresses, here is a list of the steps involved:

Step 1 The dress Front: darts; Centre Front-seam; Front fastening, tab and wrap.

Step 2 The dress Back: darts.

Step 3 Joining the dress sections: shoulder-seams; side-seams.

Step 4 Finishing the dress: armholes; collar; hem; finishing the fastening; press fasteners; buttons.

Step 1

The dress Front. Whenever you have details on a dress such as the Centre Front fastening, it is better to tackle the task before the section you're working on is joined to the remaining sections of the dress. This makes for easier handling without the bulk of the dress getting in your way.

Unpick the tacked shoulder and side-seams.

Darts. Stitch the side bust darts first. Note that slanted underarm darts must be sewn along the upper edge of the darts or else they will wring. This means that the one dart will be sewn towards the point and the other towards the base. See in the illustration how the fabric is guided through the machine in the seam line of the dart. Do not pull darts while machining; they may stretch. After stitching the darts remove the tacking and press them flat as you did for the skirt. Pay special attention to the pointed ends. Lay them over the rounded end of the ironing board so that you can mould them into the roundness of the body shape. They must not rise sharply into a point.

Moulding and shaping the fabric are secrets of good dressmaking. Sew the waist darts if you are using them. Press them towards the centre.

The Centre Front-seam. Stitch the Centre Front-seam from the pointed end of the tab stitching line to the hem. Remove the tacking and press the seam open to within 5cm of the upper end.

Front fastening, tab. The first stage is the preparation of the tab. Using the tab pattern, cut out the tab facing from lining fabric with 19mm seam allowance all round. Mark the tab pattern details on to the fabric with long tacking stitches and make single tailor's tacks through the slits along the dash line.

Pin and tack the tab to the facing with right sides together and with the facing uppermost; starting at the centre front, stitch along the top, down the right side, turn and stitch to the point. Fasten off the stitches securely at both ends so that as you work on the tab the seam lines remain secure.

Trim the seam allowance. Turn the tab to the right side and tack firmly along the sewn edge with small tacking stitches, rolling the facing slightly under, to avoid it showing.

Carefully press this edge on the wrong side of the tab, making sure that the tacking stitches do not leave impressions on the fabric as they will be very difficult to remove.

Chapter 31

The basic dress continued

In this chapter all the pieces are assembled and the finishing touches put to the dress. The tab for the dress is now made up and ready to be stitched in place.

Step 1

Front fastening, tab (continued). Before you stitch the tab to the dress, prepare the corner on the dress Front as shown in the diagram, to prevent it from fraying.

Machine stitch a row of stay stitches just outside the marked out stitching line, then cut into the corner without cutting the stay stitches.

Pin, tack and stitch the raw edge of the tab to the right dress Front on the tab stitching line but avoid catching the facing fabric into the seam. Spread the corner on the dress so that you can stitch comfortably towards the pointed end of the tab. Take care that the corner stays in position and does not drag inwards by pivoting the machine needle

A reminder of the basic dress

just inside the stay stitching at the corner. The point of the tab must be in line with the Centre Front seam.

If the fabric is thick and the seam allowance on the tab at the corner does not lie flat after pressing, trim it carefully across the corner.

Fold under the seam allowance on the facing and pin it over the seam line to cover the raw edges. Slip stitch in place by hand. Remove all remaining tacking on the tab.

To press the tab lay it full length, wrong side up, on the ironing board with the sides of the dress Front fully supported. Fold the left Front double to keep it out of the way of the iron but without dragging the Centre Front seam and press.

The wrap. To complete the Centre Front fastening make the wrap on the left Front edge. Using the tab pattern as your guide cut the facing with 19mm

seam allowance from the lining fabric but without the pointed end. Instead, extend both sides of the tab pattern to the length of the point and cut straight across the lower edge, not forgetting the seam allowance. It is not necessary to mark the seam line of the facing strip as you can use the marking on the dress Front for your stitching lines.

Pin and tack the facing to the left Front edge of the dress with right sides facing. Stitch the facing and fabric together, starting at the centre Front, along the top edge, and down the Front, leaving the lower edge unstitched.

Trim the seam allowance and turn the facing into the dress. Tack firmly along the sewn edges and press carefully.

Turn under the long raw edge on the facing until it meets the meet line for the tab and sew it to this line with a slip stitch. Working on the inside of the dress, lay the wrap over the tab and you will see that the Centre Front seam folds over too. To make the seam lie flat and open, cut into the seam allowance as shown, press the seam

open and press wrap over tab. Oversew the raw lower edge of the wrap facing by hand, catching the seam allowance of Centre Front seam into stitches. To hold the wrap in position, make several small stitches at the lower edge of the wrap catching it to the stitching line of the tab.

Give the tab and wrap one final pressing and the fastening detail is complete.

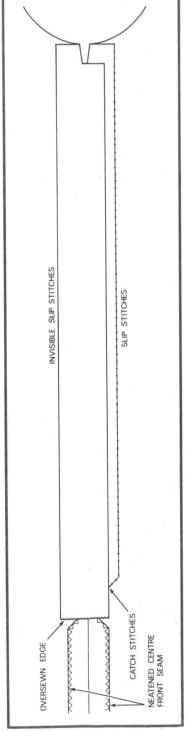

Finished stitch wrap inside

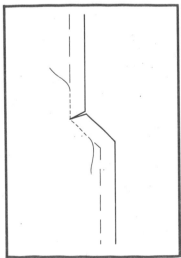

The stay-stitched corner

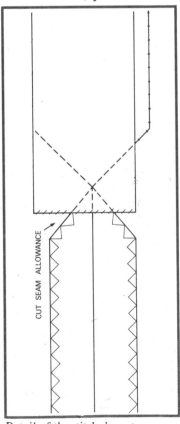

Detail of the stitched wrap

Step 2

The dress Back: darts. First stitch the darts at the shoulder if you are using them.

Slash the darts along the centre to within 3·8cm from the point and press them open as for a seam. This way they will lie flat when the shoulder seam is stitched and not leave a bump showing above the seam. Oversew the raw edges to neaten.

If you are darting the waist, sew the darts and then press them towards the centre.

Step 3

Joining the dress sections: shoulder-seams. Pin, tack and stitch the shoulder-seams, matching balance marks and seam lines. Oversew the raw seam edges to neaten. Remove the tacking. Press seams open.

Side-seams. Working on a flat surface lay the side-seams together. Match the side seam balance marks on the Back to the ends of the side bust darts on the Front. Pin, tack and stitch the side-seams making sure that both layers of fabric are perfectly smooth otherwise the side-seams will not hang straight.

Neaten the raw seam edges and remove the tacking. Press seams open. Remember to take out any impressions the seams may have made on the fabric by pressing under the seam allowance.

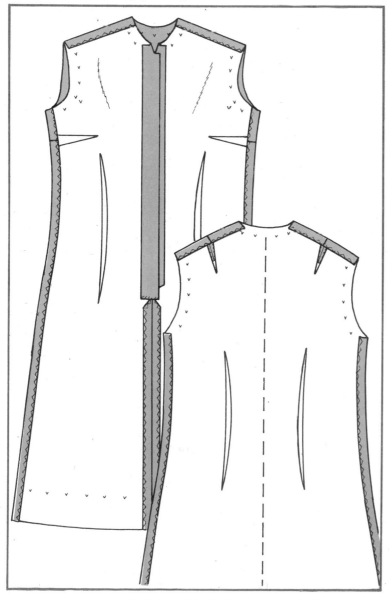

Step 4

Finishing the dress. When you make a garment with sleeves it it is important to finish the neck line first because it is essential to see if the firm fit of the collar effects the armhole line over the shoulders. But when you make a sleeveless dress it does not matter if you finish the armhole edge first.

The armhole edge is finished here so that you can see the technique more clearly.

The armholes. First measure the size of the armholes along the seam line.

Find the true bias of the facing fabric by laying one side of a 45° set square to the selvedge of the fabric and mark the diagonal of the fabric with pins or tailor's chalk (see layout of facing fabric on page 115).

Cut 3·8cm wide bias strips of fabric and join them as shown on the diagram to make up the length required for the armholes plus 5cm for ease and 2·5cm seam allowance.

The bias strips will have to be curved to follow the curve of the armholes. To do this place one bias strip on the ironing board and press round the outer edge gently stretching this into a curve as you press; then press in the fullness along the inner edge of the curve so that the material will be as flat as possible.

Turn under 13mm seam allowance at one end of the bias strip.

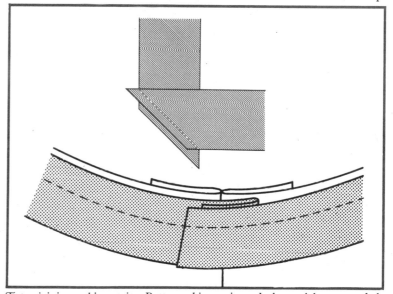

Top: joining a bias strip. Bottom: bias strip tacked round lower armhole

Starting at this end and working on the outside of the dress with right sides facing, pin the inner curved edge of the bias strip around the armhole seam line. Start at the top of the side-seam and only take 5mm seam allowance. The inner curve on the bias will still be a little full and you will have to ease the fullness into the under arm curve of the armhole seam.

Let the end of the bias overlap the turned under seam allowance as this will make for a secure join and also give a little extra stretch where you need it.

Because the curve of the armhole shape varies so much it is not advisable to join the bias strip in the straight of the grain where it meets at the side-seam, as is usual with a straight edge. So leave it untrimmed and unstitched until the facing is complete, then stitch it as it falls.

Leaving the overlap still unstitched tack the bias firmly in position and machine stitch it in place round the armhole seam line.

Remove the tacking stitches and trim the armhole seam allowance on the dress to the width of the seam allowance on the bias.

Snip into the seam allowance on the dress only to within a grain or two of the stitches then turn the bias to the inside. Roll the seam

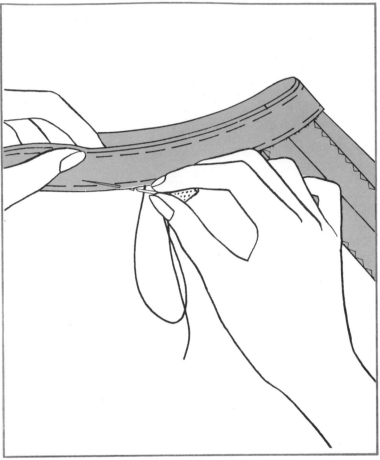

Hand sewing the armhole facing position

edge slightly to the inside to stop the bias showing and tack in place. Press the tacked edge gently. Turn the raw edge of the bias under for about 13mm and pin and tack it to the dress. Now carefully hand-sew the bias in place.

Slip stitch the lapped ends of the bias in place.

Remove all tacking stitches and give one final pressing.

Face the other armhole similarly.

The collar. First let's deal with enlarging the collar. If you had to make the neck line larger you will also need to cut a new collar pattern.

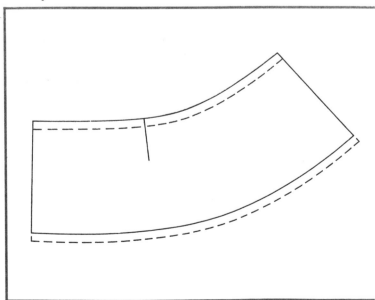

Enlarging the collar

Measure the new stitching line round the neck edge of the dress. Halve this measurement and deduct 6mm.

To find this length on the collar pattern measure into the collar from the neck edge and draw a new stitching line inside and parallel to the original neck stitching line of the pattern.

Mark the new position of the balance marks. Then cut the pattern along the new stitching line.

Place the cut pattern on a sheet of paper and pencil round it. Then add the amount you trimmed off the neck edge to the outer edge of the new collar pattern so that the collar therefore remains the same width as before.

Using the new pattern cut the collar from the dress fabric. Do not forget to place the Centre Back of the pattern on the fold of the fabric or to add and mark with tailor's tacks the 19mm seam allowance all round the outer edges.

Before you can make up the collar you will need to cut out an under collar.

Fold the facing fabric in the position shown in the layout and cut out the under collar, allowing only 16mm for seams. This will make

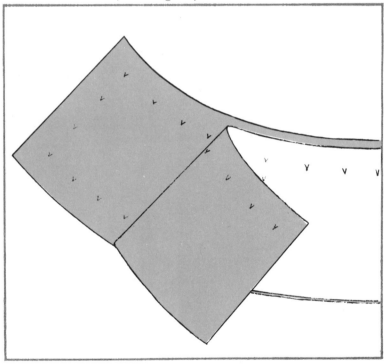

Smaller under collar in place over collar

the under collar slightly smaller and you will see why later.

Before removing the pattern, mark the balance marks. Remove pattern and mark the ordinary seam allowance 19mm on the neck edge of the under collar but do not mark the seam allowance on the outer edge.

With the outer raw edges level, pin and tack the collar and under collar together around the outer, not neck, edge using the seam line on the top collar as your guide.

Working with the under collar uppermost stitch round the collar leaving the neck edge open.

Remove the tacking cotton, cut the seam allowance off across the corners and trim it along the stitched edges.

Now turn the collar to the right side and you will see why the under collar is cut slightly smaller than the collar; this is to prevent the under collar showing on the outside.

Tack along the stitched edges rolling the upper collar edge under so that both pieces lie perfectly flat. Press lightly.

With the right side of the outer collar facing the wrong side of the dress pin, tack and stitch them together along the neck edge with

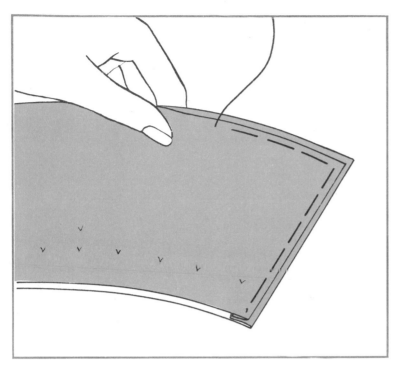

Rolling the collar edges under

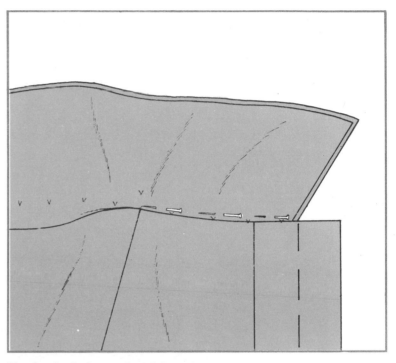

Turning in the lower edge of the under collar

the ends of the collar meeting on the Centre Front lines on the dress Fronts.

Trim both seam allowances and snip into the allowance on the collar only. Press the seam into the collar.

Turn in the raw edge on the under collar for a full 19mm seam allowance and pin. To avoid strain at the centre front you may have to adjust the depth of the seam allowance on your under collar. Snip into it as for the collar then tack it to the stitching line so that the seam is just covered by the folded edge.

Slip stitch neatly in place.

Remove all tacking and press.

The hem. After you have checked the hem turn it up and finish it exactly as for the skirt in Skirtmaking Chapter 13.

Finishing the fastening. All that remains to be done is to stitch on the press fasteners and buttons.

To find the correct position for the press fasteners it is necessary to work out the button positions first.

Use 8 buttons to trim the tab. Mark the place for the first button 2·5cm down from the neck edge. Measure the remaining length of the tab and work out equal distances for 7 more buttons having half a button distance between the last button and the pointed end of the tab. Mark the button positions along the Centre Front line with pins so that you can see them on both sides of the tab. Stitch on the press fasteners first, one under each button position. Sew the ball part of the fastener to the tab and the sockets to the wrap. To find the socket positions on the Centre Front line of the wrap fold the tab over and mark the corresponding positions with pins.

To hold the top corner of the tab under the collar when it is fastened, sew on a press fastener as shown in the picture.

Finally sew one button over each of the other press fasteners on the outside of the tab.

Give the dress one more careful pressing and it is ready to wear.

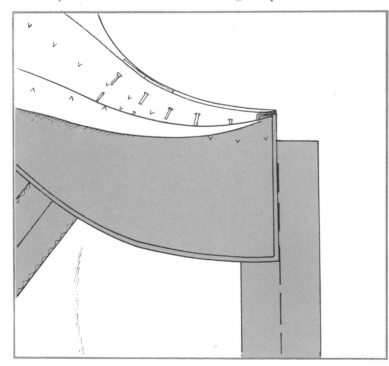

Pinning the collar to the dress

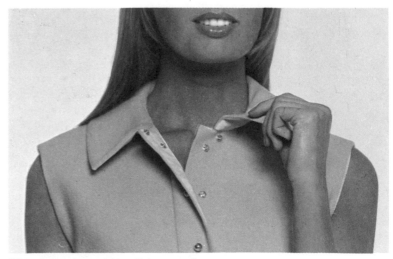

This shows the position of the press fasteners

Chapter 32

The pinafore conversion

In this chapter the basic dress pattern from the Golden Hands Graph Pages on pages 112 and 113 is converted into a pinafore style—a day version, and one for the evening with a widely flared skirt. The day version has front body darts and on the evening version the front shaping is achieved by slanting bust darts instead of the usual darts.

Full instructions are given for increasing a skirt flare —as much as a full circle if you wish. Suitable fabrics, the new patterns and the layouts for both versions are given here so that you will be ready to start making up in the next chapter.

The secrets of achieving perfect proportioning

Cutting the basic pattern to create new styles is fun and being able to do it shows real progress in dressmaking. At the same time, it is very important to know where to cut the pattern because misplaced seams can mar a garment.

Decorative seaming, whether vertical, diagonal or horizontal, is very attractive, but all seams must be considered in relation to the length and width of the finished garment.

By careful seaming and proportioning you can create a definite line, such as a square, elongating or flowing line. But if your body shape is already square, or if you are tall and thin, a similar line will only serve to accentuate it and you will need to alter the proportions to suit you.

Proportioning does not mean that you must have equal lengths of bodice and skirt when the garment is finished. It means that all parts of the garment divided by seams remain in good proportion to each other when the garment is worn, and do not emphasise figure faults or make the garment look clumsy. Nor should the outline of a design be destroyed by bad positioning of seams—they should be both a figure flattering as well as a style enhancing factor.

Finding the correct position for the horizontal seam

The position of the horizontal seam on the pinafore is determined by your figure type, height and size. See Generally Speaking Chapter 5 on figure types before you read the following paragraphs.

To find the cutting line for the horizontal seam, first read the instructions for your figure type, then modify them according to your height and size.

Figure type
Standard: 13cm below the waist line.

Large bust: first consider all the information given in Generally Speaking Chapter 5, relating to the problems of a large bust, before deciding to make the pinafore. The cutting line must be determined very carefully but unless the bust is very much larger than the hips the cutting line should be around hip level. This gives emphasis to the widest part of the hips, thus helping to balance the large bust proportions.

Leave plenty of seam allowance on bodice and skirt horizontal seams to allow for adjustments when fitting.

If your bust is very much larger than your hips pin the Front and Back pattern pieces together along the side- and shoulder-seams over strips of paper. Slip the pattern over your shoulders and pin. Place a length of dark coloured tape round your body over the pattern where you think the cutting line for the horizontal seam should go. Pin the tape down and look at the line from the front and sideways, to see if the position is right for you.

Large hips: all figure types with larger hip proportions should cut the pattern around hip bone level, 8cm to 10cm below the waist. This puts the emphasis of width on a narrower part of the body.

Height
Short, 160cm and under: there is no way to create the impression of length through horizontal seaming, but the pinafore can look right for you provided the sections are perfectly proportioned.

Mark the cutting line 8cm to 10cm below the waist line, but when you are cutting out the dress leave at least 5cm for the horizontal seam on both bodice and skirt so that you can check and perhaps adjust the seam line on the tacked garment. This way any adjustments made will not interfere with the length. Here is a guide to the proportioning for short figures.

For a day length pinafore, the skirt should look a little shorter than the bodice. For a full length evening pinafore you may be able to drop the horizontal seam line if your hip proportions are good.

Medium to tall, 163cm to 176cm: see instructions under Figure Type where the cutting lines given were for average heights.

Very tall, 179cm and over: most tall people have to cope with the problem of a long waist or long legs, or both, and as the horizontal seaming divides these lengths it presents no real problem. However, the following will help you to determine the right position for the seam.

Pin the Front and Back pattern pieces together along the side-and shoulder-seams over strips of paper. Slip the pattern over your shoulders and pin it.

Place a length of dark coloured tape round your body over the pattern where you think the cutting line for the horizontal seam should go. Pin the tape down and look at the line from the front and sideways, to see if the position is right for you.

Size
Small to average: see previous instructions under Figure type and Height, which were based on small to average sizes.

Larger sizes: this problem must be taken into consideration when making the pinafore.

If your bust size is over 96cm you should use the darts on the pattern and fit the bodice. A loose look will only add to your size while the gentle flare of the skirt on a fitted bodice, combined with a carefully positioned horizontal seam, will create a very pleasant line.

Suitable fabrics

Whether for day or evening wear, choose the fabric so that it is suitable for the style of the dress you are making. Fabrics with horizontal, vertical or diagonal design details are not suitable as the design would interfere with the cut of the pinafore dress, especially the day dress with its topstitching.

Fabrics to suit the geometrical appearance of the day length pinafore are:

☐ Firmly woven tweed and worsted woollens
☐ Double knit wool, polyester and heavy cotton jerseys.

Fabrics to suit the soft look of the evening pinafore are:

☐ Wool, silk and rayon crepes
☐ Light-weight wool and polyester jerseys
☐ Pure silk and rayon satins.

Fabric requirements

Day length pinafore. The following amounts are for the given pattern length. If you want to make the skirt longer, don't forget to add the extra skirt length required on each pattern section to the amount.

140cm width, without one way—sizes 82cm and 87cm, 1·60 metres; size 90cm, 1·75 metres; size 96cm, 1·85 metres; sizes 102cm and 107cm, 2·10 metres.

140cm width, with one way—sizes 82cm and 87cm, 1·60 metres; size 90cm, 1·75 metres; size 96cm, 1·95 metres; sizes 102cm and 107cm, 2·10 metres.

90cm width, without one way—size 82cm, 2·65 metres; size 87cm, 3 metres; size 90cm, 3·10 metres; sizes 96cm, 102cm and 107cm, 3·20 metres.

90cm width, with one way—size 82cm, 2·90 metres; size 87cm, 3 metres; size 90cm, 3·20 metres; size 96cm, 3·35 metres; sizes 102cm and 107cm, 3·45 metres.

Evening pinafore: the following amounts are for a dress length of 147cm. If you want to make the skirt longer, don't forget to add the extra skirt length on each pattern section to the amount.

140cm width, without one way—sizes 82cm and 87cm, 2·65 metres; size 90cm, 3 metres; size 96cm, 3·10 metres; size 102cm, 3·35 metres; size 107cm, 3·45 metres.

140cm width, with one way—size 82cm, 3·10 metres; sizes 87cm, 90cm and 96cm, 3·20 metres; sizes 102cm and 107cm, 3·45 metres.

90cm width, without one way—size 82cm, 4·35 metres; size 87cm, 4·50 metres; size 90cm, 5·05 metres; size 96cm, 5·15 metres; sizes 102cm and 107cm, 5·50 metres.

90cm width, with one way—size 82cm, 5·95 metres; size 87cm, 6·10 metres; sizes 90cm and 96cm, 6·20 metres; size 102cm, 6·30 metres; size 107cm, 6·40 metres.

By careful proportioning and seaming, pinafore style dresses can suit all figure types ▶

Making the new pattern

First, make sure you have plenty of paper handy for making adaptations to the Basic Dress Graph Pattern.

Then copy and cut out the Front and Back of the Dress Graph (pieces 1 and 2 in the Graph Pages).

Next, mark your waist line on the new pattern. To determine its position use either the corrected bodice toile pattern (see Toile-making Chapter 22) or use a measuring tape.

Front: square neck line

Mark out the new neck line (figure 1).

Measure 5cm along the shoulder-seam from the neck edge and mark. Measure 13cm down, make another mark and connect to the Centre Front edge by a straight line, using a tailor's square or set square. Measure back along this line 9·5cm to 10cm depending on how wide you want the neck line to be, and mark. Connect this point to the original mark on the shoulder-seam.

Cut out the new neck line as shown in red.

Back: neck line

Mark off the same distance from the neck edge along the Back shoulder-seam as you did for the Front. Then, measure 3cm from the neck down the Centre Back line and connect both marks with a curved line (figure 2).

Cut out the new Back neck curve.

Centre Back-seam

If you want to make the pinafore fitted, it is necessary to curve the Centre Back-seam slightly before you start dividing the pattern for the bodice and skirt.

Draw a gentle curve (figure 2) through the waist from a point about 10cm below the waist line to a point about half way between the waist line and neck. Make sure the curve tapers gradually back into the original line.

If you are also using the Back darts, you must compensate for the Centre Back curve by drawing the darts a little less deep, or the Back becomes too fitted.

Any further adjustments necessary to make the pinafore more fitted should be left until the fitting stage.

Cut out the Centre Back curve.

Horizontal seam

Measure your correct horizontal cutting line at equal distances below the waist line across both Back and Front pattern pieces and draw in the new lines.

Measure the side-seams of the bodice to make sure that they are the same length on the Back and the Front. Also check that the skirt Back side-seam is the same length as the skirt Front side-seam.

Since the Back and Front skirt patterns are very much alike mark the pieces clearly

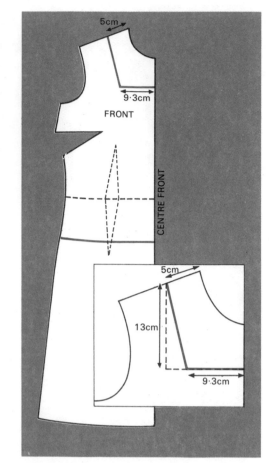

1. Making the square neck line on the Front ▲
2. Making the new Back neck line on the Back and curving the Centre Back seam ▼

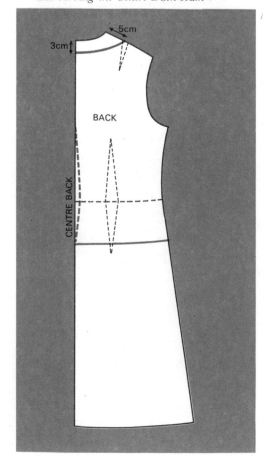

Front and Back and mark in the Centre Front and Centre Back, before cutting along the horizontal lines.

Also mark the Centre Front line on the bodice as 'fold', since there is no seam in the bodice Front.

Cut the pattern along the horizontal lines.

Back and Front facings

Here is a new type of facing to finish the neck and armhole edges of the dress.

To avoid the bulky finish which two separately cut facings would make over the shoulders, the neck and armhole facings are cut in one piece.

Lay the Centre Back and Front of the bodice pattern pieces to the straight edge of a sheet of paper and draw around the top edges (figures 3 and 4). Remove the patterns and draw in the inside lines of the facings as shown.

Reduce the width of the facings a little over the shoulders as shown by the red dash lines (figures 5 and 6). This ensures a perfect finish when the facings are stitched in place and avoids showing a roll along the edges. Cut out the facing patterns.

The skirt darts

If you are not fitting the dress with body darts use the skirt pattern as it is, ignoring the darts. But if you are stitching body darts you must deal with the darts in the skirt before cutting out the dress. Here are two ways to do this.

Method A. Leave the darts in the skirt in line with the body darts so that they look like one long dart after stitching.

Method B. Alter the shape of the skirt pattern (figure 7). This method will also add a little more flare around the hem.

To achieve this, first fold the darts on the pattern pieces to meet along the stitching lines and hold them securely in position on both sides of the pattern with sticky tape.

Lay the centre of each skirt pattern piece to the straight edge of a piece of paper, wider than the pattern, and pin along the centre line.

Slash each pattern from the hem upwards to the end of the dart. Spread the slash until the pattern lies flat and pin down. Draw around the new pattern shape, remove the original and cut out the new skirt pattern. Transfer Back and Front markings.

Increasing the skirt fullness

The diagram (figure 8) shows you how to add width to the skirt and obtain the lovely fullness shown in the evening version of the pinafore dress. The short skirt can also be made with an increased flare.

Using this method you can even increase the skirt until it is a quarter circle, for a circular skirt, but you would need to increase the number of slashes to get a good waist curve.

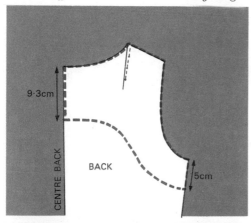

3. *Making the front neck and armhole facing* ▲
4. *Fold off dart and then make back facing* ▼

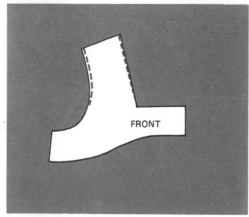

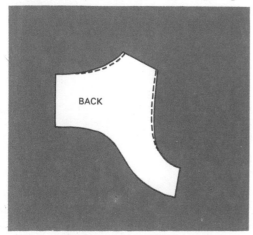

5. *Reducing the shoulder width of front facing* ▲
6. *Reducing the shoulder width of back facing* ▼

Step A. First prepare the Back and Front skirt patterns as shown in figure 7, then make two more slashes evenly spaced between the slash for the darts and the side-seam. Make all three slashes to within 3mm of the waist line, which means cutting through the darts.

Step B. Pin the centre of each skirt pattern piece to the straight edge of a sheet of paper large enough to accommodate the extra width and length needed for the evening skirt.

Step C. Following figure 8, add 61cm to the width of the hem of the short skirt by spreading each slash 5cm along the hem line. Pin the pattern down. You will notice that the waist line starts to curve up and lift considerably towards the side-seam. This is correct to retain the waist measurement.

Step D. Draw around the pattern edges with pencil and extend the side-seam. Plot out the new hem line, an equal distance from the original, using a ruler, and draw in the new curve. Cut out the new skirt pattern.

Making the pattern
for a slanted side bust dart

For the soft moulded look of the evening pinafore the front body darts are dispensed with and the side bust darts are slanted.

The slanting of the side bust dart should be by about 45 degrees. Although this may vary from person to person it should however not be more than 45 degrees. If you alter the dart by that amount you can always lessen the slant without much trouble should it be too steep for you. This will be done at the fitting.

To make the new pattern, pin the Front bodice pattern to the straight edge of a sheet of paper wider than the pattern. Draw round the pattern and into the dart. Remove the pattern.

Extend the upper side-seam (figure 9) downwards as shown. Then turn the end of the dart upper stitching line downwards through 45 degrees, make a mark on the extended side-seam and connect the point of the dart to it.

To find the lower stitching line, measure the distance between the original dart stitching lines at the side-seam and mark off this distance between the new stitching line and the side-seam. Draw in the dart lower stitching line from side-seam to point.

Draw a straight line from the dart point through the centre of the new dart to meet the new side-seam and then connect it to the dart lower stitching line at the original side-seam, as shown.

Cut out the new pattern but do not cut out the dart yet, as it may not be in the correct position.

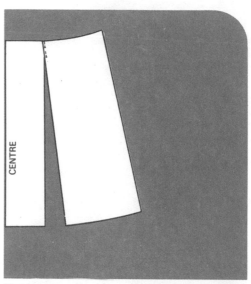

7. *Folding off the dart on the skirt pattern* ▲

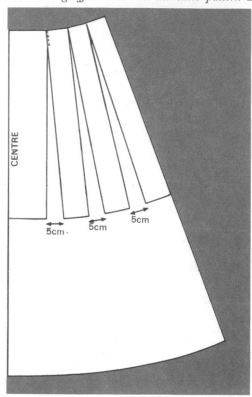

8. *Lengthening skirt and increasing the flare* ▲
9. *Altering the slant of the side bust dart* ▼

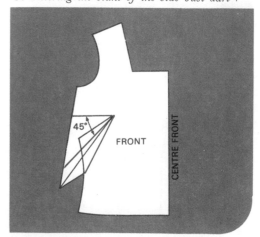

Day length pinafore

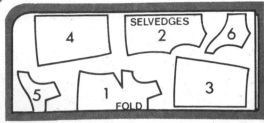

▲ *140cm width, with & without one way, sizes 82 & 87cm*

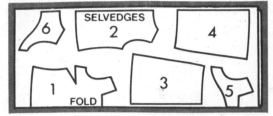

▲ *140cm width, without one way, sizes 90cm & 96cm*

Layouts for the pinafores

The layouts given here are for the day length pinafore without extra flare, and the evening pinafore. If you increase the flare on the skirt, you may need extra fabric. Using these layouts as a guide, first make a trial layout on paper before buying the fabric to calculate how much extra you need.

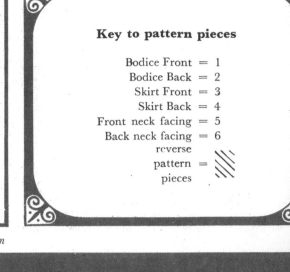

Key to pattern pieces

Bodice Front = 1
Bodice Back = 2
Skirt Front = 3
Skirt Back = 4
Front neck facing = 5
Back neck facing = 6
reverse pattern pieces = ⧄

▼ *90cm width, without one way, sizes 82cm & 87cm*

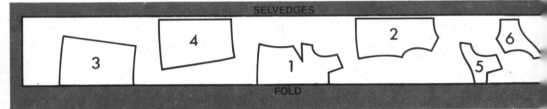

▼ *90cm width, without one way, sizes 90cm & 96cm*

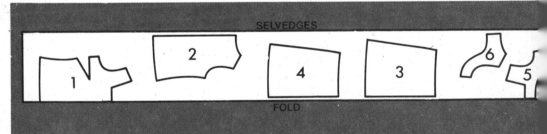

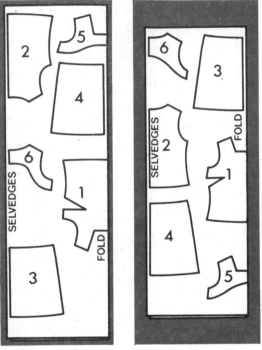

▼ *90cm width, without one way, sizes 102cm & 107cm*

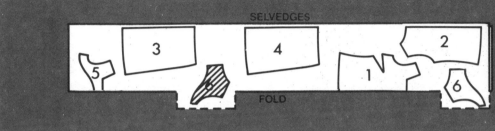

▲ *140cm width without one way, sizes 102 & 107cm* ▲ *140cm width, with one way, sizes 90cm & 96cm*

▼ *140cm width, with one way, sizes 102cm & 107cm*

▼ *90cm width, with one way, sizes 82cm & 87cm*

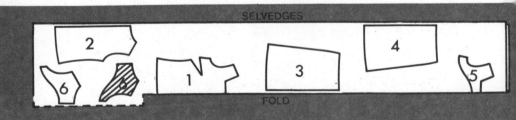

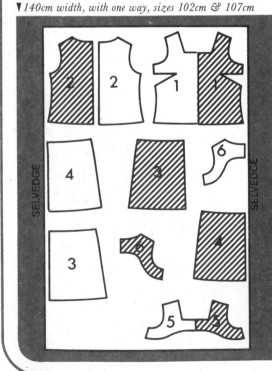

▼ *90cm width, with one way, sizes 90cm & 96cm. Alternative layout for section between red lines on layouts for without one way fabrics, sizes 90cm and 96cm* ▼ *90cm width, with one way, sizes 102cm & 107cm Alternative layout for section between red lines on layouts for without one way fabrics, sizes 102cm & 107cm*

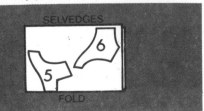

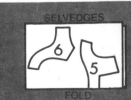

Evening pinafore

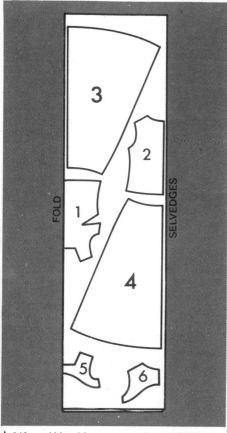

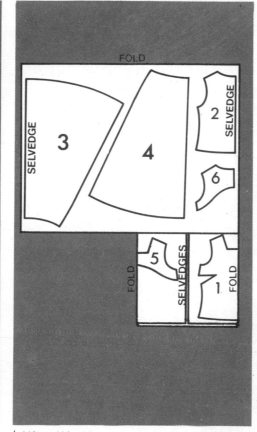

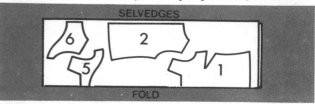

▲ 90cm width, without one way, skirt layout for all sizes

▲ 90cm width, without one way, bodice layout sizes 82cm & 87cm

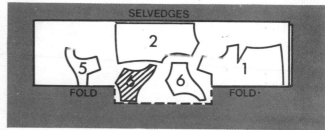

▲ 140cm width, without one way, sizes 82 & 87cm
▼ 140cm width, with one way sizes 82 & 87cm

▲ 140cm width, without one way, sizes 90, 96, 102 & 107cm
▼ 140cm width, with one way, sizes 90, 96, 102 & 107cm

▲ 90cm width, without one way, bodice layout sizes 90cm & 96cm
▼ 90cm width, without one way, bodice layout sizes 102cm & 107cm

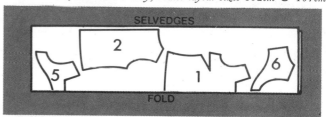

▼ 90cm width, with one way, skirt layout for all sizes

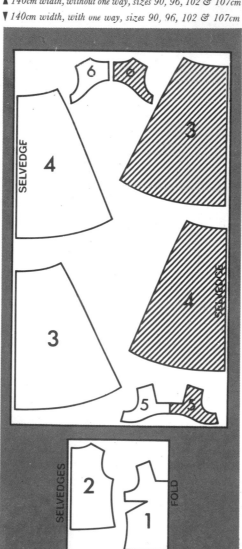

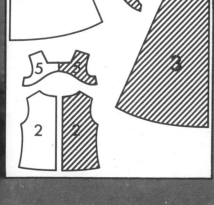

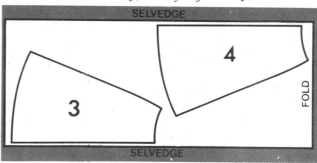

▼ 90cm width, with one way, bodice layout sizes 82cm & 87cm

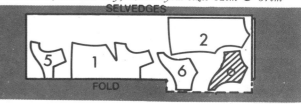

▼90cm width, with one way, bodice layout sizes 90, 96, 102 & 107cm

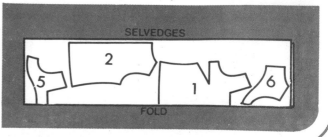

Chapter 33

Pinafores easy and elegant

The two elegant pinafore dresses from the last chapter are cut out and completed here. Separate sets of instructions are given for the day length pinafore—both with and without flare—and for the evening pinafore. Follow the making-up steps in the order given for the quickest, most successful results for making pinafore dresses.

Notions

First make sure you have all the notions at hand. For all the pinafores you will need:

☐ 60cm zip
☐ 1 or 2 reels of buttonhole twist and thicker machine needles for topstitching
☐ No. 1 hook
☐ If you are lining the dress you will need suitable lining fabric 0·25 metre less than the dress amount for without one way fabric
☐ If you are increasing the flare of the skirt you will also need 0·50 metre soft interfacing suitable for the fabric you are using.

Day length pinafore

These instructions are for the day length pinafore without extra flare on the skirt.

Making up steps

Here is a quick run through of the making-up steps:

☐ Cutting out   ☐ The lining
☐ Marking up   ☐ The facings
☐ Assembling and tacking ☐ The pocket flaps
☐ Fitting   ☐ Making up the skirt
☐ Stitching the bodice ☐ Topstitching
        ☐ Finishing: zip, lining, hem

Cutting out

Lay the patterns on the fabric using the appropriate layout for your size and fabric width from the previous pages.
For topstitching the Centre Front-seam in the skirt and the horizontal seam, you will need extra-deep seam allowances. The top-stitching can vary between 6mm and 13mm from the seam, so decide on the width and add an extra 13mm to give you the correct width for these seam allowances.
For all other seams allow 19mm, and 6·3cm for the hem.

Marking up

For those who now feel confident working with paper patterns it may no longer be necessary to tailor's tack in a continuous line around all the pattern pieces. Select strategic points only, such as where seams meet, or important shapes, or special seam distances for detail (figure 1) and make just enough continuous tailor's tacks to guide you, so that you can follow the continuation of the seams without difficulty.
Drawing lines with chalk is another quick way to mark details on fabric, but these lines can be so easily lost when handling the work. You would then have to refer back to the pattern, which could result in inaccurate copying, and you may even have to start un-picking. A little extra effort at the beginning is well worth while.

Assembling and tacking

Pin and tack the darts, side-seams and shoulder-seams of the bodice, leaving the Centre Back open. Press lightly.
Pin and tack the skirt seams and press lightly.
Pin the bodice and skirt along the horizontal seam line, carefully matching centres and side-seams. Pin and tack, then press this seam into the bodice.

Fitting

If you want to wear the pinafore over blouses and jumpers wear one for the fitting, otherwise you may fit the dress too tightly.
Pay special attention to the armholes, since a thick sweater will need extra room. If you have to increase the size of the armholes all round, bear in mind that should you want to wear the pinafore dress on its own a large armhole can look very ugly. So try on the dress both ways and reach a compromise.
Make sure the horizontal seam line is straight and at the same level back and front.
If the seam is not level, adjust as follows:
Provided the general hang of the dress is good, just lift or lower the seam line as required, remembering that you must let out from one side of the seam what you take in from the other, otherwise you will upset the hang of the dress.
If the hang of the dress is wrong, go through all the fitting stages of the basic dress in Dressmaking Chapter 30. Then finally check the horizontal seam and adjust as above if necessary.
Correct all the faults, then tack the garment together again for a final fitting.

Stitching the bodice

Stitch all the darts. Then press the body and shoulder darts towards the centre. The shoulder darts must lie flat, so if the fabric is thick make an open dart; slash along the centre towards the point as far as the scissors will allow, and press open. If the fabric frays, just slash the dart past the shoulder-seam line and press the rest of the dart flat.
Press the side bust darts flat or open.
Stitch the bodice side-seams and press.
If you have fitted the dress closely to the body you will notice that the curve of the side-seam through the waist line has deepened. This makes it difficult for the seam allowance to lie flat after press-ing and, as you turn the garment to the outside, you will see that the side-seam is strained at the top and bottom.
To enable the seam allowance to follow the contours of the seam, snip into the deepest part of the curve, to within 6mm of the stitching (figure 2).
To stop the points of the snipped seam allowance curling, round them off (figure 3), then oversew them carefully to prevent fraying which would weaken the seam at this point.
Neaten all stitched seam edges.
Do not stitch the shoulder-seams yet.

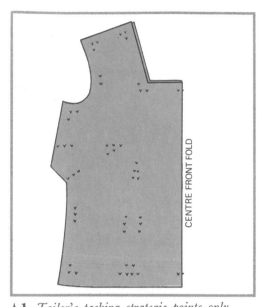

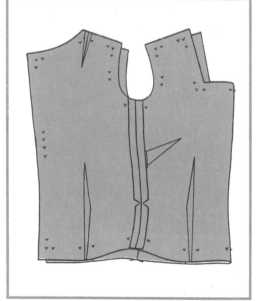

▲ 1. *Tailor's tacking strategic points only*
▼ 2. *Snipping the bodice side-seam at the waist*

The evening pinafore has soft, clinging lines ▶
▼ 3. *The snip at the waist, curved and neatened*

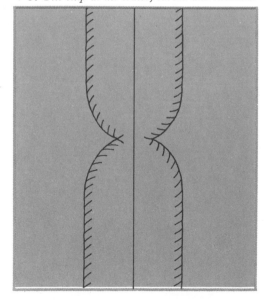

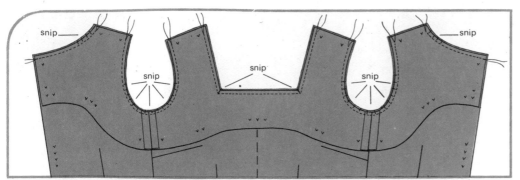

4. *The all-in-one facing stitched in place round the neck and armholes*

5. *The shoulder-seam stitched with facing open*

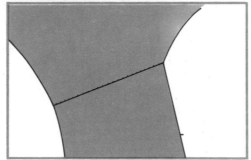

6. *The hand-sewn shoulder-seam on the facing*

The lining

If you are lining the dress it is time to make up the lining for the bodice.

Cut out the lining as for the dress but without facings.

Stitch the darts and seams as for the dress, leaving the shoulder-seams open. Press and neaten the seams.

Pin and tack the lining to the bodice, with wrong sides facing. See that the raw neck and armhole edges are level and that centres and seams coincide.

The lining seams should face the wrong side of the dress, and dress and lining fabric are used as one when the facings are attached.

The facings

Stitch the facings together in the side-seams, leaving the shoulder-seams unstitched. Press the side-seams open and neaten the lower raw edge.

With right sides facing, pin and tack the facing to the dress, matching seams and centres carefully.

Stitch the facing to the dress (figure 4) round the neck line and armholes. At the shoulders, stop stitching at the point where the stitching line meets the shoulder-seam, as shown. Fasten off the threads securely. Do not stitch the shoulder-seams yet.

Trim and snip the seam allowance where shown and turn the facing to the inside. Tack along all stitched edges and press.

With right sides facing, pin and tack the shoulder-seams of the dress only (figure 5), paying special attention to the ends of each seam. These must coincide absolutely or you will have a step where one side only

projects when the seams are finished.

Stitch and press the shoulder-seams open and work the allowance under the facing. Trim the shoulder seam allowance on the facing to 9mm and fold it under, so that the edges almost meet over the dress shoulder-seam (figure 6).

Slip stitch them together by hand and press.

The pocket flaps

To break the length of the horizontal seam, you may like to make pocket flaps as shown in the day length version of the pinafore. These are entirely optional and only serve to decorate, so you need not apply tailoring techniques.

To make a pocket flap, cut a strip of fabric from the remnants 16·3cm long by 10cm wide. Fold it lengthwise, right sides facing, and stitch 6mm seams across both ends (figure 7).

Turn to the right side, edge-tack and press. Topstitch around the outside edges, to match the topstitching you will be making on the dress.

Pin and tack the flaps to the horizontal bodice seam line, 7cm to each side of the Centre Front line, taking only 13mm seam allowance on the flaps (figure 8).

Making up the skirt

Stitch the skirt seams, remembering to leave the opening for the zip in the Centre Back. Press seams open and neaten them. Pin, tack and stitch the skirt to the bodice along the horizontal seam line, matching centres and side-seams. If you are lining the dress don't catch the lining into the seam. Press the seam open.

Topstitching

Measure out the distance of the topstitching from the seam line along the horizontal and Centre Front-seams (figure 9).

Then, using buttonhole twist, start topstitching the horizontal seam on the skirt from the right Centre Back to the Centre Front. Pivot the work on the needle when you have reached the corner of the 'T' shape at the front, and continue stitching down the Centre Front-seam towards the hem.

Topstitch the left side of the skirt, but this time start stitching from the hem, to the left of the Centre Front-seam.

To topstitch the bodice, work from the left side of the Centre Back towards the right side. Where the fabric is especially thick, such as over the seam allowance of the pocket flaps, pause before you stitch over the extra thickness and ease the pressure foot on to the work.

Finishing: zip, lining and hem

The unlined dress. Insert the zip into the Centre Back opening, starting 13mm down from the neck edge and using the lap over method as in Skirtmaking Chapter 13, p41.

To finish the neck edge, fold under the raw edge of the facing and place the fold over the zip tape but leave it clear of the teeth. Hand-sew it firmly to the tape and press. Stitch a No.1 hook and work a bar on the neck edge to hold it together.

Neaten all raw edges and make the hem.

7. *The pocket flap folded and stitched*

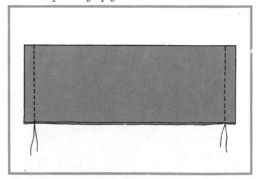

8. *The topstitched pocket flap in position*

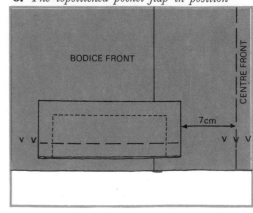

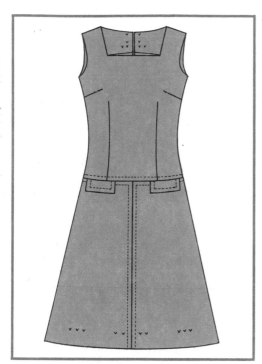

9. The topstitching lines on skirt and bodice

The lined dress. Before you insert the zip, cut the lining along the neck edge just inside the stitching so that the seam allowance on the Centre Back opening and facing can be folded back free of the lining.

Insert the zip, leaving the lining free. Start the zip 13mm down from the neck edge and use the lap over method as in Skirtmaking Chapter 13.

Make up the skirt lining as for the top skirt, but without topstitching. Join it to the bodice lining along the horizontal seam line and press both seam allowances up into the bodice.

Neaten the raw edges and make the hem on both dress and lining.

Fold the Centre Back seam allowance on the lining over the zip tape and sew it down by hand. Then fold under the raw edge of the facing and place the fold over the zip tape, clear of the teeth. Hand-sew it firmly to the tape and press. Stitch a No.1 hook and work a bar on the neck edge to hold it together.

Both versions. Give the dress a final pressing and, when pressing the topstitching, lay it over a double blanket to preserve the roundness of the stitches made in buttonhole twist, taking care that the edge of the seam allowance does not leave an impression on the outside of the fabric.

Day length pinafore with extra flare

This is worked as the pinafore without extra flare except for the topstitching. Because of the increased flare on the skirt

the top edge is very curved and when the horizontal seam has been pressed open the skirt horizontal seam allowance falls short of the skirt width (figure 10). To enable the seam to lie flat, the seam allowance will have to be snipped and therefore becomes unsuitable for topstitching. If you did topstitch it the snips would show up as dents on the outside.

There are two ways to topstitch this seam.

Method A. After stitching the horizontal seam, press the seam allowance on the skirt and bodice together into the bodice. Trim the seam allowance on the bodice to 3mm less than the width of the topstitching. Tack the seam allowances together to the bodice and just work the topstitching on the bodice.

Method B. Topstitch the skirt before sewing the horizontal seam and underlay the topstitching with strips of soft interfacing cut on the bias.

Decide on the width of the topstitching and measure this distance from the horizontal seam on the skirt. Mark with pins on the right side.

Using the soft interfacing, cut two bias strips a little less than double the width of the topstitching, and the length of the topstitching along the horizontal seam from the Centre Front to the Centre Back. Do not join them.

Lay the strips centrally over the pin line on the inside of the skirt from Centre Back to Centre Front and let them go just under the seam allowance on the Centre Front

10. The snipped horizontal seam on the skirt

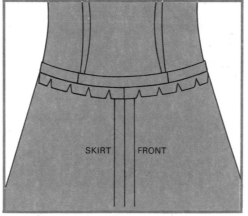

11. Bias strip tacked on skirt for topstitching

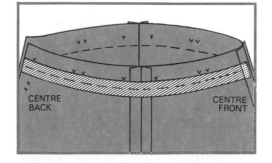

to avoid a dent in the stitching line at this point (figure 11). If the pinafore fabric is thick you should cut each bias strip at the side-seams and slip the ends under the side seam allowances.

Tack each strip to the pin line. Then, using the buttonhole twist, topstitch the skirt over the tacking line. Starting from the right Centre Back to the Centre Front. Pivot the work on the needle when you have reached the corner of the 'T' shape at the front, and continue the stitching down the Centre Front-seam towards the hem.

Topstitch the left side of the skirt, but this time start stitching from the hem, to the left of the Centre Front-seam.

Join the skirt and top. Trim the horizontal seam allowance on the skirt to 13mm, snip into the seam allowance on the skirt until it lies flat and press (figure 10).

Neaten the raw seam edges and lightly stitch the seam allowance on the skirt to the underlay of the topstitching.

Topstitch on the bodice as for the day length pinafore without extra flare.

The evening pinafore

The pinafore is ideal for evening wear. With its clever cut and subtle fit it will be a firm favourite and a very easy dress to wear.

To achieve the right look—which is soft, long, and moulds to the figure—use one of the fabrics recommended in Dressmaking Chapter 32, pl27.

When using soft fabrics, especially jersey, use as little darting as possible. Slant the side bust darts as shown in Dressmaking Chapter 32, and take any surplus fabric into the side-seams and the Centre Back-seam. This way you will avoid having to use body darts in the Front and the Back. Also flare the skirt as shown in the previous chapter.

When marking the pattern details, mark the stitching lines of the new dart on the fabric through small slits made through the pattern.

When fitting you can easily alter the slope of the dart if it is wrong—remember to make any necessary changes to the dart on the pattern for future use.

Making up and topstitching

Follow the same making-up procedure as for the day length pinafore without extra flare, remembering to press the slanting side bust darts open and to omit the body darts.

Also, if you wish to topstitch the skirt, follow the topstitching instructions for the skirt with extra flare.

Chapter 34

The shirt dress story

The shirt dress is a fashion classic. It's a style which has stayed the course through many fashion changes and which reappears, season after season, in new shapes and forms. Fabric, colour and detailing all combine to give the impression of variety although the basic style remains the same. Take as an example the styles illustrated here. They are all simple variations of the shirt dress but each has a totally different look and you can make them all from our Basic Graph Patterns.

Instructions for four of these conversions start in this chapter. They are: A. the button-through shirt dress with shirt collar and cuffs; B. the shirt dress with collar band finish; C. the evening shirt dress with tab fastening and D. the shirt dress with full, bishop sleeves.

Although the making up instructions deal specifically with these conversions, all the details are interchangeable and can be combined with garments from previous chapters to give you the full range of styles featured here. You can apply some of the techniques to commercial paper patterns as well.

So you see, all you need is a basic set of patterns, a lively fashion sense, and the field is yours!

Suitable fabrics

There simply isn't a fabric which has not been used to make the shirt dress. You can make it in a light-weight jersey or a crisp cotton for summer, warmer and heavier fabrics for winter, and more sophisticated fabrics for cocktail or evening wear.

Here is a list to assist your choice:

For summer wear: broderie Anglaise; gingham; cotton, and man-made fibre mixtures; cotton jersey.

For winter wear: most fine woollen dress-weight fabrics; cotton and wool mixtures such as Viyella; wool jersey; man-made fibre jerseys; fine tweeds.

For evening wear: all types of fine or medium-weight silks; voile; organdie; brocade and embroidered fabrics; some firm crepes.

Ideas and variations

Four conversions are given in detail. These have been selected because they entail a number of pattern adaptations, but you need not stop there.

Pockets. Go on by adding pockets to the button-through version. Topstitch the pockets in position and then topstitch the edges of the dress to match.

Sleeves. Another style could be created using the roll cuff short sleeve pattern as in Blousemaking Chapter 24, p88.

Many women like a ¾ length sleeve and this can be made quite easily by shortening the long shirt sleeve. But don't forget to make the cuffs larger as they have to encircle a larger part of the arm. If you want to link button the cuffs for ¾ length sleeves it is best to make the links with hat elastic so that they will not sit too tight.

B.   A.

From left to right:
conversion B.
Shirt dress with
collar band finish

Conversion A.
Button-through
shirt dress with
shirt collar and
cuffs

Straight-cut shirt
dress with shirt
collar, patch
pockets and
topstitching

Tunic-style dress
with tab fastening
and roll cuff short
sleeves over basic
trousers

Conversion D.
Shirt dress with
full bishop sleeves

Evening shirt
dress with head
embroided collar
and cuffs

Collarless shirt
dress with bishop
sleeves and
rouleau loop
fastening over
trousers

Conversion C.
Sleeveless evening
shirt dress with
tab fastening and
topstitching

D.

C.

The straight shirt dress. This is another version you can make. Just straighten the side-seams from the hip line down and do away with the flare. But remember that the hem line will be tighter and the buttons on the button-through version will have to bear a lot more strain.

Embroidery and beads. To decorate a plain silk shirt dress for evening wear, embroider the collar and cuffs with beads and paillettes. Choose the plastic variety which are light and will not make the collar points flop.

Belts. Belts too can make a change, but avoid the stiff and tightly buckled ones. They are meant to be worn over fitted waists and a dress cut without a waist-seam would ruckle up under them.

A. The button-through shirt dress

This conversion has a buttoned through front, a shirt collar and shirt sleeves.

The pattern
You will need the following pattern pieces from the Golden Hands Graph Pages.
From the Dress Graph Pattern, the Front and Back pattern pieces, numbers 1 and 2. From the Accessories Graph Pattern, the long shirt sleeve, shirt collar, collar band and cuff pattern pieces, numbers 8, 10, 11 and 12.

The Front. To adapt the pattern for the button-through dress first make a new pattern.
Pin the Front pattern piece securely on a piece of paper with the Centre Front 2·5cm from the straight edge of the paper. Draw round the edges with a pencil and extend the hem and neck lines to the edge of the paper.
The 2·5cm margin between the pattern and paper edge on the new pattern is the Centre Front wrap for the button fastening (figure 1).
Cut out the new Front pattern.
Space out the positions for the eleven buttonholes on the Centre Front line of the new Front pattern as shown in figure 1.
You will have one buttonhole in the collar band, so allow equal spacing between the first buttonhole on the dress Front and that on the collar band.
Leave a complete buttonhole distance between the hem line and the last button and do not try to work a buttonhole through the turned up hem.

The front facing. Copy the neck, shoulder and front edges of the Front pattern and measure out the front facing as shown (figure 1). The facing is 10cm wide along the Front and hem edge and 5cm wide at

the shoulder line.
Cut out the front facing pattern.

Fabric requirements
140cm width. Without one way—sizes 82cm, 87cm and 90cm, 2·40 metres; size 96cm, 2·65 metres; sizes 102cm and 107cm, 2·90 metres.
140cm width. With one way—size 82cm, 2·40 metres; size 87cm, 2·55 metres; size 90cm, 2·90 metres, sizes 96cm, 102cm and 107cm, 3 metres.
90cm width. Without one way—size 82cm, 3·70 metres; size 87cm, 3·80 metres; size 90cm, 4 metres; size 96cm, 102cm and 107cm, 4·15 metres.
90cm width. With one way—size 82cm, 3·70 metres; size 87cm, 3·90 metres; size 90cm, 4 metres; size 96cm, 4·15 metres; sizes 102cm and 107cm, 4·60 metres.

Notions
You will need:
- [ ] 14 small buttons (2 extra for link buttoned cuffs)
- [ ] Matching thread
- [ ] Interfacing (see below), the length of the shoulder to hem plus 19mm seam allowance

Hints on interfacing
Unlike the shirt blouse, the Centre Front edge of the dress needs interfacing.
The best type to use is a soft pre-shrunk cotton lawn. It is available in different colours so choose one to match the fabric you are using, this will stop the interfacing creating shading through the top fabric.
If you want to make the dress in a sheer fabric and have a good specialist shop near you, you may be able to obtain pure silk organza for an interfacing. This is so colourless that it can be used for most sheer fabrics. Otherwise ask at the store for the right kind of interfacing for your particular fabric.
If you find that the interfacing shows through and changes the colour of the fabric it is best to leave it out, provided the fabric has enough substance to support itself. If it hasn't, don't use that particular fabric to make the shirt dress.
It is always best to buy and try fabric and interfacing at the same time, before you are committed to an unsuitable fabric.

Lining the shirt dress
Lining the button-through shirt dress is not easy or advisable, even if the fabric is mounted straight on to the lining. In washable dresses a lining makes ironing very difficult. You also lose the shirt-like feel of the fabric and it becomes bulky.

Cutting and marking
Choose the appropriate layout for your style, size and fabric width from the layouts

included in this chapter.
Fold the fabric as shown on the layout. If you are working on a large area of a light-weight fabric, pin the selvedges and fold lightly. This will prevent the fabric rolling out of the correct fold, which could result in your cutting the sides unevenly without even noticing it.
Note: the collar and collar band are cut in the same grain of the fabric.
Remember, the pattern has no hem or seam allowance, so add 19mm for seams all round and 6·3cm for the hem.
Cut out the dress, mark the pattern details and remove the pattern pieces.
Cut out the Front, collar, collar band and cuff interfacings as you need them.

Fitting
Tack the dress, including sleeves and cuffs, together for fitting and make any necessary alterations.
For the fitting it is best to tack the Centre Front seam from hip level to hem.

Making up the Centre Fronts
Having ascertained the correct length of the dress when fitting cut out two front interfacing pieces using the front facing pattern. You will not need seam allowances along the inner edge or a hem allowance. Pin the interfacing to the inside of both dress Fronts.
Tack in position with two rows of tacking stitches: the first just outside the seam lines, and the second about 19mm in from the inner edge so that you can work on it later.
Pin and tack the facings to the right side of the dress.
Stitch in place along the seam lines of the Front wrap: that is from the neck edge down to the hem.
Layer the seam allowance by trimming as follows: trim the interfacing to 3mm, the facing to 6mm and the dress Front to 13mm.
Turn the facings to the wrong side. Edge-tack and press lightly.
Lay out the dress Fronts wrong side up. Pin and tack the loose inner edges of the facings to the dress about 2·5cm from the edge, so that the interfacing edge is accessible.
Tack the facing to the dress along the neck line.
Neaten the inner raw edge of the facing and stitch the interfacing to it with long running stitches. To do this start the stitches about 25cm above the hem line, work towards the shoulder-seam and then across, towards the neck line, so that the interfacing is firmly caught in position and so that it cannot roll or crumple during wear.

Darts and seams

Stitch the Front and Back darts and press them according to the fabric.

Pin, tack and stitch the shoulder and side-seams. Neaten the seam allowances and press seams open.

Turn under the seam allowance on the shoulder line of each Front facing and lightly hand sew it to the shoulder-seam.

The collar

Following the collar instructions for the shirt in Blousemaking Chapter 26, cut out the interfacings for the collar and collar band.

Then make up the collar and band and stitch it to the dress.

The sleeves

Again, following the shirt instructions (Blousemaking Chapters 26 and 27) cut out the cuff interfacing, make up the cuffs and make the sleeve openings. Or, if you are working on a fine fabric, make the sleeve openings as shown for the tie-neck blouse in Blousemaking Chapter 28, p111. Pleat or gather the sleeve edge and attach the cuffs.

Make the buttonholes in the cuffs now, because the weight of the garment after the sleeves have been set in can be very irritating when making small buttonholes, even though the weight is supported.

Pin, tack and stitch the finished sleeves into the armholes. Trim and neaten the armhole-seams then press them into the sleeves.

Hem, Front buttonholes and finishing

Pin and tack the hem, leaving the interfacing inside the hem. Fold in the ends of the facing over the hem and sew it down by hand (figure 3). Sew the hem, making quite sure that the seam allowance on the Front edge is turned towards the facing in the hem (figure 2), otherwise you will have a thick ridge on the outside which will force the seam to roll outwards when it is supposed to remain hidden just behind the edge of the wrap.

Check the button positions in case you had to alter the length of the dress, and then make the buttonholes by hand or machine. Sew on the buttons and give the dress a final press.

Make a tie belt from the remnants to match.

B. Shirt dress with collar band finish

The neck line is the main feature of this conversion where the collar band has been used on its own without the collar. Apart

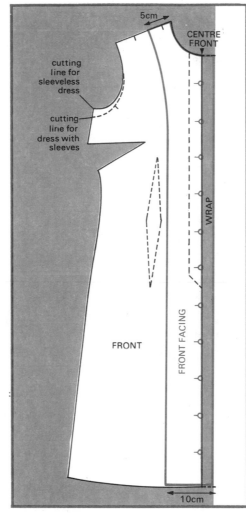

from this detail it is made with a buttoned through front and shirt sleeves as for conversion A.

The dress will look particularly attractive if the collar band and cuffs are made in a contrasting colour to the rest of the dress.

The fabric

The fabric used should be quite firm as soft fabrics would roll and the shape of the collar band would be lost.

The pattern

You will need all the pattern pieces for conversion A except the shirt collar, number 10. Also adapt the pattern as for A.

Collar band. You can make the ends square or rounded. But remember that the square ends need two small buttons for fastening to stop the corner falling down.

Fabric requirements

140cm width. Without one way—sizes 82cm, 87cm and 90cm, 2·40 metres; size 96cm, 2·65 metres; sizes 102cm and 107cm, 2.75 metres.

140cm width. With one way—size 82cm, 2·40 metres; size 87cm, 2·55 metres; size 90cm, 2·90 metres; sizes 96cm, 102cm and 107cm, 3 metres.

90cm width. Without one way—sizes

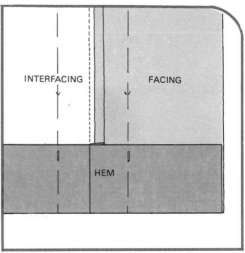

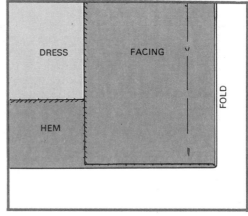

▲ *2. Seam allowance turned towards facing in hem*
◄ *1. Adapting the pattern for the shirt dress*
▼ *3. Front facing folded and sewn over the hem*

82cm and 87cm, 3·35 metres; sizes 90cm and 96cm, 3·45 metres; sizes 102cm and 107cm, 4 metres.

90cm width. With one way—sizes 82cm and 87cm, 3·35 metres; sizes 90cm and 96cm, 3·45 metres; sizes 102cm and 107cm, 4·15 metres.

Notions

As for conversion A.

Cutting out, marking and fitting

Choose the correct layout for your style, size and fabric width from the layouts in this chapter.

Cut out, mark up and fit the dress as for conversion A.

How to make the collar band

For this finish the collar band is worked in reverse to the one which you attach to a collar (see Blousemaking Chapter 26).

Here you interface the outer, not inner, section of the collar band, and, with right sides facing, stitch the outer collar band to the neck line and then hand-sew the inner section, or collar facing, to the seam line inside.

Making up and finishing

Apart from the neck finish the dress is made up exactly as for conversion A.

Layouts for the shirt dress: Conversion A

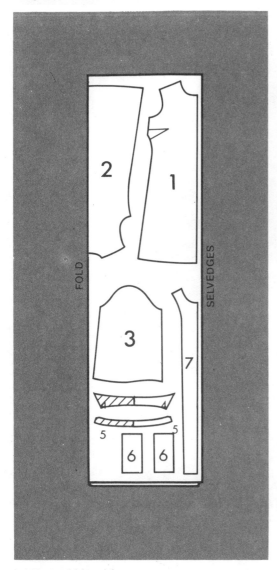

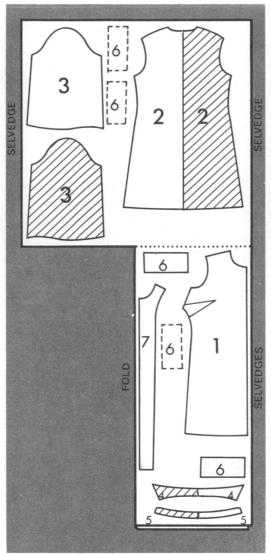

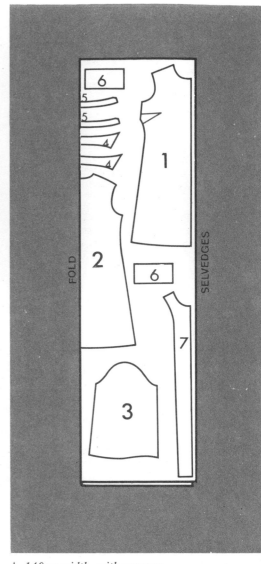

▲ 140cm width, without one way,
sizes 82cm, 87cm, 90cm & 96cm

▲ 140cm width, with and without one way,
sizes 102cm & 107cm

▲ 140cm width, with one way,
sizes 82cm, 87cm, 90cm & 96cm

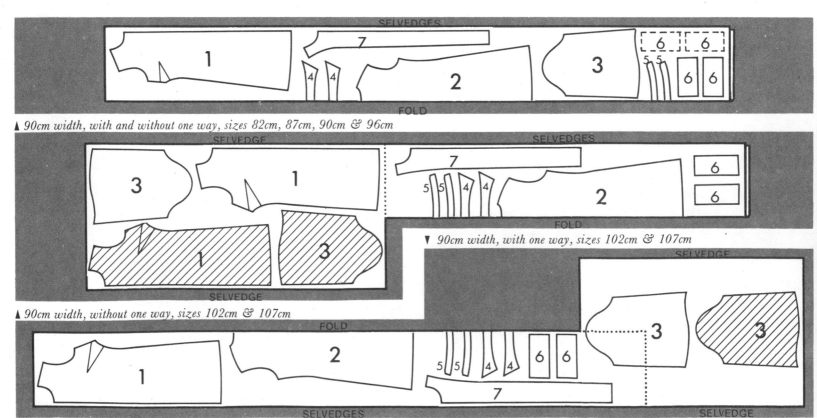

▲ 90cm width, with and without one way, sizes 82cm, 87cm, 90cm & 96cm

▼ 90cm width, with one way, sizes 102cm & 107cm

▲ 90cm width, without one way, sizes 102cm & 107cm

Conversion B

Key to pattern pieces

Front = 1   Back = 2   Sleeve = 3
Collar = 4   Collar band = 5   Cuff = 6
Front facing = 7

– – –   alternative for without one-way
////   reverse pattern pieces

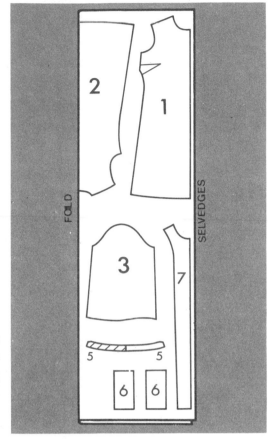

▲ *140cm width, without one way, sizes 82cm, 87cm, 90cm & 96cm*

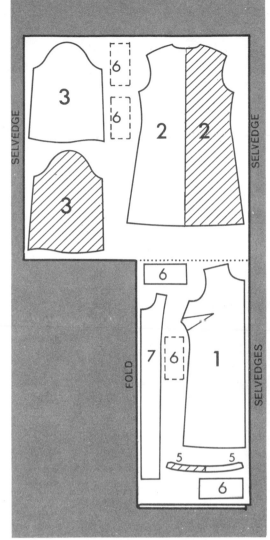

▲ *140cm width, with and without one way, sizes 102cm & 107cm*

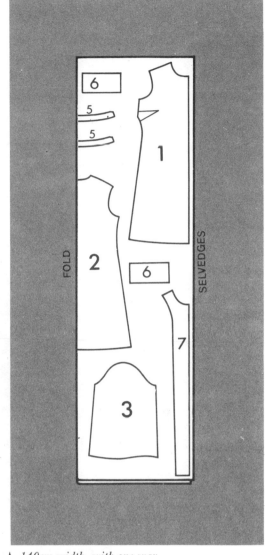

▲ *140cm width, with one way, sizes 82cm, 87cm, 90cm & 96cm*

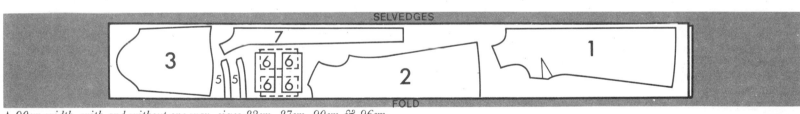

▲ *90cm width, with and without one way, sizes 82cm, 87cm, 90cm & 96cm*

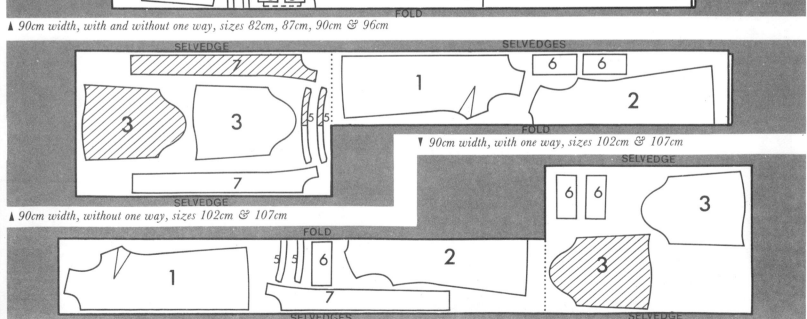

▼ *90cm width, with one way, sizes 102cm & 107cm*

▲ *90cm width, without one way, sizes 102cm & 107cm*

Chapter 35

Evening shirt dress conversion

The shirt dress story, which began in Chapter 34 with instructions for conversion A and B, continues here with this glamorous evening shirt dress, conversion C.

This style is flattering to all age groups and it is easy and comfortable to wear. It can be dressed up for really formal occasions or left plain to make the perfect dinner gown. It travels well, too. Made up in a light, printed silk you have something ideal for holiday wear—a gown in which you can feel both well-dressed and relaxed. This chapter includes the instructions for making this dress with the layouts overleaf. Also included are layouts for conversion D, the shirt dress with full, bishop sleeves. The instructions for converting the pattern and making this sleeve follow in the concluding chapter of this ingenious tale!

C. The evening shirt dress

Suitable fabrics

The fabric used will dictate the mood of this shirt dress. While all those mentioned in the last chapter are quite suitable, this style lends itself particularly well to evening fabrics.

Made sleeveless, in heavy brocade, it becomes a grand gown for formal occasions, but made in a lovely printed hand-woven Indian silk, like the one in the photograph, it becomes the type of garment which can be worn on many occasions. A characteristic of these silks is their slightly creased appearance which complements the casual look of the dress.

The pattern

You will need the following pattern pieces from the Golden Hands Graph Pages.

From the Basic Dress Graph, the Front, Back and tab pattern pieces, numbers 1, 2 and 3.

From the Accessories Graph, the shirt collar and collar band pattern pieces, numbers 10 and 11.

The right Front pattern. For this dress you need both a right Front pattern piece and one for the left Front.

First copy the Front pattern using a sheet of paper which is long enough to include the extra length needed for the evening dress. Place the Centre Front of the pattern to one edge of the paper as shown (figure 1) and draw round the pattern.

Copy the stitching line for the tab.

Measure the extra length you need for the evening dress. Starting at the side-seam measure off this amount from the hem edge with a ruler. Continue doing this along the full width of the hem, so that you retain the original shape of the hem, and draw in the new lines as shown.

Remove the original pattern and cut out the new one along the solid line in figure 1.

The left Front pattern. In Dressmaking Chapter 30 it was mentioned that a conventional wrap would be cut later, and now is the time to do this.

Place the original Front pattern on a large sheet of paper as before, but reversing it and with the Centre Front of the pattern 2·5cm from the straight edge (figure 2).

Draw round the shape of the pattern and extend the length as for the right Front.

Draw in the tab stitching line and connect the pointed end to the straight edge of the paper, drawing a straight line across. Cut out the new pattern along the solid cutting line. The 2·5cm extension above the pointed end of the tab stitching line is the wrap for the front opening.

The Back pattern. Copy the Back pattern piece on a sheet of paper long enough to include the extra length needed for the

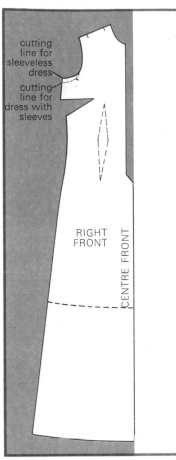

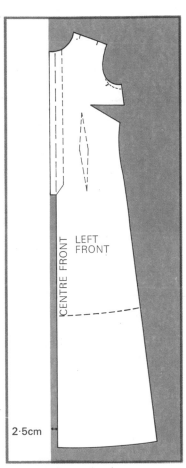

▲ 1. *Right Front showing tab stitching line and length extended*
▼ 3. *Wrap and tab facing,*

▲ 2. *Left Front showing wrap extension and length extended*
▼ 4. *Interfacing inside of wrap*

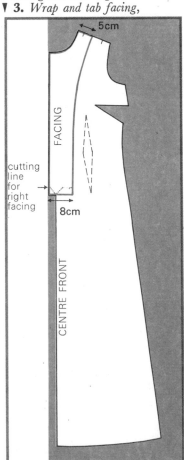

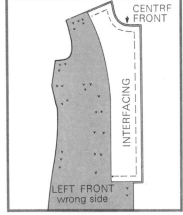

▼ 5. *Topstitching collar and band*

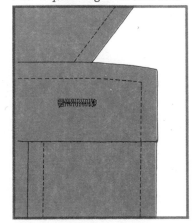

evening dress, then draw in the new hem line as for the Front pattern pieces.

Facing patterns. To make the facing patterns for the tab and wrap, pin the Centre Front of the left pattern piece to the straight edge of a sheet of paper. Draw round the shape of the neck and shoulder lines and mark the lower end of the wrap. Remove the pattern, measure out the width of the facing and complete as shown (figure 3). Cut out the facing pattern.

This outline is for the wrap facing.

For the tab facing outline pin the tab pattern piece to the front edge of the facing pattern and draw the shape of the pointed end, extending it straight to the inner edge as shown (see dotted line figure 3). Use this line when cutting the facing for the tab, but do not cut out along this line yet.

Fabric amounts

120cm width. Without one way—size 82cm, 2·65 metres; size 87cm, 2·75 metres; size 90cm, 2·90 metres; size 96cm, 3·10 metres; size 102cm, 3·35 metres; size 107cm, 3·45 metres.

120cm width. With one way—sizes 82cm, 87cm and 90cm, 3·35 metres; sizes 96cm, 102cm and 107cm, 3·55 metres.

90cm width. Without one way—sizes 82cm and 87cm, 3·70 metres; size 90cm, 3·80 metres; sizes 96cm and 102cm, 4·15 metres; size 107cm, 4·35 metres.

90cm width. With one way—sizes 82cm and 87cm, 3·70 metres; size 90cm, 4·15 metres; size 96cm, 4·25 metres; size 102cm, 4·35 metres; size 107cm, 4·50 metres.

Notions

You will need:
- [ ] 6 small buttons
- [ ] Matching thread
- [ ] Interfacing, the length of the front facing plus 3·8cm for seam allowance, or interlining (see below)

Interlinings and interfacings

If you want to line this dress do so with a fully mounted interlining chosen to complement the fabric of the dress, such as a jap silk lining for pure silks and fine rayon taffeta for brocades. The interlining is cut out the same as the dress fabric, using the layout and amount for the 90cm width without one way. It is then tacked to the fabric and used as one. This way you will not need an interfacing. If you prefer not to interline the dress you will need interfacing for the tab, wrap, collar and collar band. See the previous chapter for suitable interfacings.

Cutting and marking

To cut out the evening shirt dress you will need a really large area to work on since the full length of the dress is cut in one.

Choose the correct layout for your style, size and fabric width from the layouts overleaf. Lay up the fabric carefully, pinning the selvedges and folds to make sure that they cannot move.

The pattern has no seam or hem allowances, so mark 19mm for seams and 6·3cm for hems all round.

Cut both tab and wrap facings together, using the wrap facing pattern piece. The tab facing will be trimmed to shape later.

Note that the shirt collar and collar band are cut in the same grain of the fabric.

Cut two bias strips 3·8cm wide for the armhole facings, joining the strips to make up the required length if necessary.

Trim the wrap facing pattern piece along the dotted line for the tab facing then trim one of the facings for the tab, similarly—don't forget to add the seam allowance.

Mounting the fabric

If you are mounting the dress cut out the interlining as for the dress and tack it to the wrong side of each dress piece.

Interfacing

If you are not lining the dress, cut one collar, one collar band, one tab and one wrap facing piece from interfacing, adding seam allowance on all edges except the inner edge of the wrap facing.

Tack the corresponding interfacing pieces to the wrong side of the top collar and outer collar band sections, and the tab. Also tack the wrap interfacing to the inside of the wrap (see figure 4) on the left Front.

Stitching the Front fastening

Since it is not possible to pin the Centre Front at the top of the dress for fitting, it is best to make up the Front fastening detail before you fit. It is quite safe to do so as there will be no alteration to this particular area.

Make up the tab as you did for the basic dress in Dressmaking Chapters 30 and 31, using the front facing with the shaped end to face the tab. Do not stitch the tab and facing together along the neck edge — this remains open to take the collar band.

To avoid thick seam edges on the tab, trim the seam allowance of the interfacing to 3mm if you are using it.

Stitch the Centre Front of the dress from the pointed end of the tab stitching line to the hem. Neaten the seam and press open. Stitch on the tab and finish the pointed end inside as for the basic dress but do not fold and sew the inner facing edge to the stitching line.

Topstitch the tab 6mm from the edges.

Face the left Front of the dress with the straight ended facing. Do not stitch along the neck edge. It is not necessary to stitch across the lower end of the wrap; this often creates an unwanted thickness and it is best left open.

Trim the interfacing seam allowance to 3mm if you are using it. Finish the wrap end inside as for the basic dress but do not fold and sew the wrap facing down on the inner edge.

If you have used interfacing on the wrap, attach the inner edges to the facing with loose herringbone stitches.

Oversew the inner edges to neaten.

Fitting and finishing the dress

Tack and fit the evening dress making any necessary adjustments. Stitch the darts and seams, and finish the armhole and hem edges as for the basic dress, Dressmaking Chapters 30 and 31.

Interface collar and band (if necessary), make up, then stitch to the dress following the instructions in Blousemaking Chapter 26.

Topstitch the collar and collar band to match the tab (figure 5).

Make buttonholes and sew on the buttons to finish.

Finishes with mounted interlinings

After stitching and pressing the seams open, carefully trim the seam allowance and oversew by hand to neaten. Avoid machine finishes in any way since they tend to curl the two layers of fabric, so creating a thick and hard seam edge; this in turn makes an impression through the fabric, often showing up quite definitely on the outside.

Facings should be caught lightly to seam lines and not be firmly sewn in place. So work under the facing edge and hand-sew loosely.

To stop the interlining folding up inside the hem it is necessary to prick stitch fabric and lining together just below the hem line before the hem is turned up and finished (for prick stitch see Generally Speaking Chapter 9).

When sewing the inner edge of hems and bias facings to the mounted dress make sure that you do not sew through to the outside fabric, but only catch the interlining fabric to give the outside a smooth finish.

If you follow all the instructions given for making bias facings and sewing hems they will be quite safe and will not roll out.

Layouts for the shirt dress: Conversion C

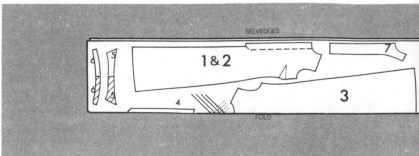

▲ *120cm width, without one way, sizes 82, 87, 90, 96, 102 & 107cm*
▼ *120cm width, with one way, sizes 82, 87, 90, 96, 102 & 107cm*

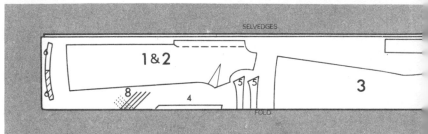

▼ *90cm width, with and without one way, sizes 82cm & 87cm*

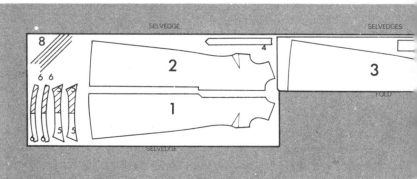

▼ *90cm width, without one way, sizes 90cm, 96cm, 102cm & 107cm*

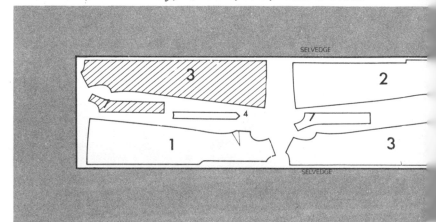

▼ *90cm width, with one way, sizes 90cm, 96cm, 102cm & 107cm*

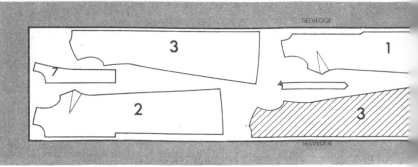

Conversion D

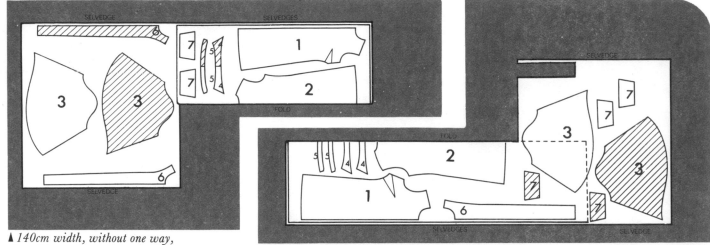

▲ *140cm width, without one way,*
sizes 82cm, 87cm, 90cm & 96cm

▲ *140cm width, without one way, sizes 102cm & 107cm*
▼ *140cm width, with one way, sizes 82cm & 87cm*

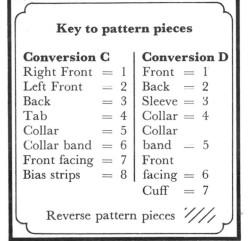

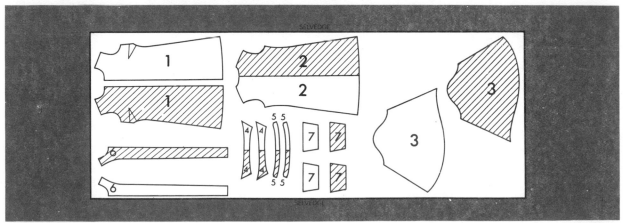

▼ *140cm width, with one way, sizes 90cm, 96cm, 102cm & 107cm*

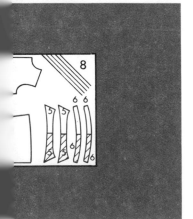

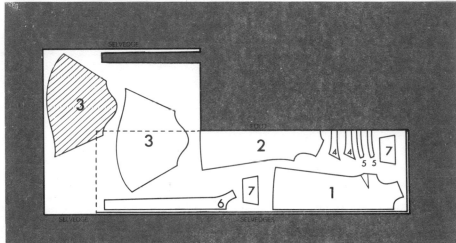

▼ *90cm width, with and without one way, sizes 82cm, 87cm, 90cm, 96cm, 102cm & 107cm*

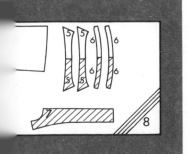

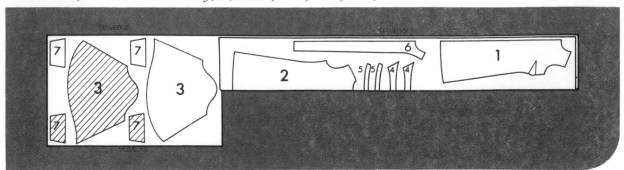

Chapter 36
The tailored jersey look

Dresses made up in jersey are most comfortable, easy to wear, allow one to move with complete freedom and, if made from a man-made fibre jersey, are also extremely practical as they wash well—many of the man-made jerseys do not even need an iron to smooth them out after washing. In addition, some of the double knits, such as Crimplene, are so hard wearing that they are almost indestructible and stay looking new after many, many washes.

This chapter gives hints on sewing jersey and how to fit garments made in this fabric. Because jersey has natural stretch, the fitting is a most important feature.

The dress illustrated here, with its smooth lines and long fitted sleeves, is an ideal style for jersey, which in this particular case is a double knit pure wool jersey with a fine, stocking stitch surface. This jersey handles very well in making up.

The dress is an adaptation of the Basic Dress Graph Pattern which is on pages 112 and 113 and you can make it from the instructions given in this chapter. These are special fitting and making up instructions for garments made up in jersey, and you will find them invaluable for other styles too.

Details of the dress include a loose lining which is stitched into the neck line with the facing and into the armhole-seams. Since there is a natural give in jersey the long, fitted sleeves can be fitted really closely and then finished with a zip opening at each wrist edge.

About jersey

Types of jersey knits

Jersey fabrics are made in a variety of textures. Starting with the plain, printed or jacquard jerseys there is the honeycomb finish and the stocking stitch finish. Generally the honeycomb surface is found on the heavier and coarser jerseys and the stocking stitch surface on the finer ones. But both finishes come in double or single knits.

Then there are jerseys with a raised surface pattern resembling a cloque. These are usually in man-made fabrics where the resilience of the fibre helps to retain the pattern shape on the surface. These are found mostly in double knits.

Added to the difference in texture is the fact that jerseys are now made in many different fibres, both natural and man-made. You will find that each jersey has different characteristics, so that when shopping for a jersey fabric you will have to bear in mind the style of the garment you are making. Once it could be assumed that jerseys only lent themselves to a particular style; this is no longer so and jerseys can be used for tailored designs as well as for the more moulded, draped or figure hugging ones. So choose the correct texture for the style you want to make.

At the time of purchase find out whether the fabric should be washed or dry cleaned.

The tailored jersey look

Although all jersey will mould well to the figure the heavier ones are most successfully used for really tailored and sculptured styles. They give you freedom of movement and a crisp looking garment without bulk, and contrary to what you may expect it does not take a clever dressmaker to combine all these qualities in one garment.

Stitching jersey

As jersey fabric spreads when under pressure, reduce the pressure on the presser foot of the machine.

Use the finest needle size you can on the machine and a thickness of thread to suit the needle size.

To stitch the seams engage the smallest zigzag stitch setting plus a stitch length setting of 12 to 14 stitches per 2·5cm. Then, as you are stitching, very gently stretch the seams to give the maximum elasticity to the zigzag stitches.

Seams which have to bear a lot of strain, such as the Centre Back and armhole-seams, should be stitched over twice.

If the machine is missing stitches as you stitch the seams, and this often happens when stitching jersey, it usually means that the combination of needle and thread is wrong. However, if your machine is very light, it may mean that the fabric is too heavy for the machine to cope with.

Curved seams in jersey

The curved seams in jersey do not usually need snipping if the seam allowance is narrow, that is 13mm to 19mm. But if you should have found a fabric which rolls and does not mould easily, then snip the seam allowance to not less than 6mm from the stitching line.

Finishing raw edges in jersey

Although the inside of a dress looks more finished when the raw edges of the seam allowances are neatened it is not necessary to neaten jersey because it does not fray. But if you want to apply a seam edge finish, make sure it is very flat and does not create a thick ridge which would make an impression through the fabric to the outside of the garment.

Zips in jersey

When inserting a zip into the Centre Back of a jersey dress make the opening 2·5cm longer than the zip, to allow for the 13mm distance from neck stitching line and 13mm for ease. If you find that the opening has dropped when you come to insert the zip it will be quite safe to ease in the surplus.

With some jerseys you may have to pin in the zip and hold the dress up to see if the fabric drops away in folds. If it does keep repinning until the folds have disappeared. It does not help to tape the opening as you will still have the same problem.

Fortunately most double jerseys will take a zip without any problems at all.

Fitting

Jersey fabrics need special and careful fitting and it is well while reading the fitting instructions for the jersey conversion even if you don't intend to make this particular garment.

The dress pattern, amount, notions

The pattern pieces

For this dress you need five pattern pieces: the Front, Back, long fitted sleeve, front neck facing and back neck facing.

Front and Back patterns. Copy the Front and Back pattern pieces from the Basic Dress Graph Pattern on pages 112 and 113, numbers 1 and 2, incorporating any correction you may have made previously for figure faults. Do not cut them out yet.

The dress is made up with a Centre Back opening and a Centre Front seam, so mark both for seaming.

As with all jersey fabrics avoid as much darting as possible and do not use the body darts. Although the dress is semi-fitted the ease is taken into the seams and the side bust darts instead.

The Centre Front and Centre Back seams are slightly curved through the waist line (figure 1 and 2). So first mark in your waist line on the Front and Back pattern pieces and then curve the centre seams as follows.

For the Front, measure 9mm from the Centre Front at the waist line and taper into the original Centre Front top and bottom (figure 1). Curve the Centre Back similarly but measure in 19mm at the waist line (figure 2).

Slant the side bust dart on the dress Front downwards by 3·8cm at the outer end, leaving the point of the dart where it is (figure 1). This will help to take in some of the fullness at the waist line of the dress.

When you have moved the dart make sure that you compensate on the side-seams as shown, so that the seam lines of the upper and lower stitching lines are the same length.

Do not deepen the dart or curve the waist line at the side-seams yet. This is done more accurately at the fitting stage.

Front and back facing patterns. Using the Front and Back pattern pieces copy the relevant top sections of each (figures 1 and 2) and make the front and back neck facings as shown. They are 5cm wide and should be trimmed shorter at the shoulder by 3mm (figure 3). Mark the Centre Front on the front facing pattern to be cut on the fold.

Sleeve pattern. Use the sleeve pattern piece number 7 from the Accessories Graph on pages 96 and 97.

Cut out all the pattern pieces.

Layouts and fabric amounts

As jersey fabrics are available in 90cm to 180cm widths it is as well to know the width you intend to buy to save you making trial layouts for 90cm, 120cm, 140cm, 150cm and 180cm widths to work out the required amount.

Before you start making a trial layout here are a few points to note. The facings are very small and can be cut from the scraps.

The seam and hem allowances are not included in the Golden Hands Graph Patterns so you will need to add 19mm for seams and 6·3cm for hems.

The hem allowance on the long fitted sleeve should be 6·3cm so that you can adjust the length at the fitting.

If you are using jersey with a heavy drop, such as a rayon jersey, allow plenty of margin between the pattern pieces on the layout since it is advisable to cut slightly wider seam allowances. Garments in these fabrics often require a little more ease because they fall so close to the body.

To start you off on your layout here is a guide for the fabric requirements for 90cm, 120cm and 180cm widths. Measure out the amounts and work from there.

90cm width. For standard sizes start with twice the dress length plus one sleeve length plus hem and seam allowances.

Large sizes may have to be cut on an open layout when it becomes necessary to add one more dress length for safety.

120cm width. For standard sizes start with one dress length plus

The long sleeved dress conversion made in a double knit wool jersey ▶

one sleeve length plus hem and seam allowances.

For large sizes the pattern pieces may have to be staggered and may require up to half a dress length extra.

180cm width. For all sizes one dress length plus hem and seam allowances should be sufficient.

Lining. Only the Back and Front of the dress are cut from lining fabric, the sleeves are not lined, nor are the facings.

Notions

☐ One 60cm zip for the Centre Back
☐ Two 12cm zips for the sleeves (optional)
☐ One hook, size no. 1
☐ Fine machine needles
☐ Matching thread

Cutting out and marking up

Cut out the jersey fabric adding hem and seam allowances.

Mark up the pattern detail with a fine soft thread, such as a number 50 tacking cotton sold for this purpose, since a sharp thread can cut the jersey stitches, resulting in nasty runs or ladders.

Fitting jersey fabrics

Fitting stages when making a jersey dress are most important. There are three fitting stages. The first is with the body of the dress semi-tacked. The second fitting stage is with the body of the dress completely tacked to include corrections made in the first stage.

The third stage is the final check up with zip, lining and sleeves tacked in position. If at this stage you make any alterations then try it on finally to see that all is well.

Preparing for the first fitting

Pin and tack the shoulder darts if used.

Pin the side bust darts but do not tack them.

Pin and tack the Centre Front seam, and the Centre Back seam from the end of the opening to the hem.

Pin and tack the shoulder-seams.

Pin the side-seams and tack them from underarm to dart and from waist to hem.

Do not press at this stage, as for other fabrics.

Before you slip on the dress remove the pins from the darts and that section of each side-seam which has not been tacked.

The first fitting

This fitting is best done with the help of two mirrors so that you can see the back as well as the front.

Fit the side bust darts first, by taking the lower dart stitching line and folding it towards the upper dart stitching line. You will then see how much more fabric you can take into the dart to get rid of the fullness above the waist line. Roll the surplus fabric into the dart by rolling the lower dart stitching line under until the front looks smooth (figure 4).

Deepening the darts does not mean that you take any more depth into the ends of the darts where they go into the side-seams (see figure 4), you only do this when you have to pin off a lot of surplus fabric into the side-seams—and this is the next stage.

Now stand relaxed in front of the mirror with both arms beside the body. The area above the waist line should look perfectly smooth without fitting too snugly to the body. There should be no upward drag lines towards the darts. If there are it means that you have taken in the darts too far down the stitching line and they must be let out.

The remaining fullness in the dress must now be pinned off at the

side-seams by deepening the curve through the waist line and over the hips.

Now fit the back of the dress.

If pinning fullness into the side-seams causes the dress to pull into the waist line and towards the sides at the back, unpin some fullness from the side-seams on the dress Back only and deepen the Centre Back seam curve until the back hangs smoothly.

The Centre Back and Centre Front should not, however, be fitted too closely to the figure but should fall into a softly moulding line.

The second fitting

Correct all the fitting faults from the first fitting and mark them on the pattern ready to cut the lining for the third fitting. Then tack the dress as corrected and try it on, making any small alterations that may be necessary.

Preparing for the third fitting

Stitch and press all darts and seams in the dress. The darts should be slashed along the centres and pressed open and the seam allowances reduced to 16mm, or less in the case of the shoulder darts. To obtain a perfect moulding at the points of the side bust darts, press them carefully over the rounded end of a press cushion.

If you wish to neaten the seam edges do so now but omit the shoulder-seam edges.

Press the Centre Back opening seam allowances as fitted and pin and tack in the zip.

Make up the lining as for the dress. The darts are stitched on the outside of the fabric, that is the side of the lining which goes to the body. This will stop the thickness of the darts making an impression on the jersey fabric. The seams are stitched on the inside of the lining as usual.

Neaten the seams of the lining as flat as possible so that they will not show through. Trim the shoulder-seams to 13mm but do not neaten them.

Pin and tack the lining to the dress round the neck line and armhole-seams (figure 5). The lining will be caught into the armhole-seams when the sleeves are stitched in. This secures the shoulder line as in some jerseys fitted sleeves can cause the shoulder-seams to drop.

Pin and tack the sleeve-seams leaving 13cm open at each wrist end for the zip opening if you intend to make the sleeves really fitted.

Pin and tack the sleeves into the armholes.

The third fitting

Slip on the dress and close the zip.

Check the sleeve fitting around the armholes and over the shoulders then fit the sleeves as follows.

Pin the sleeve openings together and fit the sleeves close to the forearm as far as the elbow. If you want to dispense with the zips make each wrist edge just wide enough to enable you to push your hand through.

The upper-arm area of the sleeves should be close fitting but not tight, so move your arms up and down to make sure that the seams will not break. All long fitted sleeves restrain your movement somewhat, even in jersey, but you must sacrifice some freedom for style. Long fitted sleeves must always be made a little longer than other sleeves as they have a tendency to work up on the arms and look too short if made the usual length. The extra length is only needed if you are fitting the sleeves really closely.

Check the length of the dress, and trim the excess hem allowance on the sleeves to make a 2·5cm to 19mm hem.

Finally check the back fitting of the dress once more, especially round the area of the zip. The zip should lie flat and the fabric round it should not bulge nor should it be held in too tightly.

Finishing the dress

Zip and facing. Stitch in the zip.

Stitch the front neck facing to the back neck facing at the shoulder-seams. Trim the seam allowance then pin and tack the facing to the neck edge of the dress, right sides together, pinning the ends of the zip tape out of the way.

Stitch the facing to the dress round the neck edge and trim the seam allowance.

Snip into the seam allowance of the lining at short intervals. The seam allowance of the jersey fabric may also have to be snipped if it does not lie easily. But before deciding to snip the jersey fabric first turn the facing to the inside and edge tack and press it to see how much resistance there is on the seam edge.

Turn in the raw edges of the lining clear of the zip teeth down the Centre Back opening and hand-sew to the zip tape. Then fold in the ends of the back neck facing to clear the zip teeth and sew to the tape.

Sew the facing to the lining with long slip stitches.

Press the top edge of the opening and close with a hand worked bar and a small hook.

Sleeves. Finish the sleeve openings before stitching the sleeves into the armholes. If you are not putting zips in the openings finish the sleeve hems in the usual way. Otherwise stitch in the zips and make up the hems as shown (figure 6), mitring the ends of each hem over the ends of the zip tape as shown.

Finally stitch the sleeves, trim the seam allowance of the armholes and oversew to neaten.

Hem. When finishing the hem use the invisible herringbone stitch as shown in Skirtmaking Chapter 15. This gives extra strength and allows the stitches to give with the fabric.

Turn up the lining hem 2·5cm shorter than the dress and machine stitch or hem in place.

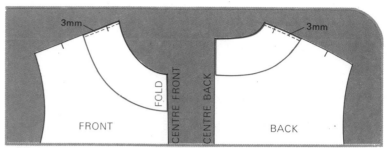

▲ **3.** *The trimmed front and back neck facings*

▼ **4.** *Deepening the side bust dart*

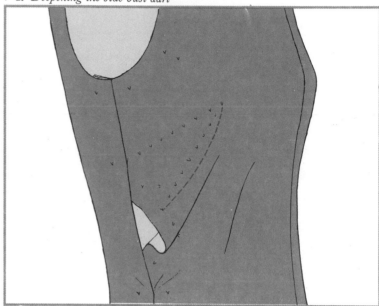

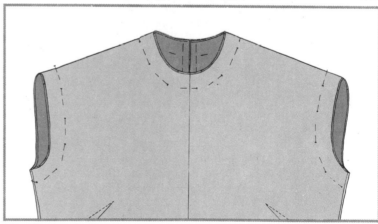

▲ **5.** *Pinning the lining round neck and armholes*

▼ **6.** *The sleeve hem with zip fastening*

▼ **1.** *The dress Front pattern*

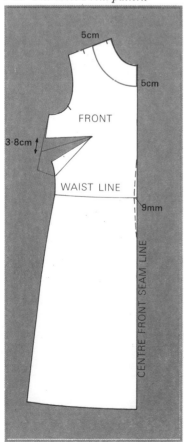

▼ **2.** *The dress Back pattern*

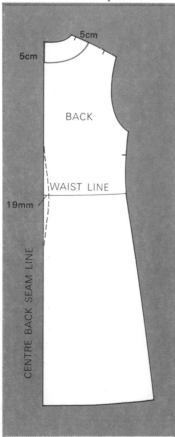

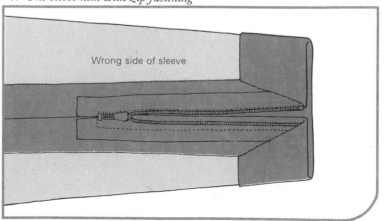

Wrong side of sleeve

Chapter 37

For the fuller figure

Rather unjustly, 'outsize' covers all sizes with hips over 107cm. But most women with fuller figures do not think of themselves as being outsize—with its suggestion of being 'out of the ordinary'—just larger than the sizes usually covered in ready-made clothes and patterns.

If a large figure is your problem, let Golden Hands help you dressmake your way out of it. You can dress just as fashionably as those with slimmer proportions if you take extra care with design, fabric and fitting. So start by finding out which of the groups below describes you best.

Group 1

This is the girl who has grown up with the 'I am different' complex—as long as she can remember people have said 'isn't she a big girl'.

She is usually tall, with good proportions, and moves well. Her bust and hip measurements vary between 107cm and 120cm.

Because of her good proportions clothes look well on her and most styles designed for smaller sizes can be adapted to suit her. She can wear frills or flowing garments and look stunning in them.

If this is your figure type however, you should avoid plain dresses with unbroken seams as they only emphasize a large area by their very monotony. The exception is the 'little black dress', but even that needs to be dressed up so that there is a focal point to break up the area of the dress.

The garments which you need to look at with caution are separates —skirts and blouses, or skirts and jackets. If wrongly proportioned they can look square and boxy, especially in the case of blouses and skirts of contrasting colours. If you wear the tucked-in type of blouse make sure that the skirt waist-band doesn't sit above the normal waist line, creating the impression of a short waist. Instead choose the hidden waist-band which sits just on the waist. Belts, too, can create a short-waisted look, so if you want to wear a belt choose a shaped one which sits lower down than a straight belt. Another point to watch is the fitting of sleeves over the shoulders. Look at yourself in a mirror and make sure that the shoulders do not look wider than the widest point across your hip line. They may, of course, have to be as wide to allow for your shoulder width, but to allow them to look wider will create an impression of largeness.

Group 2

This is the plump child who has grown up into a well-rounded adult, or what is quite often called a motherly type.

She is small and of good proportions with quick movements and her bust and hip measurements are between 107cm and 126cm.

If this is your figure type, the most important point to watch is the line of any garment—it should look narrow. This does not mean that you have to resign yourself to a perpetual straight jacket, but the garments you choose should be made of soft fabrics and any

Group 1: Junoesque type. Big but with good proportions

fullness in them should hang towards the body. Avoid stiff and bulky fabrics and fit your dresses with special care always aiming towards a straight look.

Plain colours are suitable for you but your dresses should be broken with interesting details. Some gathers in the right places can do a lot for your figure type, and so can soft body drapes or good seaming. Simulated fastenings, to avoid the thickness of wraps, can give particular interest and be most flattering.

Choose blouses and skirts in matching colours to give an impression of length. Skirts and jackets need careful proportioning and should be made in the fine woollen fabrics which can be tailored and moulded to the shape of the body.

Never try and hide your figure inside a bulky garment as this will not help to disguise your shape—it will only make you feel self-conscious.

Because your figure is inclined to be short, paper patterns invariably need adjusting so it is especially helpful to follow the toile making instructions given in Toile-making Chapter 22. By making a perfectly fitting bodice toile you will know exactly where to adjust your paper pattern.

Your figure type needs a well fitting shoulder line. Since you are more rounded than the group 1 figure you may have to allow the shoulder line to be wider than the hips. But you can fit the sleeve carefully to take as much of the fullness as possible out of the sleeve crown so that it fits smoothly into the armhole without restricting the sleeve for easy movement.

You should also watch the length of your clothes. Unless fashion dictates a very long look, make sure that the amount of leg showing is in proportion to your height.

Group 2: Motherly type. Well-developed bust and hips

Group 3: Big throughout

Group 3

This group consists of the really outsize figures with bust and hip measurements anything up to 150cm.

Usually this figure type starts as a normal size, even skinny, during childhood but throughout adult life steadily puts on weight. Her movements are slow and large because the bone structure was not made to cope with the extra circumference and weight.

This group is much more difficult to dress because, apart from the outline of the figure, there are problem areas such as bust, stomach and hips.

Plenty of room is needed in garments because freedom of movement is an essential factor for this figure type. Movements such as stooping, bending and even walking often take garments up, so that, if not carefully chosen, they can look very ungainly.

If this is your figure type then garments which allow the style to run into fullness, such as panelled skirts, are a must for you, but all fullness built into the garments should be carefully planned. Otherwise the result will be a voluminous outfit which would only make you appear larger still.

Pleats are not for you because they need to be firmly anchored to the figure to hang properly and in your case, tightly fitting garments should be avoided.

Concentrate on contour seaming over the bust, which allows for good fitting and takes the bulk of fabric out of the bodice, combined with lower neck lines and flat collars to break the width.

One of the main fitting problems is the armholes which have a tendency to be cut too large and this point should always be checked on paper patterns. There is a mistaken idea that the deeper the cut of the armhole the more freedom of movement there

is. Actually there is no extra freedom of movement to be gained from cutting extra deep armholes; they should only be large enough to allow the arm to pass into the sleeve and then sit comfortably around arm and shoulder.

In your figure type there is a tendency for the arms to tilt outwards and not hang straight beside the body. But unless you have wide and square shoulders this outwards curve of the arms means that the distance between the top of the sleeve crown and the underarm is actually shortened. So although you need extra width in your sleeves for the extra circumference of your arms you do not need extra large armholes. Later in this chapter you will be shown how to increase the sleeve size without increasing the size of the sleeve head. Pay particular attention to the length of your dresses and skirts. Walk about and move your arms when fitting to see if the garment hitches up at the back. Unless this is due to some tightness, the only way to deal with the problem is to make the back of the skirt longer than the front, enough for the garment to settle where it wants to and look even during wear.

Here are a few do's and dont's. Avoid bulky or stiff fabrics or fabrics with small all-over prints. Instead choose medium sized prints with all-over designs or, better still, those with up or down directional interest.

Choose plain dark colours with care since they emphasize a large area. A possible exception is silk with a good finish which will create subtle shading to help minimise size.

When you look at fabrics with dull finishes, choose slightly lighter colours which show a colour variation through shading. These help you to look slimmer because the colour will look slightly darker on the sides of the body.

The Golden Hands basic skirt pattern

The basic skirt pattern in Skirtmaking Chapter 10 is suitable for larger sizes: in fact you can make it as large as you like. There are, of course, certain figure problems which should be taken into account when making the pattern which are detailed below.

Making the skirt pattern

First make a basic skirt pattern in your hip size from the Golden Hands graph pattern in Skirtmaking Chapter 10. Ignore your own waist measurement and draw in the corresponding standard waist measurement of the pattern which is 30cm less than the hip measurement.
Cut out the pattern.

Altering the pattern

For a large stomach. You will need to add to the waist measurement and the Centre Front of the Front pattern piece.
First move the dart position on the Front to halfway between the side-seam and the original dart, reduce the width of the dart to 19mm and repin the length of the dart as required (figure 1).
Then lay the pattern piece on a sheet of paper and pin the Centre Front to the straight edge.
Measure the length from your waist line, at the side, to the widest part of your hips or to the top of your thighs, whichever is the wider, and mark off this distance on the pattern side-seam. From this point draw a straight line across the pattern.
Starting at the Centre Front, slash the pattern along this line to within 6mm of the side-seam. Unpin the top half of the cut pattern and make sure the lower half is pinned down securely.
Measure the difference between your waist line and that of the pattern. Then raise the Centre Front of the top part of the pattern until the space between the straight edge of the paper and the original Centre Front measures half the difference of the waist measurements. Pin the top of the pattern down securely.
This may result in a kink in the side-seam. If so, place a ruler to the upper edge of the pattern side-seam and the outer point of the hem and draw a connecting line.
Draw in the new waist line and draw round the rest of the pattern. Cut out the new Front pattern.

For a high seat. Alter the Back pattern piece. Measure the depth from your waist to the highest point of the seat and mark off this distance along the side-seam of the pattern piece.

152

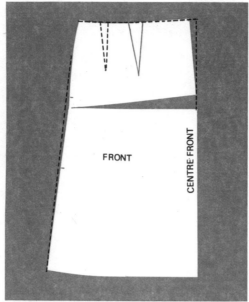

▲ **1.** *Altering the Front skirt for a large stomach*
▼ **2.** *Altering the Back skirt for a high seat*

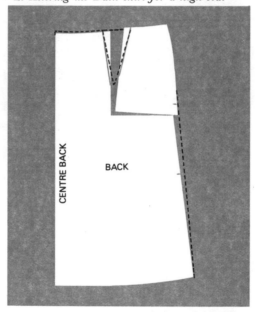

Draw a straight line through the centre of the dart towards the hem (figure 2). Then draw a straight line across the pattern from the mark on the side-seam to meet the line through the dart.
Cut out the upper side section, cutting along the lines as shown in the diagram.

▼ **3.** *Altering sleeve pattern for large upper arm*

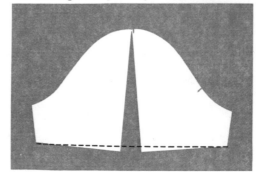

Pin the rest of the pattern securely to a sheet of paper with the Centre Back to a straight edge.
Since the pattern already includes standard ease or tolerance you have only to add extra ease over the seat, so take more depth into the dart and lengthen the Centre Back a little.
To do this, move the cut out section of the pattern outwards for 13mm and then tilt it up 13mm as shown in the diagram.
Still following the diagram, draw in the new waist line and side-seam and then draw in the new dart.
Since any extra width at the waist goes into the depth of the new dart the waist line will remain the same. As each waist fitting is different, especially on larger sizes, it is necessary to fit the waist with special care at the fitting stage.
Draw round the rest of the pattern and cut out the new Back pattern.

The basic skirt conversions

You may like to ring the changes with some of the skirt conversions. The six-gore variation (Skirtmaking Chapter 18) can be very flattering to larger sizes. The four-gore and knife-pleated skirts in Skirtmaking Chapters 16 and 17 are also suitable.

The Golden Hands Graph Pattern and larger sizes

The Graph Pattern size range already includes a perfectly graded set of patterns for larger sizes, namely the 107cm bust size. The patterns in this size are designed to take in the particular requirements of the larger figure.
Experienced dressmakers will have already realized that they can safely enlarge this pattern to take in the next size by adding to the Centre Back and Front, side-seams and armholes. But if you are not confident make a toile first to get the extra size (Toile-making Chapter 22).

The basic dress

The basic dress featured here has been made up in the largest size plus. The gentle flare and the classic detail make it a favourite for larger sizes.
To make the dress use all the pattern pieces on the Dress Graph Pattern on pages 112 and 113 and the sleeve pattern piece number 7 on the Accessories Graph. To make the short sleeve first copy the sleeve pattern as far as the cutting line for short sleeves and pin this to a sheet of paper. Straighten the slope of the under-arm-seam and add the length for the turned back cuff as shown for the blouse roll-sleeve in Blousemaking Chapter 24.

Altering the sleeve pattern for a large upper arm

To make the upper sleeve section larger without increasing the size of the sleeve head, slash the sleeve pattern through the sleeve centre to within 6mm of the sleeve crown. Spread the slash outwards as shown and make a new pattern (figure 3). You can use this method for other sleeve patterns of your choice.

Making up the dress

Make up the dress as for the basic dress in Dressmaking Chapters 29 to 31, then make up and set in the sleeve as for the blouse roll-sleeve. Make buttonholes in the tab so that it can be fastened down flat and use small decorative buttons which complement the colour of the dress.

Making a toile

It is an impossible task to cater for all figure types in each pattern size, so to deal with your personal fitting problems it is strongly recommended that you make a body toile.

When making this follow the bodice toile instructions for fitting and making pattern alterations in Toile-making Chapter 22 and the dress toile described in Toile-making Chapter 23. Also incorporate the sleeve adjustment shown here (figure 3) if necessary. Do not fit the toile as closely as the bodice toile but fit it like a dress.

For the purpose, choose a paper pattern in a basic style such as Vogue 1000. Or if your size is much over the given sizes, choose a simple waisted style from any other commercial paper pattern.

This way, you can make a perfectly fitting garment for yourself, whatever your shape or size.

It will be well worth the effort, because once you have achieved a perfect fit you will be able to use the body toile to adjust any pattern to your own personal requirements before you cut out the fabric.

Fitting on a stand

Larger sizes may find it easier to fit in the early stages on a dressmaker's stand or dummy.

Having identified yourself from the three groups of larger sizes featured in this chapter bear these points in mind when purchasing a stand. These come in many different figure types, with varying proportions, and must be chosen with great care. So it is advisable to go to a specialist shop where all types and sizes of stands are available.

They vary so much that you can even take specific points such as a rounded or straight

The Golden Hands basic dress pattern enlarged one size with simple sleeve conversion

back into consideration.

You may not be able to find a perfect fit, but if you can find a stand which corresponds to your main measurements you can make it fit you perfectly by padding where necessary.

Do not buy your stand as you buy patterns. Patterns should be bought to fit the bust measurement because this is the most difficult area on a pattern to alter.

When buying a stand it is essential to know that you hip measurement is not less than 5cm larger than the bust otherwise you will not be able to get the garment over the shoulders of the stand. If you have difficult proportions, such as a bust and hip measurement alike or a smaller hip measurement, buy the stand to fit your hip and increase the bust size by padding. If your hips are larger than normal proportions, buy the stand to fit your bust and then pad out the hip area.

Chapter 38 Frills, flounces, ruffles and scallops

This is another chapter which deals with special trims and finishes. Here are ruffles, frills, flounces and scallops, all of which you can easily add to a garment yourself.

Single edged frills

Frills are usually caught into bound or faced seams. They may be used to trim neck lines and sleeve edges on soft blouses and dresses. Children's garments, lingerie and nightwear are also favourites for the use of pretty frills.

When a frill is attached to a hem edge it becomes, strictly speaking, a flounce.

How to cut a frill

There are four basic ways to cut a frill. Which you choose depends mainly on the effect you wish to achieve.

On all single edged frills cut a full seam allowance on the edge which is joined to the garment. On the other edge the seam allowance is cut according to the finish you choose.

Cutting single width in the straight grain of the fabric (figure 1a). This type of single layer frill is most suitable for crisp fabrics (figure 2).

Cutting single width in the bias grain of the fabric (figure 1b). Single layer bias cut frills are suitable for attaching to slanted edges such as cross-over dresses. They must be cut generously to look their best (figure 3).

Cutting double width, in the straight or bias grain (figure 1c). This method of cutting is for a double, or fluted, frill. The frill is cut on a double width which is then folded lengthwise to make the fluting. Full seam allowance is, of course, added to both edges (figure 4a and b).

Whether you cut on the bias or the straight grain of the fabric depends on the width of the frill as well as on the fabric.

Circular cutting, single width (figure 1d). The circular cut frill is the type used for a waterfall effect and is therefore sometimes called a waterfall frill. It looks best when cut from fine, soft fabric. This type of frill is rarely gathered as it is cut from a circle or spiral, the inside edge being the length of the garment edge to which the frill is attached (figure 5a and b).

For long waterfall frills, two or more circles or spirals are joined together to the required length.

How to measure for the frill length

Before cutting a frill always test for effect on a short length of the fabric, and at the same time check measurements for length. The length of the frill depends in the first instance on the type of fabric you are using.

Frills in heavy fabric should not be cut too long as the fullness would add a lot of weight and bulk to the seam.

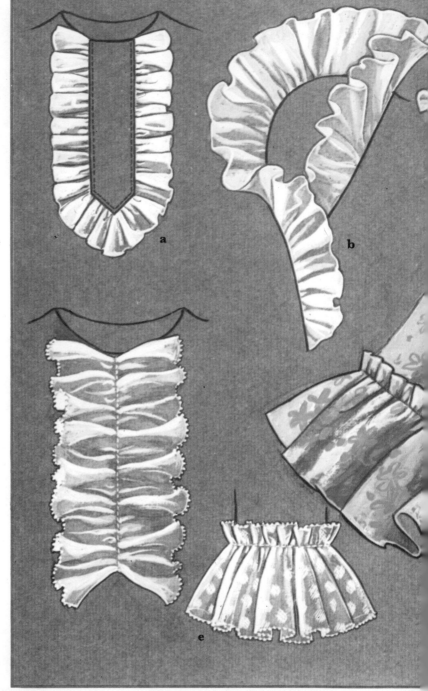

▲ **1.** *Various frills, flounces and ruffles:* **a.** *single edged frill in the straight grain;* **b.** *single edged frill in the bias grain;* **c.** *double width frill;* **d.** *circular or waterfall frill;* **e.** *double edged frill;* **f.** *fluted edged frill;* **g.** *lace ruffle*

▼ **2.** *Single frill cut in the straight grain*

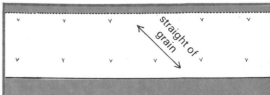

straight of grain

GARMENT EDGE

▼ **3.** *Single frill cut in the bias grain*

straight of grain

▼ **4.** *Cutting a double frill:* **a.** *straight grain;* **b.** *bias grain*

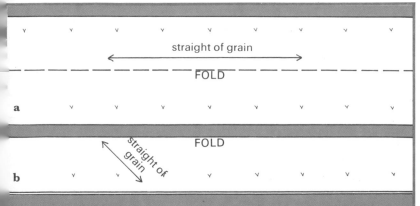

straight of grain

FOLD

a

FOLD

straight of grain

b

▼ **5.** *Cutting a circular frill;* **a.** *from a circle;* **b.** *from a spiral*

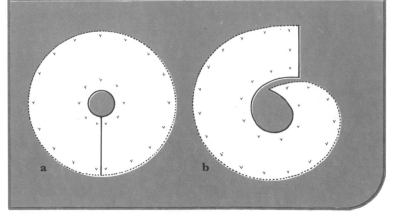

a

b

Frills in thin fabrics, however, need to have extra length otherwise they will look skimped and some fullness is always taken up into the fabric even before you start gathering it up. This applies to both straight or bias cut frills, but not to waterfall frills.

To obtain the correct length of frill for the type of fabric you are using, make this quick test.

Cut a sample length of frilling 38cm long. Make two rows of gathering stitches along one edge and draw them up so that the fabric looks nicely gathered. Measure the length of the gathered up piece and divide the 38cm by this measurement. Then use this proportion when cutting the frill.

For example, if the gathered length measures 19cm, this goes twice into 38cm. This means that for every 2·5cm of the edge to be frilled you will have to cut 5cm of frilling.

Finishing raw edges on frills

It is necessary to finish the outside edge of the frill before attaching it to the garment. It is often difficult to decide which type of finish to apply. Here are a few pointers to help you.

When dealing with single layer frills, the sewing machine can considerably reduce the work in hemming, or otherwise finishing the raw edges.

Machine hem finish. The edge can be finished with the hemming attachment on a machine, or it can simply be turned up into a narrow hem and straight stitched. For the latter, first try out the width of hem which looks best for the fabric. Roll under the edge for 3mm, then turn under again for 3mm and stitch in place. If this looks wrong try a slightly wider hem.

If you are making an ordinary machine hem on a frill, make sure that the fabric does not tighten up as you stitch. The effect may be all right to begin with but after the garment it washed you will find that the edge tends to roll.

Hand rolled finish. There is one occasion when a machine hem is strictly taboo and that is on a beautifully hand finished garment. Here a fine hand roll should be carefully applied to the garment or, of the machine finishes, a picot edge is suitable provided you are working on a fine fabric.

Picot finish. A picot edge, or picot type finish, can be applied to both bias and straight cut frills. Make sure you find out, either from your machine manual or local shop, how much to allow on the edge of the frill so that the width of the frill will not be reduced after it is finished.

Zigzag finish. You can apply a zigzag finish to frills cut on the cross, which include waterfall frills. Work over the raw edge twice to avoid weakness and, for safety's sake, allow an extra 6mm seam allowance which will be taken up in the zigzagging.

Gathering the frill

This can be done by hand or machine. A frilling attachment on a machine will gather the frill as it is stitched in place, and dispenses with gathering stitches. But do beware and follow the manual to the letter or you may well find yourself running out of fabric before you have gathered sufficient for the hem edge.

Otherwise the frill must be gathered with two parallel lines of gathering stitches along the seam line.

Attaching frills

Single frills. Whether you are using a bound or faced finish, always catch the frill into the seam when you are stitching it.

If you are attaching a frill, or flounce, to a hem edge, just stitch it to the seam allowance, with right sides facing, neaten both hem and frill seam allowances together and turn into the garment. Facing is not necessary.

To prevent the seam allowance from tilting downwards, you can assist by topstitching through all layers of fabric, close to the edge of the hem.

Double frill. The frill is folded length ways and pressed. Gather and attach as for single frills using the two layers of fabric as one.

Double edged frills

A double edged frill (figure 1e) is an attractive variation of frilling and is applied to the surface or stitched onto an edge of a garment. The frill is cut on the cross and both edges are finished with a fine hem, either hand or machine.

It is then gathered with two rows of stitches along the centre or nearer the top edge as required, and stitched to the garment between the rows of gathering. The gathering stitches are removed carefully after stitching.

Double edged frills can be made on the sewing machine with a frilling attachment, but the same precautions apply as for single frills.

Fluted upper edge (figure 1f). A pretty variation of the double edged frill, which you can use when attaching it to the hem line of a skirt, is to make a narrow fluted frill of the upper edge.

To do this, cut an extra 8cm onto the required width and turn under the upper edge 3·8cm. Make one row of gathering stitches on the right side of the fabric 2·5cm down from the folded upper edge, then make a second row parallel to the first. Draw up the gathers to fit the hem edge, pin the gathering over the seam line and stitch in position. Carefully remove the gathering stitches.

Ruffles

Traditionally, frills of lace are described as ruffles. A ruffle (see figure 1g) is made from wide lace edging or flouncing, gathered into a rouleau or bias strip binding, and attached to the neck or sleeve edge of a garment (figure 6).

Ruffles are rarely taken into seams since the texture of the ruffle fabric, in most cases, varies from the texture of the garment fabric.

Scallops

Scalloping (figure 7) is an easy way to decorate a garment. All that is required is some simple arithmetic and careful measuring. Scallops must be evenly spaced, as any miscalculations will be very noticable in their shapes.

Scallops are most easily applied to a straight edge where the grain of the fabric will assist you when stitching.

When applying them to a rounded edge, the decreasing factor in the length of the base line of the scallops must be taken into account.

Whether you apply scallops to a straight or shaped edge, it is always done best with the aid of a template, shaped to the edge of the garment (figure 8a).

The ideal measurement for the depth of the scallops is a third of the width. Measure out the scallops on the template first. Draw them on in pencil and you will then see if your calculations are right and that you have the correct number of scallops to fit along the edge.

If you are left with odd measurements, leave the depth of each scallop as it is but widen the base line to take up the extra length (figure 8b). Conversely, if you have too little length, decrease the width of the base line on each scallop to accommodate all the scallops evenly (figure 8c).

When applying scallops, cut a facing to the exact shape of the edge to be scalloped. Then carefully mark out the scallops with tailor's tacks on the facing fabric piece, using the shaped template as

▲ **7.** *Various applications of scallops*

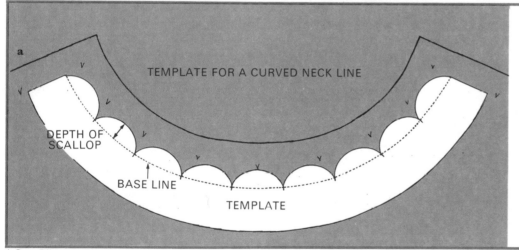

TEMPLATE FOR A CURVED NECK LINE

DEPTH OF SCALLOP

BASE LINE

TEMPLATE

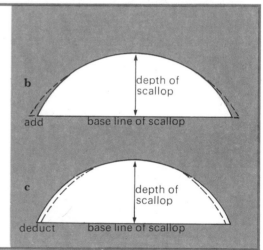

b

depth of scallop

add   base line of scallop

c

depth of scallop

deduct   base line of scallop

▲ **8a.** *The template for the scallops on a curved neck line:* **b.** *widening the base line;* **c.** *reducing the base line*

your guide (figure 9a).

If the scalloped edge needs interfacing, such as round a neck line, tack the interfacing in place.

Then tack the facing in place, right sides together, and stitch the facing to the garment along the line of tailor's tacks. Trim the seam allowance round the scallops to about 9mm if the fabric is thick layer the seams (figure 9b).

Turn the facing to the inside, thus turning out the scallops, edge-tack and press. Remove the tacking and the scalloped edge is complete.

Here is one final hint for making smooth looking scallops. If you find that after trimming and turning out the scallops they still don't lie flat, make small V-shaped notches in the seam allowance round the deepest section of each shape. This will prevent points and puckers on the shaped edges, even in the firmest fabrics.

▼ **9a.** *Marking out the scallops on the facing;* **b.** *trimming and notching the scalloped edge for turning*

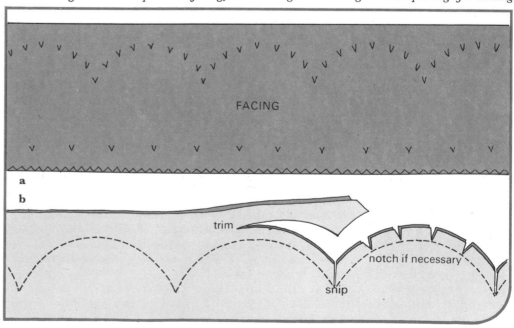

FACING

a

b

trim

notch if necessary

snip

Chapter 39

The velvet touch

If you think that velvet is a difficult fabric to make up, your fears should be dispelled after reading this chapter. It gives a description of the various types of velvet you will use for dressmaking, followed by useful tips on how to choose suitable styles, and work and handle the fabric for really successful results.

Armed with this basic velvet know-how, there is no reason why you cannot feel as relaxed handling this most romantic fabric as any other. You might start with a glamorous long evening skirt and team it with a silk, satin or crepe blouse for the exclusive look of the outfit featured opposite, from a commercial pattern. The chapter ends with special hints for making up a velvet dress and shown below are details of the dress on the facing page. When working with velvet, darts can lead to difficulties; therefore, this type of style with the shaping achieved in the contour seaming is more appropriate. And a dividing waist-seam which breaks up the vertical seam line works to the advantage of the beginner.

an alternative version included in pattern

▲ *Back and front views of dress on facing page*

Suitable fabrics and styles

Types of velvet
There are many types of velvet made from different fibres, as well as combinations of fibres, such as velvet with a cotton base and silk pile.

Their weight differs considerably too. Velvets are made as heavy as coating and as light as chiffon, and between these extremes are the easily worked dress velvets.

The most common and well known velvet is Lyons velvet, which is firm and usually made in pure silk. Rayon velvets are also common: they are made entirely from rayon and then treated for crease resist-

ance. Both Lyons and rayon velvet have short pile which makes them ideal for the beginner.

Panne velvets are also good for the beginner but are not always available as they are dependent on prevailing fashion. The nap or pile of panne velvet is brushed quite flat and in one direction. These velvets are often printed and the pile gives depth to a printed design.

French street or coat velvets are quite light in weight, but the pile is somewhat deep and it becomes a little more difficult to work. Recently a velvet has appeared appropriately named Miracle Velvet. This has a most luxurious surface but can be treated almost like an ordinary flat weave. This velvet is made from a continental man-made fibre, the appearance of which resembles ordinary artificial silk. It can be washed successfully and it is also quite inexpensive.

Since Miracle Velvet is suitable for washing it is the obvious choice for garments in light colours.

Cotton velveteen is a different type of fabric. Here the base and pile are both made of cotton. Velveteen is made to resemble velvet but the construction of the weave is different. This fabric presents no problem in making up.

Choosing the velvet
As the textures of velvet vary, consider the fit and hang you require for the style of garment and choose the velvet accordingly. If you are a beginner use a short nap velvet to get used to working on velvets before attempting the longer pile ones. So look for a good close pile with a firm handle which will allow you to work with the fabric without too much slipping.

Choosing a suitable design
Avoid styles which rely on heavy darting for the fit as darts are difficult to press in velvet.

The beginner should also avoid styles which are cut in one with no dividing waist-seam. It is best to learn to sew velvet on smaller sections of a garment as the seams are easier to control.

The pattern which is featured in this chapter incorporates all the above qualities and is therefore a particularly suitable design.

General hints

Supporting fabrics
Interfacing. It is rare for velvet garments to need interfacing, especially when there is a loose lining attached to the neck and armhole lines.

Facings. Facings must be kept to a minimum to avoid heavy rolls on the edges of the garment. It is best to face velvet garments with matching silk bias facings which are neat and firm.

Interlinings. Few velvets benefit from inter or underlinings and the stitching of seams in underlined velvet can become a nightmare, since the whole seam appears to move.

To support full skirts in velvet always construct a suitable under garment and do not use stiff linings or underlinings. Stiff fabrics will catch the pile on the inside of the fabric and slowly drag it out, resulting in bald patches all over the surface.

Hand-sewing
Hand-sewing should be practised on a scrap of velvet. If the stitches are made too timidly they only catch the loops of the pile where it is anchored into the weave and gradually pull it out. So make sure you catch the weave but don't allow the stitches to mark the pile.

Background: evening dress from a Vogue pattern in rayon velvet
Foreground: velvet skirt with crepe blouse also from a Vogue pattern ▶

Seam finishes

Seam finishes in velvet garments should be done by hand as a machine finish can cause a seam edge to tighten and roll, making it appear cockled on the outside. Do not be tempted to use pinking shears as this will only encourage fraying.

Zip fasteners

It is often mistakenly thought that you require a fine zip to fasten a velvet dress. Fine zips usually come with a fine tape and as you stitch the fine tape to the seam line through the folded thickness of the fabric it is pulled with the stitches into the depth of the pile and there is no control or anchorage to hold the stitches in position. It does not matter how much you try, your zip will always look cockled.

So always use a strong dress zip with a cotton tape. This is slightly stiff and firm and will allow you to sew it in position without puckering.

Tools for ironing velvet

For ironing velvet you should use a needleboard.

Needleboards are squares of wire pile anchored to a firm base. The fabric is then pressed with pile down on the needleboard. It is worthwhile buying an expensive one as a cheap needleboard can ruin the velvet.

You can of course draw your seams over an ordinary iron standing on its end and covered with a damp cloth. To do this open the seam allowance and draw the seam section by section over the iron, patting the velvet gently on the outside with a soft brush.

Needleboards are obtainable in the haberdashery departments of some stores. But if you cannot find what you are looking for try one of the specialist shops selling dressmaker's equipment. They will also stock very narrow strips of needleboard which you lay over a sleeve board to press the seams in fitted sleeves.

Stitching velvet

When stitching velvet the pressure of the upper presser foot on most sewing machines needs to be reduced unless the machine is self-adjusting. To test for this place two scraps of velvet face to face and make a row of tacking stitches as for a seam line. Stitch along the seam line. If the seam begins to wring loosen the pressure and stitch again. Repeat until the fabric stops wringing and the seam remains flat.

For stitching velvet use a fine soft thread such as pure silk sewing thread. Carefully adjust the stitch tension on the machine since the fabric is thick and a tightly set stitch tension will cause it to pucker.

159

Chapter 40

Successful dressmaking with checks and stripes

A very important aspect of dressmaking is using a fabric to its best advantage, and making full use of checks and stripes is as exciting as creating a new design. Take a simple pattern, make it up cleverly in a checked or striped fabric, and the result is a garment with well projected detail.

Fixed fashion rules, such as lengthways stripes for the large figure and checks for the small, have long been discarded. Provided the size of the design on the fabric is right for the proportions of the garment, and the proportions of the garment suit the wearer, there is no reason why large figures should not wear checks and small figures wear bold stripes.

This chapter gives advice on choosing the fabric and selecting the right style, and finishes with the all important aspects of cutting and fitting to help you achieve the best possible effect for your figure type.

▲ *Checks for a dashing trouser suit*

Buying the fabric

Checks

With such a variety of checks available it is impossible to cover every aspect of making a purchase in one of these fabrics. However, there are some rules to observe which can be applied to most types of checks.

The main consideration must be matching the checks. So first look to see if the design is balanced (figure 1). Does the colour repeat regularly, or are there colours in the lengthwise weave which are not repeated in the crosswise weave or vice versa? If so, you must treat the fabric as you would for one way.

Also look to see if there are the same amount of threads in the lengthwise pattern as there are in the crosswise pattern. If there aren't, the fabric must again be considered as one way. And even if the same amount of threads have been used in each direction, one

thread gauge may be greater than the other, thereby making the pattern irregular. A check may even look regular when in fact it isn't. Skirtmaking Chapter 19 shows you how you can make a simple test to find out.

Stripes

The first consideration is the repeat of the design. This can create width if the pattern is bold and the colours show an obviously wide pattern repeat. For a slim look, the stripes should not be spaced out too far apart.

Striped fabrics are made in two ways—horizontal and vertical. If you want to combine horizontal and vertical stripes in one garment, make sure they are designed well and make an interesting combination.

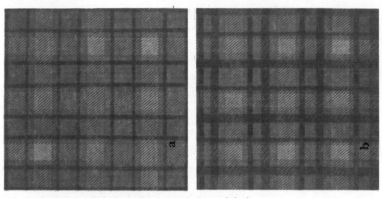

▲ **1.** *Left: balanced design; Right: unbalanced design*

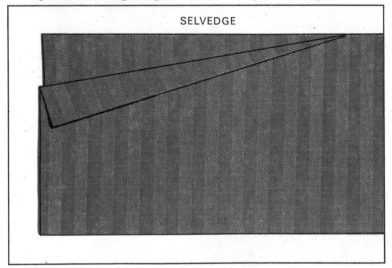

▲ **2.** *Distortion on the selvedges of a striped fabric*

Checking the fabric finish

As the fabric is unrolled on the shop counter, lift one selvedge and see if the corresponding selvedge meets it correctly. Look at the stripes and checks and see if the finish has distorted the pattern on the cloth so that they do not meet from side to side (figure 2).

Although some of these fabrics can be folded quite easily after the length has been cut off, others are very resistant to folding since they have been carelessly finished and dragged. Here one side is so much out of line it cannot be used for making up.

If you are in doubt, a good assistant who is familiar with the merchandise should be able to advise you. If, however, you cannot get assurance, buying the fabric could lead to disappointment.

Far right: wide stripes perfectly aligned. Top right: effective use of checks on a cape coat. Right: checks cross cut on a skirt. All five designs in this chapter from Vogue Patterns

Choosing the right style

Checks and stripes have an all-over geometrical and predictable design. But the figure shapes they have to cover have rounded contours which are quite unpredictable. Since every figure is different, it is not possible to design an ideal checked or striped pattern for all figures. It is up to each dressmaker therefore to choose her style, at the same time observing the few golden rules given below.

O Use large checks or wide stripes on large areas uncluttered by detail. Never distort the geometry of the design with unnecessary breaks, seams or darts. Only use them if they actually enhance the style and the design of the fabric. Figures 3 and 4 show a good and bad usage of large checks.

O Avoid darts as much as possible. A wrongly placed dart will cut or distort the design. If darts are unavoidable, try to move them so that one side of the dart seam line remains in the straight or the crosswise grain of the fabric.

O Rounded edges on collars, cuffs and pockets are not suitable for all types of checks or stripes. Confine them to small checks and fine stripes.

O Closely fitted garments, such as dresses and tailored suits, look best in small to medium sized checks.

O If the style has lots of detail such as pockets, yoke, collar, it is best to use small checks, otherwise the detail will be lost in the background of the fabric.

Designing for checks and stripes

A clever dressmaker can have fun designing for these fabrics. The illustrations in this chapter give ideas for styles which show checks and stripes to advantage.

A simple and most effective idea is to choose a fabric with light and dark alternating colours which are repeated regularly. Make a pleated skirt using the dark sections for the pleat distance and the light sections for the pleat depth. As the pleats spring open, the light colour is revealed, creating a pretty striped effect.

Cutting notes

Be prepared; making a garment in checks and stripes takes longer than making a garment in other fabrics. Attention to detail starts on the cutting table where you must take great care to match the design. Be especially careful when cutting the long sections where a mistake could be disastrous.

Before cutting make the necessary adjustments to the length and width of the

▲ *Trouser suit with band cross checked*

▲ **3.** *A good choice of style for large checks*

▲ **4.** *An unsuitable style choice for large checks*

pattern and do not take a chance by adding or cutting off the pattern on the layout.

When pinning down the pattern, make sure that all corresponding pattern pieces are pinned in the same check or stripe. Start matching from the hem upwards (figure 5). If matched from the underarm section downwards, any ease or side bust dart would throw the pattern out of line. If you are not sure what adjustments will be necessary to the side bust darts, add 5cm to the hem line at the Back and add extra seam allowance to the armhole line. Then, should you have to lift fabric into the dart, you will have enough

length to re-cut the Back to line up the fabric pattern.

Matching checks and stripes for set-in sleeves is often difficult, especially if severe adjustments have been made to the armhole line at the fitting.

To allow you some play on the sleeve crown, cut the whole sleeve head with at least 2·5cm seam allowance (figure 6). Be sure to mark out the seam line around the sleeve head carefully so that if you should have to let out on the sleeve crown, you will be able to compensate on the underarm to avoid a large armhole.

Yokes, pocket flaps and collars must always be cut with special care (figure 7).

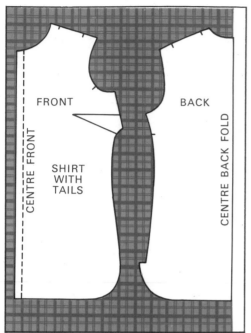

▲ 5. *Matching checks on a pattern from the hem*

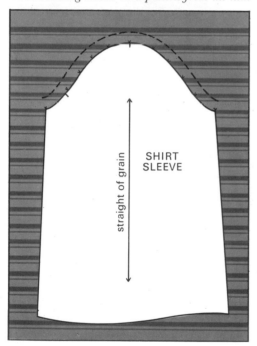

▲ 6. *Cutting 2·5cm seams on a sleeve head*

Make sure that the checked or striped pattern continues through the pocket or yoke. Tilted pockets must be adjusted precisely to the straight of the grain line on the pattern so that, although the pocket is cut on the cross, the pattern continues across the garment.

When cutting a collar from prominent coloured checks or stripes, lay the complete collar pattern on the fabric to see that the colours repeat on both collar ends similarly. If not, it is best to cut the collar in two halves with a Centre Back seam, making sure that the pattern lines coincide. Careful attention to detail is important.

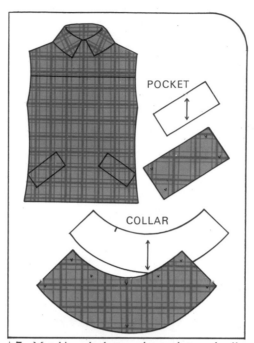

▲ 7. *Matching checks on yoke, pockets and collar*

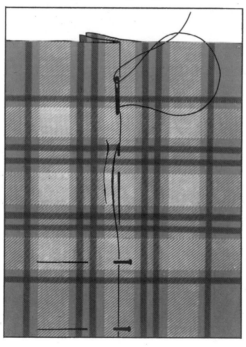

▲ 8. *Slip-basting a seam*

Preparing for fitting

Mark out the pattern detail with care since fitting alterations on these fabrics are movements of consequence. Altering one section may make it out of line with a corresponding section which must then also be adjusted to re-align the pattern.

Tack the sections together quite firmly and gently press the seam allowance to get as smooth a fit as possible for the first fitting.

Slip-basting

It is often difficult to match the straight grain lines of vertical seams such as the

Centre Back seam in a skirt. This can be made easier with slip-basting.

Slip-basting is a method of tacking where one side of the seam edge is folded on the outside of the fabric along the straight of grain line and brought to meet the other seam line in the corresponding grain line. To tack the seam together, work through the folded edge into the flat fabric as shown, slip-basting along with small stitches (figure 8).

Although slip-basting will help you match the lengthwise grain lines, do not rely on it to give you enough anchorage for matching the horizontal lines of the fabric pattern. You cannot control the tension of the tacking stitches well enough, and after slip-basting it is always necessary to pin or retack from the inside, having laid the fabric flat.

Shaped seams

Pinning and tacking shaped seams requires a great deal of care. Since the seam runs through the bias of the fabric it is so easy to accidentally drag the seam edge.

Use pins at right angles to the seam line to give you extra control over the edge and allow you to pin together matching pattern lines.

Fitting

The obvious lengthwise and crosswise grain lines and pattern lines are your fitting guide. Make sure they hang well and are not tilted or dragged to one side.

Directional design will emphasize deviation, and figure faults are more obvious.

But if the fabric design is cleverly adjusted and incorporated into the fitting of the garment without affecting the straight and crosswise directional pattern, you will see that your dress allows you to forget your problems.

It is often said that the waist-seam and hem must continue in the pattern line. This, of course, is wrong. If a figure fault makes the straight waist pucker, it is essential that the fullness is taken off into the waist seam. But do check that the crosswise grain continues around the figure perfectly horizontally.

Allow the waist-seam to follow your natural waist line and to hide the adjustment make a belt wide enough to suit you. When making the hem, remember that the checks or stripes will only go straight around the hem if the garment is cut perfectly straight from hips to hem line. If the skirt is cut with a flare, however slight, your hem line will be rounded and not run in the line of the fabric pattern.

Working with suede and leather

With the vast advances made by the tanning industry in the last decade, a greater variety of skins is now available to the home dressmaker than ever before. This has resulted in a growing interest in the use of leather and suede which is being nurtured by the major pattern companies, who are including more and more patterns in their ranges for leather and suede skins.

Despite the growing interest, however, dressmakers still tend to shrink from the relatively simple task of making a garment in this medium. Certainly leather and suede requires care in handling, plus know-how, but the rewards of working with such rich and beautiful 'fabrics' are great.

This chapter gives information on buying skins, choosing styles, fitting and making up. There are also many ideas for decorative stitching and using leather for appliqué and patchwork. The chapter concludes with advice on the important aspects of care and cleaning.

Buying the leather and suede

Types of skin

Briefly, for the purposes of this chapter, skin can be split into two distinct groups: sheep and cow.

Sheep. This animal provides those soft, velvety suedes and fine leather skins which are so much in demand, and from which most of the better quality ready-to-wear coats and skirts are made. Because of their suppleness, sheep skins are suitable for coats, skirts, waistcoats, trousers and a variety of accessories.

Sheep skins are available in sizes between ·46 and ·74 metres square, in a wide range of colours.

Remember, area is length by breadth, and as all the skins are animal shaped, the approximate dimensions across the furthest points for say ·65 metres square are 90cm by 71cm (figure 1).

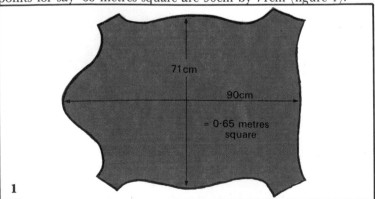

71cm

90cm

= 0·65 metres square

1

Sheep also provide chamois-type skins which are mostly oil dressed and undyed skins, similar to the wash leathers you can buy in the shops. New techniques, however, are making ranges of

subtly dyed washable skins more easily available to the home dressmaker.

Cow. This animal supplies soft, fine calf leather in addition to a tough, long pile, double sided suede in the form of suede splits. Although suede split is used extensively in the boot and shoe industry, it is equally suitable for making skirts and jerkins.

Both calf leather and suede split are available in a good range of colours. In size, calf skins average 1·11 metres square and suede splits 1·58 metres square.

Choosing the right pattern

If you're new to suede and leather, choose as simple a pattern as possible, without sleeves and preferably panelled. A panelled style is less likely to lose its shape when worn and you can utilise more skin when cutting out. A skirt or waistcoat, where intricate seaming and cutting is not required, is an obvious choice.

If you want to be more ambitious in your choice of style just bear in mind that the size and shape of the suede and leather skins will impose certain, obvious limits. For instance; it is unlikely that you would be able to cut a full length coat piece from shoulder to hem from one suede skin, and so a dress or coat will have to have seams at waist or hip level and, for all practical purposes, set-in sleeves.

Also, as each section of a garment, such as a Front, or Back, or long sleeve, usually takes one skin, you may need to relate your style choice to your purse!

An effective and also economical idea is to make only a part of the garment in leather or suede, such as the front bodice of a coat. But if you decide on this course of action be very careful to choose a woven fabric which 'works' satisfactorily with the skin.

How many skins will I need?

It's all a matter of square metres! As skins vary in size, the number you will need depends on the type of skin you are using. The supplier will be able to advise you when you buy the skins.

As a starting point for your calculations, here is a rough guide to the number of sheep skins (of ·56 to ·65 metres square) you will need for particular garments.

Short skirt, length 38cm, hips 86cm	Longer skirt, up to midi length	Bolero style waistcoat
1 skin	2 skins	1 skin

Long line waistcoat	Hip length jacket	¾ to full length coat
2 skins	4/5 skins	6/7 skins

If you have selected a pattern which specifies leather or suede, it usually states the type of skin to use and the square footage required. So, if you work to the pattern, all you need to do is to go to the supplier, who will help you convert the square metres into number of skins.

If, however, you wish to use a different type of skin to that stated on the pattern, or you have selected a pattern which does not specify the use of skins at all, it will be necessary to convert the fabric amount into square metres, or number of skins. Again, you will need to seek the advice of the supplier.

Here is another chart, also based on sheep skin (·56 to ·65 metres square), as a further guide to your calculations.

Fabric Amount 90cm wide fabric	m 0·46	m 1·18	m 1·85	m 2·31	m 3·00	m 3·70	m 4·16
Equivalent number of skins	1	2	3	4	5	6	7

Making up

Equipment

Although there are many fine and expensive gadgets on the market for leather work which you could use, the following is a list of the essentials.

- ☐ Sharp scissors
- ☐ Clear adhesive tape (to secure the pattern when cutting)
- ☐ Stapler (to secure seam allowances when stitching), and staple remover
- ☐ Adhesive such as Evostick, or rubber solution glue (for sticking down seams)
- ☐ Brown paper (for pressing)
- ☐ Tissue paper (for use when stitching seams)
- ☐ Medium/heavy sewing machine needles or special, triangular leather needles (size No. appropriate to the make of sewing machine)
- ☐ Glover's needles (as used for glove making) for hand-sewing
- ☐ Pure silk thread or synthetic thread (the thread must have a certain amount of elasticity as skins stretch slightly)
- ☐ Ball-point or felt tip pen (for marking out the pattern details)

Checking and preparing the pattern

Before you start cutting make sure that you check the pattern for size and make any necessary alterations. If you are not sure whether the garment will need alteration, it is a good idea to make a mock garment in cotton calico first, as any adjustments made after machining will be unsightly.

If you are using a commercial paper pattern, trim all seam allowances on the pattern tissue to 6mm.

If any pattern piece is larger than the skin, decide where it would be best to have a join in the garment and cut the pattern accordingly, adding a 6mm seam allowance to both pieces.

Where a left and right pattern piece is required, make a copy of that pattern piece and label it 'left', label the other 'right'. This will help you to avoid the classic mistake of cutting two left sides and will also help you to juggle the pieces around on the skin. Likewise, you will have to make another half of any pattern piece where the layout calls for placing on a fold.

Cutting out

When you are placing the pattern pieces on the skin, ensure that the maximum area is utilised, at the same time making a note of any blemishes on the right side.

If you are working with suede, you will have to decide whether or not you can afford to be a purist and keep all the pattern pieces running in the same direction. On a good suede you can get away with ignoring the nap; the surface is very flexible and it will be difficult to detect the direction of the pile when the garment is being worn.

Once you are satisfied with the placing of the pattern pieces, secure them with clear adhesive tape on the wrong side of the skin. Mark all the cutting lines and darts using a ball-point or felt pen. Cut from the neck edge of the skin using very sharp scissors. Place corresponding pieces together when cut and staple the seam edges together within the seam allowance. This will prevent the pieces sliding apart during machine stitching.

Fitting

Try on the 'stapled together' garment for fit and adjust if necessary. This is a very crucial moment. Do remember that you cannot erase the marks made by a line of stitching if alterations prove necessary at a later stage. The first row of stitches must be the final one. On suede it is just possible to make slight alterations after stitching as the pile acts as a disguise, but on leather it is impossible.

▲ *Long jerkin with thonging, in soft, supple suede from a Vogue pattern*

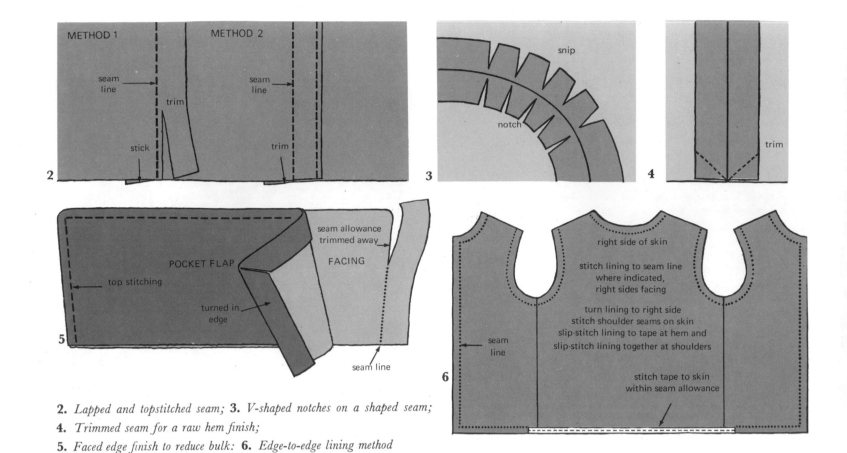

2. *Lapped and topstitched seam;* 3. *V-shaped notches on a shaped seam;*

4. *Trimmed seam for a raw hem finish;*

5. *Faced edge finish to reduce bulk:* 6. *Edge-to-edge lining method*

Stitching

○ Use tissue paper under the leather when stitching. This will prevent the feed teeth of the machine from damaging the skin, and the tissue can easily be torn away after stitching.

○ Reduce the pressure on the presser foot and do not force the leather under the needle. You will either break the needle or damage the skin.

○ Use a sewing machine needle of medium to heavy thickness or a special leather needle. Change the needle immediately if it shows signs of becoming blunt and punching holes in the leather.

○ Use longer stitches than for fabric, about 8 to 10 stitches to 2·5 cm and stitch slowly without stretching.

○ Do not stitch sharp corners but round them off very slightly. This will make it easier to turn the corners out.

○ Staple the seam allowances together when stitching. The staple remover will facilitate removal of the staples after stitching.

○ For topstitching you will find a roller foot a useful attachment (see Generally Speaking Chapter 2).

○ For all hand-sewing, use glover's needles.

Finishing

Seams and darts. Make plain seams and where seams are subject to strain or stretch, stitch narrow straight tape into those seams.

Cut darts open. To remove excess bulk on seams and darts pare away (or skive), the under surface of the seam allowance, either with a razor blade or by using one of the scissor blades turned on its side.

An alternative way to finish a seam is to lap the seam allowances and topstitch them (figure 2). This reduces bulk and is particularly suitable for shaped sections. Press plain seams and darts open. If you are using a bulky skin it will help if you first pound the seams open with a heavy wooden object such as a rolling pin or a meat hammer; for fine skin, just finger press the seams open.

Then press using a warm iron (a hot iron will stretch the skin) over brown paper or a dry pressing cloth. Use no moisture. The seam allowance can then be topstitched or stuck down with adhesive.

Here's a good tip when applying the adhesive, but to make use of it the adhesive must be perfectly fresh. Pour the liquid into a clean, empty washing-up liquid bottle and replace the top. The nozzle makes an excellent applicator.

Edges. Where an edge is curved, cut V-shaped notches into that edge to enable it to lie flat (figure 3).

Hems. Hems can be left raw as leather does not fray, or they can be glued down using the technique described above. If you decide to leave a hem raw, cut back the seam allowance as shown (figure 4).

Facings. On unlined garments facings can be used to give a certain amount of body. To reduce bulk on the faced edge, trim the seam allowance on the facing to the seam line before stitching and turn back the seam allowance on the garment edge. Place the raw edge of the facing seam line to the folded garment edge and topstitch (figure 5).

This is also a useful tip for the edges of collars, revers and pocket flaps.

You can, if you wish, omit the facings altogether, turn back the raw edges and either topstitch them or glue them down.

Sleeves. With most domestic skins it is possible to set in sleeves in the normal way, even to ease in the skin around the sleeve head. Also, you should have no problem in machining the sleeve-seams. If, however, you do find there is too much bulk for machining, sew in the sleeves by hand using a very firm back stitch.

Interfacings. Where the pattern calls for interfacing, use a non-woven type, such as Vilene, appropriate in weight to the skin you are using. In some cases a pre-shrunk tailor's canvas may be suitable. But it is always best to ask about the right type of interfacing before buying.

Linings. Stitching a lining into a leather garment can be tricky as you cannot slip stitch successfully onto skin. The answer is to stitch tape to the seam or hem allowance, or facing, and slip stitch the lining to the tape. Or, make an edge-to-edge lining as shown in figure 6.

Use a strong, durable lining such as

166

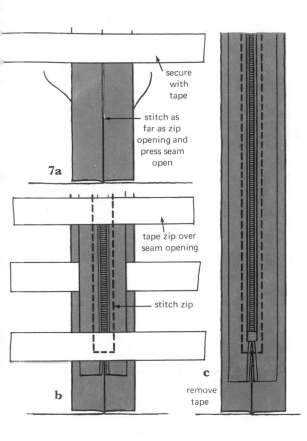

7a, b, c. *Steps in inserting a zip: secure with tape before stitching*

Tricel, otherwise you will find that the skin outlasts the lining. Even so, you may have to replace the lining.

Make skirt linings fractionally narrower than the skirt to prevent seating. When finishing the waist on lined skirts, attach the lining to the waist-seam before applying the waist-band. Then make a hidden petersham waist-band (see Skirtmaking Chapter 14).

Zips. Zips can be inserted in the normal way either by machining or hand-sewing. To hold the zip in place while stitching use clear adhesive tape on the wrong side of the garment (figure 7). This can easily be torn away when the stitching is completed.

Buttonholes and eyelets. You can make bound buttonholes quite successfully in soft leather or suede, or the buttonhole edges can be zigzagged by machine.

Alternatively, if buttons are part of the finished effect, a useful ploy is to dispense with buttonholes altogether and use covered buttons with press studs on the reverse side. These are generally easier than buttonholes for most dressmakers to cope with and look just as good.

Eyelets used in conjunction with thonging can make a very attractive fastening, especially suitable for casual garments such as the jerkin illustrated on the previous page. Making eyelets is a relatively simple job with an eyelet making kit which you can buy in most large stores or leather goods shops.

Different ways with leather

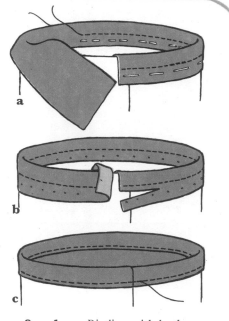

Binding

To bring a new look to an old jacket or blazer, and to save you the expense of buying a new one, apply a leather binding to the frayed edges.

Using a stapler, secure the strip of leather over the garment edge and stitch in place (figure 8a). Remove the staples and trim away the leather, together with the staple marks, leaving the edges raw (figure 8b). When you want to join the binding, simply overlap the raw ends and complete the stitching (figure 8c).

If you want to add a little interest to an otherwise plain coat, you can bind pocket flaps and collar with strips of leather using the method described above.

8 a, b, c. *Binding with leather*

Decorative stitching

Saddle stitching can be both decorative and useful (figure 9). It is useful instead of topstitching for keeping seam allowances in place without the need for gluing. For added effect work light coloured saddle stitches on a dark background, or vice versa.

For fine skin you can use embroidery thread for the stitches. For heavier skins waxed thread is more suitable.

Zigzag stitching can be very effective for joining two pieces of skin without bulk (figure 10a), or for decoration (figure 10b). Thonging can be used as a surface decoration. Worked over stitched seams or raw pocket edges, it looks rather like giant oversewing stitches (figure 11). Use an eyelet punch to make the holes for the thonging and be sure to select a small hole setting to prevent the thonging slipping about too much.

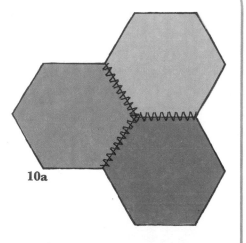

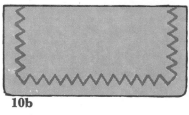

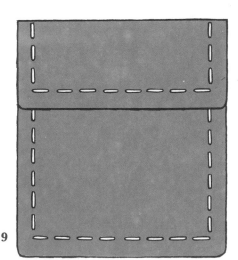

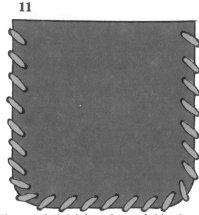

9. *Decorative saddle stitching on a pocket;* **10a.** *Zigzag stitch joining pieces of skin;* **b.** *Zigzag stitch used to decorate a pocket;* **11.** *Thonging used as surface decoration*

12-16. *Give all sorts of commercial paper patterns a personal touch with leather or suede appliqué (figures 12, 14). Or make up only certain portions of a garment in a contrasting skin (figures 13, 16). Leather or suede used in patchwork (figure 15) is another idea.*

Appliqué, patches and patchwork

With appliqué, you can achieve some striking effects by using simple shapes in various colours and applying them around a hem or sleeve edge, or on the bodice of a garment (figure 12). Use an existing design or work out your own design on paper first. Apply the shapes by zigzagging or hand-sewing over the raw edges; you can also straight stitch close to the raw edges. An interesting variation of appliqué is seen in figure 13, where suede is applied to the pocket area and is then extended into a belt.

Patches of leather or suede can be used as pockets, to repair worn elbows in jackets or to make colourful belts and bags (figure 14). Apply the patches as for appliqué.

Patchwork is definitely for the patient worker but with clever colour combinations the effect can be quite beautiful and well worth-while.

For patchwork choose a simple skirt or waistcoat pattern (figure 15). Choose geometric shapes for the patches, such as squares, oblongs and hexagons (ready cut patches are available, or you can cut your own using a template), and make up areas of patchwork slightly larger than the size of the pattern pieces. When stitching the patches together, place them edge to edge and zigzag over the raw edges, or use plain seams. Then simply make up the garment using the areas of patchwork

as if they were plain leather or suede. Whether you are working with appliqué, patches or patchwork, you can use off cuts of leather or suede, bought as such, or make use of the unworn parts of an old leather garment. Also, in addition to those featured here, you will be able to find many more commercial paper patterns which you can easily adapt to these ideas.

Sectional uses for leather and suede

An extension of the appliqué idea is seen where sections of leather and suede are built into a garment. For instance, suede yokes can be teamed with woven fabric for added interest, or a suede front added to a coat or a man's waistcoat (figure 16). Here again, there are many patterns which can be adapted for this purpose.

Care of leather and suede

If you've taken a lot of time in making a garment in leather or suede, it really is worth-while having it professionally cleaned by experts. Take time to 'shop around' as a lot of firms specialise in this sort of work and it's worth seeking them out even if you do have to send the garment by post to have it cleaned.

Today a lot of suede is washable, and not only that which is guaranteed to be so. Before you plunge your new suede skirt into water, do check with the supplier

that it is safe to do so. If you have a scrap of suede left over, try this piece first. If the result is satisfactory, and you decide to go ahead, be prepared for some dye loss and no guarantee from the supplier if anything goes wrong.

Wash with a liquid soap and rinse really thoroughly, adding a few drops of baby oil to the final rinse to keep the skin supple.

After rinsing, gently squeeze out as much water as possible without wringing—do not lift up the garment while it is still full of water. Place the garment on a thick towel and gently pat out any excess moisture.

Dry garments by pinning them up by their linings or by placing flat on a large wire tray away from direct heat. When doing so, do not stretch the garment but just smooth it out so that it will return to its original shape. When dry the skin will feel a little stiff so rub the sueded surfaces together and then press as already described.

For general grubbiness, use a proprietary cleaner. Oil or grease marks must be treated by a specialist dry cleaner—do not attempt to remove them yourself. If you get mud on the garment, let it dry before removing with a soft brush. Suede brushes, so called, are for shoes and shoes only—if you were to use one on a fine, soft suede skin you would be rewarded with a very ugly bald patch!

168

Chapter 42

Reversible and double-faced fabrics

Sewing with reversibles can be challenging and exciting as these double-sided fabrics enable you to present two different faces to the world. Although some of the sewing techniques involved may be a little more complicated than with ordinary fabrics the end result is well worth the effort, and remember—you do get two garments for the price of one!

What is a reversible fabric?

Reversible or double-faced fabrics are those in which either or both sides of the material can be used as the top fabric. Although the weave of certain cloths can give this effect, a true reversible consists of two fabrics held together by a random thread and firmly woven together at the selvedge. The two parts of a reversible fabric can be gently pulled apart revealing the threads which hold them together (figure 1).

Some reversibles consist of two layers of fabric lightly bonded together. These should not be confused with laminated or bonded fabrics, where one cloth is purely a backing for the other.

There is a wide variety of reversible materials available: combinations of checked or plaid fabrics reversing to show one plain colour; two contrasting plains; knubbly tweeds with plains—the variations are endless.

Choosing a pattern

To make a reversible garment, choose a simply styled pattern where all details can work on both sides of the garment. Avoid collars which have too marked a roll, details such as pockets slotted into seams which cannot be made reversible, and complicated fastenings. A pleat in the front or back of a garment may have to be taken out to make a garment reversible.

By their very nature reversible fabrics are firm and often bulky, and are best suited to loose swinging styles than to anything too closely fitted. You should avoid gathers, pleats or soft draping.

A poncho or a cape is an ideal garment for a first attempt at working with reversibles (figures 2a and b).

Figure 2c shows a wrap-over skirt pattern which can be very easily adapted to a reversible fabric, while figure 2d shows a suitable waistcoat. For a reversible coat or jacket choose a loose fitting wrap-over with raglan or kimono sleeves (figure 2e).

Special techniques for reversibles

Seams and darts

There is, of course, no right or wrong side on a reversible fabric, and the following seams can be worked on either side of the garment, depending on the effect you want to achieve.

Flat-fell seam. This is the seam most commonly used.

Cut a 19mm seam allowance and stitch a plain seam. Press the seam open (to give a good crisp finish) and then to one side. Separate

▲ **2.** *Reversible fabrics at their best:* **a.** *a cape,* **d.** *a waistcoat,* **f.** *a tabard*

the layers on each seam allowance and layer them as shown (figure 3a), leaving the top layer 19mm wide and trimming the bottom one to 6mm.

Turn in the raw edge of the top layer, tack over the trimmed seam allowance and either slip stitch in place or machine close to the fold (figure 3b).

Strap seam. Here the seams are stitched normally and pressed open. The layers are separated and trimmed to different widths, and then covered with a bias strip cut from one layer of the reversible fabric (figure 4). Alternatively, you could use a bias strip of matching or contrasting lighter-weight fabric or a fancy braid. The 'strap' is best slip stitched in place to leave the reverse side of the fabric unmarked.

Plain seam. Separate the layers to a depth of 3.8cm at the edges to be seamed. With right sides facing stitch two layers together (figure 5a) and press the seam open. Then turn in the seam allowances on the other two layers and slip stitch together (figure 5b).

Darts. Pull the fabric apart to the point of the dart so that the dart is accessible. Stitch the dart on the inside of each fabric layer and press open (figure 6).

Facings, interfacings and linings

A reversible garment will have none of these.

Collars and sleeves

Collars. To make a collar separate the two layers round the outer

▲ **b.** *a poncho,* **c.** *a skirt,* **e.** *a coat*

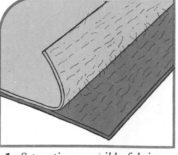

▲ **1.** *Separating reversible fabric*

▲ **3.** *Making a flat-fell seam*

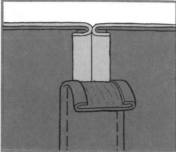

▲ **4.** *A strap seam*

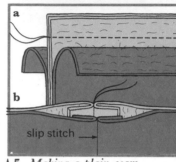

▲ **5.** *Making a plain seam*

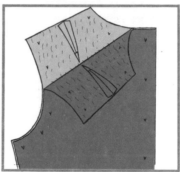

▲ **6.** *Stitching the darts*

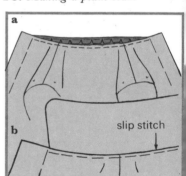

▲ **7a** and **b.** *Inserting a collar*

collar edges for 3·8cm, then turn in the seam allowances and slip stitch together. Separate the neck edges of the garment and clip the curve of the neck on both layers to within 3mm of the stitching line. Turn the seam allowances to the inside, tack each edge separately and press so that you get a smooth edged pocket into which you can insert the collar (figure 7a).

Clip the seam allowance along the neck edge of the collar and insert between the garment neck edges, matching centres and notches. Slip stitch each edge of the neck to the collar separately (figure 7b).

Sleeves. Raglan or kimono sleeves can be stitched to the garment using any of the seaming methods above, but set-in sleeves should be attached in the same way as the collar.

Hems and edges

There are two ways of finishing the edges of reversible fabrics. One method is to trim the seam allowances to the seam line and bind the edges with braid or a bias strip cut from one layer of the fabric.

For the second method, trim the hem or seam allowances to 16mm. Separate the two edges to a depth of 3·8cm, turn in the seam allowances and slip stitch the edges together. Additional top stitching will give a really firm, crisp finish.

Pockets

Only patch pockets are possible. Separate the layers round the edge of the patch, turn in the seam allowances and slip stitch to-

gether. Slip stitch the pocket to the garment.

Fastenings

Choosing fastenings for reversible garments can be a problem. Wrap-over styles are the simplest and often the most effective, and will look the same whichever side of the garment is worn outside. A simple tabard with side slits or a blanket-type poncho present no difficulties either (figure 2f).

For fastening a simple waistcoat or coat try some of the novelty closures such as buckles, clips, frogging or toggles which can create an unusual effect.

Another idea is to make rouleau loops, inserting them into the edges before finishing, and close with lacing. Punched eyelet holes closed with lacing is another possibility.

Zips. These are simple to insert but are not suitable if either layer of fabric is very thick. To insert the zip separate the layers along the zip opening to a depth of 3·8cm. Turn in the edges of each layer along the seam line and press lightly. Sandwich the zip between the folded edges and stitch in place in the usual way.

Buttons. You can fasten the garment with buttons. Either make two sets of buttonholes and fasten them with link buttoning or make one set of buttonholes and sew on two sets of buttons. The button-holes are best made by hand but they can be worked by machine. Bound buttonholes are also possible if carefully made. Separate the layers along the buttonhole edge; work the front of the bound buttonhole in the top layer of fabric and finish the bottom layer as you would for the facing (see Know-How Chapter 44).

Chapter 43

Working with simulated fur fabrics

The wearing of fur has long been a sign of wealth and position which, until recently, nothing could emulate. But today simulated furs have done just that, and the home dressmaker can buy fur as simply as buying a metre of cloth.

This chapter deals with the techniques of handling fur fabrics, giving advice on choosing the fabric, the right style and making up.

The aversion to trapping wild animals for their skin is growing and this is where fur fabric really comes into its own. There is a wide variety of fabric weight and colour to choose from and so long as the pattern you choose is simple and unfussy, a coat or jacket in this material will be as simple to make and as successful as in any other fabric.

Jacket by Vogue in Mongolian lamb fur fabric

Simulated fur fabrics and how to handle them

The most exciting aspect of today's simulated furs is their wide range and variety. Some are exact replicas of real furs, while others are wild and colourfully imaginative fabrics bearing no relation to any animal's skin.

Close imitations are often hard to distinguish from 'the real thing' since their colourings and markings are carefully copied. The fabric can also be grooved to give the impression of real fur pelts sewn together. 'Wild life' by the metre includes leopard, mink, seal, otter, Mongolian lamb and pony.

Some fur fabrics, with either smooth or curled hairs, are permanently brushed in a swirling pattern just like an animal's skin. Others have a distinct one-way nap and must be treated just as you would normal napped fabric.

The facts about simulated furs

Basically, simulated furs are pile fabrics with either woven or knitted backings. Those with knitted backings are normally more flexible than those with woven backings, which are stiffer and often more difficult to handle.

The backing can be of quite a different fibre to that of the surface pile. Backings are usually of cotton or man-made fibre while the surface pile may be of man-made fibre, such as rayon, nylon, or polyester, or of a natural fibre such as mohair or wool. Sometimes the backing is printed or PVC coated to be used as a reversible fabric, although here the layers cannot be separated as with ordinary reversibles.

Simulated furs are available mainly in 120cm or 140cm widths.

Cleaning. For woven backed simulated furs the manufacturers recommend fur cleaning, and it is important to realize that this process is quite different from ordinary dry cleaning. Most reliable dry cleaners today have a fur cleaning service.

Simulated furs with knitted backings are mainly washable but they must always be hand-washed and with extreme care. After washing the fabric will benefit from a good shake which lifts the pile.

Choosing the pattern

Simulated fur is soft and luxurious and can never be crisply tailored. Look for a style which will make the most of your fabric rather than trying to chisel it into an unsuitable shape.

By its very nature this fabric is dramatic so play up this quality by choosing simple uncluttered lines. Remember that seams will not show in fur fabric and that clever details will be lost.

Remember, too, your own figure shape; fur is bulky and will add extra centimetres, so use it to draw attention to your good points and minimize your larger features by combining the fur with plain fabric. For example, if you have heavy thighs in comparison with the rest of your figure, wear plain dark trousers with a gay fur jacket.

Avoid patterns with gathers or pleats; besides creating an enlarging effect your machine may not be able to stitch through too many thicknesses. For the same reason avoid intersecting seams wherever possible.

Do not limit yourself to those patterns which suggest fur fabric, as many others may be suitable, but for your first attempt it would be best to choose a simple shape.

Adapting the pattern for simulated fur

Having accepted the principle that when working with fur fabric excessive bulk is undesirable, you must now try to remove unnecessary thickness wherever possible in the pattern you have chosen.

If the Centre Back seam is parallel to the grain line, trim off the seam allowance and place the stitching line to a fold (figure 1).

Similarly, to adapt the pattern you can dispense with the Centre Front wrap seam by cutting the Front and front facing in one. Place the Centre Front line of the facing over that of the Front and pin (figure 2).

Alternatively, you can cut the facings in a plain firm fabric so as to avoid having two layers of fur fabric down the front.

The garment could also be lined to the edge.

To add a realistic touch to a grooved mink fabric why not emulate the furrier; shorten the pattern to allow for a band of horizontal stripes at the hem line or a single band at the cuffs, such as you might find on a real mink (figure 3).

Checking the pattern

Of course the first rule when making any garment is to check the pattern measurements. This is particularly important when working with fur fabric as it is not easy to alter seams in this fabric. For this reason it is a good idea to first make up a mock garment in calico.

Try the mock garment on, remembering that the fur fabric itself will look far bulkier. Make any necessary alterations and transfer them back to the pattern, or take the calico garment apart and use it as your pattern.

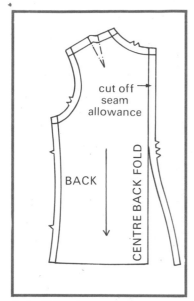

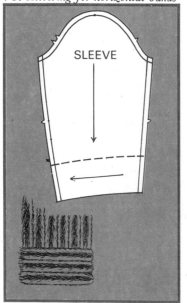

▲ 1. *Trimming at the Centre Back Butterick pattern in Terylene Sherpa pile ►*

▲ 2. *Joining Front and front facing*
▼ 3. *Allowing for horizontal bands*

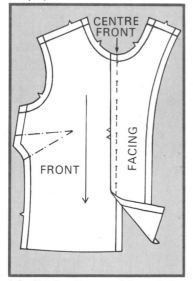

Choosing underlining, interfacing and lining

It is not usual to underline simulated fur fabrics since they have plenty of body. Interfacing, however, is usually very necessary to prevent the weight of the fabric from stretching out of shape at vital areas, such as neck line, armholes, hem and cuffs.

As fur fabrics vary so much in weight and texture it is safest to enquire when buying about the correct interfacing to use.

When choosing a lining for fur fabric bear in mind that the fixative with which many fur fabrics are treated makes their backings stiff, and this may wear away a lining which is too fragile. So choose a medium to heavy-weight durable lining such as Tricol taffeta or lining satin. Although more expensive an insulated lining, such as Milium, is often a good idea for a simulated fur which may not be as warm as it looks.

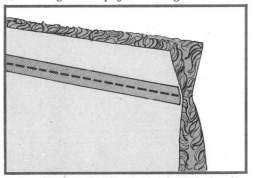

▼ **4.** *Using seam tape for stitching seams*

▼ **5a.** *Shaving the pile;* **b.** *teasing out the pile*

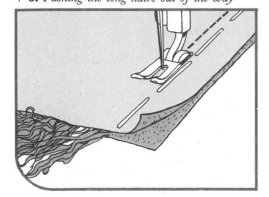

▼ **6.** *Pushing the long hairs out of the way*

If you are using a washable fur fabric make sure that the lining you choose is also washable.

Cutting out the pattern

Lay out simulated furs with a distinct one-way nap as for one-way fabrics. With long-haired fur fabrics always make sure the nap runs downwards.

However, furs with a curled, swirling pile have no nap to consider.

Remember that prominent fur markings must be matched as carefully as a patterned fabric.

Open out the fabric, place it with the pile side down and lay out the pattern pieces on the backing. If you are using the calico pattern you will already have two of each pattern piece, if not, remember to reverse pattern tissues to match.

You will be able to pin the pattern in place on short-haired furs, but where the pile is long and thick use clear adhesive tape to secure the pieces.

Use very sharp scissors when cutting and to avoid cutting the pile lift the fabric with one hand and carefully cut through the backing only. For thick fur fabrics it may be necessary to use a one-sided razor blade instead of scissors.

Mark the pattern details with tailor's chalk or a soft lead pencil. Since fur fabric tends to fray very easily notches should be marked and not cut out. All markings can safely be chalked or pencilled on the back of the fur fabric since the pile will prevent them showing through to the right side.

Stitching and finishing

First test the stitching on scraps of the fur fabric before you attempt any seams on the garment itself. The heavier the fabric, the thicker and stronger the needle and thread will have to be. A thread with elasticity, such as pure silk or one of the new synthetic threads, gives good results.

Use a stitch length of 8-10 stitches to 2·5cm.

Simulated furs with flexible knitted backings should be stitched with a narrow zigzag stitch.

Fur fabrics with PVC coated backings should be stitched with a roller foot on the machine.

A roller foot is also useful if you have to stitch directly onto the right side of the fur. Alternatively, you can cover the surface of the fabric with a strip of tissue paper.

Seams. Plain seams are the most suitable for fur fabrics. If the fur fabric has a slippery long piled surface, tack the seams carefully before stitching.

Simulated lambs-wool or similar fur fab-

rics lock together well and can be pinned. Seams in heavy fur fabric can be held together with paper clips.

When joining simulated fur to a flat fabric tack it securely in place to prevent it slipping and stitch in the direction of the nap with the flat fabric on top.

With seams subjected to strain, use seam tape in with the stitching (figure 4).

After stitching shave the pile from the seam allowance with a safety razor or scissors (figure 5a). Then use a pin to tease out the pile from the seam (figure 5b).

With long-haired fur fabrics it is easier to shave the pile from the seam allowance and push the remaining hairs towards the right side before you stitch the seam (figure 6).

Trim enclosed seams (collar seams or faced seams) as close as possible, layering them to reduce bulk. Stitch these seams twice, reducing the stitch length at corners, to make them as strong as possible.

Pressing. Most seams can be finger pressed open and rubbed on the inside with a thimble to make them lie flat. Use an iron sparingly, testing first on fabric scraps. Dry press with a cool iron on the wrong side only, using a needleboard or towelling to protect the pile.

Finishing the seams. After stitching and pressing finish the seam edges carefully. They can be bound with bias binding, over sewn by hand or finished with a wide machine zigzag stitch.

You can also slip stitch the seam allowance to the backing, thus finishing it and holding it flat at the same time.

On heavier fur fabrics seam allowances can be glued back in place with an adhesive such as Evostick.

Darts. Cut darts open and trim, then shave and finish seam allowances as you would on a plain seam.

Fastenings. Machine made buttonholes work successfully in some fur fabrics but are usually best avoided. Instead, use soft leather or imitation leather and make bound buttonholes, using the method described in the following chapter.

Imitate the fastenings used on real fur coats such as large hooks and eyes or frogging, or make a mock button opening with large covered press studs underneath the buttons.

Zippers. Zippers are best sewn in place by hand. Shear the pile from the seam allowance to prevent it catching in the teeth of the zipper.

Lining. Linings can be slip stitched in place in the normal way through the pile, but if you have difficulty shave the pile away on the edges of sleeve hems and facings.

Chapter 44

Bound buttonholes, stitched yokes and piping

Nothing gives away the careless dress-maker quite so distinctly as haphazard finishes. To avoid such a situation, this chapter gives hints on the perfect buttonhole, as well as several methods of decorative seaming.

Bound buttonholes

There is one basic technique for making bound buttonholes which is varied according to the type of fabric used.

The fabric
The fabric on which the bound button-holes are being made must have some depth into which the extra fabric used for binding the buttonhole can sink, otherwise the binding will create bulk and rise above the fabric surface.

Fabrics which fray easily must have the fraying arrested first. This is achieved by lining the binding for the buttonhole as well as the area for the buttonhole itself. Fabrics which fray even after these precautions are unsuitable.

The size
When using thick coating fabric make sure the buttonhole is not less than 19mm long. If shorter there will not be enough length to work it properly and the button-hole will look lumpy.

Unlike hand-worked buttonholes, which have a solidly stitched edge, bound button-holes are soft and give a little, so it is not necessary to make an extra allowance

The jersey of this simple, fitted coat is a suitable fabric for bound buttonholes.

when measuring out the length of the buttonhole—the buttonhole can be made to the exact diameter of the button. However, if the button is exceptionally thick add half the thickness of the button to the length for ease.

Stitch size
The stitching needs to be very firm and small as it comes very close to the button-hole opening.

Engage the smallest stitch setting on your machine and stitch two layers of fabric together. The stitches should be about the size of a pinpoint.

Width

The buttonhole width depends on the type of fabric you are working on. If made in thick fabrics the buttonholes should be about 9mm wide, but in thin fabrics you can make them quite narrow—about 5mm to 6mm wide.

Making the buttonholes

Here are step by step instructions:

☐ Measure out the buttonhole positions and length and mark them as shown (figure 2).

☐ For each buttonhole cut a strip of fabric on the cross 5cm wide and 3·8cm longer then the buttonhole length. Working on the outside of the garment, lay the strip centrally over the buttonhole position with right sides of the fabric facing (figure 3).

☐ Working on the wrong side of the fabric stitch the outline of the buttonhole, shaping it into a perfect rectangle and carefully pivoting the work on the needle at each corner (figure 4). Run the last stitches over the first stitches as shown, to prevent the buttonhole from splitting.

☐ Using sharp, pointed scissors, cut into the stitched area as shown (figure 5) taking care not to cut the stitches at the corners.

☐ Pull the binding fabric to the inside (figure 6). Then lay each buttonhole seam allowance over the edge of a sleeveboard and press the seam allowances away from the opening as shown.

☐ **Small buttonholes.** For small buttonholes turn the work to the outside and gently roll the folded edges of the binding so that they meet along the centre of the buttonhole with equal width to each side (figure 7). Lightly tack along the opening as shown.

Turn the work to the inside and gently pull the horizontal edges of the binding fabric to make the rolls continue evenly beyond the opening of the buttonhole. Catch them together permanently with matching thread (figure 8).

☐ **Large buttonholes.** Large buttonholes are made as above but each rolled edge must be worked separately. As it is rolled it must be secured with small prick stitches along the fold of the seam line on the right side (figure 9). Do not pull the stitches tight into the fabric or they will make dents which will show in the finished work.

Tack along the opening (figure 10) then stitch the ends of the rolled edges together on the wrong side as shown in figure 8.

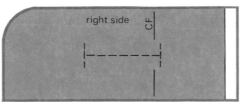
▲ **2.** *The marked out buttonhole*

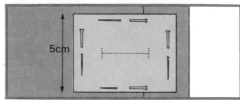
▲ **3.** *The bias strip laid over the buttonhole*

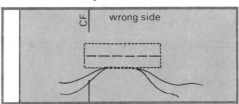
▲ **4.** *The stitched rectangle for the buttonhole*

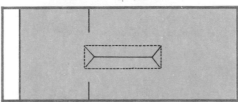
▲ **5.** *Cutting the buttonhole*

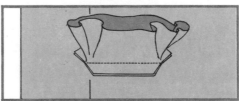
▲ **6.** *The binding pulled through the opening*

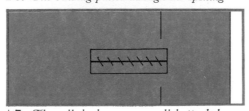
▲ **7.** *The rolled edges on a small buttonhole*

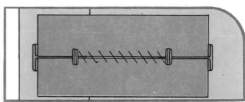
▲ **8.** *The rolled edges sewn at the sides*

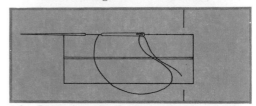
▲ **9.** *Large buttonhole: the prick stitched edge*

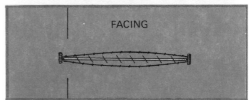
▲ **10.** *The tacked opening of a large buttonhole*

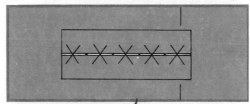
▲ **11.** *The facing cut for the buttonhole opening*

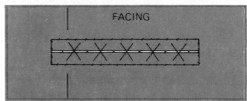
▲ **12.** *The facing cut for a thick buttonhole*

▲ **13.** *The finished buttonhole*

☐ With the tacking stitches still in place, carefully press each buttonhole. Then, while the work is still warm from the iron, gently pull the ends of the rolled edges of the bias strip to settle them into the fabric and fix the shape of the buttonhole. Remove any impressions made in the fabric by pressing under the binding fabric strip.

Turn the garment facing over the buttonholes and tack the front edge of the facing firmly in position.

Feel the buttonhole through the facing fabric and make a cut through the facing to the length of the buttonhole opening. Turn in the edges of the cut and hem them to the buttonhole (figure 11).

If the ends of the cut are tight you must make the snip a little longer to take away the strain.

Make a small bar across each end as shown, to strengthen the opening.

On heavy fabric it may be necessary to cut the facing as for the buttonhole since the turning of the raw edges makes it necessary to make a cut very much longer than the opening of the buttonhole (figure 12).

☐ Lightly press over the hemmed edges, remove the tacking thread from the rolled edges of the buttonhole and give a final pressing (figure 13).

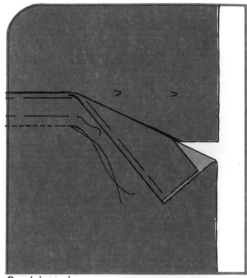

8. *A lapped seam*

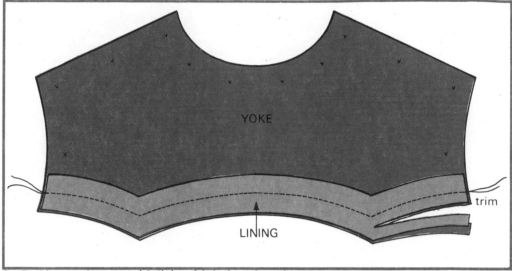

9. *Backing a yoke-seam with lining fabric for a lapped seam*

trim

YOKE

LINING

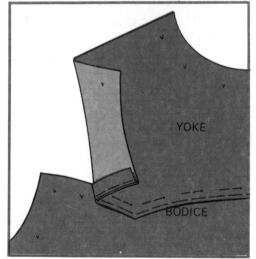

YOKE

BODICE

10. *The lined lapped seam pinned in place*

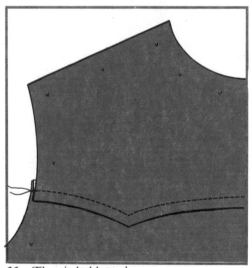

11. *The stitched lapped seam*

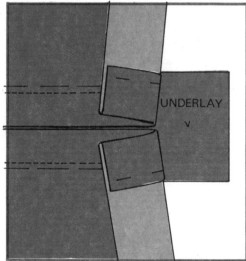

UNDERLAY

12. *A channel seam*

Stitching yoke-seams

The way yoke-seams are stitched usually determines the character of the garment. Lapped seaming (see below) is used for sporty versions and ordinary seams give a formal look. Topstitching creates a casual effect which softens the appearance and also brings out good detailing.

In addition to lap seaming two other seam types are dealt with here, the slot, channel or open seam and the piped seam, both of which add an interesting change of detail.

Lap seaming

In lap seaming the seam allowance along one seam edge is turned under, tacked and pressed. It is then lapped over the corresponding seam allowance, with the fold meeting the stitching line, and stitched the required distance from the folded edge (figure 8).

A lapped yoke-seam on a bulky fabric can result in a rather thick seam, especially

if the yoke-seam is shaped. To avoid this, first back the yoke-seam with strong matching lining fabric (figure 9). To do this cut a strip of lining fabric to the shape of the seam and twice the width of the seam allowance, in the same grain of the fabric. Pin it to the yoke, right sides facing.

Stitch the fabric and lining together along the yoke-seam line, trim the seam allowance to about 9mm and turn the lining to the inside. Edge-tack and press the stitched edge.

Pin and tack the lined edge to meet the seam line of the corresponding section (figure 10) and topstitch in place (figure 11).

Channel, slot or open seaming

The seam line in this kind of seam is not stitched together. Instead, the seam allowances are turned under, tacked and pressed, and brought to meet over an underlay, then topstitched in position (figure 12).

This type of seaming is easy to work and can be very effective on a yoke. Figure 13 shows how a designer has used V-shaped channel seaming as the main feature of a design.

There are two ways to work this type of seam.

i. Here each seam allowance is turned under, tacked and pressed. The folded edges are then brought to meet along the centre of the underlay and tacked in place and stitched.

ii. First tack the seam together, right sides facing, and press open. Place the tacked seam centrally to the underlay, stitch to each side and then remove the tacking. This method can only be used on straight seams.

Here are a few do's and don'ts.

○ Always cut the underlay so that the straight of grain runs in the same direction as the straight of grain through which the seam goes. If you ignore this precaution the underlay will wring during wear.

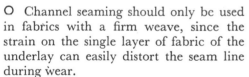
13. *Channel seaming in a Vogue pattern*

11. *A yoke-seam finished with piping*

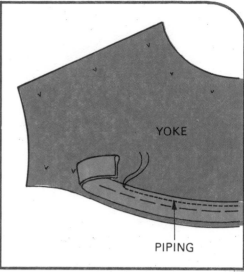
15. *Stitching the piping in place*

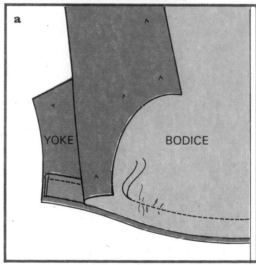
16a. *Method (i) for attaching the piped section* **b.** *method (ii)*

○ Channel seaming should only be used in fabrics with a firm weave, since the strain on the single layer of fabric of the underlay can easily distort the seam line during wear.

○ Never make a channel seam where one seam line of corresponding sections has ease built in for fitting purposes; that side of the open seam would always tilt or stand away since it has more length.

○ If the seam is used on areas which are subject to strain when sitting, such as the bust or hips, allow more ease in the garment to avoid the seam edges gaping.

Piping

Apart from attractive stitching the seam line of a yoke can be finished with piping (figure 14).

Piping can give increased importance to a seam in plain fabric or will bring a yoke out of the background of a patterned fabric.

How to pipe
For the piping, cut a bias strip twice the width of the seam allowance plus 6mm. Cut the strip long enough for the length of the seam to be piped and do not make any joins.

Fold the piping strip lengthways and press. Pin and tack the folded edge 3mm over the seam line, seam allowances level (figure 15).

Stitch the piping to the seam line as shown.

To join the piped section to the corresponding section, work in one of the following two ways.

i. Pin and tack the piped section to the corresponding section as for ordinary seaming and stitch together, stitching over the first row of stitches as shown in (figure 16a).

ii. Fold under the seam allowance of the piping and the piped section, and pin and tack it to the seam line of the corresponding section ready for topstitching.

Work the topstitching close to the folded

piped edge as shown in figure 16b.

Precautions
Before deciding to pipe a seam here are a few practical considerations.

Piping introduces thickness into seams which creates a lot of bulk. This bulk produces problems when laundering a garment. While the main parts of the garment become too dry for ironing the piped section is still wet. So special attention is required when the garment is pressed.

In addition, piping often needs hard pressing, so make sure that the fabric of the garment can withstand this before pressing.

There are very few fabrics which can be used successfully for piping. One suitable fabric is cotton piqué. Here the back of the weave is constructed so that wringing is resisted when it is sewn into the seam. It is also quite rigid and will prevent buckling when inserted between two layers of fabric.

Chapter 45

Godets and gussets

This chapter deals with godets and gussets. Both are seam insertions which every dressmaker should know about. As the exact cut of these is decided by the design of a particular garment it is impossible to give general advice on cutting. But it is particularly important that these insets be perfectly applied, and there is much to be said on the technique of application which apply to all.

Godets

Godets (figure 1) are cut to suit the design of a garment. Their function is both ornamental and practical, and the rest of the garment is cut so that the godet becomes a necessary addition to the design.

Cutting a godet

Godets come in varying degrees of a circle, depending on the effect the designer is trying to achieve. They are basically cut as follows:

Full godet. This is cut in a full 180 degree semi-circle with the straight lengthwise grain through the centre of the godet from point to hem, and with both seams in the crosswise grain (figure 2a).

Medium full godet. Here the godet is cut in a 90 degree quarter circle with the centre of the godet from the point to hem going through the lengthwise grain of the fabric and the seams through the bias of the fabric (figure 2b).

Soft fall godet. For a really soft fall cut the centre of the 90 degree godet on the bias of the fabric so that one seam line is on the crosswise grain and the other on the lengthwise grain (figure 2c).

This cut is also suitable for sunray pleating.

Suitable fabrics

When choosing a fabric for a garment with godet insertions select a soft but firm weave. The fabric must not have the dead drop of a crepe jersey since this would make the godet look untidy, although some jerseys are suitable.

Inserting godets into seams

The method for inserting godets varies with each design. Given here is the method most commonly used.

These instructions go a bit further than most pattern instructions in concentrating on the finish for the point of the godet where a certain skill comes into play.

First prepare and stitch the seam to where the godet starts. Fasten off the threads securely and press the seam open.

Stitch one side of the godet to the open end of the seam line and press the seam open or away from the godet according to the pattern instructions. Make sure that the godet seam line meets the end stitch of the upper seam line and fasten off the threads securely.

▲ **1.** *The straight panelled six-gore skirt conversion with godets*

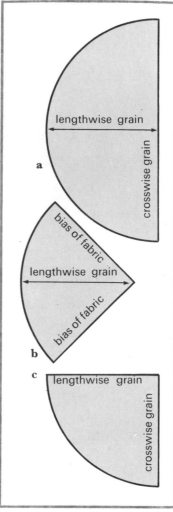

▲ **2a.** *Full godet;* **b.** *medium full godet;* **c.** *soft fall godet*

Stitch the other seam line of the godet similarly.

The junction of the upper seam line and the godet point is usually very weak indeed. This is how to strengthen it.

Unfold the seam allowance at the point of the godet and spread it over the end of the upper seam (figure 3a).

Turn the work to the outside and make a tiny bar catching in both sides of the upper seam and the underlying godet seam allowance (figure 3b).

Turn the work to the inside again and gently press the seam allowance back into position.

Gussets

Gussets are cut according to the purpose they have to fulfil, and it is most important that the gusset is related exactly to the cut of the garment.

Although gussets are inserted to give freedom of movement, they should never be inserted just because something is too tight. Gussets are an integral feature of the design and the width they provide is no more than has been left out in the cut of the garment. As the exact shape of the gusset has been carefully determined by the cut of the rest of the garment, the cutting of gussets is a complicated process which requires much expertise. Because of this the instructions for gussets must be limited to their application.

First, it is most important that you follow the grain line in the pattern. You will have seen badly cut gussets inserted into the

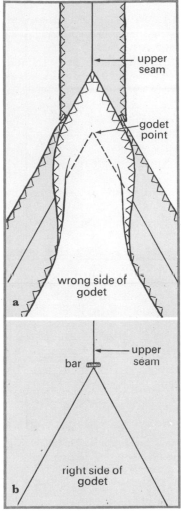

▲ **3a.** *The seam allowance spread over the upper seam;* **b.** *the bar*

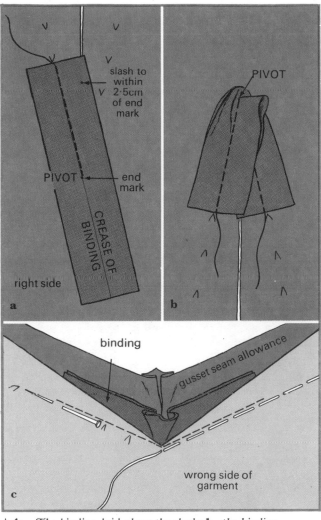

▲ **4a.** *The binding laid along the slash;* **b.** *the binding stitched;* **c.** *the gusset pinned and tacked in place*

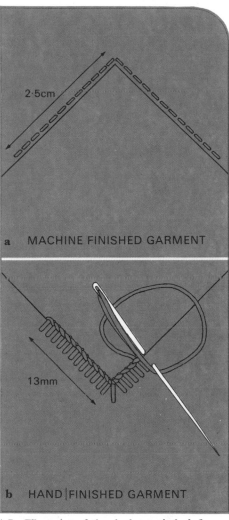

▲ **5.** *The point of the slash topstitched;* **b.** *buttonhole stitches worked into the point*

underarm seams of a garment which droop and pull adversely with every arm movement, and look very ugly indeed.

Hints on inserting gussets

The underarm gusset is the most commonly used in dressmaking. It is often inserted into a slash made in the fabric, which goes through the sleeve and into the side-seam line at the underarm.

It is essential that the point of the slash is secured firmly to avoid tearing. The methods for this are given below and are chosen according to the fabric type and finish used.

Method 1. This method uses seam binding and is suitable for most fabrics. It requires practice as the application of the seam binding is done completely freehand; tacking and pinning is impossible.

Working on the outside of the garment, first mark the end for the slash clearly and mark seam line. Slash to 2·5cm of the end mark. Cut 6·3cm of matching 16mm wide seam binding. Fold and press this lengthwise to obtain a centre crease for stitching. Open the pressed seam binding and lay half of it to the left of the mark for the end of the slash, with the crease of the seam binding just outside the seam line (figure 4a).

Stitch along the crease line to meet the mark for the end of the slash. Do not withdraw the needle but pivot the work carefully so that you cannot lose your position.

Turn the seam binding around the needle ready to lay it over the other seam line then, with the help of a pin, manoeuvre the doubled up seam binding around the needle to one side and out of the way

of the downward row of stitches. Stitch along the crease line to the end of the seam binding as before (figure 4b).

Carefully slash between the stitching to within one or two grains of the end. As you spread the slash the seam binding should lie flat across it.

When inserting the gusset, fold the seam binding over and towards the raw edges of the slash, leaving the seam line free. Pin and tack the gusset into position following seam line as marked (figure 4c). Stitch and press as recommended in the pattern instructions.

For fabrics where seam binding is too heavy, cut a strip 16mm wide from the selvedge of the fabric and fold, press and apply as for seam binding.

Method 2. This method makes use of top stitching to strengthen the points of the slash. It is suitable only for firmly woven fabrics —loosely woven fabrics must be mounted for extra strength.

Insert gusset into slash as above but without reinforcing the ends. After stitching, press the seam allowance towards the garment and away from the gusset.

On machine finished garments topstitch round the point. Working on the right side stitch close to the seam starting 2·5cm down from the point, working around it and continuing 2·5cm down the other side (figure 5a).

On hand finished garments, work fine buttonhole stitches into the point. Work the stitches on the right side using fine sewing thread. Start 13mm from the point, work into the point and along the other side, catching the edge of the seam and the seam allowance into the stitches (figure 5b).

Chapter 46

Various fastenings in dressmaking

The tone of a garment, casual or formal, is often set by the kind of fastening used on it, and in many cases a fastening may be the only fashion detail on a garment.

Fastenings can be functional, in which case they have to be very firmly and carefully constructed, or they can be purely decorative, as in the case of a simulated buttoned tab. Sometimes, however, a fastening can be both functional and decorative and a perfect example of this is a dress with a Centre Front opening fastened from neck to hem with rouleau loops. A functional fastening in quite a different mood is the fly fastening, shown on the opposite page. This is a Vogue Paris Original Pattern.

Previous chapters have dealt with some buttoned and tab Centre Front fastenings, also rouleau loop and tie fastenings, and have shown the methods of constructing these so that you can apply them to any garment you wish. This chapter gives two more types of fastenings, which are buttoned and zipped fly fastenings, to provide you with further ideas for completely changing the mood of your favourite styles.

Fabrics and fastenings

The fastening on a garment should be very carefully planned as it must not only suit the style of the garment but also the fabric it is made from. The basic construction must be correct if the fastening is to retain its shape for the life time of the garment, and also to ensure that it does not break down and so make the garment look worn out before its time.

The weight of the fabric used is the deciding factor, and a lot of dressmaking experience is required to make the right decision.

On bulky fabrics the position of the fastening is also important, especially if you have certain figure problems.

Fastenings should always remain flat and not rise from the surface of the garment in a high ridge. If this happens it could be the result of faulty construction.

Fly fastenings

Fly fastenings are concealed fastenings used when it is necessary for the surface of a garment to retain an uncluttered look and when the cut of the garment is more important than the detail. They are mostly worked into a seam line, such as a Centre Front seam or panel seam.

Although fly fastenings are often closed with a zip, the traditional way to close them is with buttonholes set into a button bar attached to the underside of the right front.

For demonstrating the fly fastenings a dress with a Centre Front seam and no waist-seam has been used.

Buttoned fly fastening

The pattern. You will need pattern pieces for a right Front, left Front, right front facing, left front facing, back neck facing, Back. Use a right Front pattern without wrap (figure 1).

Make a right front facing 5cm wide at the shoulder edge and 8cm wide down the front, the shape of the front and neck edges as shown (figure 1).

For the left Front add 3·8cm to the Centre Front edge for a wrap (figure 2), then make a left front facing 5cm wide at the shoulder edge and 8cm wide down the front.

Make a back neck facing 5cm wide (figure 3).

Lining. Both right Front edge and right front facing need to be lined.

Make a lining pattern 5cm wide, as in figure 4, and use this pattern to cut the lining for both.

Cutting out. Cut facing and lining pieces with seam allowance all round.

Making up. To avoid showing seam edges at the neck edge of the fly fastening, start the buttoning 6·3cm down from the neck line. Line the right Front and right front facing as shown (figure 5). To do this, place the lining and fabric together, right sides facing and Centre Fronts coinciding, and stitch the Centre Front starting 6·3cm down from the neck edge. Snip the seam allowance at the top of the stitching and turn the lining to the inside.

Working on the facing, tack and press the lining to the inside of the facing and make a row of vertical buttonholes 19mm from the Centre Front edge to fit 16mm diameter flat buttons.

Join the right and left front facings to the back neck facing at the shoulder-seams.

Place the joined facing to the garment right sides together. Starting at the snipped seam allowance on the right Front, stitch the facing in place up to the neck edge round the neck and down the left Front.

Turn the facing into the garment, pin in place and edge-tack.

Pin the buttonholed section of the facing to the garment a fraction inside the front edge to avoid the facing showing. Tack it firmly.

Measure in 3·8cm from the edge of the right Front and top-stitch as shown (figure 6), catching in all layers of fabric.

Fasten the neck edge with a press fastener or reversed button and buttonhole (figure 7), and sew on the other buttons.

Zipped fly fastening

The pattern. You will need patterns for a Back, right Front, left Front, right front facing, left front neck facing, back neck facing. Make right Front, right front facing and back neck facing patterns as for the buttoned fly fastening (see figures 1 and 3).

Make a left Front pattern as in figure 8, adding 13mm to the Centre Front edge, also make a left front neck facing as shown.

Cutting out. Cut all edges with seam allowances.

Making up. Complete the garment first. Stitch the right front, back neck and left front neck facings at shoulders. Place on garment, right sides together. Starting at the bottom of the fastening on the right Front stitch up to the neck and round the neck.

Fold under the seam allowance on the left Front along the zip stitching line, then pin and tack the folded edge close to the zip teeth. Stitch firmly in place (figure 9).

Fold the faced right Front edge over the zip so that the Centre Front lines meet (figure 10a) and tack down firmly.

Topstitch the zip in place on the right Front working on the right side of the fabric, catching in all layers of fabric plus zip tape. If the opening is in a seam which continues below the fastening, finish the lower end of the topstitching with a half mitre.

Snip into the seam allowance on the left Front as shown (figure 10b). Fold the neck facing on the left Front opening over the zip tape and hand-sew in place. Fasten the top with a hook and eye.

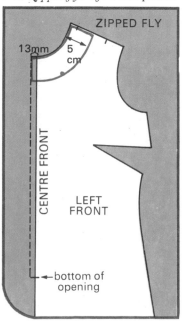

A Vogue pattern

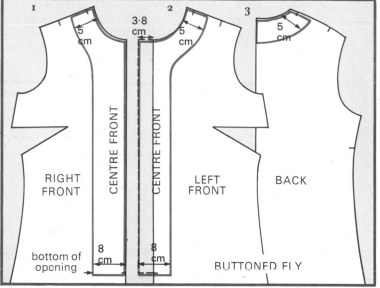

▲ *Buttoned fly:* **1.** and **2.** *right and left Front patterns:* **3.** *back neck facing*
▼ *Buttoned fly:* **4.** *Lining pattern;* **5.** *The lined right Front and facing*

RIGHT FRONT

CENTRE FRONT

CENTRE FRONT

LEFT FRONT

BACK

BUTTONED FLY

3·8 cm

5 cm

5 cm

5 cm

8 cm

8 cm

bottom of opening

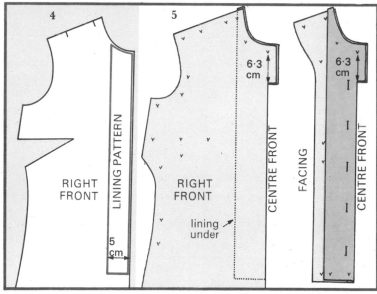

RIGHT FRONT

LINING PATTERN

RIGHT FRONT

CENTRE FRONT

FACING

CENTRE FRONT

lining under

6·3 cm

6·3 cm

5 cm

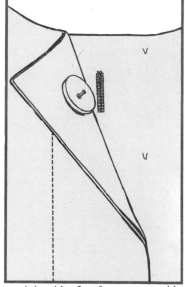

▲ **6.** *Topstitching the right Front*
▼ **7.** *Reversed button and buttonhole*

▼ **8.** *Zipped fly: left Front pattern*   ▼ **9.** *Zip stitched to left Front*   ▼ **10.** *The completed fastening:* **a.** *from right side;* **b.** *from wrong side*

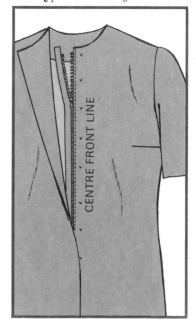

ZIPPED FLY

13mm

5 cm

CENTRE FRONT

LEFT FRONT

bottom of opening

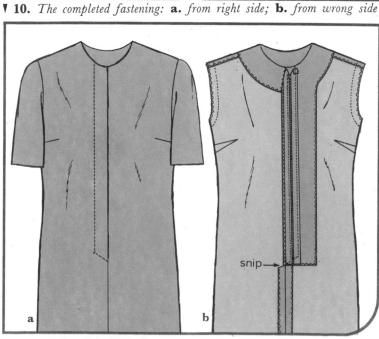

CENTRE FRONT LINE

snip

a

b

Chapter 47

Start with a pop-over pinny

Every little girl needs a pop-over to keep her clothes clean, and if it's got a pretty pocket for her best teddy or hanky it will be fun to wear. These next four pages include a trace pattern complete with instructions for hand or ma-chine sewing. Even if you're not terribly confident about your dressmaking, it's simple enough to make. Experienced dressmakers will enjoy think-ing up other pocket designs based on basic pram shape.

Fabric requirements

0·60m of gingham, 90cm wide. 0·35m of contrast fabric for pocket, or piece 28cm by 35cm. 2·75m of bias binding (for machine finish only). Two buttons. Sewing thread or embroidery cotton.

Lay-out and cutting

Fold gingham selvedge to selvedge and lay out the pattern pieces as shown in the diagrams. Cut ONE pocket in gingham and ONE pocket and loop in contrast fabric.
Mark out seam allowance on all pattern pieces and cut out along these lines.

Making up

Make line of tacking down the Centre Front on fold. Join side-seams and shoulder-seams. If you work by hand, use back stitch or running stitch. Overcast raw edges.

If you work by hand

Turn under, pin and tack seam allowance on neck, arm-holes and around hem up to the top of Centre Back. Press lightly in position. Work around these edges with alternating blanket stitch. This not only looks attractive but ensures that you catch the folded edge every time. Make stitches about 5mm apart.
For pram pocket, turn under seam allowance all round, snipping corners on contrast fabric and gingham. Tack together and work same blanket stitch all round pram.

If you work by machine

Take bias binding, open fold on one side and lay to seam allowance, right sides facing, around neck, armholes and hem. Ease into curves at neck and armholes, pin and stitch together. Turn bias binding to the inside and tack in position. Stitch to pop-over and press, taking care not to stretch edges.
For pram pocket lay gingham and contrast fabric pieces together, right sides facing, and stitch. Leave 90cm opening to pull fabric inside out. Snip corners and turn pocket through. Finish opening. Tack round edge to shape and press lightly.

To make loop, by hand and machine

Fold fabric in half lengthwise and stitch. Pull through to outside with the aid of safety pin. Press flat.

To stitch pram pocket to pop-over and finish

Lay centre of pocket to Centre Front of pop-over, with wheels about 3·8cm from bottom edge. Tuck loop for handle under end of pram and stitch, following dash line on pattern. If you stitch by hand, use firm back stitch and do not sew over the blanket stitches.
To fasten pop-over at back, attach two pieces of ribbon at neck and tie, or make two loops for buttons on right side of Back and attach where shown on pattern. Sew on buttons opposite the loops.

Some pretty bright ideas

Of course there's no need to stick to the pram pocket if you have other ideas for motifs, or if you are making more than one pop-over. Use the pram for the basic pocket shape—but adapt it in different ways.
You can make the pram, minus the wheels, into a boat, and appliqué a white or coloured sail to the front of the pinny. Or, make a basket, with a handle, and then appliqué bright flowers, or richly coloured fruits.

▲ Pop-over seen from the back

▲ Pop-over front, with pocket

▼ Layout on 90cm fabric, with pram pocket on contrast piece

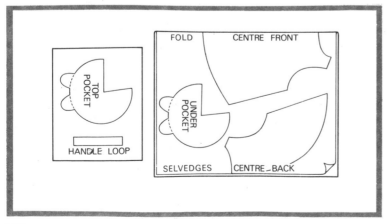

Pattern for pram pocket

Solid black line: stitching line for pram. Arrows indicate corners for snipping.
Dash line: for stitching pram to pop-over.
Seam allowance to be added: 6mm all round pram.

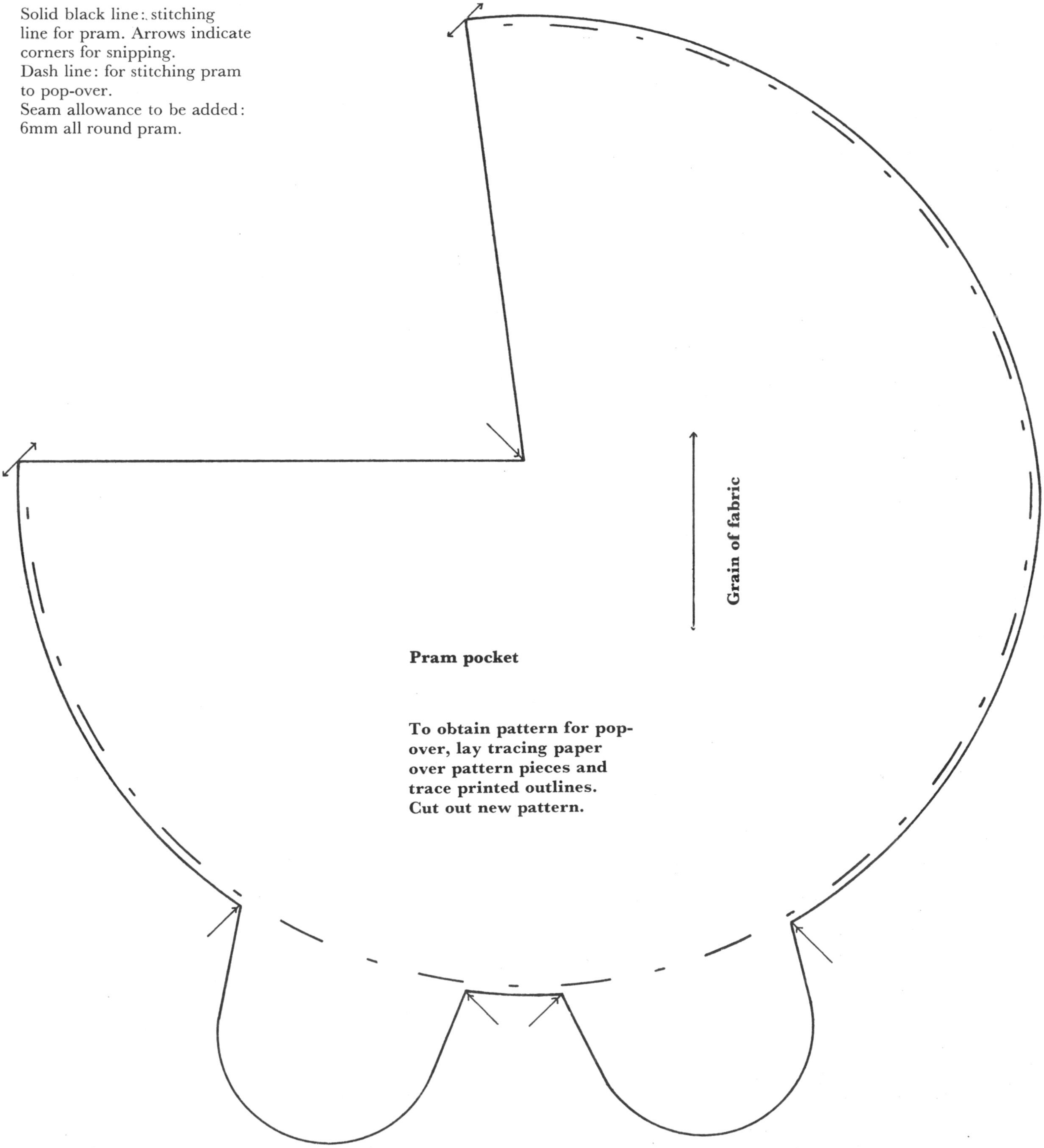

Grain of fabric

Pram pocket

To obtain pattern for pop-over, lay tracing paper over pattern pieces and trace printed outlines. Cut out new pattern.

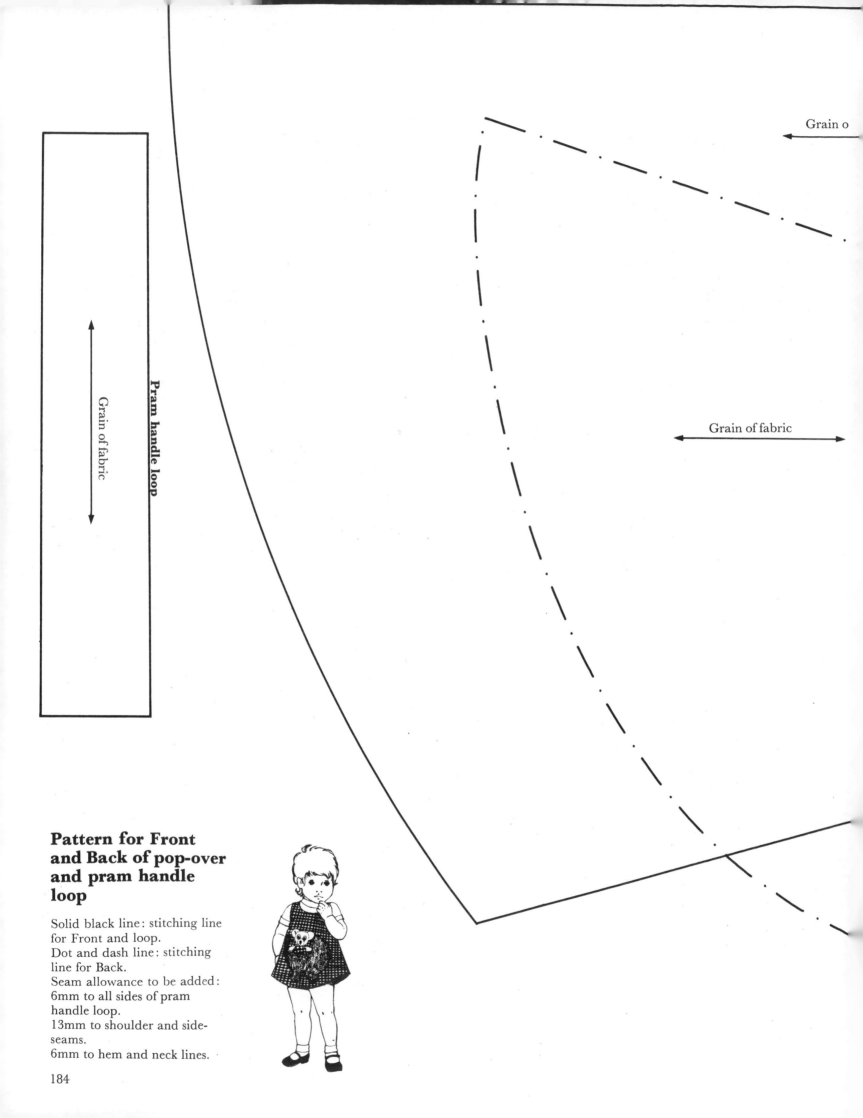

Grain o

Grain of fabric

Pram handle loop

Grain of fabric

Pattern for Front and Back of pop-over and pram handle loop

Solid black line: stitching line for Front and loop.
Dot and dash line: stitching line for Back.
Seam allowance to be added: 6mm to all sides of pram handle loop.
13mm to shoulder and side-seams.
6mm to hem and neck lines.

184

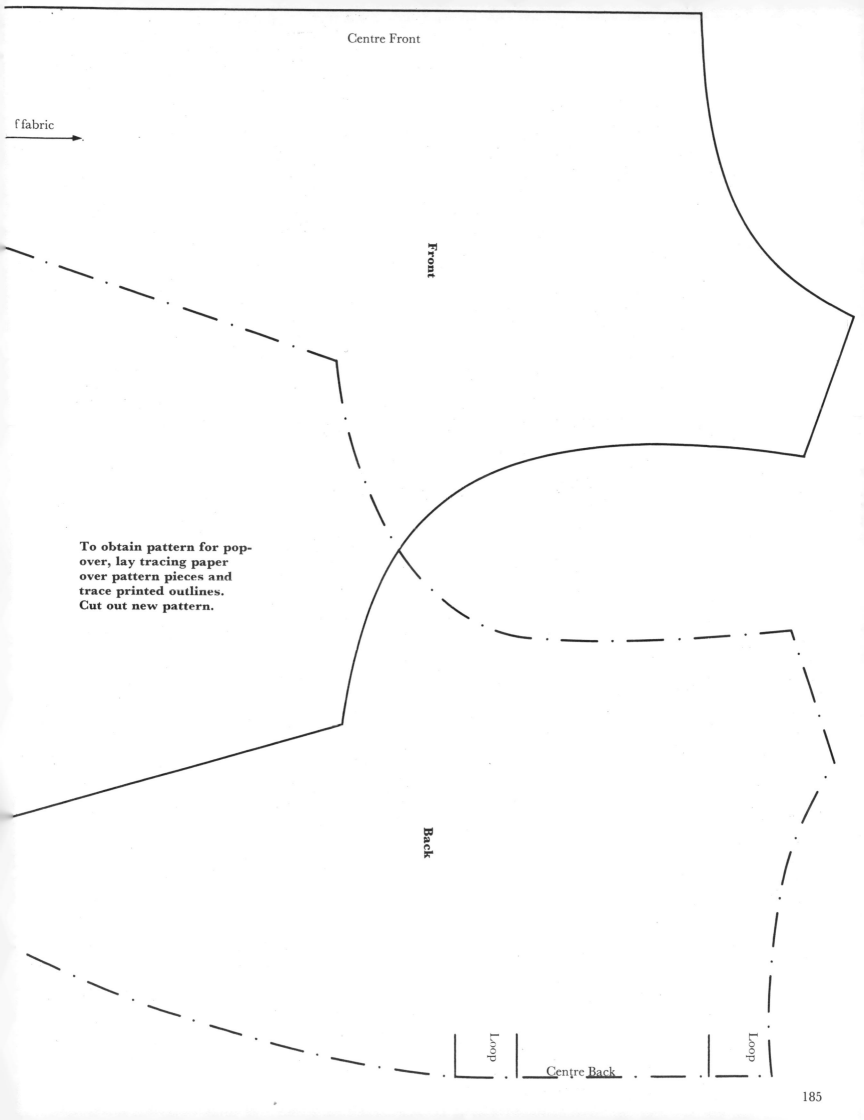

Centre Front

f fabric

Front

To obtain pattern for pop-
over, lay tracing paper
over pattern pieces and
trace printed outlines.
Cut out new pattern.

Centre Back

Back

Loop

Loop

Loop

Centre Back

Chapter 48

Angel top

Angel tops are the most useful garments in a toddler's wardrobe. Made in a light fabric, with matching knickers, an angel top becomes a pretty summer dress—or in soft wool, in a colour matched to tights, a warm winter play outfit. Angel tops in wipe-clean fabrics provide a protective cover-up for messy mealtimes and, at the other extreme, they can be the prettiest of party dresses made in broderie Anglaise.

You will need:

☐ 1·50m 90cm wide fabric ☐ 0·95m 6mm wide elastic ☐ Matching thread
☐ Graph paper for the pattern (or ordinary brown paper will do). If you are making the angel top in broderie Anglaise edging, to find the amount you need add together the width across the widest point of both sleeves and the width across the hem line on the Back and Front, plus an extra 15cm for seam allowances. If you have difficulty in finding an edging which is as deep as the length of the garment, overlap and stitch two rows together.

The pattern

The angel top fits sizes 1 and 2 and is in 41cm and 46cm lengths. There are four pattern pieces, Back, Front, sleeve and facing. Make the pattern first from the instructions overleaf.

The layout

Fold fabric to take in Back and Front. Place pattern on double fabric as shown, with Centre Back and Front on fold. Fold remaining fabric selvedge to selvedge, place centre front of facing on fold.
The pattern has no seam or hem allowance so add 19mm to all seams (except on the outer edge of the facing) and 5cm hems at the lower edge of the sleeves and hem edge.
Cut out the fabric and mark the pattern outline, stitching lines and balance marks.

Making up in six easy stages

1. Sewing sleeves to Back and Front

With right sides facing, match the balance marks on the front armhole edge of the left sleeve to those of the corresponding Front armhole. Pin, tack, and stitch the seams. Then match the balance marks of the back armhole edge of the sleeve to those of the corresponding Back armhole. Pin, tack and stitch as before. Repeat for right sleeve. Oversew raw seam edges to neaten and press seams towards sleeve.

2. Joining the facing

Align the two Centre Back edges of the facing, with right sides of fabric together, and stitch a short seam from neck edge to the balance mark, leaving the lower end open. Press seam open. The unfinished end of the seam provides the casing opening.

3. Stitching on the facing and making the casing

With right sides of fabric together, place facing round neck line, with raw neck edges level, balance marks and Centre Backs and Fronts matching. Pin, tack and stitch along neck edge.
Trim the seam allowance and then clip into it close to the stitches. Turn facing to inside of garment, tack along edge and press.
If the edge is inclined to roll, as on a springy fabric, top stitch through dress and facings close to the edge. Turn in the raw edge of the facing 6mm and tack.
Pin the facing flat into position round the inside of the neck edge. The folded edge should just cover the lower stitching line and the balance marks on the facing should meet the armhole seam.
Tack in place and stitch close to the edge, along lower stitching line.
Turn the garment to right side, make another row of machine stitches along the upper stitching line and the casing is finished.

4. Sewing the sleeve and side-seams

With right sides facing, pin, tack and stitch the left underarm sleeve and side-seams in one operation; starting at the wrist edge stitch to the underarm and then down the side seam to the hem edge. Repeat on right side.
Oversew raw seam edges and press seams open.

5. Making the sleeve casing

Turn in the lower edge of sleeves 6mm and tack. Turn up the hem allowance so that the folded edge falls just over the upper stitching line. Make the casing as before but leave a small opening in the upper stitching line for the elastic.

6. Finishing

Cut three pieces of elastic, one to fit the child's neck, the other two to fit the wrists. Thread the elastic through the casings and sew the ends firmly together. Slip stitch openings in casings to close. Turn up the hem to the required length and give all seams and edges a final pressing.

Alternative finishes

Since this garment is so quick and easy to make, you'll want more than one. Try ringing the changes with a different finish on the neck and sleeves.

Angel top with bound edges

Cut off the pattern midway between the stitching lines for the casing around the neck, and do not allow for sleeve hems.
Lay out the pattern pieces as before, but place the Back pattern parallel to the selvedges and 19mm in from the edge, to allow for a Centre Back seam.
Sew a Centre Back seam leaving 10cm open at the top.
Loosely measure the child's neck and wrists and gather the neck line and lower sleeve edges to these measurements.
Cut bias strips to the length of the measurements, adding 2·5cm for neatening the ends, and bind the gathered edges.
Use loop and button fastenings to close the back neck opening.

Angel top with back buttoning

To make a quick slip-over for playtimes or mealtimes, fasten the angel top all the way down the Centre Back with buttons.
When laying out the pattern for this version, place the Centre Back parallel to the selvedges, 8cm from the edge of the fabric. This will give you a 2·5cm wrap on each side and 5cm for the self facing.
Make the buttonholes along the Centre Back line.

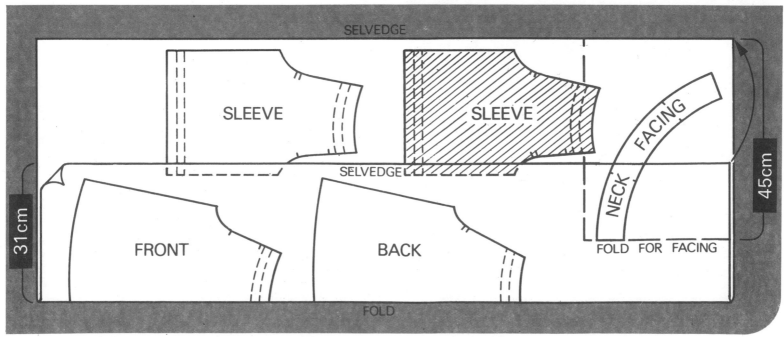

SELVEDGE

SLEEVE

SLEEVE

NECK FACING

SELVEDGE

31cm

45cm

FRONT

BACK

FOLD FOR FACING

FOLD

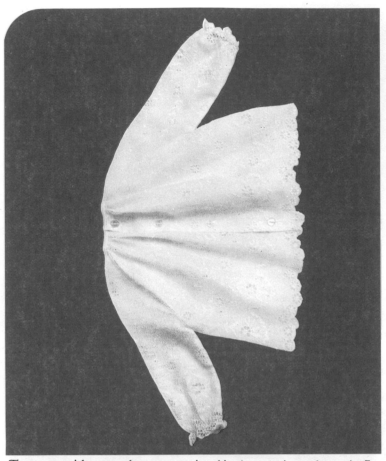

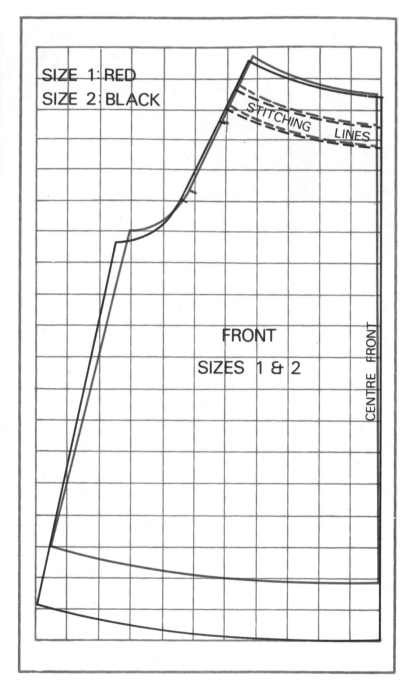

Two ways with an angel top—pretty in white ▲ or gay in a colour print ▼

The pattern

Each square on graph represents a 2·5cm square.

All the pattern pieces are without seam or hem allowance.

To make the patterns cut the following pieces of graph paper (or brown paper if graph paper is not available):

For the Front cut a piece 48cm by 28cm.

For the Back cut a piece 48cm by 28cm.

For the sleeve cut a piece 43cm by 28cm.

For the facing cut a piece 33cm by 25cm.

If you are using brown paper, you'll find it easier to plot the pattern if you draw up all the pieces into 2·5cm squares. Do make sure though that you draw the lines very carefully and absolutely straight or the pattern will not be accurate.

To make the pattern for size 2, copy it to scale from the graphs, using the outer solid black lines.

To make the pattern for size 1, copy to scale from graphs, using the solid red lines, except where black and red lines merge.

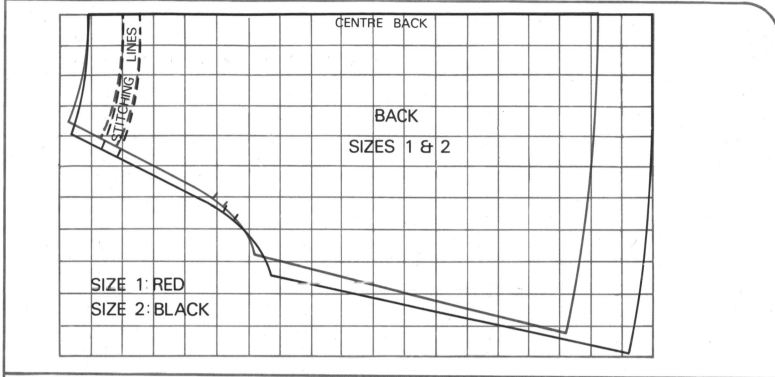

CENTRE BACK

BACK

SIZES 1 & 2

STITCHING LINES

SIZE 1: RED
SIZE 2: BLACK

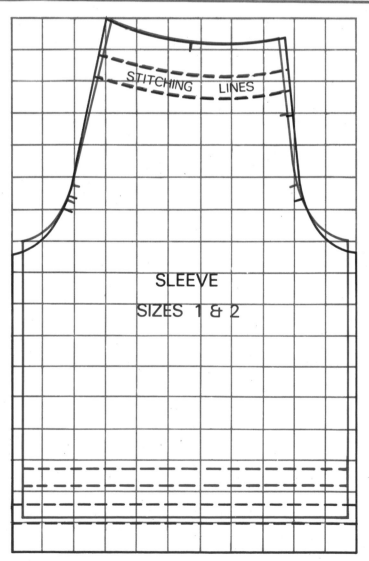

STITCHING LINES

SLEEVE

SIZES 1 & 2

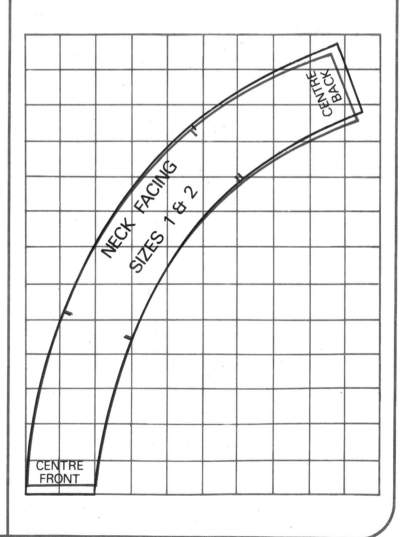

NECK FACING

SIZES 1 & 2

CENTRE BACK

CENTRE FRONT

Chapter 49

Sewing for Children

A great little dress

Here's a dress to delight a small member of the family. It's a basic pattern, shown here made up in cotton needlecord and trimmed with a sparkling white detachable collar.

This little dress is given in three sizes, to fit a 60cm, 66cm and 70cm chest. The patterns are on graph and each dress consists of three pattern pieces only. It's quick and easy to do and yet it's versatile enough for you to be able to make a whole wardrobe of excitingly different little dresses for all sorts of occasions from this one pattern.

Dressmaking for children can be easy and fun

You can make up this dress in different types of fabric with various trimmings and here are some ideas to get you started.

For play, make it in hard-wearing cotton or needlecord and add big patch pockets. For parties, as a complete contrast, make it in something light and filmy. Choose plain or embroidered organdie, organza or voile for a top dress, then stitch it to an underdress in matching or contrasting cotton lawn or taffeta. For a really delicate look, trim it with lace or add frills.

For holidays and beach wear, make a sleeveless version in towelling and, to make it really practical, stitch a row of apron pockets across the front to hold all those pretty pebbles and shells gathered on the beach.

There are many excellent washable wools available for making cosy and practical winter dresses and you can add detachable collars and cuffs to quickly change the appearance of each dress. You'll see how to make these in the next chapter.

The basic pattern

The patterns on graph are in three sizes: 60cm chest, length 57cm; 66cm chest, length 61cm; 70cm chest, length 67cm. Each square represents a 2·5cm square.

To copy the pattern, use graph paper or any firm paper drawn up accurately into centimetre squares. Before you begin, select the pattern size you want and cut the paper into pieces just large enough to accommodate each pattern graph. Then copy the outline of the pattern to scale.

It is easy to adjust the length of the pattern by adding to or deducting from the squares between the lower edge of the armhole and the hem line. Do not add or deduct at the hem because, as with the flared skirt pattern, the flare of the dress will be affected. If you need to cater for in-between sizes, select the larger of the two sizes and pin off the difference at the fitting.

Making fitting easier

Small children often get very fidgety if they have to stand still to be fitted and sometimes a fitting session can finish in tears and bad temper. You may only have an hour or two during the school

Key to graphs for the child's basic dress

The patterns are in three sizes
60cm chest, length 57cm
66cm chest, length 61cm
70cm chest, length 67cm
Each square on the graph represents a 2·5cm square
The patterns do not include seam allowance

Colour key to sizes
Size 60cm chest = ⎯⎯⎯⎯
Size 66cm chest = ⎯⎯⎯⎯
Size 70cm chest = ⎯⎯⎯⎯

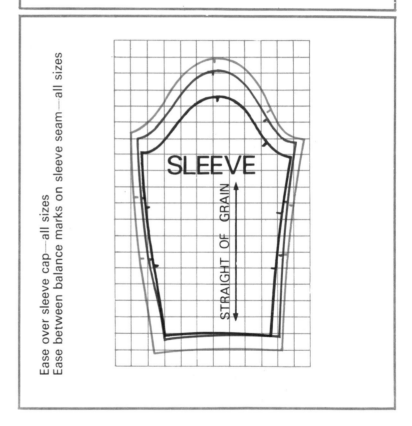

day when you can get down to some dressmaking and it may be difficult to get beyond the fitting stage.

One way to help you over these problems is to make a mock dress for the child (this is not quite the same as a toile—it's not necessary to make a toile for a child—but to be successful, children's dresses do need careful fitting).

Make it from sheeting or calico as for the blouse bodice toile and it's a good idea at the same time to cut out a miniature dress for the child's doll. The child can copy all the fitting stages and it will keep her busy too while you do your work.

Cut out the mock dress as if it was the real one with 19mm seam and 6·3cm to 8cm hem allowance. Pin and tack the Front and Back together along the side and shoulder-seams. Leave the Centre Back-seam open so that it is easy to slip on and off. Put the mock dress on the child and pin it together down the Centre Back.

The first fitting

With most children, there are four special fitting points—dropped shoulders, chubby neck, chubby arms and a high tummy. All these points affect the fitting of a dress.

Ease into Back between side-seam balance mark and armhole — sizes 60cm and 66cm chest

FRONT

STRAIGHT OF GRAIN

CENTRE FRONT

Ease into Front between shoulder balance marks — all sizes

BACK

STRAIGHT OF GRAIN

CENTRE BACK

Dropped shoulders. Pin off the required amount from the outer edge of the shoulder seam. Snip the seam allowance around the lower armhole until the creases running towards the underarm have disappeared, both back and front. Mark a new underarm seam line with pins or pencil if necessary.

Chubby neck and arms. Snip the seam allowance around the neck and armholes until the dress lies flat. Mark the new seam lines.

A high tummy. If the dress juts out in front, make a side bust dart as shown on the pattern for size 70cm chest. If you are using this size already, lift a little more fabric into the dart. In either case, the amount you take into the dart must be added to the hem line at the side of the dress, otherwise the hem allowance will be reduced.

The child with a high tummy often stands very erect which will make the dress appear rather tight across the chest and full across the back. If you can avoid it, do not alter the width across the back because this is needed for movement—add width across the front instead. This means making a new Front pattern but this is not difficult.

To make a new Front pattern, lay the pattern piece on a large sheet of paper, pinning the Centre Front to one straight edge. Measure 10cm from the edge and slash the pattern from the hem to within 3mm of the shoulder. Spread the left half of the pattern piece until the opening at chest level is about 13mm wide. If this results in too much flare at the lower side-seam, trim the flare as shown in diagram 1. Straighten the shoulder line and cut out the new pattern.

The second fitting

Make up the mock dress just as if it was the real one, except for the neck line. Trim off the seam allowance along the seam line to fit perfectly around the neck. Put in the sleeves to give you the correct setting for them and turn up all hems.

Try the dress on the child again. When you are satisfied that it fits, cut the dress into sections along the stitching lines. Place the sections flat, over the pattern pieces, and transfer all the alterations. Having done this, your problems are solved because you can use the pattern again and again with only a brief check on the fitting now and then.

About hems

It is a mistake to think that a child's dress will last longer if it is made with a really deep hem and often little dresses are made with hems up to 15cm deep. The truth is that this adds a great deal of weight to the garment and can make it look quite shapeless. Bear in mind, too, that when a dress becomes too short for a growing child, it affects not only the hem but also the length between shoulder and underarm and this, in turn, makes the sleeves too tight. Of course it may be possible to alter the dress but it is rather a waste of time to go to this trouble if the dress is only going to be worn once or twice before the seams split. Making a dress 'on the big side' is not the answer either, because the sad result would be a new dress which is shapeless turning into a dress which fits only when it is worn out! The answer is to make a dress which fits well right from the start, then the child can enjoy wearing it and you can be proud of having made it. A hem of 8cm to 10cm, if you want to allow extra, is quite adequate and will give the dress a good life of two or three seasons.

About neck line finishes

Another important point to watch when making children's dresses is the neck line finish. This section is rubbed a great deal during washing and it has to withstand a lot of wear so a good, firm finish is necessary.

To hold the neck line in shape, make a rouleau-type bound

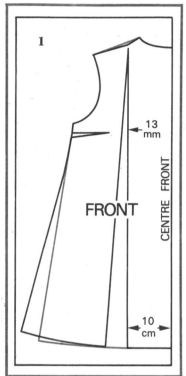
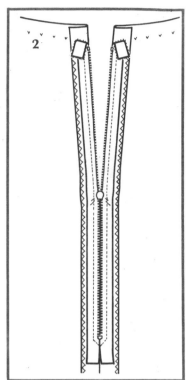

1. *Making a new Front pattern*   2. *The zip tape ends sewn in place*
Detail of the finished neck line, bound with a bias strip ▼

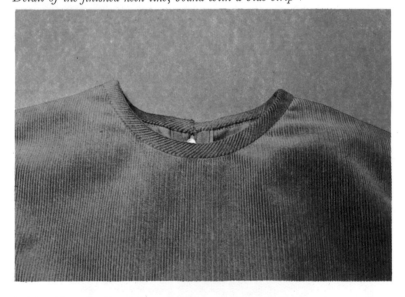

finish (described under making up instructions). Apart from being very hard-wearing, it looks neat and will also withstand the repeated stitching which is necessary when changing detachable collars for washing.

A flat bias facing is an alternative finish but does not give such a strong neck edge. This is because the seam allowance inside the bias must be snipped close to the seam to lie flat.

It is not advisable to use conventional fabric facings for children's dresses because they become worn and very untidy after frequent washing.

Fabric requirements for the child's dress

You will need

☐ for 90cm wide fabric, twice the dress length plus the sleeve length and hem and seam allowances

☐ for 140cm wide fabric, the dress length plus the sleeve length and hem and seam allowances.

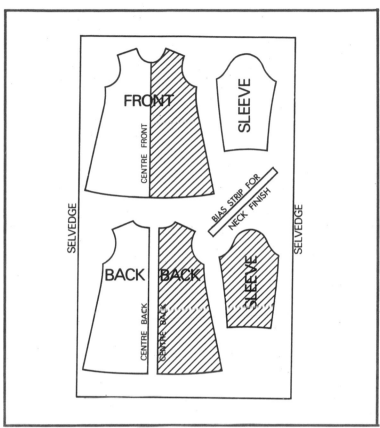

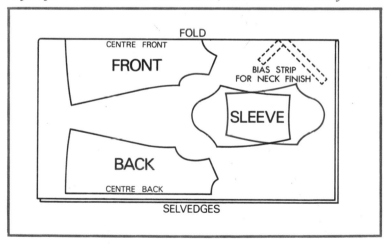

Layout for the child's dress on 90cm width, with and without one way ▲
Layout for a child's dress on 140cm width, with or without one way ▼

☐ zip (30cm for size 60cm chest, 35cm to 40cm for sizes 66cm and 70cm chest, depending on the dress length)
☐ one hook, size 1 for the neck fastening.
If you want to be really economical when calculating the fabric length, make a trial layout on paper first. You can then measure the material required from your own layout and buy the exact amount of fabric.
If you decide to add pockets or frills, don't forget to take this into account when working out the amount.

The layout
Copy one of the layouts illustrated or use the layout you made on paper to calculate fabric amount.
On your own layout, place the Centre Front of the pattern on the fold and the Centre Back to the selvedges, allowing for a Centre Back seam. Make sure that the grain line marked on the sleeve

pattern piece lines up perfectly with the grain of the fabric.
Pin all pattern pieces down securely and mark round them. Mark all pattern details not forgetting the end of the zip opening. Cut out the dress adding seam and hem allowance.

Making up
As this basic dress is so simple, you can make it up in six easy stages. It's easier still if you have made and fitted a mock dress first.

1. Seams and darts
Pin, tack and stitch the small side bust darts (if you need to use them) and press them towards the hem.
Pin, tack and stitch the side and shoulder-seams and the Centre Back seam below the zip opening. Neaten all seam edges and press the seams open.

2. The zip
Stitch in the zip as for a straight seam, leaving one inch between the zip teeth and the raw edge of the neck line. Turn back the ends of the zip tape at an angle so they will not show and hand-sew them down, as shown in diagram 2.

3. Making the sleeves and stitching them into the dress
Pin, tack and stitch the sleeve seams, neaten seam edges and press the seams open. Gather in the ease round the sleeve caps and pin the sleeves into the armholes, matching balance marks and seams. Stitch, remembering to work with the sleeve uppermost. Neaten seam edges and press the seams into the sleeves.

4. Binding the neck line
First, to hold the shape of the neck edge and to prevent it from stretching, machine a row of stay stitches along the seam line. Trim off the seam allowance 3mm from the stay stitches.
To bind the neck cut a bias strip from the dress fabric (or an equally strong contrasting fabric) 2·8cm wide and 13mm longer than the neck edge measurement.
Pin and tack the bias strip to the neck line on the outside of the dress, right sides facing and raw edges level, leaving 6mm at each end for turning. Stitch in position taking 6mm seam allowance to bring the stitching line for the binding 3mm below the stay stitching. Do not trim any more fabric off the seam allowance as this is now your guide for the width of the binding.
Turn in the 6mm seam allowance at each end of the bias strip and turn under the raw edge. The amount you turn under depends on the thickness of the fabric you are using but the folded edge should meet the stitching line when turned to the inside of the dress.
Never force the bias strip over the neck edge or it will cockle. If the bias strip is tight, let out the folded edge a little until the bias strip can be turned over the raw edge without strain. Slip stitch the folded edge to the stitching line and close the ends of the binding. Finish with a hand-made bar and hook.

5. Making the hems
Turn up the hem allowance on the dress and the sleeves. Make the hem in the usual way on the dress but for the sleeves, use a firmer hemming stitch. Sleeve hems are easily caught by little fingers in a hurry to get dressed.

The finishing touches
Press the dress and all seams and hems from the inside, taking as much care as you do with your own dresses. This final touch is not only necessary but it also justifies all your dressmaking efforts.

Sewing for Children

Chapter 50

Towelling playsuit for a girl

This chapter includes general tips on towelling fabrics, as well as instructions for a girl's beach playsuit with knickers.

Types of towelling
There are three main types of towelling and they are mostly available in 90cm to 100cm widths.

Double sided towelling. This has loops on both sides of the fabric and most plain colours are reversible.

It is warm and cosy, but the depth of the loops makes it difficult to fasten with buttons and zips.

Single sided towelling. Here the loops appear only on the top surface of the fabric. Garments made up in this towelling can be finished with conventional fastenings.

Stretch towelling. This usually has loops on one side of the fabric.

It is particularly suitable for swim-wear as it dries quickly and can be moulded to the body.

Cutting out
When pinning patterns on towelling do not use too many pins as pinning through thick fabric reduces the size of the pattern.

Seams in towelling
The seams in towelling don't present any problem. Make ordinary seams on single towelling and flat-fell seams, 13mm to 19mm wide, for double sided towelling, depending on the thickness of the fabric (for flat-fell seams see Blousemaking Chapter 24).

Facings in towelling
Neck and armhole facings cut in towelling fabric should be avoided. Instead, bind the

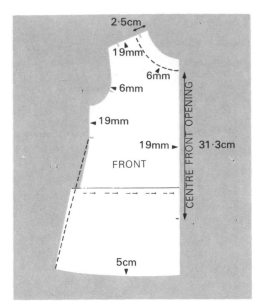

▲ **1.** *The new shortened Front dress pattern*
▼ **2.** *The new shortened Back dress pattern*

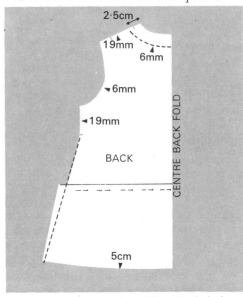

▼ **3.** *Pocket hem folded outside and stitched*

edges or use bias strip facings for a neat finish without bulk.

Pressing towelling
When pressing towelling you will get a slight flattening of the loops, but if you brush over the loops with the flat of your hand while they are still warm they will quickly rise again.

Girl's towelling dress

The dress pattern
This is made from the child's basic dress pattern in the previous chapter, which comes in sizes 61cm, 66cm and 70cm chest. Make the Front and Back pattern pieces from the graph, altering for size as necessary.

The length. As the beach dress is worn short with the knickers showing, the basic pattern needs to be shortened.

Do not shorten it at the hem line; towelling is a lot more bulky than most fabrics and it would make a very narrow garment if you did. Instead, shorten both pattern pieces by making a fold about 18cm above the hem line to the depth required and pin.

Then pin the Front and Back to a piece of paper, draw round the pattern pieces and straighten the side-seams as shown (figures 1 and 2). Remove the original pattern and cut out the new one.

The neck line. Lower the neck line on both the Back and Front of the new pattern by 2·5cm as shown (figures 1 and 2).

The seam allowances. The garment has a front zip opening, so mark the Centre Front to be cut with seam allowance.

Mark the Centre Back to be cut on the fabric fold.

The seam allowances on the pattern vary because of the finishes used for towelling, so mark them too. Mark 6mm seam allowance at neck line and armhole edges and 19mm for other seams. Also mark a 5cm hem allowance. This will act as a reminder when making up as it is difficult to tailor's tack towelling fabrics.

The pocket and daisy patterns
The bucket-shaped pocket is another type of patch pocket.

Trace the pocket pattern overleaf and cut out. Also trace and cut out separate patterns for the daisy petals and centre.

To find the position for the pocket on the dress, place the pocket pattern on the Front pattern piece 6mm up from the hem and with the upper edge 3·8cm from the Centre Front. Draw round it.

If the hem is rather curved, tilt the pattern so that it is level with the hem line and check the position at the fitting stage.

Fabric amounts and notions
To find the amount of fabric needed make a layout on paper the same width as the towelling, using the Back, Front and daisy petal pieces. The pockets and daisy centres are cut from contrasting fabric.

Allow for seam and hem allowances. Also allow for three bias strips to finish the neck and armhole edges. These should be

4 times the width of the finished rouleau plus 3mm.

If the fabric you choose is with one way, make allowance for this when calculating the amount.

Draw round the pattern shapes so that you can use the paper as a layout at the cutting stage.

You will also need a 30cm zip and matching thread.

Cutting out

Lay out the pattern using your paper layout as a guide. Do not forget to place the Back on a fold and cut the Centre Front with seam allowance.

Mark all the seam and hem allowances with pin lines except for the daisy, which has no seam allowance. Cut out. Also cut out the three bias strips.

Cut out 2 pocket shapes and 2 daisy centres from the contrast fabric.

Marking the pattern details

Tailor's tack only where it is absolutely necessary, such as at balance marks, darts (if you are using them), and seam ends. Also mark the pocket positions with single tailor's tacks through slits made in the dress pattern.

Mark the end of the opening for the zip in the Centre Front 31·3cm from the neck edge.

Don't mark the seam lines but keep the pattern at hand and measure them out as you stitch up the garment.

Fitting

Pin and tack the dress for fitting and make any necessary corrections.

Inserting the zip

Stitch the Centre Front seam below the opening mark, then tack the opening together. Neaten the seam allowance and press the seam open.

Insert the zip using the straight seam method (Skirtmaking Chapter 14), but sew it by hand with small firm back stitches. Stitching by machine will make the surface loops tilt in opposite directions.

Sew the zip to the seam allowance with felling stitches.

Making up the pockets

Pin and tack the daisy petals on to each pocket piece, working very close to the edges and using a matching sewing thread. If you have a zigzag on your machine follow the instructions for appliqué in the machine manual but engage a slightly larger stitch width to appliqué the daisy. For hand appliqué use a closely worked oversewing stitch in matching sewing or embroidery thread, catching through all

Girl's beach playsuit made in colourful towelling with daisy petal pockets

layers of fabric.

Appliqué the daisy centres similarly.

Press the appliqué then finish the pockets.

Fold the 3.8cm hem allowance at the top to the outside of each pocket and stitch at the sides as shown (figure 3).

Neaten the raw edge, turn the hem to the inside and sew by hand.

Fold under the remaining seam allowance and tack.

Position the pockets on the dress. Pin, tack and topstitch close to the edge. Press.

Finishing the dress

Pin, tack and stitch the side and shoulder-seams, neaten the raw edges and press the seams. Also stitch the darts if used.

Using the bias strips bind the neck and armholes as for the basic dress.

Finish the hem in the usual way and give the garment a final pressing.

Girl's towelling knickers

The pattern

The pattern overleaf will fit a 76cm hip and corresponds to the largest dress size. Instructions for making the pattern smaller follow.

Trace the Front and Back pattern pieces. The tracing will only give you half a Front and Back but you will need to complete the pattern pieces for an open layout.

Making the pattern smaller

To shorten. Measure the child through the crutch from Centre Front to Centre Back and compare the measurement on the pattern.

Divide the difference by 4 and deduct this amount equally from the waist and the depth of the crutch on both Back and Front pattern pieces.

To make narrower. If the child's hips are less than 76cm deduct the difference in equal amounts from the centres and side-seams of both Back and Front pattern pieces until you have the correct width.

Fabric amounts and notions

To find out the amount of towelling needed make a layout on paper as for the dress. If you are making up the dress as well include the pocket and daisy centre patterns in this layout.

As you can see by the straight of grain marking the knickers are cut in the cross of the fabric to give maximum comfort during wear.

You will also need 1 pack of bias binding, knicker elastic to fit the waist and legs, and matching thread.

Cutting out and marking

Using your paper layout cut out the fabric and mark the pattern details as for the dress.

Making up

The seams. Because the knickers are cut on the cross ordinary seams will tend to curl, so an open flat-fell seam is used with zigzag stitching.

With right sides facing, stitch the side and crutch-seams, using a shallow zigzag. Press the seam allowance to one side.

Trim the inside seam allowance as for flat-fell seaming (Blousemaking Chapter 24) and trim the top seam for a flat-fell, but without the allowance for the turning. Generally these seams should be as narrow as possible, but to make allowance for towellings which fray, leave 6mm on the inside and 9mm on the top.

Then, using a number 3 zigzag setting, work over the raw edge of the double seam allowance to make the open flat-fell. If you don't have a zigzag on your machine, make ordinary flat-fell seams.

The waist and leg casings. Neaten the raw edge of the seam allowance at the waist.

Turn the waist-seam allowance to the inside and stitch in place with the same number 3 zigzag setting, or, if you are using a straight stitch, turn under the edge first. Don't forget to leave an opening in the seam to insert the elastic.

To make the casings at the leg edges finish them with bias binding.

With right sides facing, raw edges level, stitch one edge of the binding round the leg edges. Turn the binding completely to the inside and machine stitch the other edge in place, neatening the ends.

Slot elastic into the waist and leg casings to finish.

196

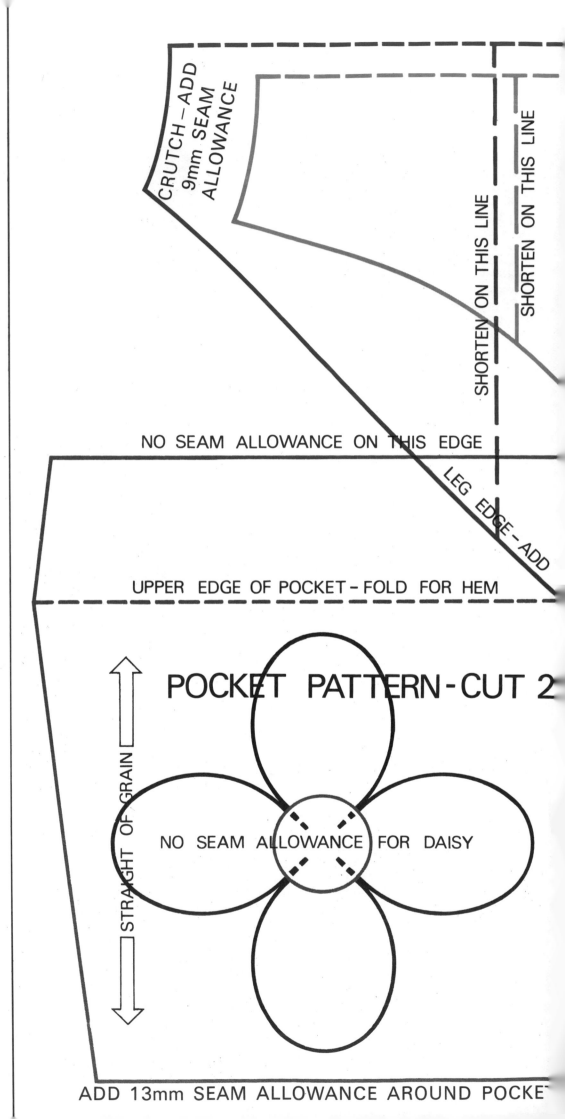

CRUTCH—ADD 9mm SEAM ALLOWANCE

SHORTEN ON THIS LINE

SHORTEN ON THIS LINE

NO SEAM ALLOWANCE ON THIS EDGE

LEG EDGE – ADD

UPPER EDGE OF POCKET – FOLD FOR HEM

POCKET PATTERN – CUT 2

STRAIGHT OF GRAIN

NO SEAM ALLOWANCE FOR DAISY

ADD 13mm SEAM ALLOWANCE AROUND POCKET

TRACE OTHER HALF OF PATTERN FROM THIS LINE

KNICKER PATTERN

FRONT —— CUT 1
BACK —— CUT 1

SIZE: 76cm HIP

WAIST LINE—SHORTEN HERE—ADD 19mm SEAM ALLOWANCE

EG EDGE—ADD 6mm SEAM ALLOWANCE

mm SEAM ALLOWANCE

STRAIGHT OF GRAIN

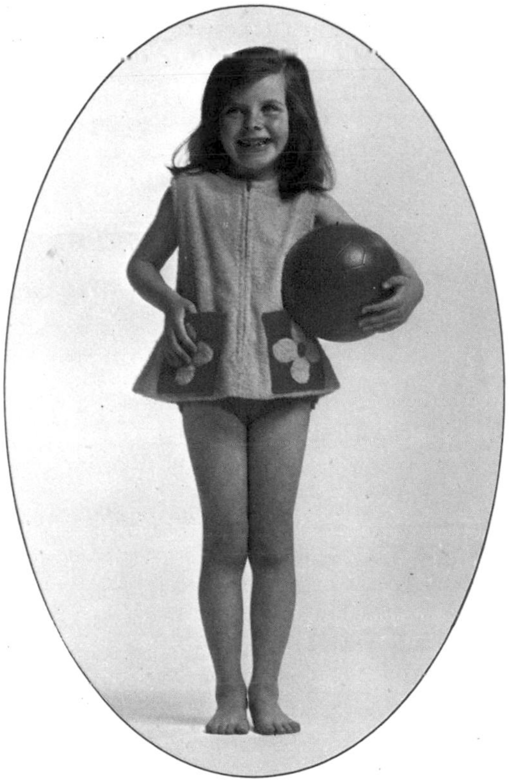

SIDE—SEAM—ADD 9mm SEAM ALLOWANCE

Chapter 51

Converting the child's basic dress

This chapter shows you how to use the child's basic dress pattern in Sewing for Children Ch. 49 to create new styles—A: the dress with a straight waist-seam and straight sleeves, either long or short, and B: the dress with a shaped waist-seam and full, ¾ length sleeves. For both styles the bodice is fitted and the skirt fully gathered.

The size range is the same as for the basic dress, that is, to fit a 60cm, 66cm and 70cm chest.

A special feature of these dresses is the high waist. A waisted dress for a growing girl has a very short life span because the waist-seam is never in the right place for long, and even if there is enough fabric to let it down, it is a difficult task. But if the waist-seam is designed to be cut high it will not look out of place even after two or three season's wear, and it's a simple matter to make any adjustment to the length at the hem line.

Choosing the right conversion

To decide which conversion to make the child's figure shape must be taken into consideration.

A. Dress with straight waist-seam. The seam goes almost straight across the body and is only suitable for really slim children. This style is not suitable for larger children because the shape of the seam would need to be severely adapted, and would never hide the problem of a high tummy.

B. Dress with shaped waist-seam. This shape is kinder to sturdily built children, it is not so rigid and allows for more freedom of movement.

Making the bodice patterns

The basic pattern. For both conversions make the basic dress pattern from the graph in Sewing for Children Ch. 49, and make any necessary pattern alterations.

Marking the natural waist line. For both conversions, first find the natural waist line before marking and cutting the high waist line.

Pin a tape firmly round the child's natural waist line and take the following measurements on both Back and Front pattern pieces:
i) centre neck to tape ii) inner shoulder to tape iii) outer shoulder to tape.

Mark each measurement on the pattern pieces as you take it (figures 1 and 2) and draw a line across the patterns connecting the points. This gives you the natural waist line.

A. Dress with straight waist-seam

To find the high waist-seam on both Back and Front pattern pieces draw a line parallel to the natural waist line, 3·8cm above it (figure 3). Cut the pattern along this line.

Mark the position for a waist dart on the Front pattern piece 8cm from the Centre Front line and 5cm long (figure 4). Draw in the dart 19mm deep (figure 5).

Make a dart similarly on the Back bodice pattern but make it 8cm long and 2·5cm deep.

Now check the high waist line for size. Measure the waist less the darts on the Front and Back bodice pattern pieces and note. Measure the child 3·8cm above the waist line tape and add 5cm to this measurement for ease. The child's measurement plus ease should equal twice the pattern measurement.

If the bodice width needs adjusting then adjust the side-seams.

Pass the ease in the upper Front side-seam (or the dart in the largest pattern) into the waist-seam (figure 5) so that the length of the side-seams on Back and Front are equal. Ignore the side-seam balance marks on the new pattern.

B. Dress with shaped waist-seam

On both Back and Front pieces draw a line parallel to the natural waist line and 2·5cm up from it.

On the Front pattern piece make a pencil mark on the Centre Front line 5cm above the natural waist line. Starting 8cm in from the Centre Front on the new waist line make a curve to this point (figures 6 and 7).

Cut out Front bodice pattern along this line and cut the Back bodice along the high waist line.

Mark the position for a waist dart on the Front pattern piece 8cm from the Centre Front line and 6·3cm long (figure 7). Draw in the dart 19mm deep (figure 8).

Make a dart similarly on the Back bodice pattern piece which is 9·3cm long and 2·5cm deep.

To check that the high waist measurement is right, measure the waist less the darts 2·5cm above the cutting line on the Front and Back bodice pattern pieces and note. Measure the child 5cm above the waist line tape and add 5cm to this measurement for ease. The child's measurement plus ease should equal twice the pattern measurement.

If the bodice width needs altering then adjust the side-seams.

Pass the ease in the upper Front side-seam (or the dart in the largest pattern) into the waist-seam (figure 8) so that the length of the side-seams on Back and Front are equal. Ignore the side-seam balance marks on the new pattern.

▼ **1.** *Front: marking natural waist*

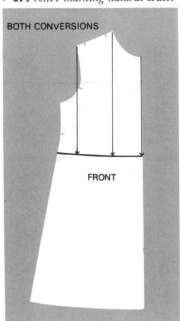

BOTH CONVERSIONS

FRONT

▼ **2.** *Back: marking natural waist*

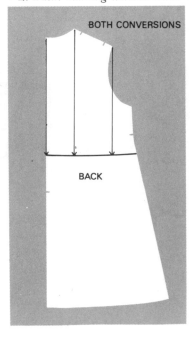

BOTH CONVERSIONS

BACK

▲ *The dress with straight waist-seam and short sleeves in a pretty print*

▲ *The dress with shaped waist-seam and full, ¾ sleeves in white cotton*

▼ **3.** *Finding the high waist line*   ▼ **4.** *Measuring for Front· dart*

▼ **6.** *Curving the Front waist line*   ▼ **7.** *Measuring for Front dart*

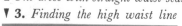

A

FRONT

3·8cm

A

BODICE
FRONT

5cm   8cm

▼ **5.** *Drawing dart, passing ease*

A

BODICE
FRONT

ease
or
dart

19mm

B

FRONT

2·5cm   5cm

8cm

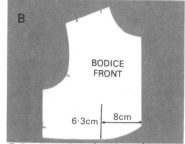

B

BODICE
FRONT

6·3cm   8cm

▼ **8.** *Drawing dart, passing ease*

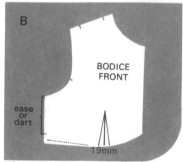

B

BODICE
FRONT

ease
or
dart

19mm

allowing 5cm spacings at the waist and 9·3cm to 10cm at the hem.

Draw round the new outlines. Mark in the centre lines and straight of grain before removing the original patterns to avoid mistakes.

Cut out the new pattern.

Making the sleeve patterns

For all sizes make the sleeve pattern from the graph for the girl's basic dress in Sewing for Children Ch. 49, making any alterations necessary.

The long, straight sleeve
This is the same as the sleeve pattern for the girl's basic dress.

The short sleeve
Mark off the desired length of the sleeve on the sleeve-seams and cut across the pattern.

The full $\frac{3}{4}$ length sleeve
The full $\frac{3}{4}$ length sleeve is the most practical for children. It is long enough to be warm and full enough to be unrestricting during play. It is also a very pretty sleeve with its fullness gathered into elastic around the lower edge.

Using the basic sleeve pattern, measure the length of both sleeve-seams and pin the amount allowed for ease in the back of the sleeve into a dart (figure 11). Then make three equally spaced lengthwise slashes from the wrist edge to within 6mm of the top as shown.

Lay the pattern on a sheet of paper and spread each section 5cm apart at the wrist.

Add a little more width at the seams by extending them outwards for 2·5cm at the lower end and tapering into the original side-seam between elbow and armhole. Draw each line in a gentle curve so that there is no kink where it joins the original seam again.

As the pattern is spread, the lower edge of the sleeve, between the centre and the sleeve-seam, will curve downwards on the sleeve back. This is correct and necessary for the sleeve to remain in place around the wrist when the arm is moved.

Draw in the new sleeve outline, copy the balance marks on the sleeve head and cut out the new pattern.

Take the child's measurement for the $\frac{3}{4}$ sleeve length and reduce the length of the pattern as required, allowing 19mm for the drop of the fullness.

Alternatively, you can leave this sleeve long, gather it into a cuff and make an opening as you did for the shirt sleeve in Blousemaking Chapter 28.

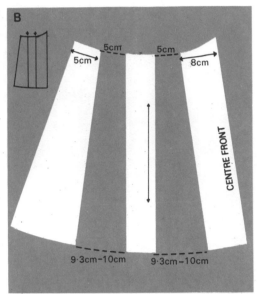

▲ 9. *Widening the Front skirt pattern*
▼ 10. *Widening the Back skirt pattern*

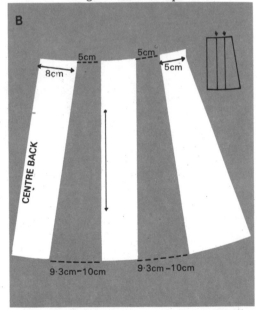

▼ 11. *Altering the pattern for the full sleeve*

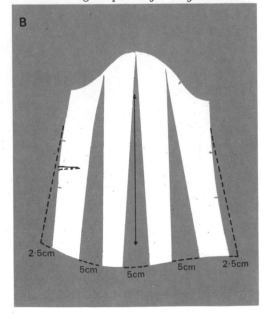

▲ *Details of the back view of Dress A*

Making the skirt patterns

A. Dress with straight waist-seam
To make the gathered skirt, square off the Back and Front skirt sections as you did for the dirndl in Skirtmaking Chapter 16 and cut out the new pattern.

B. Dress with shaped waist-seam
The skirt for this version is cut fuller at the hem than version A.

Slash Back and Front skirt pattern pieces in two places, the first 8cm from the centre lines, the second 5cm from the side-seams (figures 9 and 10).

Use the centre sections of the Back and Front pattern pieces for the straight of grain.

Place all sections on a sheet of paper and spread each skirt pattern piece as shown,

Fabrics, layouts, amounts and notions

Fabrics

There are many types of fabric you can use to make up these little dresses, and they can be patterned or plain, soft or crisp.

The dresses can be made from remnants left over from other dressmaking because the individual sections of the pattern are quite small.

You could cut the skirt, sleeves and neck trimming from one fabric and use a contrasting fabric for the bodice, or perhaps a matching spot print in contrasting colours.

Checks can be used effectively by cutting the bodice on the cross. Stripes too can be cut for effect and look very attractive.

You could try mixing textures on skirt and bodice, such as a jersey knit bodice and woven skirt, to make a pretty winter dress.

Layouts

Using the layouts in Sewing for Children, 49, as a guide, lay the pattern pieces on paper to the width of the fabric you will be using.

Bodice. For both versions place the bodice Centre Front to the fabric fold and cut the Centre Back for an opening. Allow 19mm for seams.

Skirt. Place the Centre Front for version A to the fabric fold. The Centre Front of version B and the Centre Backs for both versions are cut for seaming.

Allow 19mm for seams and 6·3cm for hems.

Sleeves. Allow 19mm for seams.

Allow 3·8cm hems on the short sleeve and the long, straight sleeve. But for the hem of the full, $\frac{3}{4}$ length sleeve allow only 19mm as it is finished off with a bias strip.

Binding. Mark out a 2·8cm wide bias strip for binding the neck edge as on the basic dress layout.

If you are making the $\frac{3}{4}$ length sleeve, mark out two bias strips 3cm wide to the length of the lower edge of the sleeve, plus 13mm seam allowance at each end.

Notions

- ☐ Zip (30 cm for size 60cm chest, 35cm for size 66cm chest, and 40cm for size 70cm chest)
- ☐ One hook, size No.1, for the neck fastening
- ☐ Matching thread
- ☐ 6mm wide elastic for the full, $\frac{3}{4}$ length sleeve

Amounts

Measure the overall length of the paper to find the fabric required and mark round each pattern piece so that you can use it for a layout when the patterns are removed.

Cutting out

Cut out the fabric using the paper layout as a guide.

Tailor's tack round the pattern edges, taking special care on the curved seams, and mark all other pattern details.

A. Dress with straight waist-seam

Preparing for fitting

Pin and tack the waist darts.

Pin and tack the bodice Front to the bodice Back.

Tack the skirt together at the side and Centre Back seams, not forgetting to leave an opening for the zip.

Run a row of tacking stitches round the top of the skirt. Then pin and tack the skirt to the bodice in the waist-seam, gathering the skirt to fit the bodice.

Pin and tack the sleeve-seams. Tack the sleeves into the armholes.

Fitting

Check the sleeves for length.

Make sure that the fitted bodice sits well and is not strained by tight seam allowance on neck and armholes. If either is tight, carefully snip the seam allowance until it lies flat.

Although the bodice is fitted it should not be too close to the body. There must be room enough for energetic movements during play.

The gathered skirt on the flat bodice will give the impression of a close fit but is, in fact, quite roomy.

A special fitting point: children with high shoulder blades usually have a hollow back and the Centre Back-seam on the bodice may need to be taken in at the waist.

To do this, unpick the waist-seam a little to each side of the Centre Back. Pin off the amount along the Centre Back-seam by which the bodice must be taken in. Draw up the gathers on the skirt so that the seam allowance on the Centre Back-seam of the skirt remains the same. Repin, tack and check fitting.

Unpick the waist-seam and take out the sleeves ready for stitching.

Making up the bodice

Stitch the darts. Press them open or flat if the fabric is heavy, and towards the centres if the fabric is light.

Stitch the side and shoulder-seams, neaten raw edges and press.

▲ *Details of the back view of dress B*

Making up the skirt

Stitch the Centre Back-seam as far as the zip opening and stitch the side-seams. Neaten the raw seam edges and press them open.

Make two rows of gathering stitches along the full length of the waist-seam.

Joining the skirt to the bodice

Pin the skirt and bodice waist-seams together on the side-seams and centre markings.

Draw up the gathers on the skirt between the pins and distribute them evenly until the skirt fits the bodice waist-seam. Pin, tack, and stitch.

If you are using a jersey knit fabric, reinforce the seam with a length of 6mm seam tape to stop the stitches from breaking. To do this pin and tack the tape over

the stitching line and make another row of machine stitches along the waist-seam, catching in the tape.
Press the waist-seam into the bodice and neaten the raw edges together.

The sleeves
The straight sleeve. Make up the sleeves and set them in the bodice as for the girl's dress in Sewing for Children Ch. 49.
The short sleeve. Make up the sleeves and set in as for the straight sleeve.

Inserting the zip
Pin under and tack the seam allowance along both Centre Back edges and press. If the seam has remained on the straight grain of the fabric, insert the zip using the straight seam method (Skirtmaking Chapter 14). If, however, the seam has been curved for a better fit, use the lap over method shown in Skirtmaking Chapter 13.

Finishing
Finish the neck edge and the skirt hem as for the girl's basic dress.

B. Dress with shaped waist-seam

Tacking and fitting
Tack the bodice as for version A.
Tack the skirt centre and side-seams.
The gathers on the skirt do not extend into the high point on the Centre Front, but start level with the waist darts on the bodice. To find the right place measure across the skirt pattern from the Centre Front, 2·5cm below the point. If you have followed the instructions for making the dart, this measurement will be 6·6cm. Mark the measurement to each side of the Centre Front of the skirt. Gather the top of the skirt to fit the waist-seam.
Tack the shaped bodice waist-seam flat over the skirt waist-seam but do not snip the seam allowance yet.
Tack the sleeve-seams, then tack in the sleeves gathering the lower edge so that they can be checked for length.
Fit as for version A, then unpick the waist-seam and remove the sleeves for stitching.

Making up the bodice
Stitch the bodice as for version A.

Making up the skirt
Stitch the Centre Front seam, neaten and press open.
Stitch the side-seams, and the Centre Back seam as far as the opening for the zip. Neaten and press open.
Gather the skirt. Make two rows of gathering stitches to each side of the Centre Front, as marked for fitting,

working towards the Centre Back.

Joining the skirt to the bodice
Snip the seam allowance of the Centre Front on the bodice point as shown (figure 12). Then fold the seam allowance along the stitching line of the waist-seam into the bodice. Pin and tack into position.
As you work on the curved edge place the pins at right angles to the edge and make sure that the seam does not pucker.
Lay the folded edge of the bodice over the seam allowance on the skirt to meet the seam line as marked, and pin together at the side-seams and Centre markings. Draw up the gathers until the skirt fits the bodice.
Tack the bodice waist-seam firmly to the skirt waist-seam, and topstitch along the folded edge, making a perfect pivot at the point on the Centre Front (figure 13).
Press the seams and neaten the raw edges together.

The full ¾ length sleeve
Stitch the sleeve-seams, neaten and press. If the seam allowances are a little tight, carefully snip them until they lie flat. Neaten the raw edges where the seam allowance has been snipped.
To finish the wrist edge on each sleeve make a casing for elastic to hold in the fullness.
To do this fold under the seam allowance at each end of the bias strip and tack. Lay the strip to the sleeve edge, right sides facing. Pin and tack to the hem line so that the folded ends meet at the sleeve-seam, taking no more than 9mm seam allowance on the bias strip (figure 14).
Stitch the strip to the sleeve and trim the sleeve hem allowance to 9mm.
Turn the bias strip to the inside of the sleeve, edge tack and press.
Fold under the raw edge on the bias strip so that the casing is 16mm wide. Pin, tack and stitch the folded edge to the sleeve, topstitching close to the edge.
Remove the tacking and press the casing. Cut a length of 6mm wide elastic to fit comfortably around the child's arm and slot into the casing. Stitch the ends firmly together. Sew the opening in the casing together by hand.
If you are using a fine fabric it may be possible to use the hem allowance on the sleeve edge to make the casing.
To do this, pin and tack the hem allowance to the wrong side and turn the raw edge under so that the channel is wide enough to take the elastic.
Topstitch to the sleeve along the inner folded edge, leaving a 13mm opening in the seam through which to thread the elastic.

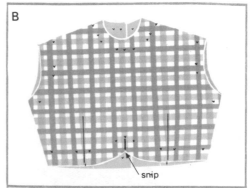

▲ **12.** *Snipping Centre Front bodice waist-seam*
▼ **13.** *Topstitching the bodice waist-seam*

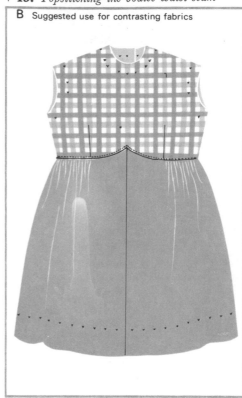

B Suggested use for contrasting fabrics

▼ **14.** *Finishing the wrist edge with a casing*

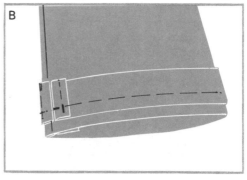

Insert the elastic as before and hand-sew the opening to close.
Set the sleeves in the bodice as for the girl's basic dress.

Inserting the zip and finishing
Insert the zip as for version A.
Finish the neck edge and the skirt hem as for the girl's basic dress.

Pretty undies for little girls

Children's undergarments must be designed and made for practical wear. The fabrics and trimmings must withstand hard wear and frequent hard washing, usually in a washing machine. Fabric manufacturers realise this so there is a wide choice in apparently delicate fabrics and trimmings which will answer these requirements perfectly.

When you are selecting the fabric and trimming make sure that they are of the same type of fibre, such as cotton trimming for cotton fabric. This is most necessary as the wrong combination can lead to disappointing results when you wash and press the finished garments.

About finishes

Although lace and similar trimmings are very pretty they are also often very expensive. But if you often make undergarments you should watch the trimmings counter of your local store. At sale times they frequently sell off batches of narrow lace in varying amounts which are much cheaper than when cut from a complete length.

For everyday undergarments you may like to use less costly methods for the trimming, so here are some suggestions for doing this.

Frills. If you want to make fabric frills for petticoats there are several economical ways to finish them.

You can stitch the hem of the frill with a pretty shell stitch, as shown in Generally Speaking Chapter 2, or a machine scalloped border is an attractive alternative. If you are working a shell finish this can be repeated around the neck and armholes. You can attach the frill to the garment with a narrow lace insertion, and narrow lace trimming can be applied to the hem of the fabric frill for a most attractive finish.

Neck and armhole edges. These edges, which come into close contact with the body, must be given particular attention because they can chafe and irritate young skins.

So, if you know that your child's skin is very sensitive, avoid a self rouleau finish for neck and armholes and buy a length of ready-folded soft cotton bias binding and make a bias bound edge finish.

The leg edges of knickers must also be kept soft so that they do not chafe or irritate. This will be discussed in the making up instructions which follow.

Petticoat

The pattern

The child's dress pattern in Sewing for Children Ch. 49 is altered to make the pattern for the petticoat.

First copy the Front and Back pattern pieces and then adapt them as follows. Since little bodies tend to get very hot when undergarments hang around them in folds some of the ease should be taken from the pattern. To do this take 3mm from the Centre Front and Centre Back and 3mm from each side-seam. This will reduce ease by 2·5cm all round (figure 1). Increase the size of the armholes by drawing a new armhole line 13mm inside the pattern edge as shown. Also cut the neck line wider by drawing in a new line 16mm from the previous one.

Measure the length required for the petticoat and shorten the pattern.

If you are using a wide trim make sure you reduce the length accordingly, to ensure that the finished petticoat will not be too long.

Before you cut the pattern consider whether or not you want to be able to lengthen the petticoat later.

As a frilled hem line has no hem allowance make two narrow rows of tucks parallel to the hem line, the folded depth of each being 9mm. To allow for this on the pattern add 3·8cm to the length. Cut out the new pattern and mark the following allowances on the pattern edges: 13mm on the side-seams and shoulder-seams; 3mm on the neck line and armhole edges (except for a shell stitched finish when you will need 6mm); 6mm on the hem line; and 13mm on the Centre Back seam.

Cutting out

Make a layout as shown in Generally Speaking 4, and calculate your fabric requirements.

The Centre Front is placed on the fabric fold and the Centre Back is cut for seaming. Also allow for rouleau binding and frills if you are cutting them from the fabric. Frills can be cut on the straight or the bias of the fabric, and should be 2½ times the width around the hem to gather up the frill generously.

Remember to add the seam and hem allowances given. Cut out the fabric.

You will also need

- ☐ Hem trimming 2½ times the width around the hem line
- ☐ One small button for fastening the Centre Back
- ☐ Soft cotton bias binding (optional)
- ☐ Matching thread

Fitting and making up

After cutting remove the pattern. It is not necessary to tailor's tack except for marking the position of the ease in the side-seam.

Keep the pattern beside you and refer to it for the seam and hem allowances as you pin and tack ready for fitting.

Apart from the general hang the most important fitting point is to make sure that the fabric clears the tender folds of skin around the underarm.

Check that the Centre Back opening is long enough for the petticoat to go over the head without causing tears over a damaged hair style!

You are now ready to stitch.

Make French seams (see Blousemaking Chapter 26) for the shoulder and side-seams and press them towards the Front of the garment.

Stitch the Centre Back seam as for ordinary seaming, as far as the end of the opening, and finish off the stitching securely.

To neaten the opening turn in the seam allowance and make a row of topstitching 6mm from the edges of the opening. If the Centre Back has not been cut on the selvedge turn in the raw edge to neaten it before topstitching.

Finish the neck and armhole edges with a rouleau or bias binding.

Stitch on a button and work a hand made loop at the top of the back opening to close it.

If you are making tucks, pin, tack and stitch them on the outside of the garment then press them down (figure 2).

Finishing the hem line

If you use a hem finish of ribbon slotted broderie Anglaise as shown here work as follows.

Pin and tack the hem allowance to the outside of the petticoat and pin the ribbon slotting section over the raw edge so that the fold of the hem line meets the frill (figure 3).

Tack in place.

Pin and tack the upper edge of the ribbon slotting to the garment.

Working on the ribbon slotting section only, topstitch the trimming in place. To do this work one row of stitches along the lower edge of the slotting catching in the folded edge of the hem line. Then work another row of stitches along the upper edge of the slotting just inside the edge (figure 4).

The ends of the trimming should be stitched together by making a French seam through the frilled section only and snipping the seam allowance in the ribbon slotting so that the ends can be turned in flat to avoid bulk (figure 4).

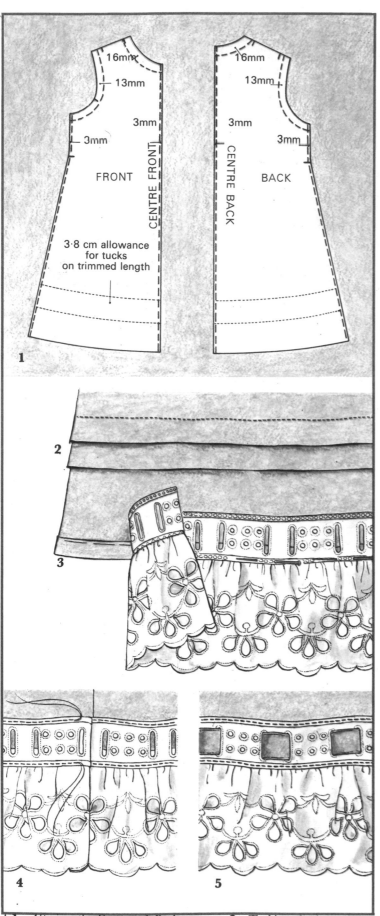

1. *Altering the Front and Back patterns* **2.** *Tucking the hem edge* **3.** *Pinning broderie Anglaise to hem* **4.** *Stitching broderie Anglaise to hem* **5.** *Ribbon slotted frill.*

The petticoat and knickers ►

Slotting in the ribbon

Use a brightly coloured narrow ribbon to slot into the trimming (figure 5).

Slot it in and out of the eyelets, overlap the ends, and hand-sew them together. Alternatively, you can start the slotting at the Centre Front leaving enough ribbon at each end to make a pretty bow. This way, if you are not quite sure if the ribbon will withstand the same washing treatment as the garment, you can easily remove it for washing.

Alternative frilled edge

If you are making a fabric frill, pin and tack the gathered edge of the frill to the hem allowance of the petticoat, right sides facing, raw edges level, and stitch as for an ordinary seam.

Trim the seam allowance and neaten carefully. Press the seam allowance upwards and then topstitch along the hem line on the outside for extra strength. If you are attaching the frill with lace insertion, make the frill less full and stitch one edge of the insertion over the raw gathered edge of the frill. Neaten the seam allowance on the frill carefully, then stitch the other edge of the lace insertion to the hem line of the petticoat.

Knickers

The pattern

Copy the knickers pattern from the graph in Sewing for Children, 50. Mark seam allowances on the pattern edges as follows: side-seams, 13mm; crutch-seam, 16mm for flat-fell seaming (Blousemaking Chapter 24); leg edge, 6 mm; waist-seam, 19mm.

Cutting out

Make a layout preferably from paper, and calculate your fabric requirements, remembering that the knickers are cut from single layers of fabric on the cross-wise grain.

Remember to add the allowances as given. Cut out the fabric.

You will also need

☐ Broderie Anglaise edging, with a deep plain edge, to trim the leg edges (figure 6). For each leg you will need the length of the leg hem measurement plus 8cm for ease (for other trimming get twice the length of each leg measurement

☐ Soft knicker elastic for the legs and waist

☐ Matching thread

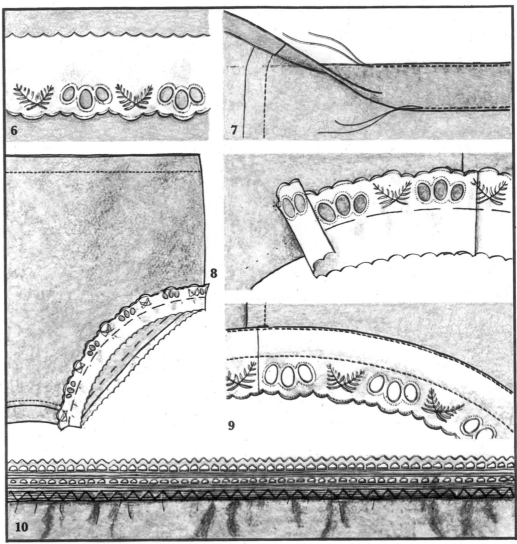

▲ **6.** *Broderie Anglaise trimming for knickers*   **7.** *Casing at waist of knickers*   **8.** *Broderie Anglaise tacked to leg edge*   **9.** *Leg trimming stitched in place*   **10.** *Soft wide elastic stitched to waist*

Fitting and making up

As for the petticoat, it is not necessary to tailor's tack the pattern detail, but keep the pattern next to you to check on the seam allowances as you tack them. Make a flat-fell seam for the crutch-seam. Then stitch the side-seams with a French seam (Blousemaking Chapter 26). Press the seams towards the Front.

To make a casing at the waist edge, turn under the raw edge 6mm then the remainder of the seam allowance and stitch the lower fold in place (figure 7). Also stitch the upper fold to avoid it rolling over.

Finish the leg edge with the broderie Anglaise edging. With right sides facing, pin and tack the seam line of the leg edge close to the embroidery (figure 8). Overlap the ends at the side-seams, and ease the trimming onto the seam line so that when the leg edge is turned up the broderie Anglaise will follow the curve and not pull in the fabric.

To make the casing for the elastic, turn under the raw edge of the broderie Anglaise and topstitch the folded edge to the knickers (figure 9).

Leave a small opening in which to insert the elastic.

Plain leg finish. For a plain finish use soft bias binding and make a casing as for the sleeve hems in Dressmaking chapter 36, figure 14.

Alternative waist finish. If you want to avoid the thickness of an elastic casing around the waist line, use the soft type of elastic which can be stitched to a raw edge (figure 10). This is available in varying widths from 13mm upwards. When cutting the knickers for this finish take off the depth of the elastic from the waist edge and allow about 6mm seam allowance.

Neaten the seam allowance carefully since the elastic is stitched to the open seam allowance.

Pin the elastic over the seam allowance and topstitch in place with a machine zigzag stitch.

Chapter 52

Collars and cuffs

This chapter includes trace patterns for Peter Pan, puritan and yoke collars, also a simple cuff. They are designed for the girl's dress in Sewing for Children Ch. 49 but instructions are given for lengthening or shortening the patterns so that you can use them for any simple dress.

Collars

Suitable fabrics for collar making

Cotton piqué is a traditional fabric for making trimmings such as collars, and it is the most useful. It is very hard wearing, and collars made in this fabric will always look crisp and retain their shape even after frequent washing.

For really pretty collars, you can use organdie or lace but, naturally, in these fabrics they will be quite delicate and require more careful handling.

Collar making does not end with plain collar shapes—there are many ways you can trim them using braid, lace edgings or embroidery. A very pretty idea is to embroider a realistic little butterfly on one side of the collar to look as though it has just settled there.

Fabric requirements and notions

You will need
☐ 0·25m of 90cm wide fabric for the Peter Pan collar
☐ 0·35m of 90cm wide fabric for each of the puritan and yoke collars
☐ One packet of soft cotton bias binding

The collar patterns

These patterns will fit a dress neck opening of 38·5cm.

Trace the collar patterns using the instructions given overleaf. Cut out the patterns.

To make any of the patterns larger, cut along the two dash lines and lay the sections on a sheet of paper. Divide the extra collar length required by four and spread each cut section by this amount. Pencil around the new outline and cut out the new pattern. To make the patterns smaller, divide the amount by which the collar is to be shortened by four and fold off this amount along both dash lines. Lay the altered pattern on a sheet of paper, pencil around the new outline and cut out the new patterns.

Cutting the collars

You will need four collar pieces to make the Peter Pan and puritan collars and two pieces for the yoke collar.

Fold the fabric, following the layouts given overleaf. Be very careful to lay the patterns on the correct grain, otherwise when the collar is stitched on it will not lie well around the neck of the dress. The Centre Front of the yoke pattern is placed on the fold as shown. Cut out, allowing 9mm seam allowance on all edges.

Making the collars

All the collars are made up in the same way except that the Peter Pan and puritan collars are made up in two sections and the yoke collar in one.

Lay two corresponding collar pieces together, right sides facing. Pin, tack and stitch around the outer edges, leaving the neck edge open.

Trim the seam allowance to 6mm and trim across the corners to remove the bulk. If necessary, make 'V' notches round the front curves on the Peter Pan collar so that the seam allowance inside the collar will lie flat when the collar has been turned out. Do not notch the seam allowance on the puritan or yoke collars because the notches will show as dents from the outside.

Turn the collar sections to the right side, tack the stitched edges and press.

On the Peter Pan and puritan collars overlap the seam allowance at the Centre Front and hold together with a catch stitch as shown in the diagram.

Stitch the collar along the neck edge, snip into the seam allowance, and finish the raw edge with bias binding.

Press the collar. Then press the bound edge to the underside of the collar, ready to sew in position on the dress. As you press the binding under the neck edge, stretch it so that it follows the shape of the collar.

Attach to the dress with long slip stitches.

Using organdie and lace

Organdie. If you use this fabric, make the collars as described in the previous paragraphs but trim the seam allowance to 5mm or, if the organdie is particularly firmly woven, to 3mm. This is because the seam allowance will be visible through the fabric.

Lace. Some patterned lace is constructed in such a way that you can use the pattern to form a pretty edge simply by cutting round the outline. If the outline of the lace pattern is corded, as with guipure lace, and you can avoid cutting through this outline when cutting out the collar, you need not finish the outer edge any further. But if the lace is liable to fray, use a fine whip stitch over the pattern outline to secure the edge and finish the raw neck edge with bias binding as before.

If the lace you are using does not allow you to cut in this manner, cut the shape for a top collar from the lace and an undercollar from organdie or organza. This will highlight the pattern of the lace and you can stitch the collar as if you were using plain fabric.

Trimming the collars

A little lace edging can turn an ordinary collar into a party-goer. For washable collars use cotton lace which will stand up to handling and ironing.

Most fine cotton lace edgings can be gathered or pleated, without being bulky. Just make sure to ease in sufficient fullness to allow the outer edge of the lace to remain nice and full too. Nothing looks worse than lace gathered on the inside of the curve and flat on the outer edge.

To make sure that you buy enough trimmings, measure along the edge of the collar and buy at least twice the amount. If the lace is very fine, much of it will disappear in the gathers so you'll need two-and-a-half times the length of the edge of the collar.

Guipure daisy or bobble chain trimming are especially pretty. These cannot be gathered so you simply stitch them to the outer edge, on top of the collar. Just remember to ease the trimming to follow the roundness of the edge, otherwise it will turn up and over during wear.

You can give a really decorative look to an organdie collar for a rich velvet dress by using either double-edged lace which is drawn up through the centre to make a double frill, or a fine slotted lace

1. *Peter Pan* **2.** *puritan* **3.** *yoke*

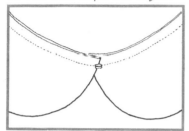

Overlapping the seam allowance

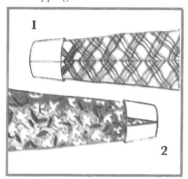

1. *Tube-shaped cuff* **2.** *pointed cuff*

The child's basic dress with lace cuffs and Peter Pan collar ▲

with ribbon slotted through the centre. Buy extra ribbon and you can make tiny bows to sew along the lace at intervals.

The lace collar, too, will look even more lacy if you trim the edge with matching lace edging.

Cuffs

Cuffs are another pretty form of trimming, either used on their own or made to match a collar. They can also be put to good practical use to lengthen sleeves which have become too short.

A point to remember when using cuffs as a trimming: sleeves should be shortened 13mm because the roll of the cuffs will add to the sleeve length.

Cuffs are easy to make and just as interchangeable as collars. You can use the same list of suitable fabrics, too.

Fabric required: for the cuff pattern given here, you'll need 0·15 metres of 90cm wide fabric.

The pattern: trace the pattern from the outline overleaf. Lengthen or shorten as necessary, using the instructions given for the collars but dividing by two instead of four.

Cutting: lay the pattern on the correct grain and cut four pieces (two for each cuff) allowing 9mm seam allowance all round.

Two ways to stitch the cuffs

Tube-shaped cuffs. Stitch the ends of each of the four sections to make four tubes. Then, with right sides facing, pin, tack and stitch two matching sections together along the upper, wider, edge. Trim the seam allowance, turn the sections out, edge-tack and press. Stitch along the lower raw edges of each cuff and finish with bias binding.

Pointed cuffs. With right sides facing, pin, tack and stitch two matching sections along the sides and upper, wider, edges. Trim the seam allowance, turn the sections out, edge-tack and press. Stitch the lower raw edges together and finish with bias binding. You can trim the cuffs using the methods given for collars.

Attaching the cuffs

For both types of cuffs, attach the narrower edge of the cuff to the sleeve. Use long slip stitches and sew the cuff to the inside of the sleeves, 13mm from the hem.

Position the tube-shaped cuffs with the cuff seam corresponding with the sleeve-seam and the pointed cuffs with the open end opposite the sleeve-seam.

Roll them up, over the edge of the sleeve and make small catch stitches under each cuff where it meets the sleeve seam. With pointed cuffs, sew each point down invisibly. This will prevent the cuffs from rolling down.

Self cuffs

You can also use the cuff pattern to make cuffs from self fabric and attach them to the sleeves permanently.

Simply stitch the lower raw edge of each cuff to the seam allowance of the sleeve, turn both edges under and face with a bias strip.

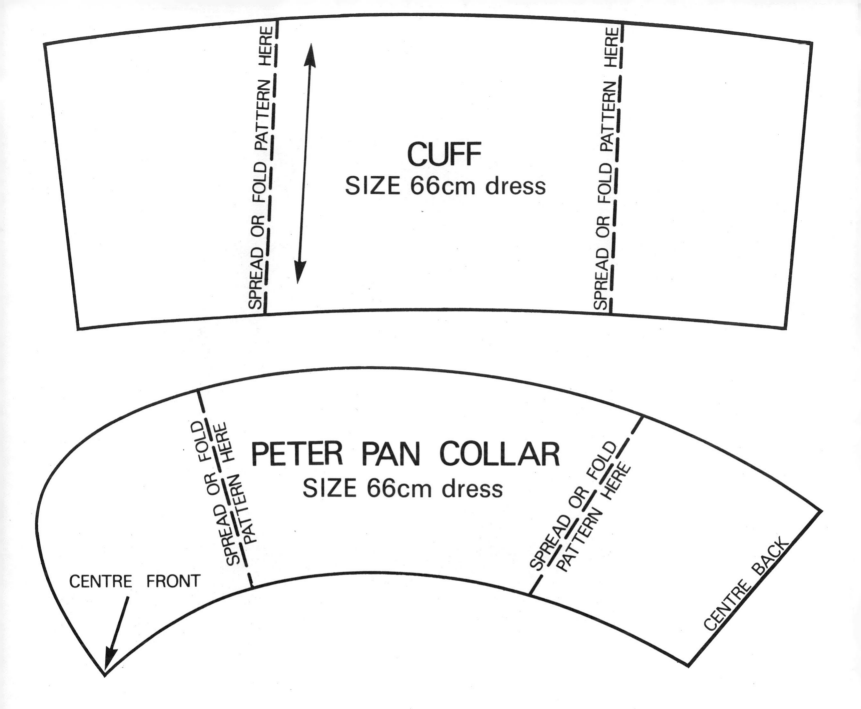

CUFF
SIZE 66cm dress

SPREAD OR FOLD PATTERN HERE

SPREAD OR FOLD PATTERN HERE

PETER PAN COLLAR
SIZE 66cm dress

SPREAD OR FOLD PATTERN HERE

SPREAD OR FOLD PATTERN HERE

CENTRE FRONT

CENTRE BACK

The patterns

Trace patterns are given here for three collar shapes and one cuff shape designed for the child's dress in Sewing for Children Chapter 49. For all patterns the size is for the dress size 66cm chest.

All patterns are without seam allowance.

The dash lines on the patterns indicate where to lengthen or shorten them.

The straight of grain for the Peter Pan and puritan collars is the straight edge along the Centre Back. The straight of grain for the yoke collar is the fold edge of the Centre Front. The straight of grain for the cuff is indicated on the pattern.

Layout for the Peter Pan collar on 90cm wide fabric without one way

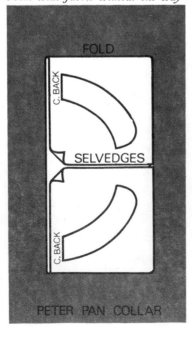

FOLD

C. BACK

SELVEDGES

C. BACK

PETER PAN COLLAR

Layout for the puritan collar on 90cm wide fabric without one way

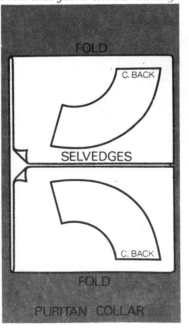

FOLD

C. BACK

SELVEDGES

C. BACK

FOLD

PURITAN COLLAR

Layout for the yoke collar on 90cm wide fabric without one way

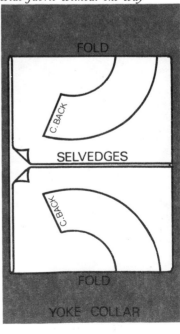

FOLD

C. BACK

SELVEDGES

C. BACK

FOLD

YOKE COLLAR

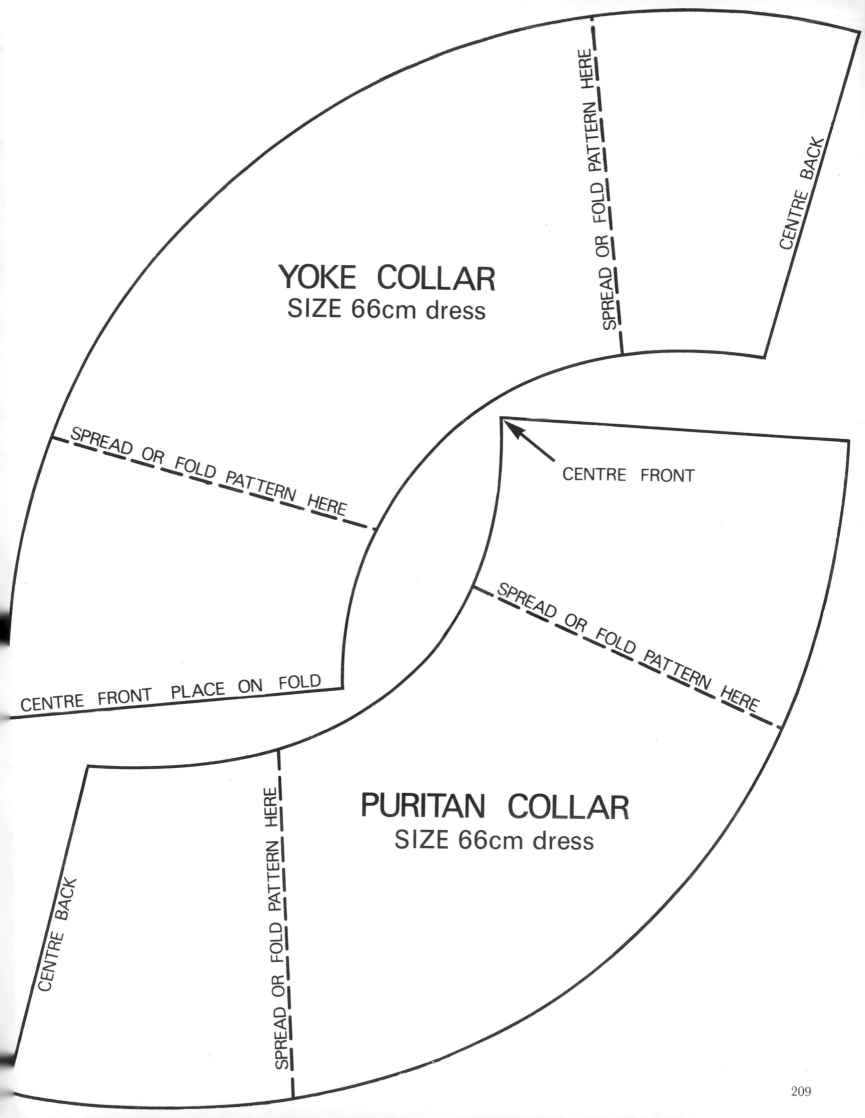

YOKE COLLAR
SIZE 66cm dress

SPREAD OR FOLD PATTERN HERE

CENTRE BACK

SPREAD OR FOLD PATTERN HERE

CENTRE FRONT

CENTRE FRONT PLACE ON FOLD

SPREAD OR FOLD PATTERN HERE

PURITAN COLLAR
SIZE 66cm dress

CENTRE BACK

SPREAD OR FOLD PATTERN HERE

Chapter 53

Playsuits in stretch towelling

Designed for active 1 to 7 year olds, trace patterns for these s-t-r-e-t-c-h towelling outfits are overleaf.

General hints

The patterns all include 6mm seam allowances, the hem allowances are also included in the patterns but they vary with each garment and are given in the instructions.

The seams on stretch towelling should be sewn on a swing needle machine with the stitch width set on the shallowest zigzag but with the stitch length set for an ordinary straight stitch. After stitching, zigzag or overlock the raw seam edges together to neaten, unless otherwise stated.

Use a synthetic thread. This has a certain amount of stretch in it and is recommended for stretch towelling.

When cutting out place the patterns on the wrong side of the fabric, but take care to follow the direction of the pile, which is indicated by arrows on the cutting diagrams, and to match up stripes if you are using a striped towelling.

If you have to press do so with a warm iron on the wrong side of the fabric.

A. T-shirt and crawler

Measurements

For a baby about 1 year old, weighing 8·62 to 12·25 kilos and measuring 38cm from neck to crutch over nappy. Instructions for altering the size are given below. See figure 1 for details of the garment.

210

1. *T-shirt and front and back views of the crawler*

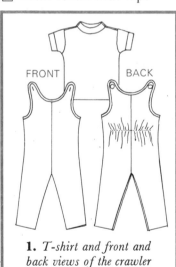

2. *Front, Back and sleeve patterns for the T-shirt A*

Fabrics and notions

For the T-shirt you will need:
- ☐ 0·50 metres 90cm wide plain stretch towelling
- ☐ 0·15 metres 13mm wide press fastener tape

For the crawler you will need:
- ☐ 0·80 metres 90cm wide printed stretch towelling
- ☐ 0·60 metres 13 mm wide press fastener tape
- ☐ 10cm 13mm wide tape
- ☐ 0·25m soft 6mm wide, elastic
- ☐ Two 13mm diameter buttons

For both:
- ☐ Tracing paper and pencil for the pattern
- ☐ Matching thread

The T-shirt

The pattern. Identify the T-shirt pattern in red from the trace patterns. Trace the top of the body pattern with both Back and Front neck lines and extend the body by 20cm (figure 2).

Also trace the sleeve pattern as shown.

Cutting out. Following the layout (figure 3) fold the fabric, place the pattern pieces on the double fabric, and cut one Back, one Front and two sleeves. Also cut two sleeve bands (a) each 13cm by 5cm, two neck bands (b), one 15cm by 5cm for the Front and one 16·3cm by 5cm for the Back, and four shoulder facing strips (c) each 3·8cm by 8cm.

Making up. Fold the sleeve bands in half lengthways, wrong sides facing. Stretching them to fit, stitch the sleeve bands to the right side of the sleeves taking 6mm seams (figure 4). Then zigzag the raw edges together as shown.

Similarly fold and stitch a shoulder facing strip to each shoulder-seam. Then fold the front shoulder facings under (figure 5) and trim to fit at the neck edge. Leave the back shoulder facings extending.

Lap each Front over the corresponding back facing. Tack and stitch them together at the armhole edge (figure 6). Insert each sleeve with the notch to the shoulder-seam and stitch.

Then stitch the sleeve-seams and side-seams in one operation. Zigzag the hem edge to neaten. Turn up 19mm and sew by hand or zigzag in place.

Fold each neck band in half, right sides facing and stitch the short ends. Turn to the right side, then stitch to the neck as for the sleeve bands. Using a zipper foot on the machine, stitch press fastener tape to the shoulders (figure 7).

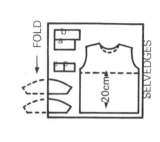

3. *The cutting layout for T-shirt A*

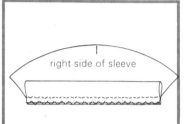

4. *The sleeve band stitched to the right side*

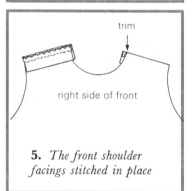

5. *The front shoulder facings stitched in place*

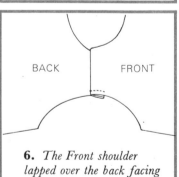

6. *The Front shoulder lapped over the back facing*

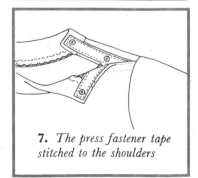

7. *The press fastener tape stitched to the shoulders*

Playsuits in stretch towelling. Left: for a 1 year old, crawler in a pretty print with plain T-shirt. Above and below: for a 2-3 year old, jumpsuit in plain towelling with contrast trim and for a 4-5 year old, striped T-shirt with plain shorts. Right: for a 6-7 year old, short legged jumpsuit with sleeves in stripes.

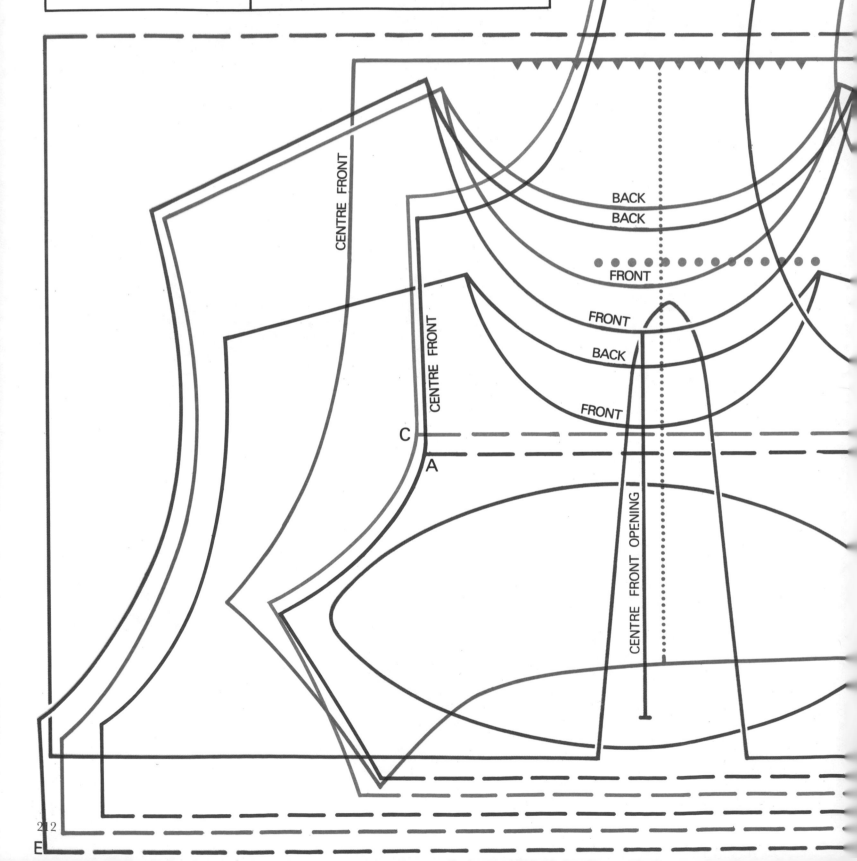

Trace patterns for children's towelling play suits

All patterns include 6mm seam allowance unless otherwise stated in the instructions. Hem allowances are also included but these vary with each garment and are given in the instructions.

Key to trace patterns

			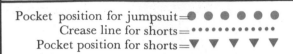
T-shirt and crawler	Jumpsuit	T-shirt and shorts	Short legged jumpsuit

Pocket position for jumpsuit = ● ● ● ● ● ●
Crease line for shorts = • • • • • • • •
Pocket position for shorts = ▼ ▼ ▼ ▼ ▼

CENTRE FRONT

CENTRE FRONT

CENTRE FRONT

BACK

BACK

FRONT

FRONT

BACK

FRONT

C

A

CENTRE FRONT OPENING

E

214

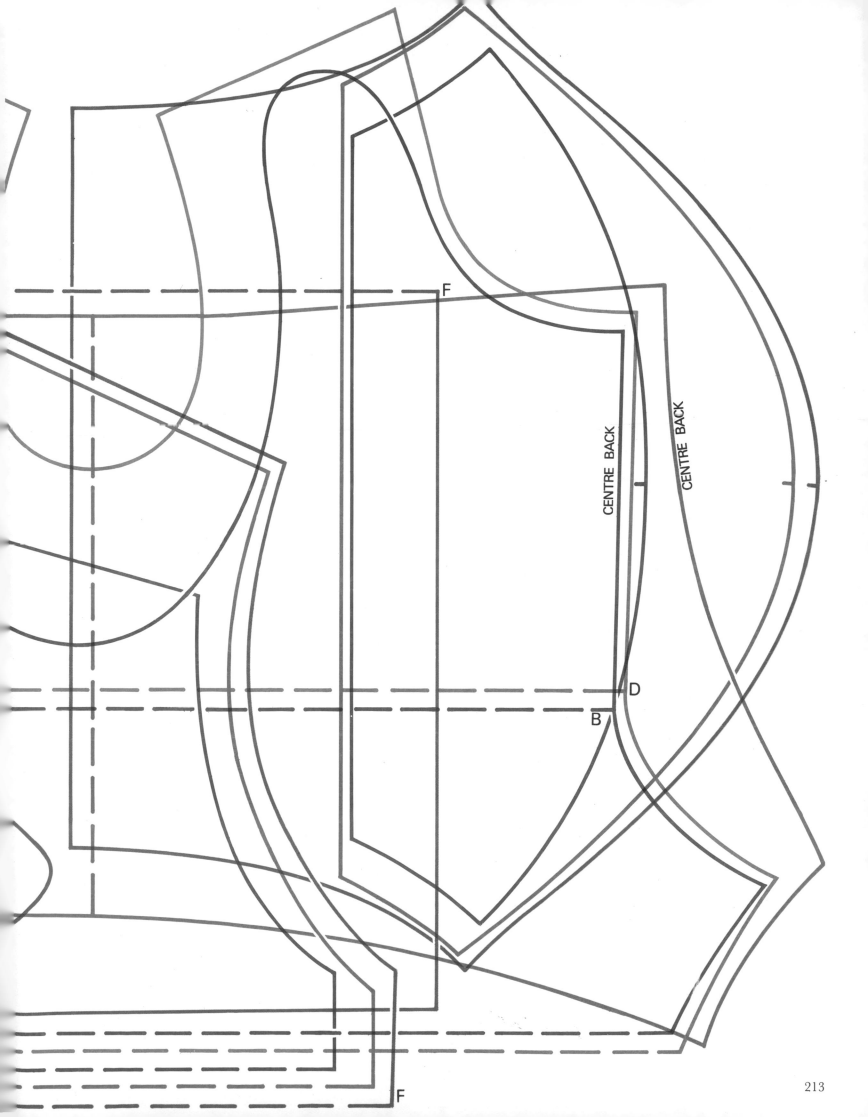

CENTRE BACK

CENTRE BACK

F

D

B

F

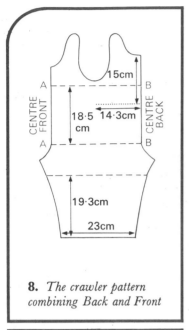

8. *The crawler pattern combining Back and Front*

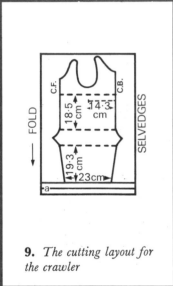

9. *The cutting layout for the crawler*

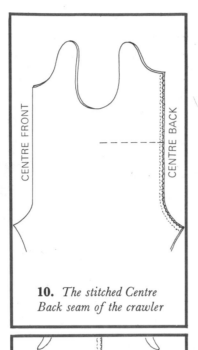

10. *The stitched Centre Back seam of the crawler*

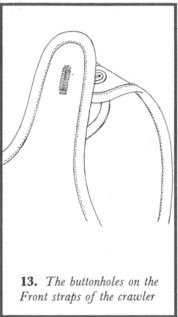

11. *The elastic stitched to the Back of the crawler*

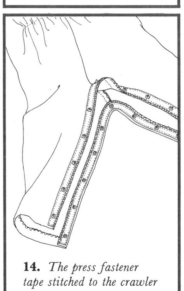

12. *The continuous bound top edge of the crawler*

13. *The buttonholes on the Front straps of the crawler*

14. *The press fastener tape stitched to the crawler*

The crawler

The pattern. Trace the crawler pattern letting in 18·5cm at the AB dash line and extending the leg end for 19·3cm (figure 8). Taper each leg-seam towards the ankle to make 23cm as shown.

Mark the position for the elastic on the Back, 15cm down from the neck edge on the Centre Back seam and 14·3cm across.

To alter the size of the pattern, lengthen or shorten the body and legs as required at the horizontal dash lines.

Cutting out. Following the layout (figure 9) fold the fabric, place the pattern on the double fabric and cut out. Also cut two strips (a) each 90cm by 2·5cm

from one end as shown, for the neck and armhole binding.

Making up. Stitch the Centre Back seam (figure 10).

Cut a piece of elastic 15cm long. Stitch it to the Back with a zigzag stitch, stretching it to fit the marking on each side of the Back (figure 11).

Stitch the Centre Front seam. Join two narrow ends of the binding strips to make a continuous strip. Starting at the Centre Back, place the right side of the binding strip to the wrong side of the garment, raw edges level. Tack and sew round the neck and armhole edges. Cut off the excess binding.

Fold to the right side, turn in the seam allowance and top-

stitch in place (figure 12) neatening the ends.

To close the shoulders, make buttonholes on the Front straps (figure 13). Cut two pieces of tape 2·5cm long and place to the wrong side of the Front shoulder straps to underlay the buttonholes. Work 19mm buttonholes 19mm from the ends as shown.

Sew buttons on the back shoulder straps to correspond, again underlaying with tape on the wrong side for reinforcement.

Zigzag the leg-seam and hem edges to neaten. Turn up the leg hems 19mm and stitch firmly.

Using a zipper foot stitch the ball half of the press fastener

tape along the back leg section to the right side, 3mm in from the edge (figure 14).

Turn the Front leg edge under 13mm and stitch the matching socket half of the press fastener tape to the wrong side over the turned edge.

B. Jumpsuit

Measurements

For a 2 year old boy or girl; chest 53cm, inside leg 28cm, shoulder to crutch 46cm. Instructions for altering the size are given below. See figure 15 for garment details.

Fabric and notions

☐ 0·95 metres 90cm wide stretch towelling in main colour and 0·25 metres in contrasting colour
☐ 2·5cm plastic buckle without prong
☐ Tracing paper and pencil for the pattern
☐ Matching thread

The pattern

Trace the jumpsuit pattern letting in 18·5cm at the CD dash line and extending the leg end for 25·5cm (figure 16). Taper each leg-seam towards the ankle to make 26·3cm as shown.

To alter the size of the pattern, lengthen or shorten the body and legs as required at the horizontal dash lines.

Mark the top of the pocket position as shown on the trace pattern. Mark the belt loops, one on the Centre Back 19·3cm down from the neck line and a second one, in line with the first, 6·3cm in from the Centre Front.

Cutting out

Following the larger layout (figure 17) fold the main fabric, place the pattern on the double fabric and cut out. Also cut out three belt loops (a) each 5cm by 2·5cm.

Following the smaller layout (figure 17) cut from contrasting fabric one belt (b) 61cm by 8cm, one neck binding (c) 47·3cm by 5cm, two armhole bindings (d) 20cm by 5cm and 1 pocket (e) 10cm by 7cm.

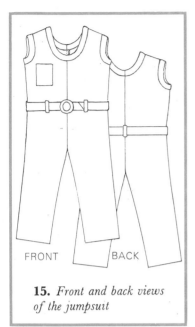

15. *Front and back views of the jumpsuit*

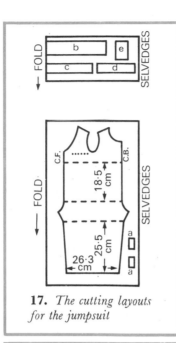

17. *The cutting layouts for the jumpsuit*

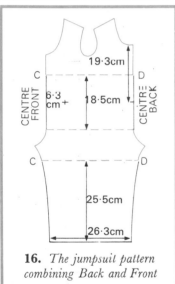

16. *The jumpsuit pattern combining Back and Front*

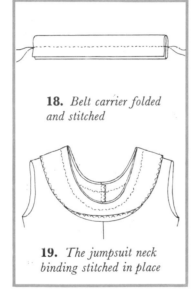

18. *Belt carrier folded and stitched*

19. *The jumpsuit neck binding stitched in place*

Making up

Zigzag the top 7cm raw edge of the pocket, fold in 13mm and tack. Turn under the remaining pocket edges for 6mm and topstitch the pocket to the jumpsuit at the position marked.

Stitch the Centre Back seam (as for the crawler, figure 10). To make the belt carriers fold them in three lengthways and stitch through the centre (figure 18). Then fold each end under 6mm and topstitch the carriers to the jumpsuit where marked. Stitch the Centre Front, leg and shoulder-seams.

Zigzag the leg hems to neaten. Turn up for 3cm and firmly hand-sew or zigzag in place. To bind the neck edge stitch the

narrow ends of the neck binding together to form a circle. Zigzag along one edge of the binding.

With right sides facing place the remaining raw edge of the binding round the neck, raw edges level (figure 19). Stitch, taking 13mm seam allowance. Turn the binding to the inside and topstitch in place over the first seam line.

Similarly form circles of the armhole binding and attach as for the neck binding.

Stitch the long edges of the belt, right sides facing, and stitch one narrow end tapering it to a point. Turn the belt to the right side through the open end.

Fold this end over the bar of

the buckle and stitch firmly with two rows of stitching.

C. T-shirt and shorts

Measurements

For a 4 year old boy or girl; chest 56cm, waist 56cm, hip 61cm. Instructions for altering the size are given below. See figure 20 for details of the garment.

Fabric and notions

☐ 0·50m 90cm wide striped towelling and 0·50m plain towelling.

☐ Four 13mm diameter buttons

☐ 0·70m soft 2·5cm wide elastic

☐ Tracing paper and pencil for the pattern

☐ Matching thread

The patterns

Identify the T-shirt in green from the trace patterns. Trace the top of the body pattern with both Back and Front neck lines and extend the body by 24·3cm (figure 21).

Also trace the sleeve pattern.

Trace the shorts pattern as shown and mark the crease line and pocket flap position. To alter the size of the T-shirt pattern add or take off 6mm at the side-seams and 3mm on the shoulder-seams. Alter the sleeve-seams and sleeve crown to correspond.

To alter the shorts pattern add or take of 13mm at the vertical dash line and 6mm at the waist edge.

Cutting out

Following the layout (figure 22) and using the T-shirt pattern, fold the striped fabric and cut out one Back, one Front and two sleeves. Also cut out two strips (a) each 8cm by 5cm for facing the left shoulder opening.

Fold the plain towelling and cut out the shorts as shown (figure 22). Also cut one pocket flap (b) 9·3cm square and one waist-band (c) 8cm by 59·3cm for the shorts, and one neck band (d) 6·3cm by 35cm and two sleeve bands (e) 6·3cm by 19·3cm for the T-shirt.

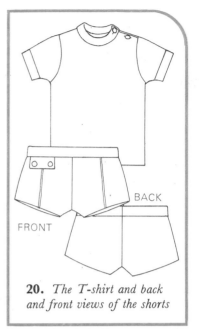

20. *The T-shirt and back and front views of the shorts*

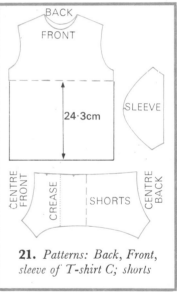

21. *Patterns: Back, Front, sleeve of T-shirt C; shorts*

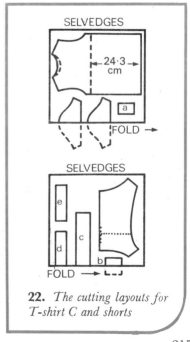

22. *The cutting layouts for T-shirt C and shorts*

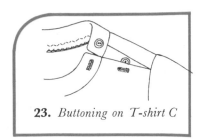

23. *Buttoning on T-shirt C*

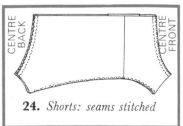

24. *Shorts: seams stitched*

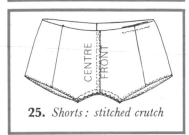

25. *Shorts: stitched crutch*

The T-shirt

Making up. Fold the shoulder facing strips in half lengthways, wrong sides facing, and stitch one to each left shoulder-seam on the right side (see figure 4). Stitch the right shoulder-seam. Fold under the front left shoulder strip and tack, leaving the back one extending. Then lap the Front shoulder over the Back extension and stitch them together at the armhole edge (see figure 6).

Apart from the shoulder-seams this T-shirt is made up exactly like the T-shirt A.

To finish, make two 13mm buttonholes on the Front left shoulder edge (figure 23) and sew buttons to the Back.

The shorts

Making up. Stretching the fabric, fold along the crease lines and stitch in the creases 3mm from the edge using a straight stitch.

Fold the pocket flap in half, right sides facing, making sure that the pile runs in the same direction as the shorts. Stitch at the sides, turn to the right side and position on the right side of the shorts with the raw edges level. Stitch on the pocket flap.

Zigzag the leg edges to neaten (figure 24).

Stitch the Centre Front and Centre Back seams (figure 24). Stitch the crutch-seam. To do this fold the shorts, right sides facing, so that the Back and Front crutch edges are level and Centre Front and Centre Back seams coincide (figure 25). Join the narrow edges of the waist-band to form a circle. Fit and cut the 2·5cm wide elastic and sew the narrow ends together. Fold the waist-band in half, wrong sides facing, and place the elastic in the fold. With the seam of the waist-band at the Centre Back, place the waist-band to the waist-seam on the right side, raw edges level, and stitch (see figure 4). Zigzag the edges together to neaten.

Turn up the leg hems for 13mm and sew firmly in place. Sew the two buttons on to the pocket flap, stitching right through to the wrong side.

D. Short legged jumpsuit

Measurements

For a 6 year old boy or girl; chest 61cm, waist 56cm, hips 63cm, shoulder to crutch 53cm. Instructions for altering the size are given below. See figure 26 for details of the garment.

Fabric and notions

- ☐ 1·05m 90cm wide striped stretch towelling
- ☐ 3 small buttons
- ☐ Tracing paper and pencil for pattern
- ☐ Matching thread

The pattern

Trace the short legged jumpsuit pattern with both Front and Back neck lines (figure 27), adding 25cm between the dash lines EF and tapering the side-seams to make the waist measurement 29·3cm. Also trace the gusset and sleeve pattern pieces as shown. To alter the size of the pattern add or take off 6mm at the side-seams and 3mm on the shoulder-seams. Alter the sleeve-seams and sleeve crown to correspond. Alter the length of the pattern at the waist line.

Cutting out

Following the layout (figure 28) fold the fabric, place the pattern pieces on the double fabric and cut one Back, one Front, two sleeves and one gusset. Also cut out a strip (a) 18cm by 63cm, shoulder to crutch 53cm.

19mm to face the Front opening.

Making up

Stitch the shoulder-seams. Zigzag the raw sleeve hem and leg hem edges to neaten. Insert each sleeve with the notch to the shoulder-seam and stitch.

Then stitch the sleeve-seams and side-seams in one operation. Tack the gusset between the legs of the Back and Front body pieces with the centre of the long curve of the gusset at the crutch point as shown (figure 29). Stitch.

Stitch the leg-seams.

Turn up the leg hems 13mm and hand-sew firmly in place. Zigzag one long edge of the front facing strip. Then place the opposite edge to the front opening, with right sides facing, raw edges level (figure 30), 13mm from the neck edges. Stitch.

Turn the strip to the inside and topstitch close to the edge of the opening.

Zigzag the raw neck edge to neaten. Then, stretching the neck edge, turn it in for 13mm and hand-sew firmly in place. Sew on the three buttons on the right of the opening and make three loops on the left edge to correspond (see figure 26).

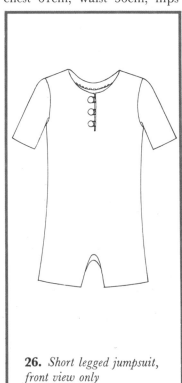

26. *Short legged jumpsuit, front view only*

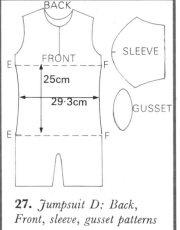

27. *Jumpsuit D: Back, Front, sleeve, gusset patterns*

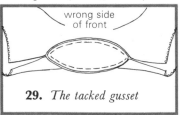

29. *The tacked gusset*

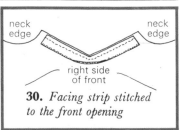

30. *Facing strip stitched to the front opening*

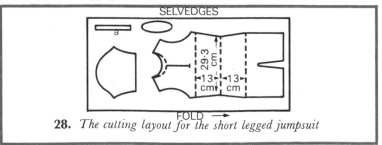

28. *The cutting layout for the short legged jumpsuit*

Chapter 54

Adaptable patterns for children's clothes

This chapter has adaptable graph patterns for day and night clothes for boys and girls from 3 to 7 years. Make the night-dress with short sleeves or turn the pyjamas into long trousers by making them up as the shorts.

Boy's tunic and shorts

Sizing

For a boy aged 4 with 58cm chest and 53cm waist; aged 5 to 6 with 61cm chest and 56cm waist; aged 7 with 63cm chest and 58cm waist.

Suggested fabrics

Denim or sailcloth.

You will need:

☐ 1.60m 90cm wide fabric
☐ 0·70m 19mm wide elastic
☐ Two 3·8cm diameter metal rings for the belt or one 2·5cm buckle
☐ Matching and contrasting thread
☐ Graph paper for patterns

The pattern

Copy pattern pieces numbers 1, 2, 3, 4, 5 and 6.
For the shorts copy the shorter length as shown on pattern piece number 1 and also draw in the side-seam and cut the pattern along this line. Draw in the pocket position on the shorts Front.

Cutting out

Following figure 1, lay out the pattern pieces on the fabric as shown.
The pattern has no seam or hem allowance so add the amounts given with the graph. Cut out the fabric and also cut

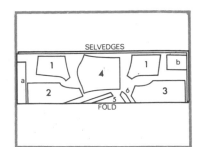

a belt (a) 76cm by 9·3cm and two pockets (b) 16·3cm by 14·3cm.

Making up

Shorts. Neaten one short edge of each pocket and then turn under for 3·8cm. Using contrasting thread make two rows of topstitching along this edge 2·5cm and 3cm from the fold. This edge becomes the top of the pocket.
On each pocket turn under the lower edge and the edge which goes nearest the Centre Front for 9mm. Tack the pockets in position on the front of the shorts, with the remaining raw edge of each pocket level with the raw edge of the side-seam. Using contrasting thread top-stitch the pocket along the front and lower edge with two rows of stitches 6mm apart. Stitch the side-seams, leg-seams and crutch seams, in that order, using contrasting thread and flat-fell seaming on the outside of the garment.
Make 19mm hems on the leg edges and stitch with matching thread.
Cut a length of elastic to fit the boy's waist and join the narrow ends to form a circle. Turn in the waist edge 3mm

▲ 1. Layout: boy's tunic and shorts

▲ Details of boy's tunic and shorts

then turn in again 2·8cm and place the elastic in the fold. Stitch the waist casing with matching thread, taking care not to stitch over the elastic. Smooth any fullness away at Centre Front, then stitch through the casing and elastic 8cm to each side of the Centre Front seam to give a flat effect at the front (see front view of shorts).

Tunic. Using contrasting thread and flat-fell seaming stitch the shoulder-seams, arm-hole-seams (pressing the seams towards the sleeves), and the side-seams and sleeve-seams in one operation starting at the hem.
Using matching thread stitch 19mm hems on sleeves and tunic.
Join neck facings at shoulder-seams and Centre Front seam. Sew to neck edge with right sides facing, taking 6mm seams. Snip seam allowance then turn and topstitch (or understitch) the facing to the seam allow-ance.
Neaten the raw edge of the facing then, using contrasting thread, topstitch to the tunic with two rows of stitches 2·5cm and 3cm from the neck edge working on the right side.
Belt. Fold in half along the length, right sides facing. Stitch, taking a 6mm seam and leaving an opening for turning. Turn to the right side and close opening.
Press, then topstitch all round with contrasting thread making two rows of stitches 6mm apart.
Firmly stitch two rings or a buckle at one end.

Boy's pyjamas

Sizing

As for tunic and shorts with the following outer leg lengths: 61cm, 66cm and 71cm respectively.

Suggested fabrics

Wool and cotton mixture like Viyella, or winceyette.

You will need

☐ 1·15m 90cm wide fabric for top and 1·40m 90cm wide for trousers and trimmings
☐ 0·70m 19mm wide elastic
☐ Matching thread
☐ Graph paper for patterns

The pattern

Copy pattern pieces numbers 1, 2, 3, 4, 5, 6 and 7. The trousers pattern piece 1 is drawn full length and without side-seams.

Cutting out

Following figure 2, lay out the pattern pieces on the fabric as shown.

The pattern has no seam or hem allowances so add the amounts given with the graph. Cut out the fabric.

Making up

Trousers. Stitch the leg-seams and crutch-seams with flat-fell seaming on the outside of the fabric.

Stitch 19mm hems on the legs. Cut a length of elastic to fit the child's waist and join the narrow ends to form a circle.

▼ **2.** *Layout: boy's pyjamas*

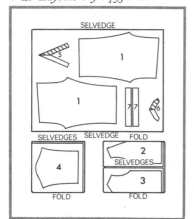

▼ *Details of boy's pyjamas*

▲ *For the girl's smock, check gingham with plain poplin—tough denim for the boy's tunic and shorts*

Turn in the waist edge 3mm, then turn in again for 28mm and place elastic in the fold. Stitch the waist casing taking care not to stitch over the elastic.

Top. Stitch seams in sleeve bands and neck band.

Stitch the shoulder, armhole, side and sleeve-seams with flat-fell seaming. Press armhole-seams towards the sleeves.

Stitch a sleeve band to each sleeve edge. To do this place the right side of the band to the wrong side of the sleeve, with seams matching and raw edges level. Stitch with 6mm seam.

Press the seam allowances towards the sleeve and stitch to the sleeve very close to the hem edge. Do not stitch through the band at the same time.

Turn the sleeve band to the right side of the sleeve, turn under the raw edge to make the band 4·5cm wide and topstitch close to the upper fold edge.

Similarly stitch the neck band to the neck edge. But before topstitching in place tack the neck band down taking care to see that the point is on the Centre Front.

Girl's smock

Sizing
For a girl aged 3 with 56cm chest; aged 4 to 5 with 58cm chest; aged 6 with 61cm chest.

Suggested fabrics
Gingham, poplin, denim or shirting.

You will need
- [ ] 1·15 metres 90cm wide main fabric and 0·50 metres 90cm wide contrasting fabric
- [ ] 0·50 metres 6mm wide elastic
- [ ] Matching thread and contrasting topstitch thread for pocket detail
- [ ] Graph paper for patterns

The pattern
Copy pattern pieces numbers 1, 2, 3, 4 and 5 from the graph.

▼ 3. *Layout: girl's smock*

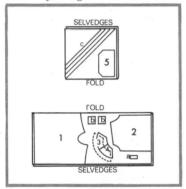

▼ *Details of girl's smock*

Cutting out
Following figure 3, lay out the pattern pieces on the fabric as shown.

Make up the other half of the Front yoke pattern and join them at the Centre Front. Cut the yokes from single fabric as shown, with the Centre Front and Centre Backs on the crosswise grain of the fabric.

The pattern has no seam or hem allowances so add the amounts given with the graph. Cut out the fabric and also cut the following: from main fabric one pocket window (a) 6·3cm by 3·8cm, and four pocket windows (b) 6·3cm square; from contrast fabric cut 2·75m of 3cm wide bias strips (c) as shown.

Making up
Pocket. Place the pocket pieces together, right sides facing, and stitch round, leaving one side of the roof open. Turn to the right side.

Using contrasting thread and a large stitch, topstitch the top and bottom of the roof and the door.

Turn in the raw edges of each window for 6mm all round and stitch them to the pocket.

Topstitch the pocket to the Front of the smock along the sides and lower edge. Back stitch the opening corners securely.

Sleeves. Stitch the sleeve-seams with a French seam.

Stitch 13mm hems leaving openings for inserting elastic. Thread a 19·3cm length elastic in each sleeve hem. Stitch ends of elastic firmly together and close the opening.

Stitch sleeves to skirt at underarm with a French seam and press seams towards sleeves.

Yoke. French seam the shoulders.

Bind Centre Back edges of yoke with contrasting bias strip.

To do this place the right side of binding to wrong side of Centre Back, raw edges level. Stitch with 6mm seam. Fold binding to right side, turn in raw edge for 6mm and top-stitch in place over the first row of stitching.

To bind neck edge join two bias strips in the straight of grain to make up 0·95m. Stitch the binding to the wrong side of the neck edge as above, leaving 30cm extending at each end to make ties.

Fold the binding to the right side. Turn in 6mm along all raw edges, including the ties, and topstitch the folded binding from end to end.

Join bias strips to length of lower yoke edge plus 2·5cm. Fold in half along the length, wrong sides together, turning in 13mm at each end to neaten. Place round lower edge of the yoke on right side, with the raw bias edge 6mm from yoke edge and bias fold upwards. Stitch in place 13mm from the lower yoke edge.

Skirt. Make two rows of gathering stitches 6mm and 13mm from the top edge of the skirt and sleeves, finishing the stitches 3·8cm to each side of the Centre Back.

Draw up to fit the yoke, matching notches to seams and leaving 13mm of skirt extending to each side of the Centre Back. Pin, then stitch, taking a 16mm seam. Trim the seam allowance to 9mm and zigzag or overlock the raw edges together. Press the seam into the yoke. Topstitch through yoke and seam allowance close to seam. Make a 2·5cm hem on the skirt. Fold in the Centre Back edges 13mm and stitch down.

Make two 30cm ties from the bias strips as for the neck ties and sew to the lower yoke edge at the Centre Back.

Girl's night-dress

Sizing
As for girl's smock.

Suggested fabrics
Clydella, brushed nylon, seersucker or winceyette.

You will need:
- [ ] 1·60m of 90cm wide fabric
- [ ] 3·20m broderie Anglaise edging
- [ ] Shirring elastic
- [ ] 1 hook and eye size No.1
- [ ] Matching thread
- [ ] Graph paper for patterns

The pattern
Copy pieces numbers 1, 2, 3 and 4.

Cutting out
Following figure 4, lay out the pattern pieces on the fabric as shown.

The pattern has no seam or hem allowances so add the amounts given with the graph. Cut out the fabric and also cut a Front opening facing (a) 10cm by 6·3cm, two bias strips (b) 3cm wide by 15cm and two bias strips (c) 3cm wide by 48cm. Cut a slit in the Centre Front of the skirt 8cm long from the neck edge.

Making up
Sleeves. With right sides facing, raw edges level, place broderie trim on sleeve hem edges. Stitch, taking 6mm seams.

Press seam allowance on each upwards, turn in the raw edges and stitch a 3mm hem. Stitch the sleeve-seams with a French seam.

With shirring elastic in the bobbin and a large stitch length, work two rows of shirring on each sleeve, 6mm apart and starting 2·5cm up from the top of the trim. Knot ends securely.

French seam the sleeves to the skirt at the underarm and press seam towards the sleeve.

Yoke. French seam the shoulders.

Cut three pieces of broderie Anglaise one 79cm long and two 18cm long. Machine gather each piece 5mm from the raw edge.

Gather the short pieces to the depth of the yoke at the Centre Front. Pin to the right side of each Front yoke piece, placing the raw edge of the trim 13mm from the Centre Front. Topstitch in place over the gathering line then zigzag raw edge of trim flat to the yoke.

Gather up the 79cm length to fit round the neck and Centre Front edges. Pin in place to the right side with raw edges of yoke and trim level. Tack.

Using the short bias strips (b), bind both Centre Front edges, taking 6mm seams.

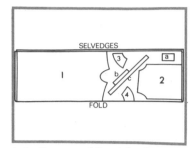

▲ **4.** *Layout: girl's night-dress*

▲ *Details of girl's night-dress*

▲ *Pretty printed Clydella is first choice for the night-dress—Viyella in contrasting colours for the pyjamas*

Join the long bias strips in the straight grain of the fabric. Place the strip centrally along the neck edge, with right sides facing, raw edges level. Stitch, taking a 6mm seam.

Stitch the strip extending at each end into a rouleau for the ties. Turn the rouleaux to the right side and complete the binding of neck edge.

Stay-stitch the yoke 13mm from the lower edge.

Gather remaining broderie trim to fit lower yoke edge with the ends extending at Centre Front. Pin to right side of yoke 6mm from the yoke edge.

Machine stitch in place along the gathering line.

Skirt. Stitch 13mm Centre Back seam.

Make two rows of gathering Stitches 6mm and 13mm from the top edge of the skirt and sleeves. Draw up to fit the yoke, matching notches to seams and leaving 6mm extending at both Front edges.

Stitch with 16mm seam. Trim seam allowance to 9mm and zigzag or overlock the edges together. Press seam upwards. Neaten the raw edges of the facing then pin the facing centrally over the Centre Front opening with right sides together. Stitch with 6mm seam graduating to nothing at the point to each side of the Centre Front opening. Slash between the stitching. Understitch the seam allowance to the facing then turn to the inside.

Hand-sew the top edges of facing to yoke seam and sew on a hook and eye at this point. Make a 2·5cm hem on the skirt.

Graph pattern: girl's smock and night-dress

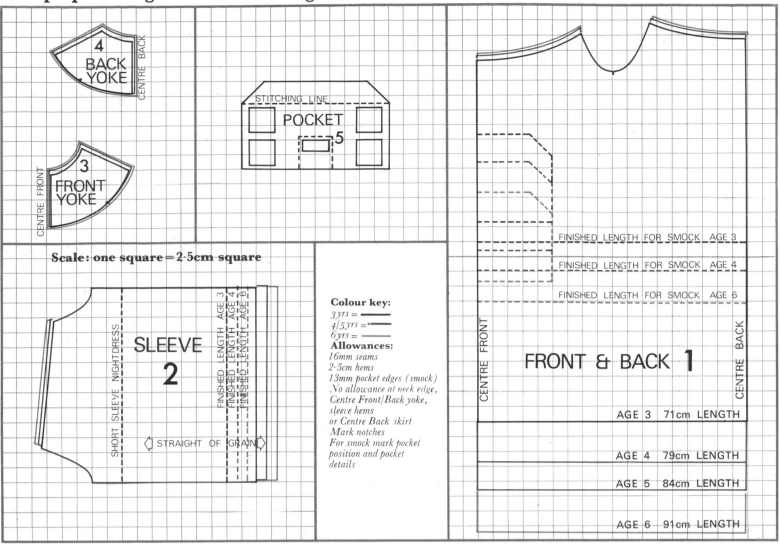

4 BACK YOKE — CENTRE BACK

3 FRONT YOKE — CENTRE FRONT

STITCHING LINE
POCKET
5

Scale: one square = 2·5cm square

SHORT SLEEVE NIGHTDRESS

SLEEVE 2

FINISHED LENGTH AGE 3
FINISHED LENGTH AGE 4
FINISHED LENGTH AGE 6

⟨ STRAIGHT OF GRAIN ⟩

Colour key:
3 yrs = ▬▬▬▬
4/5 yrs = ▬▬▬▬
6 yrs = ▬▬▬▬

Allowances:
16mm seams
2·5cm hems
13mm pocket edges (smock)
No allowance at neck edge,
Centre Front/Back yoke,
sleeve hems
or Centre Back skirt
Mark notches
For smock mark pocket
position and pocket
details

FINISHED LENGTH FOR SMOCK AGE 3
FINISHED LENGTH FOR SMOCK AGE 4
FINISHED LENGTH FOR SMOCK AGE 6

CENTRE FRONT

FRONT & BACK 1

CENTRE BACK

AGE 3 71cm LENGTH

AGE 4 79cm LENGTH

AGE 5 84cm LENGTH

AGE 6 91cm LENGTH

Graph pattern: boy's tunic and shorts, and pyjamas

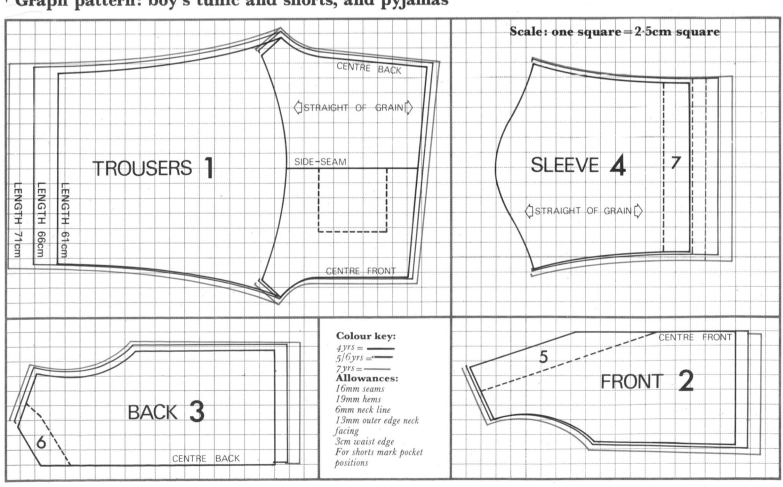

Scale: one square = 2·5cm square

CENTRE BACK

⟨ STRAIGHT OF GRAIN ⟩

TROUSERS 1

SIDE-SEAM

LENGTH 71cm
LENGTH 66cm
LENGTH 61cm

CENTRE FRONT

SLEEVE 4 — 7

⟨ STRAIGHT OF GRAIN ⟩

Colour key:
4 yrs = ▬▬▬▬
5/6 yrs = ▬▬▬▬
7 yrs = ▬▬▬▬

Allowances:
16mm seams
19mm hems
6mm neck line
13mm outer edge neck
facing
3cm waist edge
For shorts mark pocket
positions

BACK 3
6
CENTRE BACK

CENTRE FRONT
5
FRONT 2

continued overleaf

Skirt making

Making a Toile